W. E. B. Du Bois

W. E. B. Du Bois

Propagandist
of the Negro Protest

by Elliott M. Rudwick

Second Edition

*with a new preface by Louis Harlan and
an epilogue by the author*

PHILADELPHIA
UNIVERSITY OF PENNSYLVANIA PRESS

To the Memory of My Parents

PREFACE AND ACKNOWLEDGMENTS

The Reconstruction Period following the Civil War bred a countermovement in the South. An accommodation between the races was established which restored the caste status of Negroes. By law and custom the colored people were to remain an economically marginal group, politically and socially powerless, and segregated from the whites. Outside of the South, custom also demanded that Negroes should be treated as a separate and inferior people. Such conditions motivated Negroes to seek solutions to the race problem and various plans for salvation were promulgated. Three of the most important "planners" were Booker T. Washington, Marcus Garvey, and W. E. B. Du Bois. In recent years two books have treated the leadership of Washington, and others are in process. In 1955 a study of Garvey was published. The careers of the Tuskegeean and Garvey were more dramatic and colorful than that of Du Bois, and both of these men were better known to Negroes and whites than Du Bois. While several master's theses have been written about Du Bois as litterateur, as editor, and as "social theorist," until 1959 there was no published volume devoted exclusively to an examination and evaluation of his leadership.*

This omission is somewhat surprising when it is considered that Du Bois is regarded as an important figure in the literature of race relations. Impressive claims have been made about his contributions. Gunnar Myrdal and Arnold M. Rose concluded that Du Bois "set the tone" of the N.A.A.C.P. In 1925 Horace M. Bond referred to

---

* Francis L. Broderick, *W. E. B. Du Bois: Negro Leader in a Time of Crisis* (Stanford University Press).

Du Bois as "the most vital and compelling figure in the Negro world of today." Four years later, another writer announced that the Negro leader "has done more for the advancement of the American Negro than any other living man." Du Bois himself claimed that "the policy of the N.A.A.C.P. from 1910 to 1934 was largely of my making."

He popularized the theory that only college-educated leaders could save the race, and it is not surprising that, two decades ago, a college professor said, "to him the Negro intellectual of this generation, whether conscious or unconscious of the debt, owes more than to any other man of his race." However others have noted that Du Bois was pompous and "not generally liked." One critic believed that he was "unfitted temperamentally to be the leader of his race." Du Bois' tactics were not clear to some writers, and this confusion was especially evident after he contended during the 1930's that self-segregation was the colored race's only road to survival.

All of these estimates arouse the interest of the sociologist, especially one who studies the area of race relations. Over a half-century ago, Du Bois proposed that Negroes should protest against their second-class status, and at that time he maintained that direct social action was the only method which would bring freedom to his people. Precisely what were his beliefs, his leadership roles, tactics, and strategy? Did they change? When, how, and in response to what forces? What were his relations with race leaders such as Booker T. Washington and Marcus Garvey? What was his interaction with white people? What was the extent of his influence? Was he the key architect of the N.A.A.C.P.? These and other questions need to be explored.

During the writing of this inquiry I drew upon the advice and counsel of many people. I should like to express my thanks especially to Professors Jeremiah P. Shalloo and Richard D.

Lambert of the University of Pennsylvania. I also owe a great deal to Drs. August Meier and Francis Broderick, whose scholarly contributions and incisive comments have increased my knowledge of the field of Negro leadership. I am grateful to Dr. Martin Chworowsky and the Albert M. Greenfield Center of Human Relations.

There are many publishers and editors who have graciously granted permission to quote from various books and magazines:

Doubleday and Company (*Booker T. Washington, Builder of a Civilization*, Lyman B. Stowe and Emmett J. Scott); Harcourt, Brace and Company (*The Walls Came Tumbling Down*, Mary White Ovington, and *Dusk of Dawn*, W. E. B. Du Bois); Harper and Brothers (*An American Dilemma*, Gunnar Myrdal); Alfred A. Knopf (*Black Manhattan*, James Weldon Johnson) and (*From Slavery to Freedom*, John Hope Franklin); McGraw-Hill Company (*Negroes in American Society*, Maurice R. Davie); Charles Scribner's Sons (*Black Odyssey*, Roi Ottley); Viking Press (*Along This Way*, James Weldon Johnson); and W. E. B. Du Bois (*Souls of Black Folk*). Special thanks to the *Journal of Negro Education* and the *Crisis*, which permitted the use of extensive quotations from Du Bois' writings. Lastly, an indebtedness is acknowledged to the editors of *Phylon*, *Journal of Negro History*, and the *Journal of Negro Education*, who allowed me to draw from material which I originally published in these periodicals.

E. M. R.

Tallahassee, Fla.
September 10, 1959

PREFACE TO THE SECOND EDITION

by Louis R. Harlan

The year 1968 is the centennial of the birth of William Edward Burghardt Du Bois, the great Negro protest leader of the early twentieth century and the fiery symbol of Negro refusal to be treated as inferior. This occasion is appropriate for the reissue of Elliott Rudwick's authoritative and well-written life of Du Bois. Balanced judgment is the quality most needed in a biographer of any man as vibrant, complex, and controversial as Du Bois, and this judicious balance—a combination of sympathy and scholarly detachment—is manifested throughout the present biography. Rudwick is a trained sociologist specializing in race relations, as well as a historian; and this breadth of background is essential in treating such a man of parts as Du Bois, who was not only a firebrand of the civil rights movement but also a distinguished scholar, a poet, a novelist, an informal statesman of the Pan-African movement, and, in his last decades, a far-out radical. Above all, Rudwick insists, Du Bois made his greatest contribution as a master propagandist of Negro protest.

Some readers may need to learn who Du Bois was, for he lived in virtual retirement during the two decades prior to his death at ninety-five in 1963. The civil rights movement had passed him by as it went on to the new successes and new dilemmas after 1954; meanwhile, he had become so increasingly alienated from American society in these years that he had joined the Communist Party and had transferred his citizenship to Ghana. Many who have seen his photograph in the news magazines simply labeled "fellow traveler" may not know that he was the great pioneer of civil rights in America and one of the chief founders of the N.A.A.C.P. And yet, on the day he died, I was one of the crowd of a quarter-million participants in the March on Washington who paused for a minute of silent tribute to Du Bois in which the respect was unmistakable. More recently, his strong appeal to the young has been signified by the symbolic use of his name in the Du Bois Clubs of leftist youth. Controversial even in death, Du Bois is bound to be interpreted differently by those who consider him from different ideological positions. For example, it is clear that Professor Rudwick disapproves of the black nationalism which Du Bois always held under restraint and the radicalism to which he finally gave unrestrained vent. Rudwick deplores as an unrelieved personal disaster Du Bois' decision in 1961 to join the Communist Party, whereas others might consider the decision a heroic protest against the official outlawing of this extreme form of dissent. Yet, whatever interpretation the reader may prefer, the most reliable guide now available on Du Bois' career is the present book.

Born only three years after the Civil War, Du Bois journeyed on a virtual odyssey of the color line. He wandered up every conceivable avenue of assault on the absurdities that race and racial attitudes have created in twentieth-century America. Du Bois in 1903 prophesied in *The Souls of Black Folk* that "the problem of the Twentieth Century is the problem of the color line"; and at one time or another in his long life he tested every approach advocated today, from legal action, education, and cultural pluralism to black nationalism and Black Power.

Growing up in the world of nineteenth-century individualism, Du Bois as a young man sought a private and personal liberation from the burden of race through individual achievements. Early demonstrating rare intellectual gifts, he became an academic paragon—a Harvard doctor of philosophy, a student on fellowship in Germany, and the leading Negro scholar of his day. And still he was not free. He found himself unable to make friendships among white fellow students; and even after publishing two excellent books, he was relegated to teaching at inferior Negro colleges. If a man alone could not cross the color line, he reasoned, perhaps the society itself could be reformed out of the absurdities of racial discrimination through the power of social science. Professor Rudwick shows in detail how naive faith in the power of science lay behind Du Bois' pioneering Negro studies at Atlanta University early in the twentieth century.

Soon disillusioned with social science but determined to strike a blow against the "white backlash" of his day, Du Bois the man of learning became increasingly a publicist and propagandist. Breaking openly with the bland accommodationist Booker T. Washington, Du Bois started two ill-starred Negro magazines and flailed out at racial restrictions with essays, speeches, and poetry. He and fellow "radicals" in 1905 founded the Niagara Movement to demand full manhood rights for Negroes. One of the best features of Rudwick's biography is his full treatment of the struggle between Du Bois and Washington, based on the private papers of both men. The Niagarites were overpowered by white supremacy in subtle as well as crass forms and completely outgeneraled by that Machiavellian prince of Negroes, Booker T. Washington.

When white liberals, belatedly aroused to the anomaly of racial repression in a democratic society, organized the National Association for the Advancement of Colored People in 1909, Du Bois tried this interracial avenue. He became the editor of its magazine, *The Crisis,* for the next quarter-century and was for years its only Negro national officer. Subordination to white leadership was galling to the proud and sensitive Du Bois. Professor Rudwick details his substantive disputes with white colleagues and his many quarrels over real and imagined slights, but he keeps these in perspective. Rudwick knows, as Du Bois' colleagues usually did, that these personal differences were part of the price of interracial cooperation and were incidental to Du Bois' effective work as editor of *The Crisis*. His magazine's circulation was much larger than the N.A.A.C.P. membership, and his editorship gave it a distinction transcending that of an N.A.A.C.P. house organ. *The Crisis* and its editor became the leading voices of Negro expression on every aspect of race.

Professor Rudwick subtly and skillfully traces the ambivalent strains of Du Bois' response to successive crises in race relations as the twentieth century proceeded. There was a real battle within Du Bois between integrationism and racial identity, between accommodation and militancy. Even during his most active N.A.A.C.P. years, he briefly flirted with accommodationism. He endorsed Woodrow Wilson for president in 1912 in an opportunistic ploy, only to be met, once Wilson was in office, with a wave of federal segregation measures. Yet again, in the First World War, Du Bois pragmatically abandoned his socialist pacifism to endorse the crusade to make the world safe for democracy, a crusade which required him to accept segregation and subordination of Negro soldiers. In the post-war years, he swung toward black nationalism and took active leadership of the international Pan-African movement, only to swing back again as one of the sharpest critics of the nationalist mass-leader Marcus Garvey. During the 1920's, Du Bois was a patron of the Negro cultural upsurge known as the Harlem Renaissance, to which he gave an outlet in *The Crisis* and himself contributed some poetry and fiction.

The Great Depression shook the N.A.A.C.P. as it did other American institutions, and the underlying assumptions of the civil rights movement were challenged. Du Bois and others argued that the most critical problems of the Negro masses were economic and that the N.A.A.C.P. should at least temporarily abandon its traditional goals and methods to concern itself with the poverty of Negro tenant farmers and slum-dwellers. Du Bois' counsel was rejected, partly because he accompanied it with proposals of Negro cooperatives and other radical economic approaches and with some equivocal endorsement of self-segregation by Negroes. After repeated clashes, the other N.A.A.C.P. leaders ousted Du Bois.

Only after trying many other avenues out of the prison of the color bar did Du Bois turn in his last years to two radical and mutually contradictory approaches—the attempt to alter American society fundamentally through an egalitarian Communism, and flight from an America overwhelmingly white to an Africa overwhelmingly black. He became, says Rudwick, a "Prophet in Limbo." Since Rudwick's chief interest is in Du Bois as a Negro leader, he deliberately sketches these last years only briefly.

This is not the first book on Du Bois, nor will it be the last. When the Du Bois Papers are fully open to scholars, many of the gaps in our knowledge will be filled. We may wait a long time, however, for a biography as well balanced between detachment and sympathy as this one.

CONTENTS

CONTENTS

W. E. B. Du Bois

A Study in Minority Group Leadership

1. A Negro Culture and American Manhood

Three years after the end of the Civil War, William Edward Burghardt Du Bois was born in Great Barrington, a small town in western Massachusetts. The few Negroes in Great Barrington settled there long before and Du Bois' family was among the oldest residents. Du Bois described his maternal grandfather as "very dark," his maternal grandmother as a "Dutch-African woman," and his mother as "dark shining bronze." His paternal grandfather was born in the Bahamas of a union between a wealthy American of Huguenot stock and a mulatto slave girl. The offspring, Alexander Du Bois, who could have "passed" as white, was educated in Connecticut. He was a proud man who angrily refused to attend a Negro picnic, since "his fastidious soul" disapproved of identification with a disinherited group. Restless and embittered, he proclaimed he was an American and would not be forced to remain apart. Nevertheless, in the face of white discrimination, he led Negroes out of the Trinity Episcopal Church in New Haven and helped to form the colored St. Luke's Parish.[1]

Self-tossed in his conflict, he moved about, and on a trip to Haiti, Alfred, his son—W. E. B. Du Bois' father—was born. Alfred, who was "just visibly colored," was also a restless, unhappy person who wandered from place to place, and in 1867 he found himself in the valley of the Berkshires, where he met and married Mary Burghardt. He had tried many occupations—barbering, selling, even preaching; and still craving to roam, he left his wife and child and drifted away permanently. William Edward Burghardt Du Bois, in summing up his varied racial background, said he was born "with a flood of Negro blood, a strain of French, a bit of Dutch, but thank God! no 'Anglo-Saxon.' "[2] His mother returned to the "black Burghardts," and he assimilated their cultural ways, which were devoid of any African influences and represented the warp and woof of nineteenth-century New England life.

Great Barrington numbered five thousand people, the majority of whom were "middle-class" and "respectable." The "rich" farm and factory owners could not have been exceedingly wealthy, and they were few in number. They were of English and Dutch descent, as were most of the small farmers, merchants, and skilled laborers. Most of the Irish and Germans worked in the woolen mills. The Republican party controlled the town, and most of the adult males seriously took a part in the annual town meeting. The sex mores were rigid and the outstanding vice in the community was drunkenness. Emotional restraint was considered the norm, and "we were even sparing in our daily greetings." According to Du Bois, "the color line was manifest and yet not absolutely drawn," and the Negroes, conforming to the folkways of the town, organized their own social life.[3] Most of them worked as laborers and servants. In the Du Bois home, there was never a great deal of money and Du Bois' mother struggled to make ends meet by boarding a relative and working as a domestic once in a while. Oftimes, some of the whites helped the family by sending food and clothing.

Most of Du Bois' playmates were children of the well-to-do Yankees, and, like them, he learned to harbor a distrust, if not a hatred, of the town's Irish and German population. He participated in most of the childhood games and outings and regularly played in the homes of his young white friends. Great Barrington, with its rim of hills and rivers, was "a boy's paradise," and in those early, carefree years he was untroubled by the sting of racial discrimination. His first real experience of feeling unwanted and isolated came when his classmates decided to exchange visiting cards. The activity was a joyous one until a little girl refused—"peremptorily, with a glance" to accept his card.[4] A "vast veil" had shut him out, and in such moments of sadness he sought solace in the hills. He was a naturally bright boy in school and took especial delight in surpassing his white fellows in examinations or in any other kind of competition. His awareness of difference increased, even though at first he ascribed this sense of separation to his ability to recite better than the others in the class.

Gradually, he realized that some people in town considered his brown skin a "misfortune" and he knew "days of secret tears." He became very sensitive to the reactions of others, and this acute perception, born in great part of these earlier rejections, probably served to spare him from many experiences of racial discrimination. He learned to join his companions only when they indicated that they wanted him, and, when they did not, he found his amusement elsewhere. He discovered that he was less welcome when strangers or summer boarders came to town and, especially after adolescence approached, Du Bois noticed his friends seemed timid and uncertain as they attempted to explain his presence. In his recollections of this early period, Du Bois seems to minimize the extent of rejection which he experienced, and, certainly, his hurts were minor in comparison with those he heard discussed by his relatives. They, with little education and occupational status, often complained that racial discrimination had killed their chances of advancement. As a high school student, Du Bois thought that hard study would grant him immunity to the racial disabilities which kinsmen, in their work-a-day world, had described. It seemed clear to him that earnest effort in all he attempted was the only way "to equal whites."[5]

While in high school, Du Bois showed a keen concern for the development of his race, and it is probably true that no small reason for this solicitude was his sense of isolation from the whites in Great Barrington. At the age of fifteen, he became the local correspondent for the New York *Globe*, and in this position he conceived it his duty to push his race forward through capsuled lectures and other bits of instruction. Convinced that the town's Negroes were not making the most of their opportunities, he advised them to join with the whites in community betterment programs. On one occasion he counseled affiliation with some Great Barrington residents who were seeking to enforce a prohibition law. He was also annoyed that only a few Negroes bothered to attend the annual town meeting and he demanded that the race become more active politically, as a means of preserving their rights.[6]

He instructed his readers to learn more about the intentions of candidates for office. Du Bois was disturbed when he found that Negroes were not receiving their share of political jobs, and once he reminded his audience that a Republican official hired a white Democrat as night watchman, even though a Negro Republican sought the same position. As he viewed it, the Negroes should marshal their forces and establish their own political organization. Since he was taking a classics course in high school, he fancied himself as a man of letters and often used newspaper columns to persuade Negroes to cultivate an interest in literature and literary societies. After a trip through Providence, New Bedford, and Albany, he carefully reported substantial material growth among Negroes but little desire for cultural development. At the age of sixteen, Du Bois suggested his readers "consult" him before purchasing any books.[7]

The following year in 1885, Du Bois graduated from high school, and his senior oration was an account of Wendell Phillips, the anti-slavery writer. He hoped to attend Harvard College, but, having no funds, he gave up the dream—only for the time being.

Through a minister and four Connecticut churches, he received a scholarship to study at Fisk University in Nashville, Tennessee. Du Bois was excited about the chance to go into the South and especially anticipated the opportunity of meeting Negroes of his own age and educational background; he had been only too aware of his "spiritual isolation" in Great Barrington. Du Bois had formed romantic attitudes of Negro nationalism and remembered vividly "the colored world" he had seen on a picnic at Narragansett Bay, where he had been awed and entranced by this "whole gorgeous color gamut of the American Negro world." In his teens, he had heard the Hampton Quartet sing Negro folk songs and "was thrilled and moved to tears and seemed to recognize something inherently and deeply [his] own."[8] He was ready to leave New England with a feeling of tremendous expectation, for he assimilated the post-Civil War Abolitionist theory of race leadership—i.e., the Southern Negroes would prove themselves to all Americans when they were led by college-trained Negroes. Enrolling at Fisk University in the fall of 1885, Du Bois found "people of my own color . . . who it seemed were bound to me by new and exciting and eternal ties."[9]

Fisk University was founded shortly after the Civil War by the American Missionary Association, in order "to establish for the colored people of the South a University, that should adequately provide for them the advantages of Christian Education to whatever extent the capacity and energy of the race should in the future demand."[10] The future leaders of the race in the United States and Africa received large doses of Latin, Greek, and philosophy; little attention was given to industrial training as such, and the students were expected to learn "mental discipline" in order to assimilate a "broad, genuine culture." During the years Du Bois studied there, no professional schools were yet established, and all of the faculty members, except one, were white. Most of these teachers believed they were playing a profound role in the drama of racial development, and Du Bois recalled that in this period, "A new loyalty and allegiance replaced my Americanism: henceforward I was a Negro."[11]

The Great Barrington boy, who had enthusiastically attended the orderly town meetings, was shocked by the impassioned racial cleavages he observed in the South. He believed the aspirations of his people were being destroyed by racial prejudice, and he began to concentrate on a race-centered program designed to improve Negro living conditions. At Fisk he learned that Reason and Truth were The Virtues, and he planned to use them to solve the race problem. In order to learn more about the South and his race, he became a teacher in a Tennessee country school during two summers, and at close range he met the poverty, poor land, ignorance, and prejudice; beyond all else, he discovered within his people a deep desire for knowledge. A decade later he published an idealized account of these Negroes who lived and died within the shadow of a hill, separated by the "Veil" from "Opportunity." Southern mores humiliated him:

> I remember the day I rode horseback out to the commissioner's house with a pleasant young white fellow who wanted the white school. The road ran down the bed of a stream; the sun laughed and the water jingled, and we rode on. "Come in," said the commissioner—"come in. Have a seat. Yes, that certificate will do. Stay to dinner. What do you want a month?" "Oh," thought I, "this is lucky"; but even then fell the shadow of the Veil, for they ate first, then I—alone.[12]

Du Bois had also planned to write a fictional account of his summer adventure and penned a fragment of a short story entitled, "School Teacher." The slender plot concerned a bright Fisk student who was given shelter in a country store during a squall, and, while waiting for the weather to clear, he discussed Negro education with three illiterate white Georgians. Clearly, although the whites were depicted as ignorant and prejudiced, Du Bois did not intend to present them as incapable of change. In another piece, he recalled his first visit to a Negro revival meeting during this summer of school teaching and the emotionality of these rural blacks was wholly foreign to him: "The people moaned and flattened, and then the gaunt-cheeked brown woman beside me suddenly leaped straight into the air and shrieked like a lost soul, while round about came wail and groan, and outcry, and a scene of human passion such as I had never conceived before."[13]

When he returned to Fisk, he embraced his race with even greater determination than before. His early speeches revealed an affirmation of the dual themes of Negro nationalism and American heritage which were to pervade later writings. He was proud to be a Negro, but he wanted for his people all the rights to which they were entitled as American citizens. As editor of the Fisk *Herald* he wrote a piece called, "An Open Letter to Southern People." In it, Du Bois analyzed reasons for the defeat of pro-hibition amendments in Texas, Tennessee, and Georgia. He argued that Negroes voted against prohibition because whites supported it—the blacks were simply retaliating against the caste system. As Du Bois viewed it, whites neglected Negro schools to such a degree that few colored people were equipped educationally to decide on the merits of the amendment. He suggested the cleavage between the races was unnatural and unnecessary since both groups shared essentially the same concerns. It seemed to him that Negroes would be convinced of this mutuality if they were educated and if the whites demonstrated sincerity; he warned that intelligent whites would require Negro support on many coming issues because the South would not always be "solid." Du Bois carefully emphasized he understood the "inexorable laws of nature" and that he did not demand social equality or amalgamation; he reminded Southern whites unless they acted fairly, relations between the races would only worsen and become dangerous.[14]

Just as he had done in Great Barrington, Du Bois advised Negroes that blind obedience to the Republican party was an evil, and gains would be achieved through political independence. He counseled them to weigh each candidate's position on such issues as an anti-lynching law and civil rights. Although he blamed the Democratic party for the Ku Klux Klan, he was prepared to forget the past. (He even held Southern Negroes responsible for perpetuating the color line because they seemed inflexible in avoiding identification with the whites.)[15] In the election of 1888, Du Bois supported Cleveland and concluded that such a decision, multiplied by thousands, might set the balance of power process into motion and force each political party to compete for the Negro vote.

During those three years at Fisk, his comprehension of the race problem became clearer and sharper, and he resolved to fight the "color bar" in a forthright but peaceful way. He was optimistic that a solution would be found by the Negro intellectuals. He graduated from Fisk in 1888 and wrote a senior paper on von Bismarck, whom he admired as a statesman who solidified a divided land.[16] Du Bois was determined to take an undergraduate degree at Harvard College, the school which had been his first choice, and in the fall he entered as a junior. He never felt himself to be a real part of Harvard, but was able to accept isolation there because of his experience in the South.[17] Southerners refused to sit near him in class and Northern whites ignored him outside of it; on a few occasions he tried to join student organizations such as the glee club, but he did not feel welcome. It is difficult to ascertain how much of the rejection was due to his cold and aloof personality, and even Du Bois admitted that William Monroe

Trotter, who matriculated at the same time, had many white friends. Du Bois longed for companionship and wanted to be friendly with Trotter, but apparently the future editor of the Boston *Guardian* believed Negro students should not socialize with each other simply because of the accident of race, and he paid little attention to the young man from Great Barrington.[18] Du Bois agreed he probably had a reputation as an acid-tongued individual and this estimate was frequently given by people who came in contact with him.

In retreating from the white students, he argued they were preparing for another kind of world; although he opposed the color bar intellectually, he was ready "to accept the absolute division of the universe into black and white," and on the Harvard campus "the theory of race separation was quite in [his] blood." As he later wrote of the period, race became "a fetish" and he was "fanatical in its worship." In an account book which was kept during these years, he gloried in the "heart" of Africa and found it "nauseating" that the land of his forefathers should be bowing to an "Anglo-Saxon God."[19]

At Harvard Du Bois received intellectual stimulation from psychologist William James and philosopher George Santayana. Under the guidance of other professors, Du Bois' interest in history, economics, and sociology was expanded; however, a half-century later, he remembered Harvard as "reactionary" in economics and "conventional" in politics. In his academic work the subject of race was discussed and he heard lectures on biological-racial evolution; he was instructed that there were obvious differences among the major groups of mankind, and it was self-evident the lowest status belonged to the Negroes. Du Bois recalled a visit to a museum, where he viewed a group of skeletons in a progression from a monkey to a white man—with the Negro placed slightly ahead of the chimpanzee. Naturally, he did not believe in the inherent inferiority of his race; during these days he was able to accept the social evolutionary hypothesis and conclude that Negro advancement to the level of the whites could be realized within a reasonable period of time.

He gratefully accepted the friendship and hospitality which several of the professors offered, and to a small extent he was able to escape from his shell. However, he was relaxed and happy only with Negro college students and the colored community of Boston and New England—but many of these people also found him "conceited."[20] They had little patience with his Negro nationalism since they believed fervently in integration within the American society. (Du Bois charged that they were too willing to enter "under almost any conditions.")[21] His friends made many attempts to persuade him to surrender his dream and tried to convince him that he was not really a Negro, but a mulatto who should be totally unconnected with what was happening in the South. Du Bois replied he wanted to be the American they said he was, but the whites had categorized him as a Negro. He feared these intraracial cleavages, especially on the basis of complexion, and he recalled his annoyance with many mulattoes who, out of embarrassment, shunned darker Negroes. During these years, Du Bois' system of self-segregation was envisioned within a framework of temporary tactics, and eventually he hoped to arouse his fellows in an integration crusade. Yet he admitted race discrimination had forced him to feel comfortable only in the presence of Negroes and he tried to cast the "whiter world" from his consciousness.

Nevertheless, when taunted by published charges of racial inferiority, he was shrill in demanding political rights. In a rejoinder to one racist magazine article, he called upon Northern and Southern Christians to grant colored people a chance to prepare themselves for "American manhood." He announced that Southern Methodist deacons had hurt Negroes more than the Devil in Hell.

While praising the North for efforts on behalf of Negro education, he also reminded the region that its generosity did not extend to providing occupational opportunities for the same colored people whom it had schooled.[22]

In 1891 he argued that the Negro problem was "a vast economic mistake;" he declared that the Southern white oligarchy exploited its workers, and political participation would enable these laborers to protect their economic interests. Du Bois repudiated Henry Grady's statement that white-Negro relationships in Georgia were no different from employer-employee relationships in Massachusetts. In his opinion, Grady was incorrect because the desires of New England workers were recognized by their employers, who knew that economic grievances could be remedied by political action. Du Bois considered that history demonstrated a concomitance between the development of political rights and economic security. It seemed to him that the South suffered from over-rapid industrialization, complicated by political and economic ills—all of which were understandable and even excusable in the light of the region's past. He suggested that the problems of the area could be solved through the organization of a brain trust and the implementation of a university system. (As Du Bois saw it, the South had erred by attempting to use the grammar school and industrial school as the foundation of an educational program, with the university considered almost as a superfluous appendage.) The members of this brain trust were to be the creators and advisers of an educated and politically active working class.[23]

Du Bois seemed to believe there was something necessarily inherent in university education itself which would transform society into the realization of his hopes. Certainly, Harvard exhibited no worker-orientation in that period, and the status of the factory workers in New England at the close of the nineteenth century was not very high, in spite of their right to vote. Since many Southern Negroes were without the ballot, Du Bois tended to overestimate its value as a weapon of social change.

At the same time he was interpreting his theories to whites, Du Bois, who had graduated from Harvard in 1890 and was now a fellow in the Harvard Graduate School,[24] was actively engaged in admonishing Negroes to conform to those conceptions. In 1891, at the age of twenty-three, he told the Boston colored community exactly what he thought was wrong with the race. His speech was caustic and critical and he held the Negroes responsible in no small degree for their condition; he asserted that the race had made no contributions to civilization and was existing on a primitive level. He pointed out that libraries and literary societies were unused and ignored by many Negroes; even where established they were operated without imagination. He found little to praise in the literary programs and social gatherings of the Boston colored community and suggested they raise five thousand dollars a year for the support of a recreational-educational center. He indicted the Negro churches and ministry for inactivity, uselessness, and utter lack of concern for the race's education. The politicians, talkers, and resolvers were denounced, and Du Bois told his audience that, as Negroes, they should not debase themselves by embracing an "Anglo-Saxon standard of morality."[25] This talk portrayed a young intellectual who was standing alone, repelled by the low level of culture in his own racial group and just as pained by the whites who rejected him. His speech was probably interpreted by many of his listeners as an example of the worst sort of egotism. Certainly, he was prescribing a stiff dose of medicine for an uneducated people. His expectations were probably unreasonable when he suggested Negroes were not living properly unless they possessed an all-absorbing passion for knowledge.

From 1892 to 1894 he studied and traveled in Europe on a

grant from the Slater Fund, and the trip was noteworthy because it made possible the opportunity for intellectual growth and close friendships with Europeans. At the University of Berlin he studied economics, history, and sociology under such figures as Adolf Wagner, Heinrich von Treitschke, and Max Weber; from this experience came an assimilation of scientific methods of social research. He inquired into European social problems, and the Negro issue in the United States irresistibly grew in its world-wide implications. Abroad, he confirmed his trenchant opinions of white Americans and he "was a little startled to realize how much [he] had regarded as white American, was white European and not American at all."[26] From childhood until this trip, he had surveyed white people from a distance, but friendly, happy associations with a Dutch family on the boat, a summer visit with a physician's family in Eisenach, and gay outings with many other European young people caused him to review his ideas about racial barriers. Although he began to feel "more human," he was still an American Negro, and never in his life could he forget the implications of this fact. As a result of this stay abroad, Du Bois said that he stopped loathing others because they were members of the white race, and he vowed to put his new knowledge to use for the advancement of the Negro people. But the humilations of anti-Negro prejudice were to take their toll and Du Bois was to cry out in pain against discrimination and see it even where it did not exist. In the years ahead he was to develop the field of social research among Negroes, but he was never able to surrender his reservations regarding white people.

Undoubtedly Du Bois experienced something of a shock when he "dropped suddenly back into 'nigger' hating America."[27] He applied for teaching positions at such Negro institutions as Howard, Hampton, and Fisk, but there were no openings and he accepted an offer from Wilberforce College in Ohio to teach classics. From the beginning, the arrangement was an impossible one for him. ("I wore invariably the cane and gloves of a German student. I doubtless strutted and I certainly knew what I wanted.") He quickly realized that his plan to free the Negroes through the social sciences could hardly find implementation or even sympathetic reception at Wilberforce. The school had little money and was run by the African Methodist Episcopal Church. Politicians from church and state held court behind the scene and on the scene; the political intrigues infuriated Du Bois, and among his papers is a "fictional" account of "Burghardt College" and the adventures of the bishop's inept son who was granted a professorship by a toadying president living in constant fear of being removed from his position. The youthful Du Bois angrily indicted all who had sinned against the school—the "hope" of the race.[28]

He was troubled by the dogmatic religion which was the stamp of Wilberforce at the time and was nearly fired when he refused to offer an impromptu prayer while observing a chapel service. Wilberforce was the sort of place which prided itself on its religious revivals (especially liked by the more romantic students who took advantage of the opportunity for hand-holding), and classes were frequently released for devotions and fasting.[29] Du Bois was nauseated by the flood of fervor and passion, and wrote of a week-long confinement in his room—"driven almost to distraction by the wild screams, groans, and shrieks that rise from the chapel below me."

The opportunity to study the Negroes as a social system came to Du Bois in 1896 when the Provost of the University of Pennsylvania, Dr. Charles C. Harrison, offered him a special fellowship to conduct a research project in Philadelphia's Seventh Ward slums. Almost a half-century later, Du Bois recollected that "there must have been some opposition, for the invitation was not particularly cordial;" he recalled being offered a salary of eight hundred dollars for one year. In his autobiography, he claimed the figure was only six hundred.[30] Although he received a doctor's degree from Harvard the year before,[31] he said he was given the rank of "assistant instructor" and his name was not listed in the University of Pennsylvania catalogue. According to his remembrances, he maintained little contact with the faculty and none at all with any of the students, except for one occasion when he was called upon "to pilot a pack of idiots through the Negro slums." Du Bois also charged that Provost Harrison and sociologist Samuel McCune Lindsay represented a party of reformers who were seeking to prove, "under the imprimatur of the University," that the Negro voters were primarily responsible for the scandalous Republican administration in Philadelphia. He presented no verification for any of these statements.

A telegram from the University Provost to Du Bois showed the latter was paid nine hundred dollars for the year and this figure was confirmed by Harrison's report to the University trustees.[32] The monthly minute books of the trustees' meetings during the period were searched and there was only one mention of Du Bois, which took place after the Negro scholar had already started work on the project. The Provost simply asked that his action in appointing Du Bois be formally approved, and there was no indication the matter was discussed further, much less any suggestion of "opposition" to the appointment. There is no record in the minutes that Du Bois was employed with the rank of "assistant instructor," and the title actually designated by the Provost was "Investigator of the Social Conditions of the Colored Race in this city."[33]

Du Bois' bitter side-lights upon his experience in Philadelphia were in marked contrast to the temperate tone of the actual study which was published in 1899. The *Philadelphia Negro* was inspired by Miss Susan P. Wharton, a member of the executive committee of the Philadelphia College Settlement and a woman long interested in Negro philanthropy. Calling upon her many white friends for support,[34] she asked Provost Harrison "for the cooperation of the University in a plan for the better understanding of the colored people, especially of their position in this city. . . . [we] are interested in a plan to obtain a body of reliable information as to the obstacles to be encountered by the colored people in their endeavor to be self supporting."

Provost Harrison raised the funds for "a quiet, earnest effort to improve [the Negroes'] condition" by delineating the occupational areas in which they met with discrimination; this data was to be used as a basis to provide wider opportunities.

Du Bois plunged eagerly into his research,[35] because of his certainty that the race problem was essentially one of ignorance. He was determined to unearth as much knowledge as he could, thereby providing the "cure" for color prejudice. For over one year he studied a Negro ward intensively and personally interviewed several thousand people in a house to house canvass; he visited libraries and received special permission to examine private collections. He announced that he was assuming nothing and evolved a methodology to fit the conditions which he found in the field. He constructed a family questionnaire (number of members, age, sex, conjugal condition, birthplace, literacy, occupation, earnings, as well as other categories), an individual questionnaire with similar questions, a study of organizations, and a special one for servants who lived in the homes of their white employers. He curiously believed that he lessened his errors because he did not need to concern himself with "the varying judgments" of many interviewers. He was received in all but twelve homes and considered that almost universally he had established a high degree of rapport. Since one-fifth of the city's Negroes resided in the study area, he surveyed conditions in other wards, noting variations and collecting additional data on social organizations, property, crime, politics, and pauperism. He was satisfied that the section which he examined most intensively was sufficiently representative of the others. For the entire period, he lived in the Seventh Ward, and he and his young bride attended many social functions of the residents.

Du Bois found that unemployment was a serious problem and those who were working were primarily laborers and domestics; in many cases, these menial jobs were held by people with the ability to perform well in the higher status positions which were denied them because of their color; both labor unions and employers excluded Negroes from many opportunities. Negroes were living in a ghetto and met resistance when they sought housing beyond it; there was moral laxity ("fruits of sudden social revolution"), many households were poorly managed, and children were often attending school irregularly. Money was squandered on inadequate food which was often not cooked properly or nutritiously. More than a few Negroes dressed beyond their limited incomes. Du Bois concluded, "the Negro has much to learn of the Jew and Italian, as to living within his means and saving every penny from excessive and wasteful expenditures." Social institutions were examined intensively, and inevitably the Negro church was explored critically. He accused the church of "intrigue" and extravagance. The state and local governments were judged corrupt, and the Negroes, simply reflecting their surroundings, were represented as "the tool" of the party machine.[36]

The *Philadelphia Negro* is filled with Du Bois' leadership theories. He was concerned that the Negro "aristocracy" did not push the race forward; fearing they might be mistaken for the masses, they isolated themselves from them. Within the race, the lower class distrusted the higher class and turned in vain to the whites for guidance. Members of the Negro upper class rationalized their inactivity as race leaders by arguing that they refused to draw "the very color line which they protest."[37] Du Bois' investigation disclosed that the economic status of the upper group (inordinately dedicated to a higher standard of living) was nearly as unstable as that of the other Negroes, and, although many in the "aristocracy" were appreciably dependent upon the marginal masses for income, they were too insecure to be bothered about the problems of these people. Du Bois suggested that the upper class "can hardly fulfill their duty as the leaders of the Negroes until they are captains of industry over their people as well as richer and wiser."

Returning to his earlier theme of a Negro social system within the American democratic society, Du Bois emphasized that the whites had a clear right to expect the Negroes to do their utmost to solve their own problems; although he asked for white financial aid, he wanted no interference with this racial program. He declared the Negro race itself should recognize that its criminality is a "menace to a civilized people," and should take steps to improve family life. He recommended that a way be found to interest young people to forsake the brothels and gambling places and entertain themselves by more "rational means." He remarked that "the billiard table is no more wedded to the saloon than to the church if good people did not drive it there." He contended that Negroes should spend less time whining about the dearth of opportunities and more time in emphasizing edifying activities, such as lectures on physical hygiene.

Du Bois declared social services such as day nurseries, sewing schools, mothers' meetings, and parks should be organized and maintained by Negroes; it seemed to him that Negroes should also support their own building and loan associations, newspapers, stores, unions, and industrial enterprises. The hope of the race was in "the mastery of the art of social organized life." The foresight and diligence of the Negro upper class was necessary for this accomplishment, but it was imperative that the whites recognize these leaders and accord them status and power:

> The courtesies of life [can] be exchanged even across the color line without any danger to the supremacy of the Anglo-Saxon or the social ambition of the Negro. Without doubt social differences are facts not fancies and cannot be swept aside; but they hardly need to be looked upon as excuses for downright meanness and incivility.[38]

Although Du Bois' remarks indicate the hurt of a sensitive, educated Negro, he did not yet manifest the radicalism with which he became identified in later years, and he instructed Philadelphia Negroes to be "calm" and "patient" rather than "loud" and "intemperate." He believed changes would come inevitably, but slowly.

The *Philadelphia Negro* was reviewed in various periodicals. The *Nation* adjudged it "a very exhaustive study" although one which seemed "too gloomy" in view of the large number of Southern Negro migrants who were settling in Philadelphia, thus proving that living conditions could not be so undesirable in the city of brotherly love. (The reviewer did not consider that, although the Philadelphia milieu might have been perceived by the Negro migrants as superior to what was available to them in the South, the Northern conditions were not satisfactory in themselves.) The *Nation* also reasoned that, since capable Negro servants were prized by their employers, domestic labor did not need to be "degrading." This argument was a rationalization and somewhat irrelevant, since Du Bois merely pointed out that the domestic possessed low social status, earned little money, and frequently was placed in the position of having to care for her employer's children while her own roamed the streets. Du Bois had also emphasized a job ceiling which excluded Negroes from positions for which they were qualified. The *Nation* reviewer absurdly reminded the Negroes that other "races" were not given fair treatment, and, besides, social mobility involved unhappiness and possible failure. He concluded it was debatable that Negroes really lived under such traumatic conditions as people thought.[39]

The *Yale Review* termed the Du Bois study "a credit to American scholarship and a distinct and valuable addition to the world's stock of knowledge concerning an important and obscure theme."[40] The *Outlook* reported: "In no respect does Dr. Du Bois attempt to bend the facts so as to plead for his race.... All that his negro sympathies insure is that redeeming facts as well as damning ones shall be brought out. For the latter he is less apologetic than a generous-minded white writer might be."[41]

However, the *American Historical Review*[42] remarked quite pertinently that Du Bois was "perfectly frank, laying all necessary stress on the weakness of his people ... if any conclusions are faulty, the fault lies in the overweight given to some of his beliefs and hopes."

Du Bois conceived of this inductive project as only the beginning of a larger program in which American Negroes of other cities would be similarly studied. He also planned to add data on rural Negroes; since he discovered many of the Philadelphia subjects migrated from rural Virginia, he spent most of the summer of 1897 in that state and his observations were published by the United States Department of Labor.[43] He returned to Philadelphia that fall in order to address a meeting of the American Academy of Political and Social Science, where he unveiled the theoretical design for an investigative program.[44] He told the assembled scholars that Negroes did not share in the life of the nation, because they were socially unwanted and had not produced an acceptable level of culture. However, which factor was pre-eminent in accounting for the congeries of Negro problems? Negroes stressed the prejudice against them, while white Southerners (and those outside the region) emphasized cultural and racial deficiency; it seemed to Du Bois that sociology could determine just where the stress should be placed and to what extent. Such a project would enrich the social sciences significantly, because the Negro race made excellent subjects, having long been set apart and readily identifiable.

Since past researches on the Negro had been unsystematic, incomplete, uncritical, and biased, Du Bois suggested his people should be studied historically, statistically, anthropologically, and sociologically. The Negro past could be reconstructed through the collection of colonial statutes, Congressional reports, state reports, and personal narratives. Statistics could be accumulated on, among other factors, age-sex structures, conjugal conditions, occupations, and wages. The two races could be measured in a search for possible biological differences, and an exploration of the effects of amalgamation was necessary. Knowledge was also required on the extent of climatic and geographical influences. Evidences of group life could be gleaned from books, music, folklore, and from an intensive survey of the Negroes' social institutions. Naturally, the effect of anti-Negro prejudice was an important unknown; for instance, what changes did it make in connection with the race's "mental acquisitiveness," morality, criminality, and physical development?

The area of study was so expansive Du Bois believed that individual, small-scale research would be less valuable than organized programs conducted by a large university. (He also hoped the federal and state governments would contribute an appreciable amount of the statistical data.) It was his wish that a Southern Negro institution would direct this extensive program, but, of course, no school existed with the facilities which Du Bois required. Undaunted, he offered the whites an opportunity to subsidize a Southern Negro college which would collaborate with white universities. His suggestions were ignored.

He never had the opportunity again to examine another city as intensively as Philadelphia. However, in 1900, he was summoned to Chicago by some leading Negroes who were worried about the ever-increasing problem of Negro migration. He was asked to study the residents of three sample blocks. The following year he was engaged by *The New York Times* to write a series on the increasing populations and decreasing economic security of Negroes in Boston, New York, and Philadelphia. Little money was spent on these inquiries and the results are not noteworthy.

This chapter has shown that Du Bois' early life was dominated by a paradox. He sought to prove Negroes were capable of developing their own "superior" culture and he favored a separate racial social system. But he also repudiated "the color line" and wanted to overturn racial barriers. As a young man he tried to resolve the conflict by arguing that colored people should organize among themselves to prepare for an integration crusade. Since the sting of race prejudice made him feel emotionally safe only among Negroes, he seemed at times to neglect his announced end. Throughout his long career, he was to be pushed and pulled by this paradox.

He had no desire to see colored people totally assimilated in the American society, since he wished them to retain their loyalties to a Negro culture. He asserted that a colored ethos would contribute to the American way of life, complementing and elevating it. In effect, Du Bois was enunciating the theory of cultural pluralism, whereby peoples of diverse backgrounds "live together on a basis of equality, tolerance, justice, and harmony."[45] However, cultural pluralism was rejected by many whites, who ethnocentrically and racistly affirmed the inherent superiority of their group, and who maintained that accommodation between the races could be established only on the basis of dominance and submission. They demanded separateness, but not equality.

Du Bois, on the other hand, desired not only organized self-segregation, but also insisted that his people should be allowed to participate fully in the common political, spiritual, and social life of the nation. But these dual goals were contradictory, since they ignored the realities of the American milieu. A highly disciplined, almost bureaucratic, Negro social and economic system would have preserved in the minds of both races a sense of detached destinies and fostered among the colored people a glorification of separateness, thereby making it impossible for them to achieve full participation in the larger society.

Actually, the Negro world both intrigued and repelled Du Bois. He was disgusted by the disorganization, ignorance, and immorality which he saw and he condemned colored politicians, ministers, educators, and the rank and file. Yet from the contributions of these same people he was determined to construct a worthy way of life. He hoped to use the Negro university as the center of his program; the institution was to train a brain trust and sponsor systematic social research (representing the basis for social action). He called upon Negroes to establish their own social services, unions, and industrial enterprises under the exclusive direction of Negro "captains of industry." Of course, his ideas were impractical for a marginal and uneducated group. His faith in college-trained Negroes was often misplaced, since many viewed education as a symbol of status and exploitation, and not as a tool for race advancement.

He asked Negroes to be "calm" and "patient," and concluded that social reforms would come slowly and inevitably. On one occasion he even said a national election law was not as important as seeking the good will of white Southerners. After years of neglect, he was to make his reputation as one of the prominent architects of protest propaganda. For the time being, he asserted that race prejudice was caused by ignorance and social science would supply the knowledge to defeat injustice. The next chapter is devoted to Du Bois in the role of caretaker of his sociological laboratory at Atlanta University.

2. Social Reform Through Social Science

In 1897 W. E. B. Du Bois was called to Atlanta University by President Horace Bumstead. The young Harvard Ph.D. was employed to supervise the sociology program and to direct a series of conferences on Negroes which Atlanta had newly sponsored. The institution was unusual because it operated contrary to many of the Southern conventions; Negro students and white faculty shared the same dormitories and dining hall and white students who sought admission were not turned away. At least partly, because of these social deviations, Atlanta received no money from the Georgia legislature, and not a few Southerners thought of burying the school by means of oppressive taxation. Over the years, local newspapers published a spate of criticisms and the institution was accused of teaching racial egalitarianism; many Atlanta citizens viewed Northerners on the faculty as meddlers seeking to incite Negroes against whites. The General Education Board was unsympathetic with the manner in which the school was governed, since the Board advocated a rapprochement with the white South and its mores.[1]

Bumstead, a New Englander, believed strongly in the progress of the Negro race through its "exceptional men;" thus, he was attracted by Du Bois' brilliance and imagination. However, the college president was discouraged by white advisers who feared that the young Negro held no acceptable religious beliefs. Overcoming this obstacle was difficult and Du Bois had to promise to use the Episcopal prayer book when assuming his student chapel responsibilities. On many occasions the resourceful young teacher composed his own prayers; most of them were concerned with exhorting the race to cultivate thrift and industriousness.

Du Bois could not have been considered a popular teacher or colleague; respected because of his academic credentials and because of his undoubted ability, he had a reputation for being extremely "exacting and impatient." Students may have gladly accepted the chance to work under him because he was rapidly becoming an authority on Negro life, but he appeared too remote and austere to be regarded as a friendly person. Du Bois was somewhat conscious of the reactions of others and stated that while he was not always accessible, he did make an effort to drop his "mannerisms" and become "more broadly human."[2] However, his first address before the Sociological Club at Atlanta could not have won him many friends. He deprecated the previous programs of the organization, telling the membership that they talked too much and did nothing worthwhile. He commented upon the superficiality of their recent meeting on slums, announcing that they read the wrong books on the subject and erred in not embarking on an inductive study of Atlanta's deteriorated housing.[3]

Atlanta University had been influenced by the Tuskegee Institute conferences for farmers and teachers which Booker T. Washington innovated during the early 1890's. A short time prior to Du Bois' arrival on the campus, President Bumstead and George Bradford, a New England trustee, organized their program of annual conferences on urban Negro problems—probably because so many of the Atlanta students and graduates lived and worked in cities. In his autobiography, *Dusk of Dawn*, Du Bois wrote that he "peremptorily" revised the designs of the Atlanta conferences, which he claimed were meant to follow the Tuskegee pattern of inspiration and consecration. Instead, he stated that he substituted his program of science. Actually, Du Bois is at variance with what the facts seem to indicate and an examination of the first two conferences in 1896 and 1897, prior to Du Bois' direction, discloses that, although its leaders were interested in creating and re-enforcing an atmosphere of spiritual uplift and social reforms, embryonic inductive studies were made and were clearly spelled out for greater emphasis in the planning of succeeding programs. The Introduction to the published proceedings of the first conference stated:

> It was not expected that much in the line of scientific reports based upon accurate data could be presented at this first conference, but it was believed that much information could be gathered from the ordinary experiences and observations of graduates and others, and that the subject could be considered in such a manner as to arouse interest and enthusiasm, and so pave the way for collecting and digesting extensive and accurate data. Such, it is believed, has been the result of the conference held.[4]

Questionnaires were given to graduates residing in different cities, and such matters as family budgeting, earnings and occupations, and type of dwelling were to be recorded annually to note any improvements. The following year, some fifty graduates of Fisk, Berea, and Atlanta had interviewed about five thousand persons in seventeen Southern communities and Cambridge, Massachusetts. These data were transmitted for publication to the Commissioner of the United States Department of Labor. The editor of the second conference volume valued these individual city reports and anticipated using more of them during the following year.[5] In other words, Du Bois would have been closer to the facts if he had said that he generated interest in a research program already started by inexperienced men. Under his leadership the annual investigations became more encompassing and were conducted during the whole year.[6]

Du Bois' association with the conferences continued from 1897 to 1914; during that period he supervised the preparation of sixteen monographs. Since the inquiries were made by unpaid individuals on a part-time basis, Du Bois was somewhat limited in the breadth and extensiveness of his projects. In pursuing different areas of Negro life, he wanted each to have a "logical connection" with subsequent ones so that a "comprehensive whole" would gradually evolve. The first study treated mortality rates, inspiring an interest in impoverished living conditions and the manner in which they might be ameliorated. Such a focus was related to the economic foundation of the race, and the following conference dealt with *The Negro in Business*. In *The College-Bred Negro*, one year later, half of the subjects interviewed were school teachers and this fact led to an exploration of *The Negro Common School*. Du Bois began to think of the entire work as part of a "ten-year cycle," in which data on each race institution were to be published every decade; during the ten-year period all research projects were to be continued simultaneously. His "100 year" scheme was grandiose, since it was difficult to raise the meager amounts of money required for limited projects. He was unable to study politics and miscegenation because of the wrangle which such subjects would have evoked.

The Atlanta studies were of uneven quality in planning, structure, methods, and content; in order to demonstrate this disparity, one set of monographs which was poorly done will be contrasted with two studies which represent sounder research. His report, *Some Efforts of Negroes For Their Own Social Betterment*, was first completed in 1898 and repeated in 1909. However, in 1907, Du Bois received a special grant from the Carnegie Foundation and he produced a study entitled, *Economic Cooperation Among Negro Americans*, which, in part, concerned itself with the same kind of material found in the other two monographs. These three volumes leave much to be desired.

In examining "benevolent and reformatory" organizations for the 1898 work, Du Bois did not intend to inquire into all Negro communities around the country, nor to record exhaustively all appropriate activities in those cities which were observed. He selected several Southern cities, and the college graduates who collected the data were asked to record "typical examples." However, in one community, completeness was sought. Du Bois judged that the returns "seem to be reliable." Over two hundred "efforts and institutions" were studied, many of them sponsored by churches and secret societies. The church questionnaire included the following items among many others: religious denomination, number of enrolled members, number of active members, value of real estate indebtedness, religious meetings weekly, entertainments per year, lectures, literary programs per year, suppers and socials per year, concerts per year, fairs per year, other entertainments, number of literary and benevolent and missionary societies, annual income, annual budget, disbursements for charity, number of poor helped. . . . Similar questionnaires were provided for other types of organizations, and Du Bois judged that the returns from the beneficial and insurance societies were "not so full" because the enterprises were small and often changed their locations.

He considered that his presentation was of "scientific" significance because it demonstrated Negroes were not "one vast unorganized, homogeneous mass." However, race prejudice had isolated the group and caused the accelerated formation of racial institutions for which no adequate preparation had been made. Du Bois believed that more inquiries, such as this one, would provide the answer to the extent of white aid which the race required. At the conclusion of this study, Du Bois helped to prepare a series of resolutions calling for a program of racial austerity; for example, he advised that funerals should be simple, inexpensive, and without tawdry display. Having great faith in the value of co-operative businesses and consumers' associations, Du Bois offered his services as a consultant to those who wished to form such organizations.

Writing in 1898, he was not seriously troubled by the problem

43

of sampling procedures, either in the selection of his cities or in the data to be found within them. Nor did he have a passion for completeness in the one city chosen for intensive research. Although he was fortunate to obtain the services of educated interviewers, he gave few instructions beyond telling them to submit limited descriptions of some benevolent organizations within their own communities. He provided no method for checking the reliability or validity of the material sent to him, and this omission was serious since the officers of orphanages, for example, were asked to furnish statistics on their own administrations of the institutions. Du Bois succeeded in amassing an encyclopedic array of facts, often with little connection to each other, and he simply added them up when he could. He acknowledged that charitable services were performed to an unknown extent by individuals, but he made no attempt to allow for the ratio to the total picture. There are superficial lists of services and societies, and, after reading one column after another, there is a tendency to ask, "So what?" The "resolutions" do not seem to have grown out of the material presented and most of them are only exhortations which do not suggest any specific techniques to accomplish the ends sought. In declaring that churches should cut their operating expenses, Du Bois offered no yardstick which presumably might have been developed in this study. Counseling more austerity for funerals and secret societies, he failed to consider the integrating functions of ritual.

Du Bois asserted that the 1907 monograph was "a continuation and enlargement" of the 1898 account. In his treatment of the Negro church in 1907 he did not utilize any of the 1898 material on individual Negro churches; instead, he discussed the income, expenses, mission work, and many other details of the larger religious denominations. In this later study he made no reference to his handling of the beneficial and insurance societies in 1898.

The 1898 monograph contained a catalogue of various local "secret societies," giving the usual data on memberships, income, and expenses; the 1907 volume included the history and purposes of some of the larger societies, such as the Masons. The two treatments were not related to each other.

In the 1898 monograph, Du Bois mentioned several examples of co-operative businesses and a few of them were described in some detail. One of these organizations was a cotton mill named the Coleman Manufacturing Company, which was also discussed in 1907, but there was no connection made between these two examinations of the same company. Nothing was said about the development of the company in the nine years intervening; in one line Du Bois mentioned that the founder died "and a white company bought the mill and is running it with white help." Here was an excellent opportunity for a case study of the failure of a race enterprise—if more information had been gathered and related.

Some "resolutions" were promulgated by the conference committee of which Du Bois was a member, and a "crisis" was stressed in Negro organizational living, with the race depicted

> at the crossroads—one way leading to the old trodden ways of grasping individualistic competition, where the shrewd, cunning, skilled and rich among them will prey upon the ignorance and simplicity of the mass of the race and get wealth at the expense of the general well being; the other way leading to co-operation in capital and labor, the massing of small savings, the wide distribution of capital and a more general equality of wealth and comfort.[7]

This conclusion was not developed from the data presented in the monograph.

The 1909 volume, *Efforts For Social Betterment Among Negro Americans*, contained a section on methodology. Du Bois proposed to embark upon a "careful search for truth" although he admitted "mathematical accuracy" could not be expected. The conclusions were "incomplete" and the "sources are of varying degree of accuracy." He wrote to people "of standing" in various cities and asked them to compile the names and addresses of the benevolent associations about which they had knowledge. Letters of inquiry were sent directly to the groups named. Once more, he presented a cornucopia of facts; for instance, some of the questions he asked about Negro church denominations were: the number of communicants, the percentage of male and female members, the seating capacity of the churches, the value of the parsonages, and the total collection of the African Methodist Epsicopal Missionary Department from 1904 to 1908. Again, there was no connection drawn between any of the material offered in 1909 and the data given in the earlier volumes.

Obviously, the later monographs would have contributed more to social science if Du Bois had developed the data which he introduced in the earlier study on the same subjects. A selected list of orphanages or hospitals could have been studied in 1898 and re-examined a decade later. In this way, a more complete description would have been produced from which some hypotheses might have evolved. Du Bois should have placed his emphasis not on what these associations were supposed to do, but on what they actually did. He might have been concerned with the methods of leadership and the values of various approaches.

The monographs on *The Negro Artisan* (1902 and 1912) signified a more thorough and ordered contribution to our knowledge of the Negro. Du Bois recognized that he encountered a "peculiar difficulty," since much of his data came from "interested persons," although, to some extent, part of the material could be checked by "third parties." For instance, in some cases the word of the workers was validated by making inquiries of their fellow workers and their employers. The 1902 research was based upon many sources. A questionnaire was disseminated to hundreds of Negro skilled workers residing primarily in Georgia. These men described their work experiences in comparison with white artisans in the same occupations. Another schedule was sent to "correspondents" in many states who surveyed artisans in their own communities. (For example, one man described what trades Negroes entered in Memphis—whether they owned their homes and belonged to the same unions as whites.) Unions affiliated with the American Federation of Labor, and independent unions, received a questionnaire on the Negro worker; another schedule was placed in the hands of the central labor bodies in American cities, and state federations were also contacted.

As a result of these sources, Du Bois was able to provide both a list of unions which admitted Negroes and the relative proportions of the members of his race to the total membership of the unions. He could pinpoint the trades in which Negroes experienced hostility and he appended the views of labor leaders on race relations in industry. Industrial schools submitted information on their courses of study and educational leaders in all of the Southern states were asked about the kinds of manual training included in their curricula. They were also requested to comment upon the results obtained from such training. Employers in various parts of the South were asked to appraise Negro efficiency in relation to the whites and to consider whether the Negroes had shown any recent improvement. Comparative data were secured on the amount of money paid to Negroes and whites within various trades. In the 1912 survey, a similar set of questionnaires was sent to many of the same groups. Comparisons of census data for the two periods were made, in an effort to estimate whether the Negroes were holding their own in the various trades. Valuable generalizations were drawn from other data, e.g., most of the Negro trade schools were inadequate in providing their students with sufficient knowledge of a specific trade to enable them to compete satisfactorily with the whites; the schools were teaching their charges only "repair work and tinkering."

The Atlanta monographs were accorded a generally favorable reception; for example, a writer for the *Outlook* commented on *The Negro Artisan*: "No student of the race problem, no person who would either think or speak upon it intelligently, can afford to be ignorant of the facts brought out in the Atlanta series of sociological studies of the conditions and the progress of the negro.... The hand of the skilled and thorough investigator is conspicuous throughout."[8]

In 1904, a reviewer for the Southern History Association remarked: "The work done under the direction of the Atlanta Conference is entitled to the respectful and thoughtful consideration of every man interested in any aspect of the life of the American Negro. The guiding spirit of this work is Dr. Du Bois, and he is entitled to the utmost credit for what has been accomplished in the face of many obstacles confronting his undertaking."[9]

On the other hand, there were some negative comments. For instance, the *Political Science Quarterly* evaluated the monograph on *The Negro Church*: "Mr. Du Bois' theories and opinions may be correct; they are worthy of attention; but they are not well supported by any known facts, nor by the mass of valuable material here collected by himself and his fellow workers. Indeed the effect of the intermingling of facts and theories in this monograph is somewhat confusing and contradictory."[10]

In spite of the shortcomings of the Atlanta studies, what actual merit did they possess for science and society? If Du Bois must be held to his early goal of science, i.e., the ability to measure the extent of prejudice in causing the Negro problem, as differentiated from the Negroes' own cultural shortcomings,[11] his contributions are small. However, other American social scientists were hardly more successful in understanding race prejudice. Actually, Du Bois' Atlanta studies represent his efforts to introduce systematic induction into the field of race relations when other men were speculating about Negroes.

Du Bois' monument was his attempt to traverse the society, observing and counting what he saw, using the schedule, questionnaire, and interview. His method of case-counting was naive and elemental, and his questions were sometimes unsophisticated. ("Is the Sunday School effective in teaching good manners and sound morals?" "Is [church] influence, on the whole, toward pure, honest, upright living on the part of the members?")[12] But his decennial program was unique, even though none of the large universities contributed to it, as he had so much hoped. Who knows how much could have been accomplished if he had aroused real professional and financial support? Almost completely in vain, Du Bois made public appeals for help. In 1904, he said, "If Negroes were lost in Africa, money would be available to measure their heads, but $500 a year is hard to raise for Atlanta."[13] Later that year, President Bumstead informed him that the university's Executive and Finance Committee suspended publication of the last conference report until special funds could be obtained. In addition, future reports were to be sharply limited;[14] in 1905 Du Bois feared that conferences would be held biennially.[15] Somehow the studies continued, but, in 1908, President Ware (Bumstead's successor) asked Du Bois to terminate the project, and the move was only narrowly averted because of Ware's success in persuading the Slater Fund to grant a subsidy.[16]

Although his studies were lacking in systematic theory, Du Bois, through the use of his own data and that of others, made negative conclusions concerning the "common sense" generalizations held by many people of the period. For example, it was ordinarily agreed that Negroes were lynched because of well-founded accusations of rape or attempted rape. Du Bois reported, however, that in less than one-quarter of a long series of lynchings the victim had been charged with sexual assault.[17] Through comparative statistics, Du Bois also demonstrated effectively that the Southern Negro child received an inferior education, when one considered such indices as the length of the school term, the amount of school appropriations, the salaries of teachers, the value of school property, etc. Furthermore, he tried to disprove the accepted assumption that whites were the benefactors of Negro education in the South, and he estimated that Negroes paid a prominent proportion of the property taxes and indirect taxes, such as those on liquor.[18] He also asserted that Negroes should be credited with their proportionate share of state school funds received from special federal grants and the sales of public lands. This Du Bois "revelation" was widely quoted by many whites.[19]

Du Bois also repudiated the widely held view of Africa as a vast cultural cipher. In the unfolding of the Atlanta studies he presented a historial version of complex cultural development throughout many parts of Africa. Boas was quoted to prove that the glories of ancient Egypt were based upon "Negro Mediterranean culture."[20] Du Bois attempted to show that developmental processes became chaotic and stunted, not because of the inherent inferiority of the people, but as a result of the harmful influences of slave traders, geographical isolation, and oppressive climatic conditions. He was especially concerned with the incursions of the slave traders and contended that, as tribes fell apart or were forcibly joined, the more "primitive" folkways and mores were adopted.[21] He presented the natives as helpless victims, whose creative contributions were cruelly beaten down, and whose vast potentialities for growth were ignored or ridiculed.

It should be recognized that, although Du Bois stated the purpose of these Atlanta publications was "primarily scientific," he also admitted his efforts were meant to "encourage and help social reform." Undoubtedly, the attention given to the latter aim detracted from the former. Furthermore, the type of "social reform" he sought to promote naturally had its basis in the program which he developed before he went to Atlanta. In effect, the Atlanta studies served as a framework for the dissemination of his propaganda on leadership and Negro nationalism.

Since the publications covered a long span of years, it is not surprising to discover some revisions of his "social reform." In the 1899 volume, *The Negro in Business*, he deplored the fact that there were not enough Negro businessmen. He said "it gives the race a one-sided development . . . and puts the mass of the Negro people out of sympathy and touch with the industrial and mercantile spirit of the age."[22] He asked his fellows to patronize Negro enterprises, even though the prices were a little high. He considered Negro businessmen "pioneers in a great movement" that would make the race stronger and wealthier. (The 1899 conference advocated the establishment of a national "Negro Business Men's League" comprised of local and state branches. According to Du Bois, the Tuskegean Afro-American Council offered to make him the director of such a league, within its organization. The next year, Booker Washington formed the National Negro Business League. Washington was clearly familiar with the Atlanta Conference of Negro Business—as well as with other "valuable [Du Bois] studies"—and lifted the business league idea without even stating its source.)[23] In 1907, after Du Bois was influenced by American socialism, he condemned the exploitation of the common Negroes and emphasized "cooperation in capital and labor, wider distribution of capital and a more general equality of wealth and comfort." He spoke about transforming the race into a "self-supplying group" and favored the formation of a network of profit-sharing associations.

The Atlanta studies may not have improved the conditions of the race very much, but they probably did improve its morale. At a time when political and social restrictions upon the American Negroes were increasing, the Atlanta monographs must have provided many members of the race with a sense of group pride and ego satisfaction. In recording Negro achievements Du Bois was verifying the fact that the race was advancing. Negroes could also examine these volumes and find suitable arguments to account for their low status in American society, and these observations possessed the certified sanctity of "social science."

Although the studies never attained wide circulation, either among Negroes or whites, reviews of them appeared in important magazines and metropolitan newspapers. These accounts probably affected (however negligibly) some whites on at least two levels. First, white citizens learned one Negro institution of higher education was engaged in serious intellectual activity; this picture of Negroes as social scientists, and as individuals interested in the findings of social science, represented a view which was very far from the traditional racial stereotypes. Second, after reading articles or lengthy reviews of the monographs (if not the studies themselves), some white men probably concluded that Negro living conditions should be improved.

Scientific inquiries under the best of circumstances progress slowly and their effects upon the general population require even more time. But Du Bois, living in the South, was deeply aware of the seething and often erupting racist forces, and, after being confronted with "situations that called—shrieked—for action,"[24] he concluded that social research seemed futile. For example, the Sam Hose lynching was particularly harrowing to Du Bois. Hose was a Georgia Negro who killed his white landlord's wife at the turn of the century, and the Atlanta University professor hoped to publish a discussion of the case in the Atlanta *Constitution*. Before

Du Bois arrived at the newspaper office, the offender was already lynched and his knuckles were on display at a nearby grocery store. Hose's ignominious end symbolized the Southerners' refusal to consider the Negro race human enough to be accorded even elemental justice.[25]

During this period Du Bois also wrote propaganda pieces for national magazines. The separatist theme of Negro nationalism (so characteristic of the Atlanta monographs) was still evident, but, after the turn of the century, a shift became apparent and Du Bois began to *emphasize* a theme absent in the Atlanta studies—Negro civil rights. He also started to pursue direct social action tactics and in the next chapter these activities will be treated. The paradox involved in Du Bois' attempt to develop the race as a separate cultural group, and at the same time integrate its members in the United States, was ever-present. He learned to compartmentalize and move freely between his two contradictory goals.

3. The Overture to Protest:
Beginnings of the Du Bois-Washington Controversy

In 1899 the Georgia legislature was in a mood to consider the elimination of Negroes from politics and debated the Hardwick Bill which set literacy and property qualifications for voting. Although, before and after, Du Bois minimized the value of legislative lobbying, he and several others issued a statement opposing the bill. After sending it to the lawmakers, he took his case to a wider audience and wrote an article for the *Independent*. He assured readers that his protest was presented in "calm and respectful terms." The Atlanta professor did not object to the actual qualifications; he simply asked that they be applied to both races in a fair manner. He attacked the "grandfather clause" and the part of the bill dealing with a citizen's ability to interpret the Constitution. Du Bois realized both sections would transform the colored race into political pariahs.[1] The lawmakers did not enact the bill, but within a few years, Georgia (and other Southern states) effectively disfranchised Negroes by amendments to state constitutions.

In 1900 Du Bois led a group of Georgia Negroes in presenting another petition to the legislature; this time they hoped to prevent the passage of a law intended to reduce state appropriations for Negro education. As usual, the Du Bois protest was restrained and he argued that the welfare of the state was his primary concern. He contended that literate Negroes contributed more to the community because the public schools taught them to be thrifty and industrious; he suggested, if country schoolhouses closed, Negroes would become discontented, migrate to cities, and thus create labor shortages in rural districts. He observed (with tongue in cheek) that if Negroes were inherently deficient, the frustration of an educational challenge would force them to accept a lower level of aspiration. He also pointed out that an unfair division of the state appropriations would be an excuse for intervention by white philanthropists or the federal government, thereby possibly removing Southern whites from control over the Negro educational system.[2]

At the turn of the century, Du Bois was also designated spokesman for a committee of Georgia Negroes who complained they could not use the new Carnegie Library in Atlanta. Receiving no satisfaction from the board of directors, Du Bois published an account of the interview in the *Independent* as a propaganda piece, depicting an educated Negro's peremptory exclusion from a social institution which was ostensibly dedicated to the pursuit of learning. Du Bois admitted that whites needed libraries, but he asserted Negroes had greater need of them. He questioned the legality of expending public funds for the exclusive benefit of the whites. The head of the board thought a special library would be built for Negroes "in the future," probably financed by Northern philanthropists and the city of Atlanta. He added that the new white library might even come to be considered inferior to the projected Negro one, and at this point the interview was terminated "politely." Du Bois and the Negro delegation "walked home wondering."[3]

Du Bois used his talent as an essayist to publish numerous articles in popular magazines such as the *Atlantic Monthly*, *World's Work*, and the *Independent*, and his reputation increased as a leading interpreter of the Negro problem. The pieces were often impressionistic; their author was essentially a propagandist seeking the sympathy of the whites. He attempted to persuade whites that they did not know very much about his race, and that a careful study would confirm the damage which racism had done to Negroes. He observed that slavery had made large numbers of colored people careless and dependent; poorer Negroes were taught during the Reconstruction period that crooked politics represented a small, but necessary, source of income. In the face of charges that the Negro was a criminalistic race, Du Bois replied that "the first and greatest cause of Negro crime in the South is the convict-lease system." Crime was a "symptom of wrong social conditions," and, according to the Atlanta professor, colored people could hardly place their faith in a law which permitted lynchers to go unpunished.[4]

Du Bois pointed out that the race was being maligned, although it had proven itself capable of advancing.[5] In one article, he noted increases in property and land acreage as indices of racial growth. For effect, he stretched the truth and attempted to create the impression of a high degree of unity among the leaders and followers within the race. He discussed the Afro-American Council, representative of the "mental attitude of the millions," and noted that the organization had recently declared the United States government was duty-bound to protect the "life, liberty and due process" of the race and to legislate against lynching.[6] Once more, he admitted the "weaknesses" of the Negro masses and in 1901 even acknowledged "that it is possible and sometimes best that a partially undeveloped people should be ruled by the best of their stronger and better neighbors for their own good, until such time as they can start to fight the world's battles alone."[7]

He wanted to see the re-establishment of friendship and a "community of intellectual life" between "the best elements of both races." In seeking to encourage the good will of the whites, he had ambivalently minimized the effectiveness of legislative lobbying and propaganda presentations, but he did not relax his request for Negro suffrage and federal aid to education.

Du Bois even tried to frighten the whites into remedying conditions and stated that he observed rumblings of Negro resentment which could become dangerous to the established order. Southern Negroes, forced to be a party to the "hypocritical compromise," flattered the whites but whispered their "real aspirations." Northern Negroes, beaten down by discrimination, were drifting toward "radicalism." The "pent up vigor" and the "might of powerful human souls" would erupt inexorably into a strong protest, the exact nature of which Du Bois in 1901 left to the imagination of the whites. Examining a poverty-stricken rural Georgia Negro community, Du Bois foresaw the genesis of "a cheap, dangerous socialism."[8] In some of his essays of the period, the disheartened Negroes were pictured as the blundering or the faithless minority of the race; in others, the bitterness was described as more pervasive. In these articles the theme of radicalism was extremely overdrawn, probably for its shock effect. Du Bois also conveyed a higher level of unity within the race than the facts warranted. Taken together, these essays indicate that Du Bois, while accepting the separation of the Negro masses, was focusing more and more on the rights inherent in the "American creed."

In vain, Du Bois exhorted the Southern whites to demonstrate evidences of friendship and without success he had tried legislative lobbying. In 1901 he considered judicial review as a method of raising the status of the educated and more affluent Negroes, against whom a Georgia law had been passed denying them the privilege of using Pullman car facilities, even when travelling outside of the state. In reply to Du Bois' inquiry, the United States Interstate Commerce Commission suggested the name of a Negro lawyer to prepare the test case, and the Atlanta University professor, whose financial resources were small, sought the counsel of Booker T. Washington. The Tuskegean was pleased Du Bois had managed the project so well, and considerably later he agreed to contribute anonymously. Washington and Du Bois attempted to arrange an interview with Robert T. Lincoln, the president of the Pullman Company, but the latter was not eager to meet with them. After years of delay, the lawsuit was finally shelved.[9]

Du Bois involved himself in other limited social action skirmishes. In 1903 he heard that an official from the Rhodes Scholarship Foundation would visit Georgia in search of candidates, and the Negro sociologist reminded the representative that Atlanta University's faculty and students would not be invited to the scholarship conference which the white schools had scheduled. Du Bois learned that although Atlanta University might not be on the itinerary, Booker T. Washington would be consulted. The Tuskegeean was informed later that Du Bois' school had been ignored because its Mathematics Department was below caliber. According to Washington's account, he pleaded the cause of the Negro college men and had been assured the Rhodes Foundation would give them favorable consideration in the future.[10]

The Pullman and Rhodes cases are illustrations of the cooperation between Washington and Du Bois before the complete rupture in their relationship in 1904. As early as 1900, the Tuskegeean recommended the Atlantic professor for the top administrative position of the segregated school system in the nation's capital. Du Bois attended several of the Hampton and Tuskegee annual conferences and at the time called them "great" schools.[11] However, in 1901, he wrote another appraisal of Washington. Obviously the Atlanta professor had formed significant reservations which he was not ready to publicize as his own views. He observed that Washington's leadership was not a "popular" one, and that many "educated and thoughtful Negroes" (among them Paul Lawrence Dunbar) only mildly appreciated the Hampton-Tuskegee philosophy of industrial education. According to Du Bois, these men could not truly support the Tuskegeean because of

their advocacy of the Fisk-Atlanta program of higher education. Many placed their faith in racial "self assertion" and suffrage, and distrusted Washington because of his close identification with Southern whites.

On the other hand, Du Bois portrayed Washington's emphasis on industrial education as an essential link with the expansion of the Southern economy. He noted that the program attracted much-needed Northern and Southern aid. Washington was presented as the product of history and as the reflection of the industrial emergence of a nation "a little shamed of having bestowed so much sentiment on Negroes and was [now] concentrating its energies on Dollars." The "successful" Tuskegeean was a man of "evident sincerity of purpose," although the demands of the new system caused him to be "a little narrow."[12]

Relations between the two men remained cordial—at least on the surface. During the summer of 1901 Du Bois was invited to be a house guest at Washington's camp in West Virginia, but declined because of previous writing commitments.[13] The following year, however, Du Bois—concerned about the growing "breach" between the Negro colleges and industrial schools—asked the Tuskegeean to address the Atlanta Conference on the Negro Artisan.[14] Washington agreed, and in his speech he discussed the primacy of agriculture, the evils of urban life, and the superfluity of college education which left students unprepared for "fundamental . . . wealth producing occupations." His message undoubtedly succeeded in further widening the cleavage, although he recognized the contributions of Du Bois and the Atlanta conferences. Certainly, no one could quarrel with Washington's statement that agriculture would continue to be the race's basic industry for a long time, but his characterization of "parasite" jobs must have offended many of the Atlanta alumni: "I would much rather see a young colored man graduate from college and go out

and start a truck garden, a dairy farm, or conduct a cotton planta-
tion, and thus become a first-hand producer of wealth, rather than
a parasite living upon the wealth originally produced by others,
seeking uncertain and unsatisfactory livelihood in temporary and
questionable positions."[15]

About this time, Du Bois considered the possibility of an explicit
division of labor between Atlanta University (for empirical
research) and Hampton Institute (for practical applications). He
suggested that the General Education Board, and Booker T.
Washington, be approached to support the plan, although he was
somewhat hesitant and wondered if he would have independence
and "freedom" under such an arrangement. During this same
period, he was approached by Booker T. Washington's friends,
who tried to persuade him to work for Hampton Institute and
become an editor of a new Negro periodical. In the clearest terms
he demanded the right to establish editorial policy, refusing to be
controlled by the "Tuskegee philosophy." Nothing more came of
the Hampton invitation. Other backers of Booker T. Washington
told Du Bois he could have a bright future at Tuskegee Institute,
but the school's founder seemed "suspicious" of him. Du Bois
wanted to continue his annual researches and doubted Washington's
interest in them; he also feared he might be required to serve as a
Tuskegee "ghost-writer."[16] Both men came to distrust each other
and, in order to understand the controversy which became public
in 1903, the basic beliefs of Washington should be examined.

Booker T. Washington, according to white Southern leaders,
espoused "a perfect system of accommodation" between Negroes
and whites in the "New South."[17] He became the spokesman for
those who wanted the Negro race to be a labor force and not a
political force. He separated politics and economics and argued that,
when colored people had advanced economically and produced
industrious workers and successful businessmen, whites would not

oppose Negro suffrage. Washington and his followers did not seem to consider it too significant that there were many incompetent whites who were voting and many competent Negroes who were not.[18] Nor did the Washingtonians appreciate that political power could also improve, to a limited extent, economic conditions in the race. While he said he wanted nothing less than what was promised in the Constitution,[19] he emphasized that Negroes would receive "all privileges of the law" *after* they were "prepared." He believed the acquisition of property would make Negroes "conservative" voters, especially if they "consulted the whites before voting." Actually, Washington did not condone racial disfranchisement although most whites thought he did. When the Louisiana legislature sought to disfranchise Negroes in 1898, Washington complained to the lawmakers and newspapers. After the law was passed he secretly gathered names of people in Boston who would contribute money to test the law in the courts.[20] Yet he continued to minimize politics as a road to racial advancement. Paradoxically, he also served as presidential personnel adviser to Roosevelt and was consulted on both Negro and white appointments.[21]

Since ballots were not as essential as jobs, the Tuskegeean dedicated himself to training Negroes for vocational opportunities. He believed Southerners, with their long history of racism, would not support Negro education unless they were convinced a docile, efficient labor supply would result. Industrial training, therefore, evolved from an environment of expediency, but under the Tuskegeean it became the absolute principle embracing nearly every virtue.[22] Three years after he opened Tuskegee Institute in 1881, the state legislature of Alabama was so impressed it voted the school an annual appropriation. The Negro leader had discovered he gained tangible help by refusing to protest against injustice and by emphasizing harmony within the framework of the caste system. Finding so much opportunity for moral growth in "beginning at the bottom," he almost seemed overjoyed that the whites made it possible for Negroes to start with so little.

He said his people should educate themselves for those tasks which the community would permit.[23] Since he contended that the race's main concern was with industrial-agricultural pursuits, he believed the educational system must reflect that fact.[24] According to him, white and black proponents of higher education would benefit the Negro race if they recognized industrial education as the proper beginning. When property had been acquired, art and literature could then be cultivated.[25] On countless occasions, the Tuskegeean denied his program was opposed to Negro higher education.[26] However, for every statement of Washington which seemed to support liberal arts, there were many others in which he demonstrated a distrust. He made innumerable references to a young man living in a hovel, dressed in grease-splattered clothes, but busily studying a French grammar. He often spoke of the Negro boy who went to Hell in the big city after receiving the kind of education that caused him to lose interest in his father's farm.[27] Certainly, Washington was critical of the Negro colleges. It was fashionable for writers of the period to state that higher education did not really compete with industrial education and that both contributed to each other;[28] actually, the Tuskegeean, while seeming to grant Negro higher education its own small sphere of influence, proposed to make industrial education a universal training ground.[29]

After his sentiments were acclaimed at the Atlanta Exposition in 1895, it was not a difficult matter to find financial aid and co-operation from Northern philanthropists (such as Andrew Carnegie), whose economic philosophy Washington had appropriated. In 1901 he helped to form the Southern Education Board; the organization was composed of prominent educators and industrialists and subsidized Negro institutions which preached the gospel of industrial education. The following year the program was expanded and the General Education Board was established. To influential whites Washington had become the only *bona fide* representative of the Negro race.

Now that the Washingtonian ideology has been reviewed, it will be compared and contrasted with the Du Boisian program at the beginning of the twentieth century. Up to that time, Du Bois differed with Washington on many things, but he was not so far from the Tuskegeean ideologically as were other men who later regarded the Atlanta professor as the firebrand apostle of the anti-Washingtonian movement. For the most part, Du Bois and Washington respected each other, although their personalities were too different to build a friendship. With the Tuskegeean he placed his emphasis upon securing the good will of the white upper class, instead of relying primarily upon legislation to raise the status of the Negroes. Nevertheless, both men sought to prevent racist legislation from being passed and both attempted to test racist laws which had been enacted.

The two leaders pointed up Negro "weaknesses" and exhorted the race to transform itself morally and become increasingly industrious and thrifty. Washington and Du Bois argued that their race, living in a milieu of separateness, had its own destiny and its own differentness. According to Du Bois, his people were essentially musical, artistic, humble, and jocular; all of these traits provided a necessary complement to American commercialism. Washington saw his people as cheerful, devoted, tractable, and humble; these attributes served to furnish an excellent labor force for the capitalist system. Du Bois on occasion was more critical of capitalism but still supported Negro entrepreneurs. The two educators favored Negro nationalism or racial self-sufficiency. Washington's system was domestic, while Du Bois' "Pan-Negroism" encompassed the United States as well as other lands, such as Africa and the West Indies.[30]

As already shown, the major difference between the two philosophies was in connection with education. Du Bois suggested a plan centered around the Negro college, with a cultured brain trust urging the race forward; while the Tuskegeean emphasized industrial education and repudiated "abstract knowledge." It is questionable that there would have been a conflict between these ideologies if the Washingtonians had not insisted their program was so valuable it warranted universality, and if they had not annointed their chieftain as "the accepted representative man among ten million of our fellow citizens."[31] As a result, many whites begrudged Negro colleges their meager operational budgets because of the belief that such money was squandered on the teaching of useless subjects, and should have been earmarked in the first place for industrial schools, where some good could have been accomplished.[32] At a time when Du Bois watched his beloved Atlanta University starving, the Washingtonians were enjoying prosperity and ever-increasing influence.

Another difference which was slowly becoming apparent concerned the suffrage question. Both men advocated it for literate Negroes, although Washington stressed "preparation" for the ballot more than he propagandized for immediate voting. While evident before 1902, this split was to be sharper in the following months. Whites were soothed by Washington's gradualism, happy in the knowledge that nothing "dynamitic"[33] would be attempted by Negroes. Pursuant to the Washingtonian formula, slowness was actually speed because it guaranteed the race's salvation, when Negroes could "be great and yet small, learned and yet simple, high and yet the servant of all."[34] While Du Bois disavowed useless complaint, he seemed to hold Negroes less responsible for their condition than Washington did. The Great Barrington Negro protested calmly, but he presented a picture to the whites of racial discontent and incipient revolution. He wanted a rapprochement but his words suggested more urgency than Washington's.

In Du Bois' 1901 article in *Dial*, he had pointed out that there were some Negro leaders who opposed Washington's conciliatory approach. Unmentioned among the insurgents was William Monroe Trotter, who founded the Boston *Guardian*, the organ which became the thorniest critic of Washingtonian policies. The *Guardian* editor asked Booker T. Washington:

> To what end will your vaulting ambition hurl itself? Does not the fear of future hate and execration, does not the sacred rights and hopes of a suffering race, in no wise move you? The colored people see and understand you; they know that you have marked their very freedom for destruction, and yet, they endure you almost without murmur! O times, O evil days, upon which we have fallen![35]

In the sharpest language, Trotter termed Washington a political boss who masked his machine by pretending to be an educator. He resented the Tuskegeean's connections with President Roosevelt, because the apostle of industrial education, according to the editor, opposed Negro participation in politics. Trotter also criticized Washington for trusting the President (who encouraged the lily-white Republican party in the South). On one occasion the *Guardian* editor accused Washington of being instrumental in the appointment of a lily-white Republican to replace a white Democrat as Collector of Internal Revenue in Alabama; the journalist implied that a cash reward was expected for that political chore.

Trotter, besides editing the *Guardian*, was the "spearhead of sentiment" of the Boston Radicals*, a group of Negroes who had

---

* "Radicals" is used as the generic term for Negroes who were anti-Washington.

graduated from various New England colleges. By 1902 the lines of battle were becoming more sharply drawn and Trotter demanded that a man support the Washingtonians or the Radicals. He was particularly desirous of wooing Du Bois into the Radical camp, since the latter's academic achievements impressed educated Negroes. According to Kelly Miller, Trotter was sensitive to the charges of the Washingtonians that his position was visionary, and the *Guardian* editor was determined to set up an organizational structure and attract wider support for social action projects. Miller contended Trotter was aware of his own oratorical shortcomings and "began to cast about for a man of showy faculties who could stand before the people as leader of his cause. He wove a subtle net about W. E. B. Du Bois, the brilliant writer and scholar, and gradually weaned him from his erstwhile friendship for Mr. Washington, so as to exploit his prominence and splendid powers in behalf of the hostile forces."[36]

Actually it need not be hypothesized that Trotter hatched a cunning plot to secure Du Bois' assistance or that Du Bois had become his unwitting tool. By 1902 Du Bois, while not "in absolute opposition" to Washington, had moved closer ideologically to the Boston journalist. The Atlanta professor's redefinitions essentially resulted from his increasing disenchantment with the Tuskegeean's methods and platform. Du Bois could only have responded with wrath to a typical Washingtonian statement of that year: "One thousand bushels of potatoes produced by the hands of an educated Negro are worth more in solving our problems than dozens of orations or tons of newspaper articles."[37]

Nevertheless, he refused to be actively and publicly anti-Washingtonian, not only because he did not disagree with the Tuskegeean's Negro nationalism and self-help themes, but also because he believed that as a social scientist he should be removed from the tumult of a leadership struggle. According to Maude Trotter Stewart, her brother was very frustrated when he discovered that Du Bois was "just not strong in wanting to fight."[38]

In September of 1902, Du Bois attacked ideas to which Booker T. Washington obviously subscribed, but the Tuskegeean was not directly named. The Atlanta professor was critical of those who discouraged a liberal arts education for Negroes. He considered the exclusive preoccupation with industrial education was futile and reaffirmed that the only effective foundation was higher education, since "progress in human affairs is more often a pull than a push, a surging forward of the exceptional man, and the lifting of his duller brethren." Because of the "dangerous" segregation patterns, educated Negroes would serve as stewards of the race, but Du Bois clearly defined their roles as temporary. Once more, in wrestling with his conflicting desires for Negro nationalism and integration, he seemed to conclude in favor of the latter: "The present social separation and acute race-sensitiveness must eventually yield to the influence of culture, as the South grows civilized."[39]

Trotter was so delighted with Du Bois' article that he used it as the basis of an editorial in the *Guardian* which was entitled, "Two Negro Writers, But How Different." He made a stinging comparison between a selfish, unoriginal, and thoroughly unenlightened Washington; and a brilliant and resourceful Du Bois, whose contribution was "beyond all praise, with one or two exceptions it is without a doubt the very best thing that has been said by a Negro on the question of Negro education in America."[40] Du Bois' reaction to this fulsome editorial is not known, but it would have been understandable if he were overjoyed by such a reception, especially in view of the mounting atmosphere of distrust and condemnation between him and the Washingtonians. Perhaps such red-carpeting by the Boston Radicals enabled him to make his break with Booker T. Washington more easily. Within a few months, in January of 1903, Trotter wrote a front-page article announcing Du Bois would soon speak on a program sponsored by the Boston Literary Association. The following week Trotter reported Du Bois was given an "ovation" and "the presence of this educated Negro must have won over every one present to the positive advocacy of the higher education for the race, though Prof. Du Bois said nothing of that subject."[41]

During the spring of 1903, Du Bois published *Souls of Black Folk*, a book which James Weldon Johnson described as having "a greater effect upon and within the Negro race in America than any other single book published in this country since Uncle Tom's Cabin."[42] There was no doubt that the chapter, "Of Mr. Booker T. Washington and Others," created an intellectual and emotional flutter for many, and Johnson credited this analysis of racial leadership with affecting "a coalescence of the more radical elements and [it] made them articulate, thereby creating a split of the race into two contending camps. . . ."[43] Basil Mathews, one of Booker T. Washington's biographers, agreed that this essay was a crucial factor in furnishing "the anti-Washington movement, for the first time, with a coherent argument."[44] William Ferris, a contemporary Negro observer, contended that Du Bois' volume became the "political bible" of the educated segment of the race and that Du Bois was honored as the "long-looked-for political Messiah."[45] Actually, the evidence seems to indicate that, although the Radicals thrived on Du Bois' book, the Atlanta professor still refused to take an active leadership role in the promotion of a formal organization and continued "to occupy middle ground."

Whatever Du Bois' desires, *Souls of Black Folk* completely alienated him from the Tuskegeeans, and a perusal of the contents of the chapter, "Of Mr. Booker T. Washington and Others," will disclose the reasons quickly. Essentially, Du Bois said nothing that he had not stated before; this time, however, he *explicitly* indicted

Washington. It seemed to Du Bois that Booker Washington arose primarily as a compromiser between the North and South and that his ideology "practically accepts the alleged inferiority of the Negro." Du Bois observed that within the last years, his race had become disfranchised and suffered egregious losses in civil status, as well as in the support of its institutions of higher education. While the Atlanta professor admitted these deprivations were not the direct consequences of the Tuskegean's teachings, he did hold Washington accountable for their acceleration. He charged that the Tuskegean had sealed an economic bargain with the South, wherein civil rights and college degrees were unimportant, at least temporarily. Du Bois argued that the race could not forge ahead without the attainment of these very objectives which had been surrendered. He did not deny the importance of pacifying the South, but he refused to pay Washington's price which he interpreted as degradation and virtual slavery. Du Bois, acknowledging the Tuskegean had lobbied to prevent the Negroes' disfranchisement, charged the leader had also condoned the ever-tightening caste system. He proposed several "supplementary truths" to Washington's "dangerous half-truth" that Negroes bore the major responsibility for remedying their problems: slavery and race prejudice were important causes of the low status of the race; an adequate Negro educational system depended or the training of teachers by the colleges; and self-help required more effective encouragement from affluent whites. The Atlanta University professor advised disaffection from "part of the work of [the Negroes] greatest leader."[46]

After *Souls of Black Folk*, the *Outlook*, a white weekly friendly to Booker T. Washington, portrayed Du Bois as a whining, impractical racial renegade who was "half ashamed of being a Negro."[47] The Tuskegean-dominated press embarked upon a campaign to vilify and intimidate Du Bois. For example, the

Washington *Colored American* vigorously urged President Bumstead of Atlanta University to silence the professor:

> If Atlanta University intends to stand for Dr. Du Bois' outgivings, if it means to seek to destroy Tuskegee Institute, so that its own work can have success, it is engaged in poor business to start with; and in the next place, the assurance can safely be given that it will avail them nothing. Tuskegee will go on. It will succeed. Booker Washington will still loom large on the horizon, notwithstanding the petty annoyances of Du Bois and his ilk. Dr. Bumstead in his Northern campaigns has pretended to acknowledge the efficacy of Tuskegee's methods and also to recognize the necessity of the two kinds of education—the very thing Booker Washington himself does. Visitors who were at Tuskegee during the late Negro Conference will readily remember a speech made there by Dr. Bumstead, in which he declared most positively that there was no friction between the two schools, and was also most loud in his protestations of friendship and interest. Let him prove himself by curbing the outgivings and ill-advised criticisms of the learned Doctor who is now in his employ; that is, if Du Bois does not really represent him and the sentiment of Atlanta University....[48]

Perhaps the fairest analysis and evaluation of Du Bois' aims appeared in an essay by J. S. Bassett in the *South Atlantic Quarterly*. (Trotter was so pleased with this piece that he gave it front-page treatment in the *Guardian*.)[49] Unlike many others, Bassett did not view *Souls* as a frenzied, malevolent assault on Tuskegee. Since the college-trained Negroes had been all but ignored in the tumult of industrial education, Bassett held that Du Bois' defense of their interests was understandable and justifiable in any intelligent consideration of the methods to establish an interracial peace. Recognizing that Negroes did require cultured leaders as well as skilled workers, Bassett tried to allay the economic fears of the

Southerners by assuring them that there would always be an ample Negro labor force, because only a small minority would ever pursue higher education. Commenting on a popular racist book entitled, *The Negro a Beast or the Image of God*, he asked whether a "Beast" could have produced *Souls of Black Folk*.

In July of 1903 Du Bois took another step closer to the Boston *Guardian* when he too made it clear that the Tuskegeean was actually a political boss. He went further than he had in his critique of the preceding spring and unfairly increased Washington's responsibility for the anti-Negro attitudes of the whites: "He has so manipulated the forces of a strained political and social situation as to bring about among the factors the greatest consensus of opinion in this country since the Missouri Compromise."[50] The last thing Washington wanted to be called was a political colossus and friendly newspapers answered this "covert sneer."[51]

While Du Bois was willing to flail away at Washington he was still reluctant to take an active leadership role in marshalling the Radicals. He did not accompany William Monroe Trotter to the annual Afro-American Council meetings at Louisville in the summer of 1903, and the *Guardian* editor led the Radicals' unsuccessful struggle to wrestle control of the Council from the Washingtonians. At the sessions Washington was execrated as a villain who sold his soul, and a free-for-all ensued after the Council passed a resolution endorsing Theodore Roosevelt. Trotter, accurately charging Washington owned the organization, was defeated after he was unable to substitute a resolution condemning the President for not influencing Congress to help the Negroes. The Boston *Guardian* editor also damned Roosevelt for selecting white Democrats to fill political posts in the South, while sending Negro Republicans home empty-handed. The Radicals sought to generate interest for a prompt reconvening of the Council, and Booker T. Washington commissioned Emmett J. Scott, his private

secretary, to persuade Negro newspaper editors to pay no attention.[52]

The infuriated Trotter returned to Boston and on the night of
July 30–31, 1903, he led a rebellion against the Tuskegeean which
came to be known as the Boston Riot. It was this incident which
finally brought Du Bois into active leadership of the Radicals. The
Atlanta professor did not have any connection with the fateful
skirmish and did not arrive in Boston (where he stayed with
Trotter as a house guest) until after the disturbance. His first reaction after hearing about the uprising was a feeling of exasperation
and anger—at Trotter's impetuosity.[53] However, after making an
investigation, he concluded the riot was actually precipitated by a
Washington man. He fumed when the *Guardian* editor was jailed
as a provocateur, and the professor wrote a letter (which the Boston
Guardian printed) supporting the journalist. Perhaps it was this
published letter which caused some "prominent and influential
man" (George Foster Peabody, a backer of Booker T. Washington)
to broadcast the rumor that Du Bois was linked "with Trotter and
[the] conspiracy." The note certainly disturbed trustees of Atlanta
University and it was discussed at a meeting of the school's
executive committee. President Bumstead maintained complete
confidence in Du Bois, and the group took no punitive measures
against the sociologist.[54]

Nevertheless, both the President and Chaplain of Atlanta
University were anxious about the rumor. Du Bois understood
their fears and dispatched a note to Peabody, disclaiming any
responsibility for the riot. In frankness, he rejected Trotter's
excesses but respected his honesty. He asserted his friend was "far
nearer the right" than Booker Washington, who was "leading the
way backward." Naturally, this second Du Bois letter did not
please Bumstead, who had hoped the Atlanta professor would
have been conciliatory and simply acknowledge his innocence in

the Boston episode. He was unprepared for Du Bois' comparison and feared the reaction of Peabody and other Tuskegeean friends. When Atlanta University's leading trustees examined a copy of the note, there was "quite an outburst of dissent from fully half of those present." Bumstead remained loyal to his friend but seemed more conscious than ever "of the difficulty of being honest with ourselves and at the same time being judicious in dealing with those who do not agree with us."[55]

The Boston Riot itself demonstrated the plethora of emotions which were evoked and the rising tide of resistance which was evident when Booker T. Washington arrived at the African Methodist Episcopal Church for a Business League rally. For several months the Tuskegeean had prudently declined speaking engagements in Boston, the Radical capital, because he wished to avoid the kind of disturbance which finally occurred.[56] Washington's circumspection only caused Trotter to announce belligerently that the educator would not make a public appearance because of cowardice. The group at the church on that night of July 30 was a large one, since the Washingtonians, overzealous in their acceptance of the Radicals' challenge, made strenuous efforts to publicize the program and printed a long list of their prominent supporters. Many people came to the church because they heard "something" was going to happen. W. H. Lewis and T. Thomas Fortune, both Washingtonians, addressed the assemblage, and, whenever they referred to their leader, hissing sounds reverberated throughout the room. The crowd grew restless and angry. After the Tuskegeean was introduced, he was unable to say more than a few words because of the furor, and finally twenty-five policemen were called. When the Negro chieftain proceeded, he unwisely chose to unwind an old anecdote about a mule, and the Trotter men began to fume again.[57] Trotter arose and asked Washington several loaded questions on education and voting: "In view of the fact that you are understood to be unwilling to insist upon the Negro having his every right (both civil and political) would it not be a calamity at this juncture to make you our leader? ... Is the rope and the torch all the race is to get under your leadership?"[58]

The audience by this time was completely out of control; men were yelling and hissing; simultaneously, some enterprising partisans brought forth "red pepper and stink bombs." Trotter was arrested and became a martyr—his followers conducted sympathy services in Washington, New York, and Chicago.

Booker T. Washington philosophically described the Boston Riot as inevitable and his friends sought to discredit the Radicals as emotionally unstable, offering the excesses during the affair as proof. The Boston white newspapers such as the *Herald* and the *Transcript* reported the episode and held Trotter responsible. Emmett J. Scott and Washington efficiently dispatched these comments to various Negro newspapers for reprinting. Since the clippings in the white press and in most of the Negro papers were friendly to Washington, Scott was undoubtedly correct in saying that the Radicals had lost ground.[59] Washington went further and wrote to his friends that he was convinced Trotter and Company had "completely killed themselves" among all elements—Negro and white—in Boston.[60] Since Du Bois' name did not appear among the culprits, it seems reasonable to conclude the Tuskegeean knew that the Atlanta professor was not involved in the fracas. According to Washington's version, Trotter was removed from the church "in handcuffs, yelling like a baby." Actually, the Boston editor enjoyed his martyrdom and spurned an opportunity to avoid incarceration and accept probation. Though locked up, he continued to write for the *Guardian*.[61]

Two weeks after the riot, Washington wrote to President Roosevelt and told him that after a calm analysis (in a "purely unselfish ... disinterested" light) he felt only pity for the Radicals.

In his supposedly unbiased opinion, the Radicals were simply jealous of his good fortune; these men were parasites who had never come up the hard way through "natural and gradual processes." Their present life was therefore "artificial" and they believed Washington should place the race in a similar "artificial" milieu.[62] Years later, Washington recalled the night of July 30 and indicted the "intellectuals" who thought "the world owes them a living." Unbelievably, he contended that some of these educated men profited so much from protesting that they would have been unhappy if the Negro problem were solved.[63]

It is difficult to assess how much of Washington's implacable stand toward the opposition was caused by his own jealousy of their college degrees and cultural advantages. How much of his resentment of their demands for independent thinking was due to psychological uneasiness in dealing with these intelligent men, and what proportion of his unyielding attitudes was the result of guilt feelings, caused by his frustrating silences before the white philanthropists? Did Washington's antipathy for the Radicals stem in part from the historic social distance between free Negroes and those who, like himself, experienced the slave status. Most of his opponents had forebears who were free for many decades before the Civil War. They possessed a sense of reverence, perhaps even snobbishness, about their lineage. In Du Bois' own writings about his family, for example, there was an obvious sense of pride in "our free birth."[64]

At any rate, the Washingtonians were determined to have their full measure of revenge and they continued in their efforts to penalize all of the principals of the Boston Riot. Emmett J. Scott pursued George Washington Forbes, the co-founder of the *Guardian*, and tried to pull strings to have him dismissed from his Boston library job.[65] Another attempt was made in 1903 to hurt the *Guardian*. Many weeks before the July 30 disturbance, William

Pickens, a suspected Washingtonian, delivered an address in Boston on Haitian history, and Trotter said unkind things about him in the newspaper. In the fury after the riot, Washington's attorney visited Pickens and recommended the institution of a libel suit against Trotter. In October, Du Bois, hoping to quash the Tuskegee-financed suit, dispatched a letter to a good friend of Pickens.[66] Although Pickens eventually withdrew the suit, the Atlanta professor knew who had instigated the legal affair.

In the wake of the Boston Riot, Trotter's imprisonment, and the legal activities against the Boston *Guardian*, Du Bois increased his emotional commitments to the Radicals. He had painfully observed the power and implacable influence of Booker T. Washington and was filled with disgust and anger. Now he was finally able to overcome his reluctance to assume command of the social movement which was dedicated to the Negroes' prompt realization of the promises in the "American creed." A few months after the riot he led the Radicals in a fruitless attempt to negotiate an honorable peace with the Tuskegeeans; in 1905 he founded the Niagara Movement, an organization which waged an all-out war upon the gradualist approach to race relations.

4. The Radicals Fail to Effect a Rapprochement

Months before the Boston Riot, Washington had hoped that differences with some of his opponents would be resolved in a "quiet and private conference," and he sounded out Du Bois on the subject. Significantly, although Du Bois' role in the conference was not one of co-sponsorship, he was consulted throughout the planning stage; probably he was selected as the man with whom to negotiate because he was considered approachable, if not controllable. (The Tuskegeeans refused to bargain with William Monroe Trotter and the conference room was closed to him.) This conclave was the Atlanta professor's first battle test as a real social action leader and he emerged from it an aggressive planner and bargainer.

Washington solicited ideas for the parley and promised to inform Du Bois about subsequent developments.[1] The Tuskegeean desired his friend, T. Thomas Fortune, editor of the New York *Age*, to be among the conferees, although he was aware that Fortune had recently clashed with the Atlanta professor. As if to balance Fortune's presence, Washington suggested that Du Boisian Clement Morgan be invited. For the record, at least, the Tuskegeean declared he expected the assemblage to admit exponents of all schools of thought within the race. Du Bois relished his role as negotiator; in a "confidential letter" to Kelly Miller, whom he mistakenly labeled, "anti-Washingtonian," he discussed the pressures placed upon Washington to invite several men who espoused the higher education view. He appeared to know what he wanted, if not quite how to get it; he reasserted salvation did not lay in begging whites, but it rested essentially upon the promulgation of a program,[2] planned and directed by Negroes:

1. Full political rights on the same terms as other Americans.
2. Higher education of selected Negro youth.
3. Industrial education for the masses.
4. Common school training for every Negro child.
5. A stoppage to the campaign of self-depreciation.
6. A careful study of the real conditions of the Negro.
7. A National Negro periodical.
8. A thorough and efficient federation of Negro societies and activities.
9. The raising of a defense fund.
10. A judicious fight in the courts for civil rights.

The conference had been postponed from the spring of 1903 because, according to Washington, additional time was required to secure financial backing.[3] Probably a truer reason for the delay was the intraracial climate of resentment generated by the Afro-American Council meeting in Louisville and the Boston Riot. As months passed, however, Du Bois continued to be consulted about the list of conferees. By November of 1903, the Atlanta professor, although still favoring the parley, seemed even more distrustful of Washington and suspected a "BTW ratification meeting." When he sought to make certain that a key associate would be listed as a participant, Washington became displeased. The Tuskegeean suggested "personal feelings" be forgotten; reason demanded a "large" proportion of the conferees come from the South where most Negroes lived. (He also deprecated "mere theory and untried schemes" of Northern Negroes.) Du Bois was angry and hinted that he might not attend; the Tuskegeean then backed down and invited the man Du Bois had suggested. Washington instructed the conferees they would be reimbursed for all expenses and he curiously added that the money was provided so no one would consider himself obligated to "any individual or organization."[4]

The Alabama educator was dramatically resourceful and those who attended knew the cash had been coaxed from white philanthropists.

Shortly before the conference Du Bois prepared a confidential memorandum which was sent to trusted lieutenants. In this document, he divided all of the conferees into six categories; "Unscrupulously for Washington" (T. Thomas Fortune, *et al.*); for the Tuskegeean, "without enthusiasm or with scruples" (Robert R. Moton, *et al.*); "Uncertain, leaning to Washington" (Bishop Alexander Walters, *et al.*); other categories were "Uncertain, possibly against Washington," "Anti-Washington," and "Uncompromisingly Anti-Washington." According to his estimate the Radicals were outnumbered sixteen to nine, but he advised his followers to be ready to condemn the Tuskegeean and withhold support until the latter affirmed the principles of civil, political, and educational equality. Du Bois outlined possible "tactics" of the opposition and planned to withdraw if Washington strangled the meeting:

> The tactics of the pro-Washington men will take one or more of the following forms—
> a. Conciliation and compromise.
> b. Irritation and brow-beating.
> c. Silent shutting off of discussion by closure methods.
> Come prepared therefore in case of
> a. to be firm and hammer at the principles and Washington's record.
> b. to keep good temper and insist on free speech.
> c. to protest against closure or underhand methods even to the extent of leaving the meeting.
> Bring every speech or letter or record of Washington you can lay hands on so that he can face his record in print. The main issue of this meeting is *Washington*, refuse to be side-tracked. . . .[5]

Du Bois wanted to avoid being charged with nonco-operation and persuaded others not to boycott the affair prematurely. Of course he anticipated the Tuskegeean would control the conference, but he concluded his own position was a safe one since no promises had been made to the Negro leader. (Actually, Washington, who expected Du Bois to shun the meetings, was not very happy about the final list of participants.) Du Bois, counting on "a warm time," asked Clement Morgan to bring the Trotter questions which precipitated the Boston Riot, and in such a climate of distrust and dispute it was not surprising that no real rapprochement resulted.

Although Washington was of the opinion that this conference would be "the most important, serious and far-reaching in the history of our people," there is only a scanty record of what actually transpired in New York's Carnegie Hall on January 6, 7, and 8 of 1904. Even Du Bois has said little on the subject. The Tuskegeean believed the spotlight of newspaper publicity would make racial harmony even more difficult to obtain; the *Outlook* and the *Independent* carried nothing on the gathering even though they usually had shown interest in Negro conclaves. Few of the Negro newspapers gave any attention to the event. However, the Washington *Bee* editorialized that Du Bois ignominiously surrendered, and the paper wailed that the Tuskegeeans purchased the Du Boisians cheaply with chicken dinners, hard liquor, and travelling expenses. The Negro newspaper admitted the cloak of secrecy made it difficult to collect information on the assemblage, which was dubbed "the Star Chamber Conference."[6]

Among the prominent whites who addressed the group were statesman Carl Schurz, Oswald Garrison Villard, liberal editor of the New York *Evening Post* and grandson of abolitionist William Lloyd Garrison, and industrialist Andrew Carnegie, who praised Booker T. Washington much to the annoyance of Du Bois. These talks were followed by many explosive moments. (At one point a Washington partisan accused Clement Morgan of making an unauthorized transcription of the proceedings—the note-taker angrily retorted that he was writing a letter to his wife!) The Du Bois and Washington forces established a formal agreement on objectives at this Carnegie Hall conference. The South was recognized as a good place for Negro development—if the region "ultimately" yielded "political and civic equality." Negroes were asked to advocate the enforcement of the Fourteenth and Fifteenth Amendments. The ballot was "of paramount importance" and guarded other institutional interests. The conferees recommended that the race organize politically in order to secure the election of sympathetic candidates; the group also favored submitting test cases of discriminatory laws to the courts. They concluded that potential Negro leaders could profit from higher education, while the rest of the race should attend grammar schools and industrial schools. The delegates maintained that efforts should be made to reach white leaders of the North and South and that interracial conferences should be held regularly. Washington, Du Bois, and Hugh Browne, a Washingtonian, were charged with responsibility for the selection of a Committee of Twelve—which was to function as a racial brain trust.[7]

Although many of the conclusions were sufficiently general so that both sides could believe their programs had been enacted, it did *appear* that Washington shifted on the question of the "paramount importance" of the ballot. On the other hand, the Tuskegeean did not have the impression he yielded anything new (at least he attempted to convey that thought to rich white friends); he seemed assured his wisdom triumphed and that many in the enemy camp had been converted. As a matter of practicality he suggested that the unregenerates, including Du Bois, be kept under close surveillance. Robert R. Moton also agreed Du Bois needed "help" and recommended that Dr. H. B. Frissell, head of Hampton Institute, invite Du Bois there for more talks; Washington vetoed the idea because of the possibility that it might be construed by Du Bois as a "bribe" attempt. Another Washingtonian, Charles W. Anderson, the New York Collector of Internal Revenue, considered the punitive approach the only one which would work against the Du Bois men, whom he portrayed as egotistical and super-educated.[8]

In the first months after the conference, Washington and Du Bois co-operated on some of the aspects of their race advancement program. The Alabama educator, convinced that many Southern Negroes were not voting because of apathy or ignorance, suggested Du Bois, Hugh Browne, and he should sponsor the publication of a pamphlet on voting.[9] He engaged someone to write about the suffrage requirements in Alabama and was careful to submit a copy of the essay for Du Bois' examination. (The Tuskegeean's private correspondence shows that he was concerned about increasing Negro registration and voting. As a Republican supporter he secretly proposed a plank—opposing racial disfranchisement— which a friend took to the party convention in 1904.)[10] Washington also advised that Negroes should receive information on jury service and sent Du Bois a manuscript on the subject; the Atlanta professor was asked about the feasibility of using the Negro press to reprint the essay. Du Bois approved immediately, and within a short time race newspapers informed their readers that Negroes were being tried illegally in cases where jurors were barred because of racial grounds.[11]

Du Bois' movements continued to be scrutinized by the Washingtonians, and in March of 1904 Emmett J. Scott asked a friend to sound out the Atlanta professor when the latter arrived in Indiana for a public lecture. The Washingtonian scout reported that Du Bois addressed a "big crowd;" in a private "buzz" session afterward, the educator refused to commit himself about Booker Washington. Since Du Bois had not condemned industrial education in his formal talk, Scott's associate concluded that "perhaps the New York Conference did him good."[12] Others hit the trail in order to muster support for the Tuskegeean in the hinterlands; Charles W. Anderson "diplomatically" told Dr. Charles Bentley, who had recently been named to the Committee of Twelve, that Washington demanded his appointment while Du Bois favored another man.[13] The amount of latitude which Tuskegee-appointed members of the Committee of Twelve were expected to exercise at the forthcoming meeting in July was suggested in a communication to Washington from Emmett J. Scott, who presumed that associates "will stick close to you" and "do what you'd have them do." Anderson made the atmosphere of suspicion even hotter when he protested that the Du Boisians were "leaking" information and saying that Washington was buying influence among Negroes (with white funds). He tried to convince his chieftain it was utterly impossible to get along with the Du Bois men, whom he described as "cattle."[14]

On his side, Du Bois complained that in the election of individuals to the Committee of Twelve, he was virtually ignored by Washington and Browne—and a rubber-stamped "Pro-BTW" clique was created. Months later Du Bois, recalling the affair in a letter to Oswald Garrison Villard, asserted he was too ill to attend the meeting of the group in the summer of 1904. According to the account, Washington postponed the sessions for two weeks and then failed to send him an invitation to the rescheduled conference. Shortly thereafter the Atlanta professor resigned.[15] Evidence does show that on July 6, 1904, a meeting was held in New York City for the purpose of selecting "a permanent organization," and at that time Booker T. Washington was elected chairman, with explicit power to assemble the group at his own discretion. Hugh Browne was chosen secretary and Archibald Grimke (a Du Bois man) became treasurer. Three weeks later Browne sent Du Bois a form letter describing at least some of the deliberations of the parley.[16] This document contrasts with the approach and content of the "Summary of Proceedings" memorandum which was drawn up the preceding January. The July statements were conciliatory and appear to have been fashioned from the old Tuskegee mold. The July group stressed only "constructive, progressive effort" and "Negro successes," believing that intraracial "points of agreement rather than points of differences" should be emphasized. The Committee was to inquire into unfair treatment of Negroes on trains and to encourage interracial conferences, but there was no mention of higher education or the "paramount importance" of the ballot. According to Du Bois, when he received this transcription from Browne, he was asked whether the following statement should be included as one of the duties of the Committee of Twelve:

> [to] keep before the race the importance of voting at municipal, state and national elections, and especially the payment of all taxes and especially that class of taxes which are a consideration of voting.[17]

Naturally Du Bois considered this declaration essential but there was no reference to it when the paper was issued in final draft form.

The Washington-Du Bois conference of 1904 and the Committee of Twelve represented an opportunity to unite the Negro leaders into an organization which might have been a real power in directing the race. Influential whites probably would have contributed money and prestige to this general staff of Negro leadership. The catholicity of the group's goals might have preserved its structure and at the same time have permitted individual leaders, under the guidance of the entire organization, to emphasize their special concerns. No such racial assemblage could have been possible without the sustenance of Booker T. Washington, whose convictions on racial matters influenced, and in turn were influenced by, his white friends. At the same time, the absolute co-operation of the Du Bois men was necessary to the Committee of Twelve's effectiveness. If the alliance of such diverse forces was to be maintained, a genuine spirit of compromise was demanded. The Committee of Twelve failed essentially because Washington was unable to establish a reciprocal division of labor pact with the Du Boisians. This failure resulted from a belief that his system of racial amelioration was all-encompassing. Thus he denied that the Du Bois group had any valid reasons for a separate existence. Distrustful of them (as they were of him), he impugned their motives repeatedly. On the face of it, Washington and his friends argued that there were no essential grounds for dispute between the two schools of thought: "All of us are aiming at the same thing; we may be pursuing different methods, trying to reach the same goal by different roads, and there is no necessity for quarreling."[18]

However, Du Bois contended that principles were sacrificed unless he emphasized the doctrine of Negro manhood and participated in an immediate direct action struggle to secure political rights and higher education, as well as elementary and industrial education. There were distinct grounds "for quarreling" because the Tuskegeean expended comparatively few efforts on what Du Bois deemed race equality imperatives. Many of Washington's "methods" frustrated the Du Bois group. As already indicated, since industrial education possessed Tuskegeean priority, Negro institutions of higher education were given no attention. Washington's interest in other issues, such as voting, was uneven. For instance, at the January conference he agreed the ballot was "of paramount importance," but the question was ignored by the Washington-controlled Committee of Twelve several months later. Behind the scenes he opposed racial disfranchisement and publicly he stated voting was one of his ultimate objectives. However, the subject was not a strong present concern, at least not strong enough for him to make consistently unequivocal statements on behalf of Negro suffrage, or, more realistically, *to permit Du Bois and the Committee of Twelve to do so.*

It appears that the Washingtonians wanted only to use the New York conference and the Committee of Twelve for the purpose of bringing the Du Bois group into line. On the other hand, Du Bois' role in this whole affair reflected a naivete in attempting "to understand and co-operate with Mr. Washington." Desiring to present a common front before the white "enemy," he wanted to join a coalition with Washington but he demanded race unity "against the enemy and not veiled surrender to them."[19] He came to the January conference even though he disapproved of many of the conferees; his own preliminary estimate demonstrated his side would be outnumbered sixteen to nine, but he assumed the forcefulness and incisiveness of his arguments would sway Washington. Du Bois should have appreciated that his resignation from the Tuskegee-dominated steering committee would be interpreted as unyielding, unfair, and impeding. Oswald Garrison Villard, who was to be one of the founders of the National Association for the Advancement of Colored People, considered Du Bois' resignation "a great mistake."[20] In the short run it seems that his withdrawal, after having involved himself deeply in the negotiations, further diminished the prestige of the Radicals, since liberal whites had not as yet understood the implacability of Booker T. Washington. In the long run, by proving that Negro intellectuals could not establish an equitable arrangement with the Tuskegeean, Du Bois' departure hastened the formation of a new Negro rights organization. The Carnegie Hall conference and the Committee of Twelve helped to propel him into the limelight as an action leader, and during the following year he created two tasks for himself: 1. to scrutinize further and to expose the Tuskegeean "surrender" and 2. to form and direct the Niagara Movement.

By 1905 Booker T. Washington had reached the pinnacle of prestige. He had been presented to queens and dukes, received honorary degrees from great universities, and served as political adviser to President Theodore Roosevelt. Tuskegee Institute prospered and little more than a year before, Andrew Carnegie contributed six hundred thousand dollars. Leading industrialists came to Tuskegee to see its operation, and its founder became legendary. Negro educational institutions desiring support from the whites first cleared their causes with Washington, and schools were handicapped without the Tuskegee seal. Scholars and writers used the resources of the Negro information center which Washington foresightedly established at Tuskegee, and the place was acclaimed as the capital of the Negro race in the United States. To millions of whites he became the only *bona fide* interpreter of the Negroes, and national magazines begged him for articles. Financed and extolled by the whites, it was inevitable that Negroes should pay him homage. Much of the Negro press found it desirable and often beneficial to support Washington, and gradually he became the Negro Expert-On-All-Things-To-Do-With-The-Negro: "He was appealed to on any and every subject: how many bathrooms to put in a YMCA, whether or not to start a day nursery in some town, and so on. These things came into his office, but were not scattered over the country to be answered by specialists; they were answered by Washington and his coterie."[21]

Efficiently, Washington organized the "Tuskegee Machine" and relentlessly applied pressure: "Things came to such a pass that when any Negro complained or advocated a course of action, he was silenced with the remark that Mr. Washington did not agree with this. Naturally, the bumptious, irritated young black intelligentsia of the day declared, 'I don't care a damn what Booker Washington thinks! This is what I think and *I have a right to think.*'"[22]

Du Bois asserted that the whites backed the Tuskegee machine in order to perpetuate a large and docile Negro worker class. Since the "Talented Tenth" represented Negro aspiration, these intellectuals would have to be controlled and their criticisms smothered. Actually, it was possible for Negro newspapers to favor Washington in their editorial columns while simultaneously condemning Southern discrimination vehemently. One historian, August Meier, stated that Washington, who "saw some value in agitation and protest," was really "frightened" by the Du Bois group and sought to suppress them, not because they were attacking racists, but because the Radicals were not loyal to him.[23]

In his autobiography, Du Bois recalled that he despised the Tuskegee machine very early, but omitted any references to it in the 1903 *Souls of Black Folk* because the subject was too "controversial." However, long suppressed wrath and frustration came to the surface in January of 1905, when he published an item[24] in the *Voice of the Negro* charging several unnamed Negro newspapers received $3,000 in "hush money" during 1904. Du Bois also wrote a piece for the Boston *Guardian*, execrating unidentified sections of the Negro press which he accused of being paid to assail the anti-Washingtonians. Oswald Garrison Villard challenged him to present proof of the charges. Atlanta University's President Bumstead was "disturbed" because he believed that the professor's accusations, while accurate, could not be documented; even if they could, he feared that the resultant discord would be self-defeating. The New York *Age* mocked Du Bois as a "Professor of hysterics," demanding that he "stand out in the open" and name the newspapers which were receiving this secret money. Just as Bumstead feared, the paper drew Atlanta University into the foray and asked the school's administrators to examine the propriety of the professor's accusations. The newspaper also lashed out at those editors, such as Trotter, who had published the assertions, and the villains were disparagingly identified as "the precious knockers" of the race.[25] Shortly after the publication of the charges in the *Voice of the Negro*, the magazine's own editors asked the Atlanta professor for the "particulars" so that the guilty newspapers could be flailed publicly; Du Bois, who knew that he did not have sufficient evidence, retorted that he was unready to make any "further comment."

In letters to Oswald Garrison Villard and W. H. Ward, editor of the *Independent*, Du Bois stated that the newspapers which were then chastising him were the very ones which had become paid conspirators.[26] They were the New York *Age*, Chicago *Conservator*, Boston *Citizen*, Washington *Colored American*, *Colored American Magazine*, and the Indianapolis *Freeman*. However, Du Bois' proof (which Trotter dispatched to him) was quite limited to say the least. He possessed a letter from a one-time editor of the Chicago *Conservator* who alleged that he had been offered three thousand dollars to join the Tuskegeean camp. He had another deposition from a former editor of a Washington paper who presumed that the newspaper received forty dollars a month "from the outside to maintain its policy." Du Bois believed it significant that the guilty papers "print the same syndicated news (and editorials), praise the same persons and attack the same persons." For example, he showed that one pro-Booker Washington editorial appeared in several Negro papers on the same day. (The editorial discussed Washington's recent White House visit with Roosevelt: "The President is entitled to every credit for his dependence upon this representative of the race in matters affecting our best interests. . . .") Villard's reply demonstrated his faith "in Mr. Washington's purity of purpose, and absolute freedom from selfishness and personal ambition."[27] He was unconvinced by the "exhibits" which Du Bois enclosed.

Shortly after this exchange between Villard and the Atlanta professor, Booker Washington received a note from F. J. Garrison, who rationalized those Du Boisian accusations which he could not believe. For example, the Atlanta professor had asserted that the Tuskegeean employed Emmett J. Scott as a press agent, and Garrison found it "so preposterous to all who know you that it makes clear the animus of your assailants." Garrison remarked that if Washington ever sought to consolidate the Negro press, he had done so for altruistic motives (race unity). Actually, the Boston white man was not completely sure of his ground and wrote: "The support of any editor who is moved by purely mercenary considerations is not to be solicited or desired. . . . I wish when you have a chance . . . you would write me freely about this whole matter. If I blow a blast, I want to feel fortified on all points."[28]

The Tuskegeean's reply was a masterpiece of persuasion. He denied that he ever bought editorial policies or that he owned even "a dollar's worth" of any Negro newspaper.[29] In this note to Garrison, Washington misrepresented a great deal but did so with impunity because of the pedestal upon which his friends had placed him. Du Bois without financial resources, could not prove his case. Today, aided by August Meier's provocative, ground-breaking article, "Booker T. Washington and the Negro Press", and drawing upon documents in the Washington Papers at the Library of Congress, it is possible to clarify the record of the Negro leader's relationship to the Negro press.

It must be emphasized that many of the newspapers in Washington's camp followed him because they sincerely believed the economic emphasis was the surest way to improve the status of the race; others seized upon his "protest strands" and stressed those, while simultaneously condoning his conservative statements. They realized the Tuskegeean always had to be conscious of the white Southerners who were looking over his shoulder. On the other hand, there is ample evidence to demonstrate that the Negro leader established a smoothly run organization which patrolled the Negro press, influenced large sections of it against his opponents, and rewarded his allies financially in various ways. Several publications counted heavily upon his contributions. Among these before and after 1905 were the New York *Age*, the Washington *Colored Citizen*, and *Alexander's Magazine*. One editor wrote to Washington in that year, "I want you to do what you can toward the next week's paper and a little on the enclosed bill which I have not been able to meet."[30] In 1904—the year before he penned the letter to Garrison—Washington secretly invested $3,000 in the *Colored American Magazine*.[31] For several years he assumed part of the operating expenses of the magazine and during this period he not only suggested material for editorials but also advised on changes in the staff.

Advertisements were given to newspapers which supported him. As one example of this type of influence the Charleston *Advocate* is cited. Emmett J. Scott received word that the *Advocate's* editor was piqued because he was ignored by the Tuskegeeans after having praised them; consequently, he announced that he would no longer publish the blurbs which were sent from Tuskegee headquarters. Scott apologized to the editor for past neglect, sent an advertisement, and promised additional consideration in the future.[32] The editor of the Atlanta *Independent*, after publishing a "very strong and wise editorial" on Washington's Negro Business League, informed the leader of his allegiance and asked for an advertisement.[33] The Tuskegeean employed R. W. Thompson to send canned items to co-operating papers and the staff member often distributed anti-Radical material to the newspapers. Thompson sometimes wrote his own squibs and articles but frequently he was only the middleman who transmitted pieces authored by Emmett J. Scott.[34] After the Boston *Colored Citizen* referred to William Monroe Trotter as a "toad," the *Guardian* editor sued for libel in 1905, and courtroom cross-examination revealed Emmett J. Scott had actually written the offending article. The New York *Age* was another paper which often used Scott's editorials and one Washingtonian noted that a particular piece had a "*twang* decidedly 'Scottish!'" Finally, Washington and Scott began to fear their program was being praised too much, and these excesses were giving credibility to Du Bois' denunciations; ironically they were forced to issue instructions to ignore Tuskegee temporarily.[35]

Inexorably, the Tuskegee machine brought about a strong undercurrent of revolt within the race, and the Atlanta professor capitalized upon it by inviting some of his supporters to assemble at Kelly Miller's Washington home in March of 1905 for the purpose of forming a new social action committee. Du Bois, undoubtedly sensitive to the Tuskegeean's charge that the intellectuals were removed from the essential problems of the rank and file, anticipated the new organization would be "in close touch with the people and with intimate knowledge of their thoughts and feelings." Before the meeting the Washington *Bee* and the Boston *Guardian* shrilly proclaimed Du Bois their chieftain:

> There is one man upon the American continent who is entitled to the respect and confidence of a race that is oppressed, whose champion he has been since God has given him power to write and speak. One man of our race is gaining the confidence and esteem of his race and is coming more and more to be regarded as the chiefest among ten thousand as a spokesman for his race before the white American public.[36]

The Atlanta University professor was a Negro leader driven by frustration. He had begun his career as an accommodationist, but, after failing to gain the friendship of the whites and after being blocked by Booker T. Washington, he was ready to accept the plaudits and finally develop a propaganda program of pressure and agitation.

At the time of the conference, the Tuskegeean decided the New York *Age* should avoid the mention of Du Bois' name, even for the purpose of castigation. He expected this policy of not "advertising" the Atlanta professor would be adopted by other newspapers. He omitted the Atlanta press from the blackout, undoubtedly because of the potential damage to Du Bois' position at the university. Other Washingtonians were clearly worried about the "alliance . . . of offense and defense" which the Radicals were forming.[37] The rumblings of the Du Bois group grew louder and were heard even across the color line by Oswald Garrison Villard, who feared "a nasty explosion . . . which will hurt the race."[38] Within a few weeks the burst occurred and the Niagara Movement was organized.

5. Niagara Movement: The Protest

In July of 1905 W. E. B. Du Bois invited a "few selected persons" to the "secret" sessions of the Niagara Movement at Fort Erie, Ontario. Twenty-nine members of the Talented Tenth participated —many more were expected but, according to rumors, they declined at the last minute after being pressured by white friends of Booker T. Washington.[1] Inevitably, Du Bois was elected general secretary. Between 1903 and 1905 he emerged as the second most prominent living Negro. He was recognized by many as the founder of "Negro Sociology," and Negro college graduates especially considered him the representative "of the race's aspiration." For them he was an example, not of what a colored man might achieve, "but of what HE IS and HAS DONE." Du Bois was regarded as a man who had reached "the heights to which it is possible for some of us to climb."[2]

Diplomatically, the conferees proclaimed that they did not intend to condemn personalities such as Booker Washington; they realized that there would be enough difficulty in gaining public support without creating additional obstacles by appearing to be blusteringly anti-Washingtonian. J. Max Barber, an editor of the *Voice of the Negro*, declared Washington's name was mentioned only twice during the deliberations and Du Bois had admonished the group to concern itself only with "principles." Barber maintained that the Tuskegeean was not unacceptable in the movement if he supported its program. However, the *Voice* editor (demonstrating that no protest organization could be initiated in 1905 without striking direct blows at Washington) condemned "certain temporizers and compromisers" who tried to make American

Negroes accept "one leader, one policy, and one kind of education."[3] Du Bois reacted similarly when he prepared the conference
invitation list. He rejected several men as "bought" and "hide-
bound" Washingtonians.[4] Basil Mathews, one of Washington's
biographers, incorrectly stated that only "superficial observers"
believed the Niagara Movement clashed seriously with the Tuskegeeans.[5] The evidence indicates that contemporaries like William
Ferris, before choosing a battle position in what appeared to be a
hard struggle, carefully took the measure of Du Bois' and Washington's personalities, attitudes, and power.[6] James Weldon
Johnson recalled the Niagara Movement (and *Souls of Black Folk*)
divided the race into "two well-defined parties" and the "bitterness" continued for years.[7]

Du Bois was satisfied that the organization would function most
effectively with a simple structure, and the executive committee
was composed of chairmen of the Niagara Movement's state
associations. The following committees were established: Finance,
Interstate Conditions and Needs, Organization, Civil and Political
Rights, Legal Defense, Crime, Rescue and Reform, Economic
Opportunity, Health, Education, Press and Public Opinion. In his
aim for a "thoughtful" and "dignified" membership, Du Bois
eschewed an approach to the Negro masses and made his appeal to
"the very best class of Negro Americans." The platform of the
1905 Niagara sessions (while containing nothing new from the
Radicals) was written in vigorous and sharp tones. The conferees
placed the responsibility for the Negro problem on the shoulders
of the whites. The Radicals were not asking for opinions; they
were making definite demands and telling the whites what must
be done. "We want to *pull down* nothing but we don't propose to
be pulled down.... We believe in *taking what we can get* but we
don't believe in being satisfied with it and in permitting anybody
for a moment to imagine we're satisfied.[8]

For the record the following[9] were the Niagara demands:

1. *Freedom of speech and criticism*—The fluid exchange of ideas was crucial to the Talented Tenth, who refused to be pressured into silence by the Washingtonians.

2. *An unfettered and unsubsidized press*—Unless their own propaganda reached and aroused the people, the Radicals contended that Negroes would remain a captive race. The charge that the press was bought and controlled served as a solid rallying point.

3. *Manhood suffrage*—The conferees desired to participate in the American political system (North and South) on the same basis as the whites. The very term, "Afro-American," was repudiated because of its alien connotation, and "Negro American" became the designation which was approved by the delegates. (Their dislike of the term may also have been caused by its association with the Tuskegeean Afro-American Council.)

4. *The abolition of all caste distinctions based simply on race and color*—Racism was denounced as "unreasoning human savagery," and Jim Crow was condemned as an avenue for insult as well as a crucifixion of manhood.

5. *The recognition of the principles of human brotherhood as a practical present creed*—Du Bois considered the Niagara Movement's task was to interpret the real Christ to white Christians.

6. *Recognition of the highest and best human training as a monopoly of no class or race*—The Niagara men desired universal common school education; high schools and technical high schools were to be for all who wanted them. Colleges were to be available for those who could profit from them. Federal aid to education was advocated.

7. *A belief in the dignity of labor*—The Niagara Movement asserted that Negroes must have equal employment opportunities. Employers and trade unions were severely criticized for racial discrimination. Peonage was denounced.

8. *United effort to realize these ideals under wise and courageous leadership*—Constant protest was the approved method to secure Negro rights.

The *Outlook* magazine denied race prejudice was increasing and repudiated the anti-segregation stand of the Niagara men. The editor of the popular weekly maintained that certain "distinctions" were required to preserve "race integrity," and those Negroes who refused to accept a separate status automatically admitted the inferiority of their race. The magazine was also disturbed by the "whine" of the Niagara Movement and concluded the Washingtonians were the only "real leaders" who represented the sentiments of the Negro people.[10] On the other hand, the Cleveland *Gazette* praised the Niagara manifesto, and the Chicago *Law Register* agreed that human rights were never achieved without aggressive protest.[11]

Within a few months after the adjournment of the conference, local branches held meetings in various parts of the country. (In the late summer of 1905, Rev. Garnett R. Waller, a Baltimore member, told the New York branch of the movement's efforts in his city to prevent the Negroes from being disfranchised.)[12] The Niagara men claimed that memberships increased from twenty-nine in July of 1905 to fifty-four by September, and to one hundred and fifty at the end of the year.[13] Ralph Bunche considered the growth was small in view of the organization's great aims, but Du Bois (perhaps rationalizing) stated that one hundred and fifty members were sufficient for 1905. He said that if conditions did not greatly change, he had no desire to see the Niagara Movement ever exceed five hundred members. At the end of the year, the general secretary recorded there were "strong" local branches in seventeen states and plans were in progress for thirteen additional groups. Du Bois also noted that several Negro newspapers and magazines were bringing the Niagara message to the people: Chicago *Conser-*

vator, Virginia *Home News,* Cleveland *Gazette,* Maryland *Lancet,* Boston *Guardian,* Washington *Bee,* Oregon *Advocate, Voice of the Negro,* and the *Moon.*

Since the day of its inception, Booker T. Washington scrutinized the movement and plotted its destruction. On July 11, 1905, when the Niagara conference opened, Washington indicated to Charles W. Anderson that he wanted "information" on what was happening. Anderson submitted his first report by return mail and characteristically doubted the Niagara men had either "influence" or "honesty of purpose."[14] The Tuskegean was assured that "not one tenth" of those whose names appeared on a published list had actually attended the conclave, and that Du Bois (or someone equally "enterprising") padded the list for publicity purposes. A short time later, the Tuskegean conferred in New York with Anderson and the editor of the New York *Age* on methods of dealing with the Radicals. Anderson suggested L. M. Hershaw (one of Du Bois' lieutenants) should be fired from his government job. The high level strategy was to isolate the Radicals from the Negro press, and the word was passed down the line.[15] Emmett J. Scott felt certain that the Niagara men would be unable to persuade most of the race press even to reprint articles which had been published originally in friendly white publications.[16] As usual, the press blackout was ineffective, partially because the Washingtonians found it impossible to resist the opportunity to condemn the "opposition." For example, the Tuskegean's nephew, Roscoe Simmons, sent a critical editorial, originally published in the New York *Advertiser,* to various white and Negro papers. At the end of the month, Scott formally changed the strategy and advised his associates "to hammer" the Niagara Movement.[17] Throughout all of this initial planning the Tuskegean was unable to understand why some Negro newspapers still regarded the Radicals as "gentlemen."[18] Washington used his great persuasive powers to redirect a few Negro editors. For example, the editor of the Atlanta *Age* (who failed to perceive "the true inwardness" of Du Bois and devoted editorials to the Niagara Movement) was invited to take an expense-paid trip to Tuskegee Institute.

In the midst of the Washingtonians' anxiety, Bishop Alexander Walters made it known that he was prepared to return to the presidency of the Afro-American Council and initiate a "counter-movement" to Niagara. Walters proposed to bring the Radicals under his control by advocating civil and political equality. At the same time, Washington could continue to speak in conservative tones, thereby retaining white support. R. W. Thompson (a Tuskegeean aide) was delighted with the plan and told Emmett J. Scott that the reorganized Afro-American Council would be "stronger and more practical" than the Niagara Movement.[19] Scott was less optimistic that Walters (who sometimes exhibited independent tendencies) could be controlled.[20] However, the Bishop was "resurrected" (as Du Bois put it). The Atlanta professor was undeceived and denounced the Afro-American Council[21] which he said had been almost completely inactive between 1902 and 1905.

Booker T. Washington, keeping all irons in the fire, suggested that spies be employed to undermine the Niagara Movement.[22] Often Charles W. Anderson delegated a "deputy" to monitor the public speeches of leading Niagara men such as Du Bois. After one such meeting, Anderson disclosed that Du Bois' address "was a failure." He added joyously that, during the program, those in the audience who were loyal to Niagara were asked to rise, and practically all who stood were either women or boys![23] Washington used other maneuvers to discredit the new organization. He visited influential whites, such as Oswald Garrison Villard,[24] who as moderates supported both industrial and higher education. The Tuskegeean tried to convince these gentlemen to shun the movement. He also made the most of disagreements within the Niagara group, such as one involving Du Bois, Kelly Miller, and Archibald Grimke. The Tuskegean, appearing deeply sympathetic, met with Grimke, whom he found more dependable than Miller. The latter was described as too "mushy" and unaggressive; the Washingtonians hoped that Grimke's services could be used in the field of propaganda.[25]

In this power struggle the Washingtonians were strengthened by impressing the Negroes through political patronage. Furthermore, appointees could be used to perform various tasks for the Tuskegeeans, even while on government time. (For example, in late 1905 it was hoped that President Roosevelt could be persuaded to assign one more "Deputy" to the New York office of the Department of Internal Revenue. Anderson, the New York Collector of Internal Revenue, informed Washington that if a new position were created the person who filled it could devote unlimited time "to meet your purposes." Several Negroes were given political jobs and some received small increases in salary. Many Negro newspapers carried these proofs of Washingtonian potency. The New York Collector of Internal Revenue told Booker Washington that President Roosevelt ("Our Friend") had recently stressed the importance of making it clear to the Negro people that the Tuskegean's "influence" was always present whenever they were appointed to federal jobs.[26]

Washington, despite all of his resources, feared the Niagara Movement would receive aid from the Constitution League, an interracial civil rights organization founded in 1904 by John Milholland. The League (and the Niagara Movement) favored the Platt Bill, which would have reduced Congressional representation in those states disfranchising Negroes illegally. The Tuskegean opposed the bill and declared that Southerners would rather surrender Congressional seats than permit Negroes to vote.[27]

Without the Negro leader's co-operation, the Constitution League was unable to lobby effectively in the nation's capital. Milholland decided that a grass-roots movement would influence Congress and he sought the help of various Republican clubs. Since William Monroe Trotter was contacted, Washington suspected Milholland's motives, even though the white industrialist had been previously praised as a "generous" contributor to Negro causes.[28] Nor did relations between Tuskegee Institute and the Constitution League improve after an official of the latter organization asked Charles W. Anderson to supply the names of prominent New York Republicans so that Trotter could send them copies of the Boston *Guardian*! The blunder was colossal; Anderson was the sort of man who informed storekeepers that he would not buy from them unless they refused to sell the *Guardian*. He gleefully wrote Booker T. Washington that, in one week, the newspaper was "removed" from two more stores.[29]

Other reports about Milholland's defection filtered into Tuskegee headquarters, and the Negro chieftain's friends feared the Niagara Movement would be harder to defeat if the white industrialist supplied it with money. According to one informant, Du Bois had been selected by Milholland as "a strong man," and the Atlanta professor was hoping for an alliance between the two equal rights organizations. Washington's nephew observed that Du Bois, "under the guidance" of a Constitution League official, delivered an address at a New York Republican club. The Alabama educator advised one of his associates to inform the League that New Yorkers would not tolerate any "nonsense" from Du Bois or Trotter. Since no direct avenue was found to sever the connection between the Niagara Movement and the Constitution League, the Washingtonians tried to weaken Milholland's influence with the New York Republican party organization. In October of 1905, Anderson conferred with Governor Odell and informed him the

Constitution League was out for "trouble."[30] Actually, Milholland had co-operated with both wings of Negro leadership and did not wish to be considered anti-Washingtonian.[31] However, he was stuck with the reputation and later came to deserve it. Members of the Niagara Movement fervently embraced the League's principles ("enforcing the mandates of the Constitution") and Du Bois continued to speak at public meetings of the organization.[32] Niagara's *Voice of the Negro* carried an article[33] praising the League in early 1906, and such laudations appeared about the time the Atlanta professor accused Booker T. Washington of persuading the Negro press to give Milholland's group the silent treatment.[34]

Besides co-operating with the Constitution League in Philadelphia, New York, and Washington, the Niagara Movement also exchanged speakers with Trotter's New England and Boston Suffrage Leagues. Undoubtedly, the cause of racial advancement would have been served more efficiently if real efforts had been made to bring all of these groups into one organization. There were no essential differences in their ideologies, and, in the public view, all were considered radical. However in 1906, the Constitution League was the only one with white members, and for that reason it was probably suspected by some Niagara and Suffrage men. Du Bois favored a merger, but even he seemed lukewarm. He recognized the practical difficulties to obtaining unification, not the least of which was Trotter's egotistical personality. The *Guardian* editor relished only too well his big-fish-in-small-sea status. Naturally, these groups, operating separately, were no match for the well-disciplined Washingtonians.

Plans were made to hold the second Niagara conference at Harpers Ferry (for sentimental and propagandistic value) in August of 1906. Du Bois arrived there a few weeks prior to the opening session and many local Negroes were afraid he meant to "stir up trouble."[35] Not only was the Atlanta professor known as a

Radical, but his bearing suggested unbounded arrogance and prevented him from gaining the confidence of colored citizens in the community. The Niagara meetings took place at Storer College and among the speakers was Richard Greener, a Howard University professor who was actually a Tuskegeean spy. Greener's assignment was to counsel the Radicals to ally themselves with the Washingtonians—he had been carefully instructed "to get on the inside."[36] His mission ended in failure. As usual, the Niagara men vigorously blasted their enemies. Booker T. Washington, unmentioned by name, was the "third person of the trinity," who for alleged pay and publicity sold out his race. President Roosevelt and Secretary of War Taft were also condemned, and one speaker charged that the Republicans concluded an agreement with the Democrats, in which the latter would vote "correctly" on the tariff question if the former soft-pedalled the Negro rights question.[37]

Various committee chairmen reported. The head of the Health Committee asked the group to sponsor a national campaign against tuberculosis, and one member suggested that Negro clergymen should co-operate in popularizing "the gospel of cleanliness, water, and air." John Hope, chairman of the Education Committee, recommended that Niagara men prepare, for legislators and the interested public, a pamphlet on conditions in Southern Negro schools. Hope pointed out that the Niagara messages would be disseminated more widely if greater efforts were made to secure co-operation from Negro editors and ministers. He also thought that the movement should sponsor educational forums.[38]

The members of the second Niagara conference found no dearth of critics. The *Outlook* concluded that Negroes would be better off if this organization asked more of them instead of asking more for them. The white weekly agreed that colored people should vote, but only after they acquired "manhood." The magazine compared the platform of Booker T. Washington's National Negro Business League with the Niagara platform. Du Bois was described as "assertive" and Washington was considered "pacific." Washington focused on achieving an "inch of progress" rather than a "yard of faultfinding."[39] Negro critics were even harsher in their denunciations; Kelly Miller explained that the 1906 manifesto seemed like "a wild and frantic shriek."[40] The New York *Age* was still calling the Du Bois group an "aggregation of soreheads" who were jealous of Washington's success. According to the *Age*, the Niagara principles were no different from those of the Afro-American Council which Washington endorsed. The Tuskegeean was depicted as a leader of the "masses" and a victim of Negro intellectuals who attacked him because he lacked a college degree. The race needed "something cheerful" and therefore repudiated the "lugubrious" and "bitter" chants of the Radicals.[41] Actually, the Du Bois men still erred in their belief that they were the real "leaders" of the race, and they were unrealistic in failing to gauge the wide fissure between the Talented Tenth and the unschooled majority.

Near the end of the year, J. Max Barber chronicled some of the activities of the local Niagara chapters. Credit was given to the Illinois branch for securing the appointment of a Negro to the New Chicago Charter Committee—a maneuver which was considered crucial to prevent school segregation. (The Niagara men charged that local newspapers had recently exerted pressure to separate white and Negro children in the Chicago public schools.) The Education Committee of the Illinois Niagara branch was informed that the new charter would not permit segregation in tax-supported schools. The Illinois branch was also aroused when *The Clansman* opened in a Chicago theater, and Jane Addams was given the task of convincing drama critics to ignore the play.[42]

The accomplishments of the Massachusetts chapter were described. The group participated in the defeat of an amendment to the Rate Bill in Congress (legalizing segregated railroad cars).[43] The branch also lobbied unsuccessfully to prevent the Massachusetts legislature from contributing money for the Jamestown Exposition unless the state of Virginia acknowledged that all citizens, regardless of race, would be admitted on the same basis.[44]

If the Radicals would not unite under the banner of one single organization, it was even more unlikely that they would merge with the Washingtonian associations. Yet in 1906, such suggestions were made by prominent Negroes besides Professor Richard Greener. The Washington *Bee* declared that the National Negro Business League and the Niagara Movement should join forces; on reconsideration, the *Bee* decided the Business League should remain independent but the Afro-American Council and Du Bois' organization should combine.[45] The immediate background for the 1906 merger discussions was laid in a 1905 proposal by Mrs. Carrie W. Clifford, the wife of a federal job-holder. At that time, she suggested the Afro-American Council should join with Niagara, but her idea was repudiated as a Washingtonian maneuver. Shortly thereafter, the Washington *Bee* asserted that consolidation was possible if the Afro-American Council accepted the Niagara view on the reduction of Southern Congressional representation. The Jacksonville *Advocate* advised Du Bois to negotiate but the Niagara general secretary was described as "not enthusiastic." The subject was shelved for several months and in August, 1906, the *Bee* announced that T. Thomas Fortune, Washington's associate, backed the merger plan.[46] However, the editor of the *African Methodist Episcopal Review* contended that no union was possible because of the jealousies of race leaders; he substituted a motion for "federation and friendly co-operation."[47] William Hayes Ward, editor of the *Independent*,[48] also maintained that personal desires for power were not unimportant impediments to consolidation and recommended another meeting similar to the unsuccessful Carnegie Hall Conference of 1904.

Actually, unification was more impracticable in 1906 than it was in 1904. Mutual distrust prevented communication between both sides. The Washingtonians still believed their leader demanded every right for Negroes that Du Bois did and the Tuskegeean could achieve these goals while Du Bois could not. The Washingtonians ignored the difference between declaring themselves in favor of a goal and working consistently and continually toward its realization. By 1906, the Radicals were more united than they were at the time of the Carnegie Hall Conference, although they overestimated their strength and, of course, scattered their efforts among several organizations.

However, in September, the Niagara Movement was invited to send representatives to the Afro-American Council meetings and L. M. Hershaw, head of the Niagara's District of Columbia branch, accepted.[49] Shortly before the Council sessions, Washington secretly called for a "conservative" platform, and in a personal appearance before the Council he condemned "inflammatory" statements of Northern Negroes. Heeding the Tuskegeean, the Council, while opposing a segregated railroad car law and denial of civil political rights, emphasized the preservation of interracial "harmony" and "material progress."[50] Interest in a merger was significantly dampened.

The Council sessions climaxed a year of Washingtonian accommodation. Contradicting his "enemies" he affirmed that Negroes were living in a comparatively "happy period."[51] In this "happy period" various states had already adopted constitutional amendments restricting the franchise, i.e., Mississippi in 1890; South Carolina, 1895; Louisiana, 1898; North Carolina, 1900; Alabama, 1901; Virginia, 1901. His optimism remained unchanged even after the Atlanta race riots in 1906, and he rejoiced that the "better elements of both races" in the city co-operated along religious and educational lines.[52] In contrast, Du Bois charged the riots were premeditated by the whites and could be avoided in the future only by the application of Niagara principles.[53] The Tuskegeean New York *Age*, demonstrating that the Niagara men were cowards, noted Du Bois escaped to Alabama during the riot—while Booker T. Washington arrived in the troubled city and endangered his own life to aid his people.[54] Actually, Du Bois was out of the city on a research project, and when he learned about the violence he returned to Atlanta immediately. On the train, full of concern for the safety of his family and race, he composed the "Litany of Atlanta":

> Listen to us, Thy children; our faces dark with doubt, are made a mockery in Thy sanctuary. With uplifted hands we front Thy heaven, O God, crying: *we beseech Thee to hear us, good Lord!* . . . Surely, Thou too art not white, O Lord a pale, bloodless, heartless thing? . . . But whisper—speak—call, great God, for Thy silence is white terror to our hearts![55]

In early 1907, George W. Crawford, head of Niagara's Civil Rights Department, pointed out the error of waiting until the "overworked" Du Bois prodded members to action. Crawford urged each Northern chapter to lobby for state civil rights laws; he asked all Southern members to convince the railroads and legislators to improve travel accommodations for the race. Local Niagara organizations were also requested to obtain new trials for the innocent who were convicted by juries excluding Negroes. Crawford favored co-operation with men outside of the Niagara Movement.[56] Weeks before, a Niagara committee was appointed to co-ordinate activities with the Constitution League; subsequently, Du Bois became a director of the League. In a state like Connecticut, it was difficult to differentiate between the two groups, since both were organized and operated by many of the same people. The Radicals in Connecticut asked Republican candidates for Congress to support demands for a congressional investigating committee on Negro suffrage.[57]

The Niagara men hoped to invalidate racist laws by sponsoring test cases. After a Miss Barbara Pope was fined for refusing to enter a Jim Crow car when it crossed the state line into Virginia, the Niagara men successfully appealed her case. In 1907, Du Bois estimated more than six hundred dollars had been spent on the Pope litigation and the Niagara Movement was in debt two hundred and forty dollars.[58] By this time, he found it harder than ever to recruit people into the organization; however, despite constant Washingtonian pressure, he claimed a membership roll of three hundred and eighty persons.[59] Refusing to be discouraged, Du Bois, with F. H. M. Murray and L. M. Hershaw, founded a miniature monthly called the *Horizon*. Since Murray and Hershaw held federal jobs, Charles W. Anderson tried to persuade President Roosevelt to fire them, and falsely asserted that Hershaw was "*the head devil*" in the anti-Roosevelt campaign.[60] Booker T. Washington's aide-de-camp shrewdly refrained from admitting that he was more disturbed about the attacks upon the Negro educator than by those on the President.

The Niagara Movement held its third annual conference in 1907. Since the organization felt an emotional attachment to Harpers Ferry, there was some talk of meeting there again. However, between 1906 and 1907, Storer College experienced an "unexpected lessening of its annual appropriation," and friends of the institution maintained it was "injured" because the Niagara Movement met on the campus one year before. Du Bois was notified that no 1907 invitation could be extended until the Storer trustees granted formal permission.[61] It is not known what action the trustees finally took, but the third conference was held in Boston. The relatively small amount of attention which the Negro press gave to these sessions reflected the general doldrums of the organization as well as the success of the Washingtonians. It was becoming painfully apparent to many that little had been accomplished by the Radicals.[62] Du Bois realized there was "less momentum" at this third conclave, and he observed "internal strain"—a condition which he ascribed to his own "inexperience" and to Trotter's difficult personality. Shortly after the conference, Washingtonians dubbed it a "failure."[63] In two years of operation, the Niagara men succeeded in raising only $1,288.83, and during the same period they spent $1,539.23. According to the leadership, eight hundred persons attended one of the 1907 sessions, but the Washinton *Bee* commented that there were fewer than one hundred delegates—not even enough to receive a special railroad rate.[64]

At the conclave, the Constitution League was praised for its investigation of the Brownsville Affair and Roosevelt and Taft were excoriated. Senator Joseph B. Foraker of Ohio became the man of the hour for his condemnation of the evidence upon which the soldiers were dismissed from military service.[65] (Three companies of a Negro regiment were involved in a 1906 race riot in Brownsville, Texas. The men were accused of "shooting up the town" and protecting fellow Negroes who participated in the riot. President Roosevelt ordered the soldiers dishonorably discharged, but they were restored to duty in 1909.)

The Niagara conferees, angered by a recent decision of the Interstate Commerce Commission upholding Jim Crow railroad cars, put on a brave front and declared, "All means at our command must be employed to overthrow [the ruling] and change the personnel of that weak, reactionary board."[66] There were many other examples of the impotence of the Niagara men—and their soul-searching. A New York delegate announced that several congressmen informed him there was little hope of enforcing the

Fourteenth and Fifteenth Amendments.[67] Rev. J. M. Waldron was concerned with an old Niagara ailment, i.e., its failure to attract the "masses." Waldron also announced the organization might become revitalized if it co-operated with Socialists and working class whites.[68] Du Bois favored this proposition. Although he referred to himself as a "Socialist-of-the-path" and desired government ownership of basic industries, he also had some reservations because the Socialists—and white workers—discriminated against Negroes.[69]

The 1907 "Address to the World," which the Indianapolis *Freeman* called "a final shriek of despair," did not deviate in tone or approach from the addresses of the two previous years.[70] The document is probably most significant because of its political advice to "the 500,000 free black voters of the North." The Republican party was called "the present dictatorship," and the faithful were urged to vote against Taft, Roosevelt, or any other Republican standard bearer.[71] Such heretical sentiments did not seem to trouble the New York *Age*, whose new editor, Fred Moore, contended that the Radicals would have to support the 1908 Republican candidate because there was no one else for Negroes to back.[72] As usual, the *Outlook* compared the Niagara sessions with the deliberations of some other organization which the magazine considered worthy of praise. In 1907 the *Outlook* pitted the Niagara Movement, composed of men who had a "grievance," with the National Association of Colored Physicians, Dentists, and Surgeons, comprising men who had a "record." Du Bois and his followers were told that laws could not lessen "the burden of the black man's life."[73] A Niagara lieutenant reminded the editor of the white weekly that agitators performed a valuable service in awakening the nation to find remedies for its problems; he added that many of the members of the doctors and dentists association also belonged to the Niagara Movement.[74]

The Boston conference was also the scene of a rupture between Du Bois and Trotter, which seriously damaged the morale of the whole movement, and especially the Massachusetts branch. The seeds of the schism were sown the year before when Du Bois' good friend, Clement Morgan, the head of the Massachusetts branch, supported Governor Guild in his race for re-election. Trotter was adamant that Guild should not receive Negro aid because the white politician had been instrumental in securing a state appropriation for the segregated Jamestown Exposition. Trotter was rankled that Morgan, who had opposed the appropriation, wanted to vote for Guild; and the *Guardian* editor was absolutely livid when he heard the Negro leader was to be nominated for the state legislature by the Republicans, as a reward for "loyalty."

A few months later another crisis occurred. It seems that Morgan staged a social affair for money raising purposes a short time prior to the 1907 Niagara conference, and he neglected to consult Trotter on arrangements. The *Guardian* editor charged that Morgan's favorites were placed in positions of prestige at the affair. The Niagara Executive Committee sided with Trotter and ruled that Morgan should be fired. Du Bois, however, informed the Executive Committee he would resign unless they rendered a verdict against Trotter.[75] The general secretary was re-elected and Morgan remained at his old post, apparently on a temporary basis; the disharmony remained, and Mary White Ovington (a white social worker who became one of the founders of the N.A.A.C.P.) informed Du Bois that the squabble must be making Booker T. Washington happy.[76] Clement Morgan called the whole affair a "small matter . . . magnified by malcontents," and it angered him that Du Bois was being criticized vehemently.[77] Trotter carried his battle into the open and the New York *Age* noted that the *Guardian* was denouncing the Niagara leaders. Once more, Du Bois decided to resign, believing the Executive Committee had not really supported him and was therefore contributing to the "nation-wide dissension in our ranks." However, another executive session was scheduled and Morgan and Du Bois were entreated to remain at their posts. The controversy was an important factor in hastening the disintegration of the Niagara Movement.[78]

For the Radicals, the 1908 presidential campaign began early. They knew Booker Washington planned to support Taft for the Republican nomination even though this fact was supposed to be a top secret.[79] In February, Du Bois predicted Taft would run against Bryan and advised Negroes to "stay home" on election day; ambivalently, he wrote that Taft must be defeated and "it is hard to imagine . . . someone worse."[80] Practically, he could not bring himself to support a Socialist candidate, and in March he reluctantly announced for Bryan since, "an avowed enemy [is] better than [a] false friend."[81] Many Negro newspapers were stunned. The Salisbury *Piedmont Advocate* cautioned against "surrender" to the Democrats: "The Negro is not conquered by the Democrats. Wait a minute, Prof. Du Bois, let us see what the Democrats are going to do for the Negro. Did you ever hear about 'jumping out of the frying pan into the fire?' Don't do it, brother, the fire is hot."[82]

The New York *Age* reminded Du Bois that a Southern congressman, "who recently shot a Negro on a street car in Washington," also favored Bryan. Some of these gibes originated at Tuskegee Institute and Booker T. Washington personally sent the following one to editor Moore: "Hoke Smith, Ex-Governor Vardaman, Benjamin Tillman and Thomas J. Heflin are all warm supporters of Mr. Bryan. Dr. Du Bois advises the colored people to support Bryan in preference to Taft, and thus ally themselves with the above named gentlemen."[83]

Du Bois recognized, as he had years before, what a hard task it was to convince Negroes that they owed nothing to the Republicans. In his opinion, the Republican party never truly opposed slavery. He claimed that after the Civil War Negroes were enfranchised in order to serve as tools of the politicians, and, although the Republicans controlled the three branches of the national government for decades, racism was allowed to flourish. Furthermore, Negroes had even been ejected from Republican party councils in the cloudburst of lily-whiteness, and Du Bois angrily complained to the chairman of the Republican National Committee.[84] On the other hand, the Democrats of 1908 had a great deal to offer Negroes. In Du Bois' mind, the Democrats advocated corporation control, liberty for the West Indians and Filipinos, and improved working conditions for wage earners. According to the Niagara general secretary, the Democrats comprised an "impossible alliance" between the "radical socialistic" wing of the North and the Southern "aristocratic caste party," and the coalition was doomed to disintegration. However, if the Negro voters continued to oppose liberal Northern Democrats, the latter would be reluctant to break with the South. Du Bois, still chasing the balance of power dream, assumed that Negroes had the ability "to deliver with ease" New York, New Jersey, Ohio, Indiana, and Illinois—as well as to create the possibility of victory "in a dozen other states." Du Bois asserted that if Bryan won with the help of the race, both Democrats and Republicans would be impressed; but if Bryan went to the White House without Negro aid, the South would become stronger politically, "and then good-bye to the fifteenth, if not the thirteenth amendment."[85] As a reply, the Washington *Bee* published an account of Taft's speech to the African Methodist Episcopal denominational convention, in which the candidate made a ringing declaration on behalf of Negro higher education. The *Bee* editorialized that Taft's statement "took the last prop from under the Du Bois clan." The *Age* warned that if the Democrats won,

Negroes "in the border and pivotal States" would lose their right to vote.[86]

The comments of these newspapers were the fruits of Washingtonian efforts to present the Republican party to the Negro people. Ralph W. Tyler, who was an assistant auditor in the Treasury Department, organized the Republican-financed Colored Press Bureau; R. W. Thompson, who also held a federal job, was director of the Bureau.[87] Attempts were still made to punish editors who were "anti-Taft," and J. Max Barber was pushed out of his job in Chicago, allegedly on personal instructions of Booker T. Washington.[88]

In Du Bois' last editorial in the *Horizon*, prior to the election, he lectured the "winner" on the political debt owed to Negroes, who made victory possible. Although Taft won by a substantial majority and received most of the Negro votes, the Atlanta professor was consoled by the belief that "more Negroes voted against Mr. Taft than ever before voted against a Republican Candidate." While admitting that colored people did not have the influence to elect a President in 1908, he contended that in the future they would be able to muster the necessary power.[89]

Disunity among the Radicals was evident throughout 1908. They still talked vaguely of a merger and continued to squabble among themselves or spawn a new organization to add to the growing list. However, during the year, the Niagara Movement succeeded in co-operating with the reorganized Afro-American Council. For instance, both groups produced a joint statement against lily whites, and in the spring Bishop Alexander Walters was inducted into the District of Columbia branch of the Niagara Movement.[90] In March, Du Bois was invited to attend a meeting of prominent members of various Negro equal rights organizations, and Trotter loudly objected. Walters, who believed the *Guardian* editor's "narrowness" would prevent a merger of the Radical groups, pleaded with the Atlanta professor to come "if the day is to be saved." But the Niagara chieftain declined and stated frankly that he found it unbearable to work with Trotter. The conference in Philadelphia created the Negro American Political League, and Du Bois correctly observed that the delegates had not laid a foundation for a merger, but had simply increased the number of racial associations by one.[91]

Two months before the election, the fourth conference of the Niagara Movement was held at Oberlin, Ohio, and again the conclave was characterized by strenuous talk and no action. Earlier, Mary White Ovington indicated that she would speak on "The Relation of the Negro to Labor Problems," for the benefit "of the aristocrats who are in the membership."[92] The sessions revealed debility in the national organization and in the branches as well. The secretary of the Pennsylvania branch submitted a report which showed disunity and disinterest within his group. During the previous year, his organization failed to convince the Philadelphia Board of Education to desegregate Negro schools and engage a substantial number of Negro teachers. The local Niagara branch did not give the Negroes in the community a comprehensive analysis of the situation, and several Negro ministers decided to work independently and negotiate with the school board. The Niagara state secretary and the local Negro press devoted their energies to attacking the ministers. The Pennsylvania Niagara report also indicated that the group was financially bankrupt.[93] The fourth annual "Address to the Country" blasted "the Negro haters of America," who had succeeded in excluding qualified men from all areas of American life. Negroes were advised to get guns and prepare themselves for defensive action against white mobs.[94]

Booker T. Washington did not relent in his efforts to destroy the Niagara Movement, even though it was apparent the organization was on the verge of expiring. One source reported that, of the four hundred and fifty people on the Niagara membership list, only nineteen gathered at Oberlin. Another account said that fifty were actually present.[95] The Tuskegeean concluded the group was "practically dead" and asked the New York *Age* to publish an obituary which he prepared. Almost simultaneously, other Washingtonians were still trying to bury the Niagara Movement in a conspiracy of silence and had gained commitments from white newspapermen to ignore the Oberlin sessions.[96] Gradually, the Negro newspapers which supported Niagara dwindled and, in 1908, the Chicago *Conservator* capitulated to the Tuskegeeans.[97]

The following year, the Niagara Movement was still limping along; so many of the branches had become quiescent that it was news when the Columbus group held several regular meetings.[98] In August, the fifth annual conference was held at Sea Isle City, New Jersey, and it was ignored by both the Negro and white press. Almost single-handedly, the "disappointed" Du Bois tried to keep the organization going, when old reliable officers such as George W. Crawford appeared ready to give up.[99] F. L. McGhee, the head of Niagara's legal department, told the delegates that there was almost no money for legal activities.[100] In the fifth annual address, the organization claimed at least partial credit for "increasing spiritual unrest, sterner impatience with cowardice and deeper determination to be men at any cost." The general secretary's socialistic orientation was evident when he suggested his race should unite with other "oppressed" workers of the United States, Mexico, India, Russia, and the rest of the world. The conclave did elicit some typical and some odd comments from a handful of Negro papers.[101] For example, the Indianapolis *Freeman* was annoyed that Du Bois should have called the theory of inherent racial superiority "a widespread lie," and the ultra-sensitive Indiana editor suggested the use of some less "cruel" expression such as "fable" or "falsehood."[102]

Between 1909 and 1910, the *Horizon* was sinking further into the red, and Du Bois asked, "If you are not interested in yourselves, who will be interested?" The editors paid the deficit "out of their shallow pockets."[103] The year before, Du Bois tried to secure financial backing from John Milholland for a periodical to be published in New York; however, the deal was never consummated. Even when the *Horizon's* death rattle was heard in April, 1910, Du Bois still clung to the hope that he could remain in business until the 1910 sessions of the Niagara Movement. The members of Niagara were still paying their dues irregularly, and frequently were not contributing anything. The national treasurer notified the general secretary that he "had not been able to give more time" to handling the group's finances. Despite all these difficulties, Du Bois considered the members "a splendid set of people" and wanted to stage the sixth annual conference at Sea Isle City again. He had just about convinced himself that regular dues were unnecessary, and the Niagara Movement could continue to exist as a social-educational order, with its members buying adjoining lots at a summer resort. The organization never convened again as a separate entity, and, after the N.A.A.C.P. was formed, Du Bois asked all of the Niagara alumni to support it.

The Niagara Movement was the first national organization of Negroes which aggressively and unconditionally demanded the same civil rights for their people which other Americans enjoyed. The men of Niagara helped to educate Negroes to a policy of protest and taught the whites that some colored men were dissatisfied with the prevailing pattern of race relations. The organization hewed a path for younger men to follow and helped to lay the foundation for the National Association for the Advancement of Colored People.

The Niagara Movement failed for many reasons. Its program of racial equality was too far ahead of the historical period which chose Booker T. Washington as its representative. Du Bois admitted his organization had not accomplished very much and he correctly emphasized Washingtonian obstruction as an essential factor for the lack of success. The Tuskegee machine was formidable, since it consisted of powerful white friends, large amounts of money, political patronage, and large sections of the Negro press. In contrast, the Niagara men had little money and were unable to attract many wealthy whites to their side.

Furthermore, most of the members felt psychologically isolated from the Negro masses. Arnold M. Rose contended that many even regarded the bulk of the Negro race as inferiors.[104] The organization was composed of men who occupied a privileged position within Negro society and they were quite conscious of that fact. No small number considered their education as primarily a symbol of social prestige which divorced them forever from association with the masses. Aside from the higher social status which a university education conferred, such training gave these people a relatively intellectual outlook. There is a degree of social distance within any group between the educated and less educated segments, and this observation was especially true in the Negro race whose Talented Tenth was actually a talented hundredth. These educated men had an empyrean conception of human rights, which they did not effectively convey to the rank and file, who were little interested in politics. The Niagara utterances frequently seemed useless to the Negro workers. Du Bois had often said that political and economic problems were interrelated, but a major weakness of the Niagara Movement was that it spent comparatively little time on economic salvation. The ballot was regarded as the panacea.

Du Bois' personality and his inexperience as a social action leader were not advantages to the organization. He was often described as "aristocratic" and "aloof" in his dealings with the masses and the Talented Tenth as well. Du Bois was well aware of his "natural reticence" and "hatred of forwardness," but he was unwilling or unable to do anything about it. Booker T. Washington was a diplomat, politician, and tactician; Du Bois was none of these types. He "hated the role" of being a social action leader and was sensitive to Washingtonian attacks. In actuality, he was the College Professor of Niagara—giving lectures here, writing papers there, and expecting all the while that his "students" would carry his ideas far and wide. He seemed oblivious of the fact that the Talented Tenth were not the "leaders" of the race. Lastly, there is no question that the organization was weakened by the "individualism and egotism" of William Monroe Trotter. His intemperate statements made the Niagara Movement especially vulnerable, and the Washingtonians often asserted that his excesses were representative of the entire association. Du Bois was never able to control the *Guardian* editor.

Despite all of these limitations, the members of the Niagara Movement could be justifiably proud of their efforts on behalf of higher education, their contributions to legal redress, and their attempts to organize a political lobby composed of informed, independent, and articulate citizens. As exponents of the strategy of protest, they provided an answer to Washingtonian accommodation. It is true, however, that the Niagara Movement developed a hard core of uncompromising Negroes who matched in intensity the unyielding Washingtonians, and during the battle the race may not have profited very much in the short run. Nevertheless, the Niagara men, and their friends in other equal rights organizations, did promulgate a set of blueprints which were to guide many Negroes and whites.

6. The N.A.A.C.P. is Founded: White Liberals and the Protest.

About the time the Niagara Movement was in its last stage of disintegration, the National Negro Committee (later known as the N.A.A.C.P.) was founded. Du Bois was inextricably involved in its growth, and, as the new organization attained greater prominence, he rose from the defeats of the Atlanta studies and the Niagara Movement and became the Negroes' leading propagandist. The National Negro Committee owed a substantial debt to the Niagara Movement and other equal rights organizations such as the Constitution League. The Committee, assembling in New York City on May 31, 1909, stood for racial equality and had an interracial composition from the start. (Du Bois' dying group was weakened because—with one or two exceptions—the members were all Negro.) Many of the whites in the National Negro Committee were influential and articulate—Oswald Garrison Villard, Lillian Wald, Jane Addams, John Milholland, among others; many of the Negroes who held positions of leadership were Niagara veterans—W. E. B. Du Bois, J. Max Barber, J. Milton Waldron, L. M. Hershaw.

The Committee received its spark when a white social worker, Mary W. Ovington, read William E. Walling's impassioned account of the 1908 Springfield, Illinois, race riot. After lengthy discussions, Walling and Miss Ovington agreed that a permanent group protecting Negro rights should be established.[1] An examination of the private papers of Oswald Garrison Villard also reveals a 1908 reference to his own conception of a similar association.

Booker T. Washington asked him for a financial contribution to test an Alabama law which remanded Negroes to the chain gang when they failed to fulfill the terms of their labor contracts, and Villard replied that colored people obviously needed an "endowed 'Committee for the Advancement of the Negro Race.' "[2] Although Villard had a profound and naive faith in Washington during the early years, by 1909 he was becoming impatient privately, not only with Washington's leadership but also with his monopoly upon it. Villard believed President Taft and the Tuskegeean ignored Negro higher education, overpraised white Southerners for giving Negroes only economic help, and generally failed to note "the real injustices." He was also annoyed that the Negro educator devoted so much energy to his political machine—according to a rumor Villard heard, President Taft even complained the Tuskegeean "was asking too many favors."[3] The white journalist decided the time was ripe to encourage Negroes like W. E. B. Du Bois.

The 1909 National Negro Committee conference was preceded by several preliminary meetings which were attended by Miss Ovington, Villard, Walling, Dr. Henry Moskowitz, and Charles E. Russell—all of whom were white. Villard issued a "Call" on Lincoln's Birthday which was signed by many prominent whites and Negroes, among them, Du Bois; the document was unconcerned with the Negroes' economic problems and focused upon civil and political equality.[4] Villard, quite conscious of Booker Washington's "power," knew that the Negro leader was capable of weakening the National Negro Committee. Therefore, the editor of the New York *Evening Post* sought the Tuskegeean's "sympathetic interest and help." Villard invited Washington to the May 31 conference and promised that the organization would not be allied with either the Du Bois wing or the conservative branch of Negro leadership. Actually, he was not anxious to have Washington at the meetings and took pains to make it clear that a "radical political movement" might be launched.[5] Washington replied that he did not wish to attend the first conclave because he wanted to avoid jeopardizing his work in the South, and he observed that Southern Negroes, who could only advance the race in certain ways, were also performing a very useful service which could not be duplicated by their brethren in the North. The Tuskegeean was not referring to a division of labor policy and it is clear that he had little intention of lending his resources to a protest movement; he was interested only in "progressive, constructive work" for the race, rather than in "agitation and criticism." Villard, who was not disappointed by the reply, assured him the National Negro Committee would soon merit complete approval.[6]

It was inevitable that many should have judged the 1909 conference as "anti-Washingtonian"; *The New York Times* noted the conferees acknowledged they were acting without the Tuskegeean's "support," and Du Bois referred to the educator's absence as "conspicuous."[7] Since the signal flags were out, powerful white friends of Washington (such as Andrew Carnegie) also shunned the conclave. Colonel Thomas W. Higginson, who had commanded the first Negro regiment in the Civil War, condemned the conferees' program which he said would block President Taft's efforts to restore good will between North and South. According to the *Outlook*, the Negroes' "genuine friends" feared the National Negro Committee would hurt the race's cause as much as the most rabid racists had ever done, and Professor William James of Harvard thought race prejudice might increase as a result of the publicity the gathering received.[8]

The conference opened by attempting to answer the basic question of whether or not Negroes were like other men, and most of those present sought to discover a one-to-one relationship between "Science and Human Brotherhood." In Du Bois' account, a Columbia University anthropologist and a zoologist from Cornell University "left no doubt in the minds of listeners that the whole argument by which Negroes were pronounced absolutely and inevitably inferior to whites was utterly without scientific basis." Actually, both scientists were more cautious and the anthropologist said: "It is absolutely unjustifiable to assert that there is trustworthy evidence for the view that marked differences of mental capacity between the different races exist; that if they exist they are certainly of a much slighter extent than would appear from hasty observation. On the other hand, it is equally unjustifiable to assert that no differences exist."[9]

The zoologist concluded that the Negro average brain weight was lighter than the whites', and the Negroes manifested prefrontal deficiencies more frequently—the latter causing inferior "psychic faculties, especially reason, judgment, self control or voluntary inhibitions." However, he also declared that there was a great deal of overlapping between the two races. The brains of whites, Negroes, and apes were put on exhibit so that the delegates (and the press) could observe how human the Negro brains were.

In his prepared address before the conclave, Du Bois attempted to delineate the interrelatedness of politics and economics. He began with a criticism of Booker T. Washington's position and for the occasion his bitterness was masked. He was obviously trying to make a good impression on the whites in the audience and seeking to avoid, for the time being at least, the "anti-Washingtonian" label. In this climate of benignity his dispute with the Tuskegeean was only methodological not ideological, since Negro suffrage was also a Washingtonian goal. But Du Bois also said that Negroes would find it more difficult to achieve the franchise as long as demands for the ballot were soft-pedalled. His crucial point was that the hopes of a voteless group of workers could be destroyed by laborers who were permitted to vote—economic competition stimulated race prejudice and franchised white men could make occupational discrimination permanent.[10]

On June first, after the scientific papers had been read in an atmosphere of relative calmness, the frustrated Negro conferees burst into action and demonstrated that they did not even fully trust their white associates at the conference. There were two places in which white leaders such as Villard anticipated trouble, and it came with no lack of haste. The first was in the selection of a steering committee, and an outburst occurred when someone suggested that Booker Washington be appointed. Such an idea was anathema to many, but the more practical pointed out that the Tuskegeean's selection would guarantee financial support from white people. Villard seemed surprised "the whole colored crowd" was "bitterly anti-Washington," but Miss Ovington replied that the affair had been declared out-of-bounds for loyal Washingtonians. In an attempt to pacify, Villard read the letter from Washington in which the educator, recognizing his presence would place a damper over the proceedings, declined to attend. Scrutinizing the group for reactions, the white journalist observed that "Du Bois was wholly satisfied with it," and on the basis of the letter Washington was not named to the committee. According to Miss Ovington, the wrangling was interminable; about midnight the nominations committee completed its deliberations and "took a middle course [which] suited nobody."[11] Extremists such as William Monroe Trotter and Ida Wells Barnett were excluded, and they made no effort to cloak their consternation, doubtlessly sharpened by the fact that such middle-of-the-road Negroes as Leslie Pinckney Hill and Mary Church Terrell were placed on the steering committee. (Mrs. Barnett was later added to the committee.)

The second precipice was reached when the resolutions were introduced and a lengthy debate followed; the chief offenders in this battle were Trotter and J. M. Waldron. Villard was especially piqued at Trotter, whom he described as "behaving very badly" and "speaking incessantly . . . making the most trivial changes in the language, always with a nasty spirit." The session, which was hopelessly bogged down in vituperation and irrelevancy, was portrayed by Du Bois as "warm and even passionate." He related, "A woman leapt to her feet and cried in passionate, almost tearful earnestness—an earnestness born of bitter experience—'They are betraying us again—these white friends of ours.' "[12] The suspicion and hostility seemed to increase, and someone charged that a traitorous clique had captured the machinery of the organization before the meetings began. One observer thought the session was "somewhat less noisy than Bedlam." At one point in the proceedings, when a complete impasse was reached, Villard quietly conferred with William E. Walling and considered the formation of another organization—composed of more workable associates. Villard was more understanding a little later when he wrote, "I suppose we ought really not to blame these poor people who have been tricked so often by white men, for being suspicious, but the exhibition was none the less trying." Du Bois, unlike Trotter (who maintained a tenuous relationship with the National Negro Committee-N.A.A.C.P. for only a few years, since he feared that it was "too white"), succeeded in gaining the admiration of the whites. Villard wrote, "All through our committee sessions, Du Bois was most useful; his attitude and bearing were faultless and his spirit of the best. I was more impressed with him than ever before." The white journalist's high opinion of Du Bois was certainly affected by what he considered to be the Atlanta professor's more mature (restrained) attitude toward Booker T. Washington.

The resolutions which were finally adopted were echoes of what the Radicals had been saying for years. The political and economic suppression of the Negroes was sternly denounced, and the President of the United States and the Congress were asked to compel the Southern states to abide by the Fourteenth and Fifteenth Amendments. The National Negro Committee also demanded that Negro children receive their proportional share of state educational appropriations. With an obvious eye on Booker Washington, who was looking over the shoulders of the conferees, the following resolution was included:

> We agree fully with the prevailing opinion that the transformation of the unskilled colored laborers in industry and agriculture into skilled workers is of vital importance to that race and to the nation, but we demand for the Negroes as for all others a free and complete education, whether by city, state, or nation, a grammar school and industrial training for all, and technical, professional and academic education for the most gifted.[13]

Several objections were raised in reference to the first part of the preceding resolution; as written originally, the phrase, "of great importance to that race," was used, but it was amended to read, "of first importance." After Trotter and Waldron complained, the words, "of vital importance," were substituted.[14]

Trotter wanted the conference to take an anti-Taft stand because the President refused to consider Negroes for federal jobs in the South unless such appointments were approved by white Southerners; however, one white conferee reminded the conclave that Taft had recently repudiated the move to disfranchise Maryland Negroes. The group decided to condemn Taft in the first situation and praise him in the second. The National Negro Committee also passed a resolution which was very similar to Du Bois' argument that the right to vote determined the Negroes' treatment in all other institutions of American society, including the economic. Booker Washington could not have been pleased.

Washington's New York City representative, Charles W. Anderson, was active behind the scenes, not only in securing data on the conference and transmitting it to the Tuskegeean, but also in obstructing some of the plans of the Negro conferees. For instance, after he heard that "a big public testimonial" had been scheduled for Du Bois, he persuaded friends of the Washingtonians to shun the affair; happily he reported to his chieftain that the program would have to be shelved or reduced in scope. The next day, Anderson wired the Tuskegeean that Du Bois, Waldron, and Bishop Alexander Walters (among others) were meeting secretly. Booker T. Washington was also instructed that a public meeting was to be held that very evening and the leaders were due to confer secretly on the following day. Anderson confided that, as far as he had heard, Villard "is with them."[15]

Mary White Ovington emerged from the deliberations feeling "weary" but having great respect for many of the Negro conferees: "I find myself still occasionally forgetting that the Negroes aren't poor people for whom I must kindly do something, and then comes a gathering such as that last evening and I learn they are men with most forceful opinions of their own."[16]

Villard, agreeing that the meetings were a "great success," was pleased to note the New York City press had not launched into any "sensational attacks," and he seemed to think the metropolitan dailies gave the gathering fair, unslanted coverage. Actually, at least two New York newspapers did strike unfair blows in their accounts of the National Negro Committee conference. The New York *World* was apparently disturbed about the question of social equality and captioned its first story, "Whites and Negroes Mix at Conference." The subtitle was even more obvious—"Absence of Young White Women Is Deplored by One Colored Delegate."[17] *The New York Times* recorded an interview with William E. Walling ("a Socialist"), who purportedly explained that, in accordance with the National Negro Committee's aim of civil and political equality, the Negro would secure "the privilege of going where he pleases and mingling with white people, without the barrier now thrown up against him." Many of the women who attended the programs declared they were "enthusiastic supporters" of the "sort of equality outlined by Mr. Walling."[18] The *Times* man also called attention to the fact that no effort had been made to draw the color line at the conference. While the *Times* may have recorded many of the facts, it expressed them in a prejudiced manner—and omitted other pertinent details. For instance, Walling wanted the Negroes to have freedom of association, but he did not believe they should force themselves socially upon the whites, as the *Times* quotation led people to conclude.

Naturally, Southern white newspapers had only critical comments to make about the National Negro Committee. The Baltimore *Sun* announced "a sad day" would dawn for Negroes if Northern "friends" alienated them from "the good will and helpful aid of the best elements in the South." It also published a letter to the editor, in which the writer said that rich and poor Socialists hobnobbed with Negroes at the New York gathering— and the ideas expressed there could only lead the nation into a "socialistic revolution." The Raleigh *Observer*, in an article entitled, "More Fool Negroes," stated that the conclave sought to undo white supremacy and racial intermarriage had been advocated. The editor concluded he was sorry "those loud-talking agitators could not be forced to make connection with a plow and a mule."[19]

Villard's shrewd strategy after the conference was to remind Booker T. Washington that other whites besides himself planned to make certain the National Negro Committee did not become an extremist group. The white journalist proposed to ask Andrew Carnegie for money, and appreciated only too well that Washing-

ton could dry up this source simply by labelling the new organization "dangerous." Even Miss Ovington, who considered herself
"anti-Washington" and professed to be disinterested in the
Tuskegeean's endorsement, recognized that Negroes could not
afford to underwrite the movement, and this fact made limited
compromises necessary in order to secure the help of influential
people. As it turned out, white philanthropists did not wish to
become financial angels for the Committee, since they preferred to
help those in the field of race relations who stressed obligations not
rights, "harmonies" not "discords," and separation not integration.[20]

Villard kept trying to keep Du Bois from wrecking his plans.
In September of 1909 when the Atlanta professor was asked to
participate in a memorial service for William Lloyd Garrison, the
white journalist welcomed remarks about the "highest aspirations"
of the race but cautioned against criticizing the Washingtonians.
Diplomatic discussions between Villard and the Tuskegeean continued, but the Negro leader declared that he would eschew the
National Negro Committee until guarantees were given that
neither Trotter nor Du Bois would promulgate its policies.[21]
Actually the Washingtonians were never able to understand that
the moderate Villard was sincere in his dealings with them and
they constantly condemned his "unfriendly attitude." In 1910 they
feared that he, John Milholland, and Du Bois had hatched a plan
to merge the National Negro Committee with the more outspoken
and aggressive Constitution League.

Such worries made the Washingtonians step up their efforts to
recapture those sheep who had strayed. For example, Mary Church
Terrell (the wife of Tuskegeean political appointee, Judge R. H.
Terrell) was scheduled to give an address at the second conference
of the National Negro Committee in 1910, and Washington
pointedly asked the judge where he stood in this "embarrassing"

situation. While denying that he sought "to control anybody's action," the Tuskegean announced that, since Mrs. Terrell was associated with the "opposition," it would become difficult for "your friends to help you." Judge Terrell, like many another husband, was unable to keep his wife at home when she had an errand elsewhere—she delivered her speech and condemned "Northern neutrality in the [anti-Negro] crimes of the South."[22] Emmett J. Scott also worked diligently to convince friends of the National Negro Committee to break away. On learning that H. T. Kealing had been "proposed" as a member of the executive committee, he asked the fellow to see him before accepting the post. Kealing shunned the organization after belatedly discovering it was "animated by the spirit of bitterness and complaint."[23]

At its 1910 conference the National Negro Committee formally changed its name to the National Association for the Advancement of Colored People, and the officers elected were: National President, Moorfield Storey; Chairman of the Executive Committee, William E. Walling; Treasurer, John E. Milholland; Disbursing Treasurer, Oswald Garrison Villard; and Director of Publications and Research, W. E. B. Du Bois. All of the officers were still white men, with the exception of Du Bois. The conferees concluded that it was imperative to publicize the plight of the Negroes, and, contrary to Booker T. Washington, they believed such candor would not damage Southern reform efforts.[24] Villard was pained by the "silence" of the New York press and blamed the Tuskegean: "I should not be at all surprised if he had gone the rounds of the newspapers and had advised them not to print such radical utterances; it would be, to his mind, a perfectly honorable action."[25]

Although there were a few paragraphs in the *Times* and the *Tribune*, there was not anything about the gathering in the *Sun* apparently, and this omission was especially galling because the

Sun published a column-long interview with Washington, who was visiting New York City at the time. The *Times* included two accounts of the conclave and seemed to select for emphasis excerpts of two addresses which were extremist-sounding. Clarence Darrow (a "Socialist") was quoted as having suggested that Southern Negroes should protest against exploitation by refusing to work. Franz Boas, the anthropologist, was reported to have said that the resolution of the race problem would come inevitably through "amalgamation" and "the elimination of the most pronounced type of negro."[26] In his own editorial for the New York *Evening Post*, Villard stressed that Southerners, Northerners, radicals, and conservatives appeared on programs of the N.A.A.C.P.

Certainly, Washington felt contempt for the 1910 proceedings ("nonsense") and was still sure most of the white and Negro conferees possessed ulterior motives and/or were "deceived." He was shocked that the white delegates permitted Negroes to believe gains could be realized "by merely making demands, passing resolutions and cursing somebody." The Tuskegeean was comforted that the Negro masses knew the true path of advancement. Of course, he was rankled when Du Bois left Atlanta University to become the N.A.A.C.P. Director of Publications and Research; yet he must have been aware that Du Bois promised (before being employed by the N.A.A.C.P.) not to use the Association as a center of attack upon the Tuskegeean. Washington feared Du Bois' residence in New York City would unleash "evil tendencies" and he suggested that Charles W. Anderson's political club be reorganized. One delegate from each important Negro organization was to be admitted to the club, thereby creating a metropolitan "clearing house" under Anderson's domination.[27]

Du Bois was not unhappy to leave Atlanta; for years he hated the city so much he forced himself to ignore the place. He tried not to give the community an opportunity to discriminate against him and did not even ride the streetcars or attend the theaters.[28] Discontent with the city only underscored the despair he felt in connection with the Atlanta University monographs on the Negro, and he believed the studies would have thrived if Booker T. Washington had not blocked support for the project.[29] Du Bois was also convinced that "powerful interests," among them the General Education Board, withheld aid from Atlanta University's other activities because of his association with the institution. According to Professor Willard Range, the administrators of Atlanta "breathed a sigh of relief" when their "embarrassing ornament" headed for New York City.[30]

Du Bois possessed sufficient reasons to feel insecure, because he was at the lowest point in his career—not only did the Atlanta University publications fail to meet his expectations, but he was also faced with the burial of the Niagara Movement. In later years he turned on the white founders of the N.A.A.C.P., but these same people in 1910 perhaps rescued him from oblivion. The Atlanta *Independent* noted his "passing" in a stinging article which the Washingtonians reprinted. While the account was malicious and extreme, in its broad outline, the portrayal of the professor as a social isolate was substantially correct. Du Bois was depicted as an educated "stranger" among the Negro race who refused to participate in its "social life." According to the newspaper, he could not even bring himself to converse with Atlanta Negroes whom he sometimes encountered at the local barber shop.[31] Similar accusations of snobbery were to plague him for the rest of his life, and, undoubtedly, reticence or exclusiveness must be considered as a distinct limitation in the personality of this man who aspired to lead his people and transform their attitudes.

Shortly after joining the New York office of the N.A.A.C.P., he became embroiled in another fight with William Monroe Trotter. The Association wanted to celebrate the one hundredth anniversary of Charles Sumner's birth by sponsoring a Boston public meeting in January of 1911. Du Bois was asked to make the necessary arrangements and Clement Morgan engaged Faneuil Hall for the occasion. Trotter, on hearing about this move, considered his own position in Boston Negro circles threatened. Representing the New England Suffrage League and the National Independent Political League, he announced his own plans for a Sumner centenary program in Boston. Two independent celebrations would advertise that the Negro leaders were fighting again and the N.A.A.C.P. sought to avoid such an unseemly demonstration of disunity. The Boston *Guardian* editor undoubtedly counted on this fact. President Moorfield Storey, trying to calm the "disturbed" Trotter, suggested Du Bois could set up a combined meeting with all three organizations participating. In Storey's opinion, if no amiable agreement were reached, the N.A.A.C.P. should cancel its program. Since Trotter was adamant, the Association confined its celebration to New York City, but Du Bois took his own revenge and publicly disparaged the Trotter meeting. The *Guardian* editor counterattacked by complaining to Storey and Francis J. Garrison, and these white leaders severely blamed Du Bois for creating dissension. Oswald Garrison Villard concluded that Du Bois was petty, and that such behavior indicated a serious personality defect. Storey, thinking the Negro race would suffer because of Du Bois' habitual "little digs" at antagonists, hoped the leader would learn that a great deal could actually be accomplished by condemning ideas instead of personalities.[32]

The smoke had hardly diffused from the Trotter battle when Du Bois, despite N.A.A.C.P. efforts to restrain him, renewed war against Booker T. Washington. A few months before, on a visit to Europe, the Tuskegean told Britishers that race relations in America were not deteriorating—on the contrary, white and black Southerners knew the race problem was slowly being solved.

In contrast to Du Bois' impassioned utterances about lynching Washington informed audiences it was only human nature to dwell upon extreme incidents and ignore day-to-day illustrations of friendliness across the color line. John Milholland, also in London at the time, repudiated the Alabama educator's comment that "a few Negroes" could indeed use Pullman cars in the South. Milholland declared Du Bois and other "real leaders" of the race were unable to buy such accommodations.[33] Since Booker Washington received repeated assurances that the N.A.A.C.P. was not dedicated to an anti-Tuskegean platform, he asked Robert R. Moton to elicit Villard's reactions to Milholland's statement. The Alabama educator, hoping Villard would be pushed to stir up matters "in an interesting way," suggested the white editor was ignorant of Association intrigues. However, Villard asserted the N.A.A.C.P. assumed no responsibility for the personal expressions of its members and emphasized again that the organization was "not anti-Washington or pro-Du Bois."[34]

In the wake of Milholland's criticism came Du Bois' reply to the Negro leader's London speech. Authoring an "Appeal to England and Europe," he portrayed Washington in the old role of a man unable to tell the truth for fear of alienating rich white benefactors. Du Bois, intending to make propaganda hay, sent copies of the "Appeal" to prominent Negroes and asked them to subscribe to it publicly, in order to dramatize that successful men opposed the Tuskegean's pronouncements. Among those who signed were Dr. Nathan F. Mossell, head of the Douglass Hospital in Philadelphia; Bishop Alexander Walters, A.M.E. Church; and E. H. Morris, Grand Master of the Odd Fellows and formerly a member of the Illinois state legislature.[35] On the Du Bois document appeared the words, "Headquarters, National Negro Committee," and, since the Committee was incorporated into the N.A.A.C.P. only a few months before, it was not unnatural that Booker T.

Washington wondered whether the latter organization was responsible for the barrage. The New York *Sun* did attribute the circular to the N.A.A.C.P., and Washington, in dispatching it to Villard, informed him that the Du Bois "Appeal" was nothing like the earlier promises which had been made about the ideology of the N.A.A.C.P. Du Bois had signed his name with the title, "Secretary, National Afro-American Committee," and Washington charged "somebody" was trying to convey the impression that the Association sponsored the document.[36]

Villard's inquiry convinced him that a stenographer had unintentionally neglected to erase the words, "Headquarters, National Negro Committee," from the old stationery which Du Bois used, but the white journalist promised that the N.A.A.C.P. leadership would examine the entire matter at its next meeting. However, he admitted frankly that, although he sought to avoid intraracial disunity and had influenced the N.A.A.C.P. to ignore the Tuskegeean's statements of "optimism," he subscribed to (but had not been consulted about) Du Bois' "Appeal." Booker T. Washington was warned that Negro intellectuals, acquiring strength and receiving aid from increasing numbers of whites, might persuade the Association to attack the educator directly, thus rejecting Villard's pacifistic advice and possibly causing the New York editor's resignation. Perhaps Washington thought Villard was lying about everything; certainly, Robert R. Moton held the N.A.A.C.P. responsible for the Du Bois document and called Villard's version "moonshine."[37]

In Du Bois' accounts of the "Appeal," which were published in the *Crisis* (the N.A.A.C.P. monthly which he edited), he was careful to state that the essay was issued independently of the Association. He blandly asserted that no evidence existed which could have led any person to conclude that the document was the official expression of the organization he represented.[38] However, in order to show the far-reaching importance of the controversial paper, Du Bois printed responses from the London *Nation*, *Kolnische Volk Zeitung* from Germany, and the Vienna *Die Zeit*, among other periodicals. Whatever may be said about his "Appeal," Du Bois' use of language and manner of promotion certainly demonstrated he was a talented counter-propagandist, and the Washingtonians sadly realized this fact. The *Crisis* editor was absolutely delighted to reprint some reactions from American newspapers. The Raleigh *News and Courier* wrote:

> It is hard to tell which is the worst enemy of the Negro race—the brute who invites lynching by the basest of crimes, or the social-equality-hunting fellow like Du Bois, who slanders his country. Fortunately for the peaceable and industrious Negroes in the South, the world does not judge them either by Du Bois or the animal, and helps them and is in sympathy with their efforts to better their conditions.[39]

The Chicago *Tribune* observed that the high achievement of the signers of the "Appeal" proved the Negro race had made great strides. The Buffalo *Express* acknowledged the petition would result in some hostility, but judged that in the long run Negroes would profit because, if it did nothing else, it would embarrass the whites who were concerned about European public opinion. The Philadelphia *Bulletin* disagreed with this last point:

> One may lament with the petitioners that the Negro has so few opportunities or that so many are denied him, but evolution of a race is a slow matter. All history shows it. . . . The petitioners to Europe complain, too that the Negro is not received socially according to his merits. No law can affect that. It is an iridescent dream that there shall ever be social equality between the races. That, however, is apparently the secret of the restlessness of Professor Du Bois and his friends. They are educated, cultivated, refined and of high character. Their quarrel is that they are not

white. It is a tragedy that they are not, but it is a great fault with some of them, that they nurse their wrongs too much rather than trying, like Dr. Washington, to improve the race in a practical way. Certainly Europe is not going to help them.[40]

Characteristically, Du Bois' campaign for social equality was condemned as a fervent desire of the propagandist to be a white man. The theme of social equality is an important one and will be reserved for later discussion.

Although Oswald Garrison Villard had mildly threatened the Washingtonians with the possibility of an N.A.A.C.P. war upon them, he and other whites in the Association (Francis J. Garrison, Moorfield Storey, *et al.*) were still unprepared to surrender their hope that the Tuskegeean could somehow be encouraged to co-operate with their organization. The peak year in the N.A.A.C.P.'s campaign to woo Washington occurred in 1911. The year began in a characteristic and inauspicious manner when the Alabama educator wrote that Villard was influenced by "sour and disappointed" social ciphers in the Negro race. Contradicting Villard's earlier comment, the Tuskegeean declared Negro intellectuals were no longer being deceived by agitators and were entering his own camp in large numbers. Shortly afterwards Washington decided it was time to show the N.A.A.C.P. leaders he had no fear of them.[41] Villard realized only too well that he and the Tuskegeean disagreed on "fundamental philosophy" (for example, the Negro educator's silence on Northern residential segregation), but the New York editor wanted to prove himself a *moderate* "radical."

The case of the Constitution League demonstrated this point. About this time, John E. Milholland was unsuccessful in trying to merge the League with the N.A.A.C.P., and his aggressive stand against Booker T. Washington was one crucial reason that a formal alliance could not be established. Villard, fearing his organization might be blamed for future extreme statements made by Milholland's group, notified the Alabama educator that the Constitution League would not be combined with the N.A.A.C.P.[42] However, the suspicious Tuskegean thought the Association would only pretend to be conciliatory in order "to inveigle our friends into believing in their sincerity," while the Constitution League might well serve as the mud-slinging partner.[43] Because of Du Bois' close relationship with Milholland, the Washingtonians simply refused to conceive of any policy difference between the two organizations.

In February of 1911 when the N.A.A.C.P. considered the erection of a building in New York City to house its administrative offices and those of other groups dedicated to Negro advancement, Washingtonian Charles W. Anderson was invited to attend a small meeting devoted to a discussion of the project. Anderson was unimpressed by this gesture, although he asked his chieftain for instructions. He toyed with the idea of accepting the offer in order to observe whether "any important white persons" were involved, but Booker T. Washington advised a policy of judicious isolation, apparently on the grounds that Anderson's presence might be interpreted by both friends and enemies as implying a commitment.[44] Obviously, the N.A.A.C.P. was getting nowhere with the Tuskegean; however, within a month, a fortuitous incident occurred which almost brought about a rapprochement. It was not strange that the reconciliation did not last, in view of the suspicion which the two groups had long nurtured.

In March of 1911, Booker T. Washington was assaulted by a white man after the Negro mistakenly entered a New York City apartment building in search of a friend. According to a malicious rumor, he went there to call upon a white woman. Naturally, the educator was pained by the entire episode, especially after this sordid affair culminated in the trial and acquittal of the assailant.

However, the Negro leader received many sympathetic letters and telegrams from a number of people whom he considered his antagonists, and these friendly gestures motivated him to write Villard that the time had come to forget all past unpleasantness and combine "both factions." Washington advised ("as a first step") the N.A.A.C.P. to appoint three delegates to serve as its representatives at the forthcoming annual meetings of the National Negro Business League. Villard, conceiving that he was on the threshold of a historic *entente cordiale*, favored a dramatic exhibition of affection for Washington in the form of an N.A.A.C.P. resolution of "sympathy and confidence." The New York journalist appreciated that "some people" in the Association would not be well disposed to support such a motion, but he adjudged it imperative to create a climate for "peace negotiations."[45] And "peace" might fill N.A.A.C.P. coffers.

Since the beginning, the Association had financial problems and during early 1911 was forced to borrow from its anti-lynching fund in order to operate. Villard always argued the organization was in a limping condition because of Washington's opposition— which was a signal for many wealthy whites to continue their boycott. As proof of his assertion the editor cited the case of two rich Philadelphia women who ignored the N.A.A.C.P. because they feared Du Bois would transform it into an anti-Washington battleground. Villard planned to send Du Bois to meet the ladies and give them "his own assurances." Apparently, Du Bois promised Villard again that he would refrain from denouncing the Tuskegeean and would also try to convert John Milholland.[46] Such pledges were never possible to keep.

Moorfield Storey was also seeking to persuade rich white people that they possessed a "misapprehension" about the Association. Speaking for the organization's leadership, he professed a profound admiration for the Tuskegeean. Storey explained that

his own group protected Negro civil rights and therefore comple-
mented the contributions of the Alabama educator. He pointed out
that the acquisition of property was important, but many Americans required education to appreciate the Negroes' right to buy
property. Storey deplored the "ill feeling" which existed among
those who were helping Negroes and he admitted the N.A.A.C.P.
needed aid from all sources—so far as he was concerned, the
intraracial leadership struggle was a "dispute over trifles."[47]

Obviously the groundwork for the pacification of the Washingtonians was laid and, just before the annual Association convention, Villard wired Booker T. Washington, requesting from
him a friendly word to the conclave. The New York editor
explained the gesture would facilitate the designation of delegates
to the National Negro Business League meeting.[48] However,
unknown to Villard at the time, the Tuskegeeans were unwilling
to bear partial responsibility for their past misunderstandings with
Du Bois and the N.A.A.C.P. Nor were they ready to consider the
men who had been their adversaries as equal partners in an inter-
dependent program of racial uplift. The very day after Washington
received Villard's telegram, he confided to Charles W. Anderson
that strategy demanded a "conciliatory course" which would
inevitably "leave Du Bois standing high and dry." Anderson and
Robert R. Moton urged their leader to assent to Villard's "proposition," but to frame a cautious reply ("with ring of sincerity").
They told him to avoid the charge of being unco-operative—if any
future discord resulted, public opinion would recognize the fault
rested with certain N.A.A.C.P. "scoundrels." The Alabama
educator sounded like an echo out of the past when he notified
Villard that although the leaders pursued "different lines" full
agreement on basic goals could be achieved. Since the Tuskegeean
did not understand the reasons for past disharmony, he blamed
personality factors and called upon all principals to forget "personal

differences," "personal bickerings," and "selfishness." Undoubtedly, there was some sincerity in his statement but there was also
the old strong belief that Villard was negotiating because of fear
and weakness. Primarily, Washington's "co-operation" was still
part of an overall strategy to isolate Du Bois and attempt to change
the emphasis of the Association.[49]

On March 31, 1911, Villard wired Washington that the following
resolution had been voted by the N.A.A.C.P.:

> Resolved that we put on record our profound regret at the recent
> assault of Dr. Booker T. Washington in New York City in which
> the association finds renewed evidence of race discrimination and
> increased necessity for the awakening of the public conscience.[50]

The Alabama educator was deeply appreciative of the "generous
act." (As a result of this "opening wedge," the New York journalist anticipated that the Negro leader and his delegates would be
present at the 1912 N.A.A.C.P. conference.)[51] In addition to this
resolution the 1911 conclave, following the Villard-Storey approach, went on record as wishing "to antagonize no one" who
was earnestly trying to help the Negro race. The addresses of the
editor of the New York *Evening Post* and Du Bois represented
attempts to synthesize the Washingtonian economic emphasis and
N.A.A.C.P. civil libertarianism.[52]

After this conference Booker Washington adopted a dual role of
seeming to help the white journalist while hindering Du Bois. For
the first role the New York *Age* is a case in point. The paper had
disregarded Tuskegeean hints to terminate the battle with the
N.A.A.C.P. Villard, ignorant of the Negro leader's unsuccessful
attempt to effect the editorial cease-fire, asked Robert R. Moton
to fix it so that the *Age* would follow a friendly policy. A few days
later the Alabama educator also gave Moton the task of bringing
the newspaper into line. Moton shrewdly sent this note to Villard

for the purpose of demonstrating the Tuskegeean's good faith. At this juncture Washington wrote directly to Villard and assured him everything possible was being done to correct the excesses of the Negro press.[53]

The Alabama educator was implacable in his handling of Du Bois. He accused Milholland and Du Bois of conspiring to persuade President Taft to place the former professor in some ranking post, possibly as minister to Haiti. The Tuskegeean feared he would lose prestige if the Negro Radical received the appointment; besides, he counted on suggesting one of his flock for the job. However, he did not wish to request a presidential interview since he was worried that Taft might think the intraracial fracas was only a personal fight. (The President had always been told that Du Bois attacked Booker Washington because the latter was a 100 per cent Taft man. The Alabama educator was presented to Republican leaders as a martyr—crucified because of selfless service to the administration. Naturally this approach, minimizing the deeper causes of the dispute, made it difficult for Du Bois and his friends to receive much consideration from the White House.) On this 1911 occasion Charles W. Anderson asked a white friend to inform Taft's secretary that the Milholland-Du Bois "opposition to the President . . . is constant and personal." Washington, suspecting Taft hoped to promote support from Du Bois and Milholland, thought someone needed to warn the President that since these men had "no strong following" their help was valueless. Determined "to settle Du Bois forever" in the mind of the Chief Executive, Washington passed along an anti-Taft cartoon from the *Crisis*.[54] A short time later the *Crisis* editor published two anti-Taft editorials,[55] and one may only wonder whether Du Bois wrote them after the word was passed that he would not receive any consideration from the White House.

The Washingtonians kept tabs on Du Bois when he went to

London for the Universal Races Congress in the summer of 1911. Although Mary W. Ovington and John E. Milholland attended the meetings at the University of London, other N.A.A.C.P. directors were not very enthusiastic about the conclave and argued that the Association ought not to divert its attention from the race problem in the United States. Officially, the N.A.A.C.P. sent Du Bois to England "to make foreign propaganda";[56] practically, however, the organization gave his activities there little support. It may be hard to imagine why Du Bois' labors abroad were regarded as a threat by Booker T. Washington, who should have recognized the former professor's obvious weaknesses as an organizational leader and his conspicuous fondness for grand conferences. The Tuskegeean's apprehension was due to many factors, among which were the following: 1. alarm that the N.A.A.C.P. might throw its weight behind the Universal Races Congress, 2. overestimating Milholland's and Du Bois' influence among N.A.A.C.P. board members as well as the European whites, 3. fear of being ridiculed before the Europeans, 4. knowledge of Du Bois' skills in the art of propaganda writing.

Du Bois, having prepared supporters for the Universal Races Congress since 1910, announced the meetings represented just about the most important movement in the twentieth century. He wrote they were of greater account than the Russian-Japanese War, the Hague Peace Conference, or even the beginnings of socialism —because the world had not previously witnessed an international scientific conclave exclusively devoted to the concept of race. He believed quite naively but sincerely that, if members of all races and nationalities assembled and exchanged ideas, a "spiritual" bond would grow after the delegates departed from London. He thought of the Universal Races Congress as an interracial "World Grievance Committee" and anticipated this "reunion of East and West" would lead directly to world peace.[57]

Booker T. Washington, fearing Du Bois and the N.A.A.C.P. directors would denounce his approach to the Negro problem, sent Robert R. Moton to England. Moton, who received letters of introduction to various influential people abroad, did not originally plan to address the conclave and plotted instead to move "on the inside" of things in order to scrutinize "our antagonistics." After chatting with Du Bois and examining his proposed speech, the Washingtonian concluded that the N.A.A.C.P. official would not be an intemperate critic. Du Bois intended to condemn Washington's rose-colored portrait of Negro life in the United States, but references to the head of Tuskegee Institute were "purely impersonal—and very dignified." Moton seemed reassured (at least letters to his chieftain indicate such a reaction), but, in order to make absolutely certain the Washingtonians were fully protected, he decided to follow Du Bois' talk with one of his own. If Moton showed tension, Booker T. Washington was even more edgy and "anxious to hear" about the happenings in London. Unlike his trouble-shooter, the Tuskegeean did not find any "optimism" in the Du Bois address, and conjectured that, while the original talk may have been acceptable, a doctored version was disseminated underhandedly.[58]

Distinguished scientists, such as Franz Boas of the United States and von Ranke of Germany, contributed papers to the Congress and asserted "mankind is one." Von Ranke held that it was not possible to chart fixed or enclosed lines of racial demarcation, and Boas repudiated the unchangeability theory of racial development. The American anthropologist proclaimed races are "growing . . . entities." Another scientist wrote, "It is of no more importance to know how many races there are than to know how many angels dance on the point of a needle!" An Oxford University professor announced that the intelligence of contemporary primitive peoples approximated that of the Europeans—geographical and social environments were thought to hold the key to race differences.[59] The scientists urged "the vital importance at this juncture of history of discountenancing race prejudice, as tending to inflict on humanity incalculable harm, and as based on generalizations unworthy of an enlightened and progressive age."[60]

According to Du Bois "the tangible result" of the meetings was the creation of an "international committee," charged with promoting world peace through interracial co-operation. The new council was to direct a friendly inquiry into the cultures of all racial groups and publicize the dangers of ethnocentric thinking. The investigators were also directed to examine the biological and sociological results of miscegenation, collect empirical evidence of workable means of social reform among the underdeveloped peoples, and encourage such amelioration programs. The committee advocated the extension of vocational and college education throughout the world as an important means of bringing about interracial harmony.[61]

Unlike Du Bois' ecstatic reports, Miss Ovington's account of the Universal Races Congress underscored her acute concern—because the conferees were reluctant to explore the ramifications of imperialism.[62] Although the problems of China, India, and Egypt were touched upon, Du Bois admitted that "one felt the repression of those who talked on these subjects." No impolite words were to mar the drawing room atmosphere of gentility. The leaders of the conclave made it quite plain that good will was to be established first, afterwards other "difficulties" could be "readily" ironed out. However, "political issues" were simply ignored. The ground rules specified that no political resolutions were to be promulgated, nor could the organization be "pledged to any political party or any program of reforms."[63] Some of the participants wanted to set up "a permanent world organization" with machinery for widespread social action, and John E. Milholland especially supported this proposal. Miss Ovington reported she sensed "a hostile influence" to the idea. The assembly ended its deliberations and held no subsequent meetings. In August of 1914, a notice appeared in the N.A.A.C.P.'s *Crisis* magazine indicating that a second conclave was planned for Paris the following year. Some time later, Du Bois recalled that the Universal Races Congress would have left impressive legacies if World War I had not intervened.[64]

The Congress was significant because its international forum provided the prestige of scientific authority for the race egalitarians. It was intended primarily as a propaganda piece, although it failed to cause very much of a stir. The *Crisis* was the only magazine which made any serious attempt to publicize the meetings. The New York *Times* was concerned that strict racial lines be held: "There can be no universal 'melting pot.' The consciousness of physical kind persists even after a frank and generous recognition of cultural affinity."[65] Negro newspapers bestowed their praises. The *Afro-American Ledger* called the conference "the greatest event of the twentieth century"; the *Amsterdam News* termed it "the most unique and without doubt the most stupendously ambitious gathering of the students of mankind in all history"; and the Washington *American* hoped it would "become as fixed as the Hague Tribunal."[66]

In view of the fact that so little could have been accomplished—even if more publicity had been given to the affair, why did Du Bois devote so much of his attention to the Universal Races Congress? Probably the best reason was that it fulfilled a deep emotional need to get beyond the United States milieu and walk upon the international interracial stage. There he could find the acceptance and recognition which he felt were denied him in his own country. For many years he had conceived of himself as an internationalist, and some of his happiest days were those spent outside of his native land. During the conclave Du Bois enjoyed his "broadest contact" with whites. While in America he felt isolated in his relations across the color line, and when he joined whites for some function he feared and often received "deliberate insult." Consequently, he adopted a rule of infrequently speaking to white Americans. In London he was filled with the idealism of the conference and responded enthusiastically to the friendly overtures and invitations from such prominent people as H. G. Wells and Mrs. Havelock Ellis. The *Crisis* reported something of his social calendar. He was guest of honor at a dinner given by the Lyceum Club which "from time to time entertains various distinguished guests and assembles other distinguished persons to hear them speak." The hostess of the evening was Her Highness, the Ranee of Sarawak, and some of the guests were stellar attractions of London society.[67]

Du Bois was exhilarated by the cosmopolitan atmosphere of the Universal Races Congress and his lifelong yearnings for "human brotherhood" were momentarily fulfilled. In London he met Buddhists, Mohammedans, Christians, Jews, atheists, and agnostics—all in happy fellowship. As he walked about and heard many foreign languages spoken in convivial gatherings, his dream of cultural pluralism seemed to be coming true. Suddenly color appeared to be "a small and unimportant distinction." He experienced elation when he saw the dark General Legitime of Haiti conversing with milk-skinned Germans and Scandinavians.

Actually most of these intellectual conferees-of-the-world had done little to change race relations in their own countries; however, at such an international conference (their private little "World Council"), in their own eyes at least, they were enrobed in a mantle of momentary power as they issued resolutions. It gave them a profound sense of importance to believe (or at least to say) they "represented" fifty "races" and gained the "co-operation of many of the leading people of the world." Du Bois even wrote that the conference had the "support" of presidents, of parliaments, most of the membership of the Permanent Court of Arbitration and the delegates of the Second Hague Conference, twelve British governors, several British prime ministers, and more than forty colonial bishops. The conferees, by their own admission, were "the most cultivated and responsible section of humanity," but they gave little consideration to the question of how their "reasoned statements" were to reach their countrymen at home. The all-important problem of imperialism was untouched, as the delegates moved about in their vacuum.

Some may have said the London meetings were organized to assemble the theorists—men who spun "propositions" for the social actionists. However no provision was made for such a division of labor. Du Bois, of course, printed accounts of the conclave in the *Crisis* during the months after adjournment, but the "movement" was soon forgotten. There was never any organizational relationship between the Universal Races Congress and the National Association for the Advancement of Colored People. The conferees were far removed from the working-class movements in their own countries and Du Bois admitted that "the labor question was hardly touched in its main modern phases."[68] The approach adopted by Du Bois, who headed the American delegation, was typical: basically he was a propagandist leader and not an administrator. He was a man of persuasive words who cared little for implementation. As a propagandist, he used conferences to substitute for working organizations.

Through all these conclaves—including the ones during the Niagara period and the N.A.A.C.P.—Du Bois' emphasis was upon race equality and a denunciation of segregation. But elsewhere, frustrations forced him to cling to the segregated economy theory and the Negroes' separate contribution to civilization. In a letter, he wrote that the Negro race must attain more than "simply equality with other people. . . . I want the colored people to have the right to develop according to their capacity and I certainly would be disappointed if they did not develop much higher things than the white race. . . ." Examining segregation in the South, he underscored the increasing differentiation in interest and cultural tradition which existed between the two races. He thought Negroes were becoming more united in racial consciousness and more desirous of co-operating with each other.[69] He maintained that the race was prospering in its isolation by organizing its own unique system of social institutions. In the N.A.A.C.P.'s *Crisis*, he condemned whites who were manipulating the Negro separate system, but, outside of the magazine, he stressed that whites instituted a "hands off" policy and the resultant "closed circle of social intercourse" was beneficial to Negroes.[70]

Writing for *World's Work* in 1911–12, he gave an example of Negro renascence in "Black Durham":

> A black man may get up in the morning from a mattress made by black men, in a house which a black man built of lumber which black men cut and planed; he may put on a suit which he bought at a colored haberdashery and socks knit at a colored mill; he may cook victuals from a colored grocery on a stove which black men fashioned; he may earn his living working for colored men, be sick in a colored hospital, and buried from a colored church; and the Negro insurance society will pay his widow enough to keep his children in a colored school. This is surely progress.[71]

Du Bois advocated a segregated economy primarily in the South because he believed the North provided some opportunities for integration. Yet he also wrote that the "Souls of White Folk" were filled with hate for Negroes. One may only wonder how the following chauvinistic sentiment was received by the white board members at the N.A.A.C.P.: "Instead of being led and defended by others, as in the past, the [Negroes] are gaining their own leaders, their own voices, their own ideals.[72]

The conception of a differential Negro culture ran counter to the propaganda of the Association, but during this period Du Bois did not emphasize this ideology in the *Crisis*, and apparently it created no conflicts with board members.

However, there were serious clashes of opinion with the organization because of Du Bois' notion of his role as a race leader. He considered himself to be the omniscient editor, the powerful pundit, the man with a mission so large that he (and the *Crisis*) could not be subordinated to the N.A.A.C.P. By the end of 1915 his influence increased as the magazine's circulation grew, and when Booker Washington passed from the scene Du Bois became the most prominent prophet in the Negro race.

7. The *Crisis* Magazine Grows: More N.A.A.C.P. Crises Develop

Du Bois had been engaged by the N.A.A.C.P. as research director, but all available funds were spent on "constant propaganda and legal work" and nothing remained for scientific investigations. He did not relinquish his desire to edit a magazine of propaganda and news, and against the well-meaning advice of some board members he started the publication of the *Crisis*, the Association's monthly. The first issue in November of 1910 had a circulation of 1,000, but within a little more than a year 16,000 copies were printed monthly. In 1913 the circulation went up to 30,000 and about three-fourths of the copies during this period were sold to Negroes.[1] As editor, Du Bois maintained considerable independence although he worked with an advisory committee. The *Crisis* was a separate department in the N.A.A.C.P. and came to be recognized as "Du Bois' Domain." The editor believed he could make his contribution to the cause of Negro rights by publishing this journal and had no inclination to take an aggressive role in promulgating policies at sessions of the N.A.A.C.P. board of directors.[2] He preferred to make his influence felt on the pages of the magazine and freely admitted the *Crisis* was "the only work" in the Association "which attracts me."[3] Mary White Ovington described his attitude quite clearly and in so doing also divided the *Crisis* and the N.A.A.C.P. into two distinct compartments: "Du Bois was a member of the board, careful in his judgment and scrupulous in never demanding his way in matters that pertained to the N.A.A.C.P. On the other hand, he wanted complete freedom in editing the *Crisis* magazine.[4]

Although the journal was the property of the Association, Du Bois was "determined" the *Crisis* would reflect his own views because he considered that the board, composed of varied personalities, was not able to express a set of well-defined opinions on specific issues. He suggested that when the board chose to take certain positions, it could state them in annual resolutions or in the N.A.A.C.P. section of the *Crisis*. He argued that if the magazine had not discussed his own ideas in a provocative fashion, it would have been unread and of little influence. During his long career these independent conceptions brought him into many conflicts with board members.

There were other problems in publishing the journal:

> No magazine in this country addresses so varied an audience. We are talking at once to educated hypercritical reformers of refined taste to whom a mistake in color scheme, or in English usage, or in character of advertisement seems a crime; at the same time we are speaking to people who can hardly read and write. Between these we run the whole gamut of partially educated unthinking people, of well educated people with undeveloped tastes, of practical business men, etc. It goes without saying that the *Crisis* must 1. give reliable information, 2. be attractive in make-up, 3. be frank and fearless in discussion.[5]

Actually, the magazine was produced for an educated Negro public. Du Bois tried to build reader interest by publishing a series of articles which his selected audience would appreciate, and among the pieces during the first year were "Colored High Schools," "Women's Clubs," "The Colored College Athlete," and "Harriet Beecher Stowe's Personal Knowledge of the Negro Character." Another feature was "Along the Color Line" which, like a small town newspaper, contained news items about a large number of Negroes. There was also an "Opinion" section in which Du Bois treated important events from the point of view of various newspapers. The *Crisis* contained an N.A.A.C.P. section wherein important addresses and reports of the leadership were printed. The magazine's audience was advised "What To Read" among recent books and articles, and short biographies of prominent Negroes were presented in "Men of the Month."

The advertisements reflected the journal's aspiring supporters. There was an "Educational Directory" (Howard, Atlanta, Wilberforce, Fisk, Lincoln Universities, *et al.*) and a "Legal Directory." There were also announcements about schools of shorthand and barbering, and one ad declared, "We teach you all the Secrets of Real Estate, Brokerage, and Insurance Business." A large proportion of the readers were mulattoes and many light-skinned Negroes were featured on the covers. For instance, in November of 1911 a "Quadroon" appeared. ("... Born of World Brotherhood, Crowned of all Motherhood, Beauty of Heaven and Earth.") Many readers regarded the magazine reverently. For example, J. Saunders Redding recalled that in his boyhood home the only periodical the children could not touch was the *Crisis*, which "was strictly inviolate until my father himself had unwrapped and read it—often ... aloud."[6]

An editor's prerogative is to comment upon anything which he considers pertinent to his readers and he is assumed to be an authority on countless subjects. Commonly he draws unequivocal conclusions and gives unlimited amounts of advice. As *Crisis* editor Du Bois asserted all of his occupational rights, and he pontificated monthly on any area of Negro-white relations which interested and/or annoyed him. It is worthwhile to examine the gamut of his editorial reactions during the early years.

He called for resistance against the attempts which were then being made by whites to institute segregated schools in various cities outside of the South. In 1910 he asserted that separate schools invariably were inferior ones. The editor conceded that perhaps three-fourths of the Negro children "are below the average of their fellow students in some respects," but he made a distinction between achievement and capability.[7] In another editorial he condemned the disorganized conditions which allegedly existed at the New York City Colored Orphan Asylum. He concluded that the white board engaged only submissive Negro teachers and "the white teachers do not as a rule love or sympathize with their poor little black charges."[8] Du Bois also encouraged "enterprising" artisans and professionals to migrate to the Northwest and volunteered to answer all inquiries about the area. He was quite direct in warning "empty-handed" workers (lacking in skills or financial resources) not to make the trek until they improved their bargaining positions.[9] In another editorial he praised Negro resourcefulness and was delighted that Southern farmers substantially increased the value of their holdings since the turn of the century. Du Bois was a morale builder in this 1912 piece and announced that the United States Census Bureau statistics, on which his report was based, had caused a racist clerk in the Bureau to develop "a severe case of lockjaw."[10]

The *Crisis* editor thought of himself as racial adviser ex officio. He called for "systematic charity," "systematic migration," and the planned cultivation of Negro art, drama, literature, history, and pageantry. In his magazine he attempted to explain the concept of social equality and show its significance in interracial relations. In 1911, members of both races interpreted the term to mean the unrelenting desire of some Negroes to push themselves into intimate relationships with unwilling whites. For Du Bois, social equality was "simply the right to be treated as a gentleman when one is among gentlemen and acts like a gentleman." He stated Negroes were equal to whites by "divine right," and that if his race did not proclaim this interpretation segregation possessed a secure rationalization and "democracy" could not exist.[11] In the *Crisis* editor's opinion, racial separation and discrimination revealed that the whites feared their race might not be "superior"; he also observed that white people did not countenance a separate social system they could not regulate: "They do not want separate Negro schools, but Negro schools under the control of white superintendence who hold the purse strings. They do not want separate [railroad] cars, but cars which Negroes may not enter save as servants. They do not want to stop social intermingling, but they do want to prescribe the conditions."[12]

He declared that a separate racial system was "physically impossible" and suggested the only practical substitute was to deal with Negroes in terms of their particular skills, abilities, and personalities.[13]

His verbal blasts at the whites were loud and frequent; sometimes he condemned the whole "Anglo-Saxon civilization." After white men insulted marchers in a suffrage parade, Du Bois wrote: "Wasn't it glorious? Does it not make you burn with shame to be a mere Black Man when such mighty deeds are done by the Leaders of Civilization? Does it not make you 'ashamed of your race?' Does it not make you 'want to be white?' "[14]

As he had done in the Niagara period and earlier, he accused white Christian churches of being "the strongest seat of racial and color prejudice." He asserted that this social institution, the historic helpmate of the slave trade and slavery, bolted its door to Negroes, although Jesus Christ, like the average colored man, was poor and held a lowly job. The editor pressed the parallel further and pointed out that both Christ and Negroes were maligned and maltreated. As Du Bois pictured it, the returned Christ would worship among Negroes—rarely among the wealthy white congregations.[15] At times the *Crisis* denounced a particular religious denomination, e.g., the Episcopalians who prayed in "the church of John Pierpont Morgan and not the church of Jesus Christ."[16] Often Du Bois produced not criticisms but diatribes against the white church—the institution which society considers inviolate: "How long is practical Christianity going to be able to survive its own hypocrisy? Or will Christian ministers be able to keep straight faces?"[17] Such sentiments as these must have made it more difficult for the N.A.A.C.P. to recruit among wealthy whites.

Of course the Negro church did not escape censure. While Du Bois acknowledged it was a moral force which acted as a stabilizing influence upon the family and served as a laboratory in which leaders were trained, he still disapproved of many of the highest officials ("pretentious ill-trained men ... dishonest and otherwise immoral"). He had little praise for the average Negro minister, who condemned dancing and theatergoing and was "still blaming educated people for objecting to silly and empty sermons, boasting and noise, still building churches when people need homes and schools, and persisting in crucifying critics rather than realizing the handwriting on the wall."[18] Essentially, Du Bois was a rationalist who believed educated Negroes should be encouraged to work for the church, "regardless of their belief or disbelief in unimportant dogmas and ancient and outworn creeds." However, his cavalier dismissal of aspects of religion, which the majority of his race considered sacred, did not help his effectiveness as a propagandist. These dogmas which were preached each Sunday from every pulpit were hardly assessed as "outworn" or "unimportant" by church-goers.

Du Bois' editorials had clearness, sharpness, and dramatic style; the theme of protest was expressed with directness and simplicity: "I am resolved to be quiet and law abiding, but to refuse to cringe in body or in soul, to resent deliberate insult, and to assert my just rights in the face of wanton aggression."[19]

His sentences were frequently aphoristic, making it easy for readers to commit them to memory:

> Oppression costs the oppressor too much if the oppressed stand up and protest.
>
> Agitate then, brother; protest, reveal the truth and refuse to be silenced.
>
> A moment's let up, a moment's acquiescence, means a chance for the wolves of prejudice to get at our necks.[20]

Reacting to some odious incident such as a lynching, the editor could be matter-of-factly sardonic, giving the readers a sense of imperturbability which conceals a tempest:

> Let the eagle scream! America is redeemed at Coatesville. "Some people talk of punishing the heroic mob, and the governor of Pennsylvania seems to be real provoked. We hasten to assure our readers that nothing will be done. There may be a few formal arrests, but the men will be promptly released by the mob sitting as jury—perhaps even as judge. America knows her true heroes."
>
> This we said some nine months ago [1911] when the crucifixion at Coatesville was new in its horror. Some of our readers took us roundly to task at the time, but to-day we can proudly announce the fulfilment of our prophecy: The last lyncher is acquitted and the best traditions of Anglo-Saxon civilization are safe. Let the eagle scream![21]

At other times his rage thundered forth: "Let black men especially kill lecherous white invaders of their homes and then take their lynching gladly like men. It's worth it!"[22]

The dramatic movement of Du Bois' prose may also be seen in his discussion of two Negroes who, delayed by a Kentucky freight train wreck, were served in the railroad dining car—without any adverse reactions from other patrons. The two men were so grateful they wrote to the *Crisis* about their experience:

> The editor read this and read it yet again. At first he thought it was a banquet given to black men by white; then he thought it charity to the hungry poor; then—then it dawned on his darkened soul: Two decently dressed, educated colored men had been allowed to pay for their unobtrusive meal in a Pullman dining car "WITHOUT ONE SINGLE WORD OF COMMENT OR PROTEST!" And in humble ecstasy at being treated for once like ordinary human beings they rushed from the car and sent a letter a thousand miles to say to the world: My God! Look! See!
>
> What more eloquent [remark] could be made on the white South? What more stinging indictment could be voiced? What must be the daily and hourly treatment of black men in Paducah, Ky., to bring this burst of applause at the sheerest and most negative decency?
>
> Yet every black man in America has known that same elation— North and South and West. We have all of us felt the sudden relief—the half-mad delight when contrary to fixed expectation we were treated as men and not dogs; and then, in the next breath, we hated outselves for elation over that which was but due any human being.
>
> This is the real tragedy of the Negro in America: the inner degradation, the hurt hound feeling; the sort of upturning of all values which leads some black men to "rejoice" because "only" sixty-four Negroes were lynched in the year of our Lord 1912.
>
> Conceive, O poet, a ghastlier tragedy than such a state of mind![23]

Du Bois' political editorials were his major interest. In the 1912 campaign the *Crisis* endorsed Woodrow Wilson, despite the disagreement among N.A.A.C.P. board members regarding which candidate to support. Du Bois lent his aid to the Democratic standard-bearer only after perceiving (as he also did in the previous presidential election) that there was nowhere else to go. In 1912 the N.A.A.C.P. propagandist resigned from the Socialist party after deciding that Debs could not win—besides, Du Bois still could not trust the Socialists on the Negro question.[24] He was vehement in his denunciation of President Taft's "abject surrender" to racism, and termed him the worst Chief Executive in half a century. Du Bois wrote, "Any colored man who votes for Mr. Taft will do so on the assumption that zero is better than minus 1."[25] The *Crisis* editor also concluded that Theodore Roosevelt's new political party had no "respect" for Negroes. The Progressives sought white support below the Mason-Dixon line, and, at the party convention, Southern Negro delegates were turned away while lily whites were welcomed. The Progressives also shelved Du Bois' race equality plank guaranteeing the ballot to Negroes.[26]

In August of 1912, Du Bois demanded a "price" for Negro votes—enforcement of the Reconstruction Amendments and the discarding of segregation. However it became clear that Wilson had no intention of paying the price in advance, or even of acknowledging whether any part of it would be paid at a later date. The Negro leader, admitting that Wilson could not be counted upon as a "friend" of the race,[27] observed that there were "disquieting facts" about the New Jersey governor's Southern background and administration of Princeton University. (Wilson *had* "by evasion prevented Negroes from enrolling at Princeton.")[28] However, Du Bois forced himself to find the hoped-for brighter side, i.e., the Democratic candidate would not be a tool of Tillman and Vardaman or of their supporters in the Southern ruling class. The *Crisis* editor's expectation was that, if Wilson arrived at the White House "by the grace of the black man's vote," the race would receive official help to obtain political and civil rights. As usual, Du Bois predicted Negroes would constitute a "strategic" electorate (500,000) and would likely hold "the balance of power."[29]

In his last editorial before the election, the Negro journalist described Wilson as "disconcertingly vague," but neglected to share with his readers all of the factors behind his reservations. Du Bois had published an account of a pre-election Wilson interview with William Monroe Trotter and J. Milton Waldron, in which the New Jersey governor allegedly admitted he needed Negro votes and would, if elected, veto any hostile legislation which the Democratic Congress might pass. When the Democratic standard-bearer read this version, he was piqued and denied everything. He reaffirmed there would be no "unfair discrimination" in his administration and privately asked Oswald Garrison Villard's aid in ghosting a statement for Negro consumption. Du Bois was given the task of writing the declaration which the Democratic candidate was to issue as his own. The Negro editor's memorandum was hardly an extreme one—it simply indicated the Democratic party repudiated racial disfranchisement and openly and happily accepted men of both races who believed in honest government. However, Wilson rejected the statement, and in place of it he proclaimed that as a Southerner he had great affection for Negroes. Obviously, Du Bois possessed intimate knowledge of Wilson's equivocation—that he supported the candidate, anyway, only demonstrated the extent of his frustration in seeking (almost at any cost) a political berth for his people.[30]

The *Crisis* editor gambled on a dubious premise—if your friends insult you, your enemies may be kinder. After the election he was anxious about his decision; finally he had picked a winner and the victor possessed tremendous power for good or evil. Besides, Du Bois knew his own reputation as a sage was at stake. (Of course, it is questionable that he led many Negroes into the arms of the Democrats, although he calculated "at least 100,000" actually voted for Wilson.) The Negro journalist observed that Wilson's advisers "hate us" and would attempt to bar White House doors;

he pointed out that the President would have to be extremely forceful in order to gauge Negro public opinion accurately. Once more Du Bois suggested the Democratic party should dissociate itself from the victorious "Southern Oligarchy" and ally itself with non-racist elements in and out of the South.[31] Such a political alignment was hardly realistic, but the *Crisis* editor needed to conceive of it as a relatively immediate possibility so that his conscience would be allayed.

In late November of 1912, the New York *Age* struck at Du Bois and other Negro Democrats, and printed the "darkey story" which Wilson allegedly recited when he received the nomination:

> I am afraid I shan't run quite as fast as the darkey did when he was shot at just as he was getting away with the chicken. "Ah done heah dat bullet twice," he said, telling about it afterward. "Twice!" "Yes, boss, twice, suah' nuff. Ah heah dat bullet once when he pass me, and 'den agin when ah pass him."[32]

A few weeks later the *Age* published interviews with two leading Southern Democrats (one was Representative Albert S. Burleson of Texas who became Wilson's Postmaster-General), in order to demonstrate the "peril" to Negro government workers. The politicians granted the Negroes' right to menial jobs as messengers or doormen, but proposed to bar the race from higher positions. The *Age* concluded, "We suppose words like these sound pleasantly and encouragingly to the ears of such Negro Democrats as Dr. Waldron, Dr. Du Bois and others."[33]

By March of the following year Du Bois admitted Wilson's victory had been assured even without the aid of Negroes. Now he was looking to the "near future" when his balance of power concept was sure to be in working order.[34] Only a few Negroes lost their jobs during the early weeks of the Wilson era and Du Bois was not ruffled. The beginning of the Du Bois-N.A.A.C.P.

clash with the Chief Executive occurred in July of 1913 when it became evident that the Treasury and Post Office Departments were segregating Negro employees. Oswald Garrison Villard was reluctant to believe this action was "deliberate" and assumed it did not have the personal approval of the President. He informed Wilson the Republicans were making political hay from this outbreak of racial separation. Villard predicted that if it had official sanction, Negroes would become rubber-stamp Republicans again. Although the Chief Executive acknowledged the policy was inaugurated without his specific authorization, he was disposed to consider it was "as much in the interest of the Negroes as for any other reason." He presented the standard rationalizations, i.e., separation in government offices and buildings reduced irritation and contention. The President appeared genuinely disturbed that this procedure could possibly have been interpreted as an anti-Negro gesture—his subordinates had informed him that prominent Negro leaders were happy with the new approach.[35] Wilson did not identify these leaders. It is not known whether Taft-man, Booker T. Washington, was consulted, but it is doubtful the Tuskegeean would have approved in 1913. The New York *Age* asked Democrats Du Bois, Trotter, and Bishop Walters if they backed the Wilson policy; the newspaper, declaring they must have been "misrepresented," gave them an opportunity to clear their names.[36] It was hardly possible that the *Age* really supposed these leaders would have condoned the segregation of government workers—probably the newspaper was simply trying to make these "Wilsonian Democrats" squirm a little.

The N.A.A.C.P. board of directors sent the President "a very pointed letter of protest" signed by Jane Addams, W. E. B. Du Bois, Moorfield Storey, and Oswald Garrison Villard; a copy was dispatched to the Associated Press, the Negro newspapers, and 50 white denominational newspapers. Wilson's segregation-for-safety arrangement was denounced as "fallacious," humiliating, and dangerous.[37] In an editorial, Du Bois called for united Negro action. Although black Republicans were self-righteously making the Negro Democrats eat crow, the *Crisis* editor's succinct reply was, "Bad as the Democrats may prove, they cannot outdo William Howard Taft." As the days passed, more Negroes were dropped from the Treasury Department, the Chief Executive did not appoint Negroes to prestige positions, and discriminatory legislation was introduced in Congress. (Some of the many bills proposed to exclude Negroes from military commissions, establish segregated facilities for all Negro government workers, and exclude Negro immigrants from settling in the United States.) Postmaster General Burleson issued additional racist pronouncements to the press, but, despite everything, Du Bois still evidenced faith that President Wilson would not contribute to the rising tide of racism.[38]

In the summer of 1913, Villard suggested that the White House appoint a commission, composed of members of both races, to investigate the race problem in the United States and report directly to Wilson. According to the New York *Evening Post* editor's proposal, the President would then be free to decide if Congress should be advised to act on the findings of the privately financed commission. The Chief Executive seemed completely confounded. ("I never realized before the complexity and difficulty of this matter.") He said he was "absolutely blocked" by Senatorial resistance. He decided there was a compelling need for "delicacy" and feared Villard's commission would be a "blunder." As Wilson viewed the situation, the very appointment of such a study group implied distressing conditions existed between the races, and politicians were sure to be provoked by the inference. Villard understood he was being shown the door in a courteous fashion, but he reflected that the President might be influenced by the mounting pressure of an N.A.A.C.P. letter writing campaign. The journalist also thought his exchange of notes with Wilson was especially good "publicity" for the Association.[39]

Wilson had occupied the White House for six months when Du Bois protested that the Chief Executive possessed not even "the slightest interest" in Negroes, nor the inclination to remedy the race's condition. Ambivalently, the *Crisis* editor still held "the conviction that a vote for Woodrow Wilson was not a vote for Cole Blease or Hoke Smith"—prominent white supremacists in the Democratic party. He reminded the President of "a growing nest egg of 500,000 ballots," although once more the tortured Negro journalist acknowledged that the Solid South effectively barred black voters and assured itself of White House control. But Du Bois was *emotionally* bound to the old balance-of-power conception. He warned Wilson that top Democratic politicians hoped to carry New York, New Jersey, Pennsylvania, Ohio, Illinois, and Indiana by 200,000 votes, and "there are 237,942 black voters in these States." Since he had exhorted his readers to vote the Democratic ticket in 1912, the burdened Du Bois knew he was required to deliver "some apology or explanation."[40] His disillusionment was complete after William Monroe Trotter was humiliated at the White House in late 1914. The Boston *Guardian* editor went to complain about the segregation policies and unloaded a barrage of embarrassing questions. The Chief Executive proceeded to accuse the Negro, who vigorously supported his candidacy, of political blackmailing and disrespect. Du Bois reported the incident in the *Crisis* and praised the "brave" Trotter. The N.A.A.C.P. also backed the *Guardian* editor, and Chairman Joel Spingarn sent the President a disapproving letter which the *Crisis* printed.[41]

During these first years Du Bois' editorials on various subjects generally paralleled the efforts of the Association, although his expressions were frequently considered by some board members to be too outspoken. As already indicated, he indicted the church, an inviolable institution; Oswald Garrison Villard and other board members were convinced he was overreaching himself and damaging the equal rights movement. Essentially, Du Bois was not an organizational leader who could present a project to the N.A.A.C.P. board, solicit ideas, translate the product into a working program, and weld individuals into a unit to administer it. The editor believed he could be more useful to the cause of Negro rights by publishing the *Crisis* than by taking an aggressive role in the N.A.A.C.P. board sessions. As previously shown, he thought of himself as a propagandist who stirred up controversies, commented on current events related to the race problem, provided arguments for racial egalitarianism, and formulated theoretical blueprints which other men were to bring into actuality. Such a conception lessened his influence in the operation of the N.A.A.C.P.

Over the years, 1913 to 1915, there were sharp struggles between Du Bois and members of the N.A.A.C.P. board. The issue was clear-cut: how responsive to the board was Du Bois to be, and how much actual power over the *Crisis* was he to have? Association leaders (such as Villard and Joel Spingarn) believed they possessed a better grasp than Du Bois of N.A.A.C.P. "interests." Villard as board chairman decided he had the right to "control" the *Crisis* and its editor. Since Du Bois was also a member of the board, he refused to consider himself Villard's "subordinate" and demanded "independence of action."[42] In protest Villard resigned as chairman in late 1913. Early in the year, Francis J. Garrison, a leader in the Boston branch of the Association, wanted to make the organization's financial campaign more successful by disseminating a pamphlet describing N.A.A.C.P. accomplishments. Du Bois was asked to write it but, according to Villard, frequently made himself unavailable for such chores. About this time, the board chairman was developing his idea for the presidential commission to investigate the color problem and asked the *Crisis* editor to submit suggestions; he found the journalist slow in presenting a memorandum on the subject and interpreted this tardiness as an indication of disinterest. As far as Villard was concerned, Du Bois was forwarding his own designs instead of pursuing activities directly related to the immediate needs of the N.A.A.C.P. However, the chairman was unready to confront the Negro editor. Matters at the executive office of the Association were in constant turmoil because Du Bois and his secretary clashed with May Nerney, the board's executive secretary (who often threatened to resign). Villard thought the disputes would be avoided to some extent if the *Crisis* occupied other offices; however, he was convinced Du Bois was "too self-absorbed." He concluded that the Negro editor was "a very great asset but also . . . a danger."[43]

Du Bois also tangled with Villard over an article which *Survey* magazine asked the Negro to author. Later Du Bois denounced the *Survey* editors for rejecting the essay, allegedly because it contained a demand for "social rights"; and privately he accused Villard of joining the magazine in a conspiracy against him and his claim for the Negro race. In the controversial paragraph Du Bois had stated: ". . . the Negro must demand his social rights: His right to be treated as a gentleman, when he acts like one, to marry any sane, grown person who wants to marry him, and to meet and eat with his friends without being accused of undue assumption or unworthy ambition."[44]

Actually there was nothing in this paragraph or in the entire article to which Villard and the N.A.A.C.P. had not subscribed on previous occasions. Villard's objections to the essay were procedural ones. He believed that the Negro journalist, after opening the article with a statement that the Association supported the assertions, had forfeited the right to write as a private individual, and was in fact acting in the capacity of an Association executive. In effect, an official declaration was sent to the *Survey* magazine without first being cleared with the organization (and Villard). The white editor, long disgusted by Du Bois' individualism, was teaching him a lesson in organizational manners and intensifying the hostile atmosphere which existed at the headquarters of the National Association for the Advancement of Colored People.

Villard was outraged by another incident in the summer of 1913. The *Crisis* editor, arriving in Los Angeles for a lecture, was photographed with an elite Negro group, and the picture appeared in the N.A.A.C.P. magazine under the title, "Colored Los Angeles greets THE CRISIS. . . ."[45] After seeing the caption, the board chairman asserted that Du Bois "refused to recognize the *Crisis* is the organ of the Association and he cannot carry it around in his pocket." In despair Villard withdrew his name from a list of contributing editors to the *Crisis* because he "could no longer be responsible, even in that way, for its conduct." He resigned the chairmanship near the end of 1913 and charged that his "authority over the *Crisis* has been questioned." He strongly suggested the board explore minutely the nature of the relationship between the Association and the *Crisis*; he contended that the public should not be confused or deceived further—the *Crisis*, under Du Bois' stewardship, was a peculiarly personal product and not an Association organ.[46]

Mary White Ovington was saddened by Villard's decision:

> I am sick at heart over it . . . it means a confession to the world that we cannot work with colored people unless they are our subordinates. And everyone who believes in segregation will become a little more firmly convinced that he is right. And when we demand that some colored man be put in office and be given a place in which he will be the equal of a white man, we shall be told, "You can't

give a nigger a big job. Haven't you found it out yourselves." It puts us back five years.[47]

After the editor of the New York *Evening Post* stepped down from his ranking position on the board, Du Bois produced a suitably appreciative editorial—naturally, his readers had no way of knowing he was the insupportable weight on the "overburdened" Villard.[48] In January of 1914, Joel Spingarn assumed the chairmanship of the board.

About this time, Du Bois' sharp tongue and editorial autonomy created additional problems for the N.A.A.C.P. Without consulting the Association leadership and without measuring the consequences, he opened fire on large sections of the Negro press. The battle started when the Washington *Bee* denounced him as a dependent relative feasting at the table of the Association. Since the *Bee* also added that the N.A.A.C.P. neglected the Negro press, Du Bois replied that the *Crisis* did republish editorials and notes from other papers, although much of their output was not "worth reprinting or even reading." Although the Association needed the support of the Negro press, Du Bois proceeded in his own way, independently of organizational policy, to alienate Negro editors by his condescending assertion that they were inaccurate, unscrupulous, and illiterate. The *Crisis* editor was still the Tiger of Niagara—unable to realize that times had changed. Negro newspapers were enunciating the protest doctrine more frequently than in the preceding decade, and, while they often ignored the N.A.A.C.P., board strategy was to court them, not condemn them.

Within a few weeks, "a large number of editors" declared they were victims of a traitorous assault and peppered the *Crisis* with a barrage of jeers. Du Bois had indeed created a "tempest" and the N.A.A.C.P. was to be stuck with it. The Richmond *Planet* mocked the "professional bookworm" and maintained that average

Negroes had confidence in their press even though the editors were not grammarians. The Washington *Bee* remarked that the newspapers did not use "Harvardized English" because they were so busy reporting the news to the race. The New York *Age* accurately summed up the situation: "The consensus of opinion is that in alienating the good will of the Negro press, Prof. Du Bois had hindered, rather than helped, the cause of the N.A.A.C.P." Several months later the editors were still fighting back. The N.A.A.C.P. found it necessary to extricate itself from its awkward position in the fracas, and at the annual meeting in 1914 passed a resolution praising the Negro press and inviting its "co-operation." Some newspapers printed the resolution for what it was—a direct slap at Du Bois. However, the *Crisis* editor was not admitting any errors. He published the resolution in the magazine, not as a part of official N.A.A.C.P. business, but as a reprint from the Norfolk *Journal and Guide*, which "thinks that the resolution ... was by way of apology for THE CRISIS." Clearly, Du Bois wished his own readers to believe it was not. Undoubtedly, much of his attack upon the Afro-American press was motivated by a strong need to convince the N.A.A.C.P. that fearless and outspoken publications hardly existed. Therefore, his own editorial talents were essential and irreplaceable and should be free from interference.[49]

Despite the Association's declaration of confidence in the Negro press, Du Bois was not silenced and suggested that Negro editors refused to "lead public opinion" and were content in the role "of following afar with resonant brays." Perhaps some slight repairs were made when he acknowledged that the New York *Age*, among other "elements," had co-operated with him in seeking to prevent "The Clansman" from being performed in New York City in 1915. Grudgingly, he also conceded that others besides the N.A.A.C.P. participated in the campaign to prevent the passage of racist legislation in the Sixty-third Congress.[50] Board members reflected that the *Crisis* editor would have shown greater wisdom if he emphasized such examples of intraracial co-operation even more frequently.

With Du Bois continuing to go his own way, the aura of mistrust under the Villard regime was not replaced by a feeling of complete confidence between the *Crisis* editor and the new chairman, Joel Spingarn. Other board members accused Du Bois of creating disunity in the Association and some considered N.A.A.C.P. interests would be best served if the Negro resigned. In 1914 Spingarn, who was fond of Du Bois, attempted to persuade and cajole him to subordinate his efforts to the "general welfare" of the Association; the new chairman pleaded with his friend to end the practice of thinking in terms of *Crisis* and "non-*Crisis*" divisions within the organization. But Du Bois argued that friendly critics like Spingarn were deceived, and unfriendly ones like Villard and Miss Nerney were prejudiced against Negroes. He was still imprisoned by his old conception—the *Crisis*, rather than serving the N.A.A.C.P. as its interpreter to the public, was the pre-eminent division. The organization was just piddling along, but in his estimation the *Crisis* would "make the N.A.A.C.P. possible." The journal was the grand mentor of the race—it alone could teach Negroes not only how to protest, *but how to live*. After colored Americans had received sufficient indoctrination from the *Crisis* "branch," they would be better able to fit into the N.A.A.C.P. "branch." Du Bois held the opinion that "harmony" in the executive office of the Association was possible only if a separate white and Negro division existed. The man who condemned Woodrow Wilson presented a paradoxical panacea—color separation in an organization dedicated to the elimination of the color line. Actually, since Du Bois distrusted whites he preferred to see Negroes in absolute "control" of the whole Association, and longed to tie it to his old chauvinistic goal of a racial economy. In

1915, he editorialized, "I thank God that most of the money that supports the N.A.A.C.P. comes from black hands; a still larger proportion must so come, and we must not only support but control this and similar organizations and hold them unwaveringly to our objects, our aims and our ideals."[51]

However, the Negro journalist was willing to compromise. He asked Villard and Spingarn for permission to be completely responsible financially for the *Crisis*—which was to remain the official publication of the Association. He recommended that the board appoint a committee to censor material considered harmful to the organization. Villard was skeptical that Du Bois possessed the acumen or emotional stability necessary to succeed. President Moorfield Storey was ambivalent about the Negro editor's capacity for co-operation and seemed to side with Villard. Storey depicted Du Bois as a tragic figure—a classic study of a talented Negro damaged emotionally after a lifetime of being "treated as inferior by many men whom he knows to be his inferiors."[52] A week later on December 1, 1914, the board convened and worked to clarify the question of what influence the editor should have legitimately in shaping the *Crisis*. No satisfactory answer was given and the subject was tabled for a future meeting.[53] The board agreed that a *Crisis* committee should guide Du Bois, but this arrangement was not to prevent further crises.

In 1915 another round of hostilities erupted between Du Bois and Villard. The *Crisis* editor was persuaded that William E. Benson, Negro founder of Kowaliga industrial community in Alabama, was misused by whites who controlled the enterprise. Villard, who was on the board of the Kowaliga industrial school, not only regarded the criticisms as a personal insult, but also called Du Bois' unproved statements an illustration of the editor's biased and irresponsible direction of the magazine. The conflict becomes more meaningful when the relationship between Benson and Du

Bois is briefly examined. The *Crisis* editor was especially fond of
Benson, whose avowed aim was to synthesize the highest principles
of business and philanthropy. Benson believed large-scale Negro
migration to the cities was dangerous because of the dearth of
industrial opportunities resulting from labor union barriers. He
contended Southern rural conditions should be ameliorated so that
migration would be made pointless. He started an industrial-
agricultural school in 1888 and organized a company employing
Negroes to construct better, cheaper, easy-credit farmhouses for
other Negroes. Various industries were established, i.e., a cotton
ginnery, turpentine plant, and a naval stores plant. These developments were made possible through white gifts and loans. Over the
years, Negroes charged that some of the whites supported the
project for rapacious not altruistic reasons; in 1915 the creditors-
trustees demanded Benson's scalp and held him responsible for
recent financial setbacks.[54]

Du Bois was attracted by Benson's forceful personality, and it
seems clear that Kowaliga fitted some of the editor's racial economy
ideas. Of course, the two men "often disagreed in detail and fact,"
and Benson's scheme did not emphasize political rights. The
Crisis editor wrote: "Kowaliga was not a perfect thing—it was a
dream, inconsistent, illogical, but fine, big of vision and of the
stuff that remakes worlds."[55]

He felt impelled "to burst out sometime on the Benson situation," and the N.A.A.C.P. monthly carried the following brief
and slanted report which precipitated Villard's anger:

> An unfortunate occurrence is the attempt of a part of the stock-
> holders of the Dixie Industrial Company to oust William E. Benson,
> founder and president. This company was founded sixteen years
> ago. It is worth about $400,000 and has been a notable undertaking.
> Mr. Benson charges that a "Negro Education Trust" has been
> opposing him. A white man has been nominated to succeed him.[56]

The editor's comment was short because he knew quite well that a lengthy diatribe would have been blue-penciled by the *Crisis* committee. However, by indirection and insinuation he got his message across. He did not tell his readers Benson's organization was losing money, instead he informed them that "it is worth about $400,000." In announcing that "a white man" would replace his friend, Du Bois implied race prejudice. He printed Benson's accusation of persecution by a "Negro Education Trust," but did not identify the organization nor make any attempt to present its version of the dispute. (The "Trust" was Booker T. Washington and his backers.)[57] Later in the year Du Bois implied again that Benson had been exploited: "They say Benson failed at Kowaliga. I do not know. I was but the far-off onlooker who only heard. But I heard Benson."[58]

Villard was piqued because he was not consulted by Du Bois before these items appeared in the *Crisis*. He believed his advice should have been sought, not only as an active member of the Kowaliga board of directors, but also as one who had a long association with Negro industrial schools in the South. It does seem that the Negro editor should have conferred with Villard, but their relationship was probably so strained that such an interview was not possible. Also, Du Bois probably thought Villard would have tried to prevent the items from being published. The *Crisis* editor, instead of gathering evidence on the Benson case, preferred to trust his preconceptions—Villard was a racist and Benson was a martyr on the Cross of Race, "loveable . . . handsome as a god in smooth bronze beauty." These were the necessary "facts."

Mary White Ovington, without any notable success, tried to heal Villard's hurt feelings, and, as a member of the *Crisis* committee (which of course was set up to prevent such incidents from occurring), apologized for not having blocked the offending items.

The second half of her letter was a defense of Du Bois and it is probably the best one on record by an official of the N.A.A.C.P.:

> I know we can never agree about Dr. Du Bois, but I am going to make one more try at explaining my great desire to keep him on the *Crisis* and in the Association, particularly as I find people are saying, "Oh, she worships Dr. Du Bois!" as though that settled it. I do admire his genius and his business ability and I prize his friendship greatly, and it doubtless prejudices me in his favor; but if I disliked him I think I should want him on the *Crisis* just the same. For I am in accord with his ideals for the Negro, with his method of work. He does do dangerous things. He strikes at people with a harshness and directness that appals me, but the blow is often deserved and it is never below the belt. That is of immense importance to me. I find so much underhandedness, so much intrigue especially in the world of men who have little power and are struggling to better themselves, that I will accept blows, even if they fall on my own head, if they are in the open and I can strike back. . . .
>
> The *Crisis*, too, I think plays a square game. I've heard all the complaints about it of late, and but one gave any suggestion of double-dealing. That was the Survey matter, and I believe that was a mistake, not a subterfuge. Every other complaint has been of over-severe or unjust denunciation. We're trying to keep such complaints down, and we shall keep on trying, but doubtless they will come, and I appreciate your feeling that they are serious enough to warrant a change of *Crisis* editors. But I cannot agree with you. The present editor is a tremendous figure. He is head and shoulder above any other colored man we could find to fill his place, his reputation as a writer grows with every year, and he gives to our little magazine a distinction that we should find the public missed did we once remove it.[59]

In his reply to Miss Ovington, Villard reasserted that Du Bois' vehemence was weakening the N.A.A.C.P. He declared the Negro editor's influence was waning even among educated colored people and warned that within the near future the Association would have to make a choice between the two men.

A few months later Benson died. Du Bois, so emotionally involved in the fall of this man from a high position in an institution created by him, identified his own organizational predicaments with those of his old friend. The *Crisis* editor eulogized Benson and himself:

> Then came the great Tragedy of his life, the great Denial. In the presence of Death questions of merit and blame boot little. Suffice it to remember that for his cause he made the Supreme Sacrifice of Death. None can do more.
>
> They will bury him I trust at Kowaliga. All the long years the solemn pines shall sough above him. All the long years the voices of little black children shall make his silence sweet. And may God have mercy on his soul and on mine.[60]

The power struggle between Du Bois and the board was moving to a climax, and at the December, 1915, board meeting the *Crisis* editor was asked to present for evaluation a summary of his contributions since 1910, when the N.A.A.C.P. was incorporated.[61] A few weeks before, the Negro leader further increased tensions by publishing two editorials in the *Crisis*. The first was an announcement that beginning January 1, 1916, the magazine was prepared to become completely self-supporting. Du Bois made his comment with "genuine satisfaction" since he viewed the financial success of the publication as an ace card in his demand for editorial independence. In the second editorial Du Bois also attempted to justify his control over the magazine, as much to the general membership as to the N.A.A.C.P. board (which, of course, was debating the question of how much power he would retain). Although the Association paid his salary and *Crisis* office expenses,

Du Bois presented himself as the financial benefactor of the *Crisis*:

> From the beginning the editor of the *Crisis* has made himself
> personally responsible for every single debt which has been incurred.
> He has used his own salary and borrowed money to tide it over
> difficulties and given his personal notes to meet emergencies. In
> not a single case has the Association, except the editor, assumed the
> slightest responsibility or risk or advanced a single cent. There is
> both precedent and moral right that legal ownership in whole or
> in part should rightly follow such financial risk. But not only has
> the editor refused to press this point in the slightest degree but he
> has even in one case yielded to an invasion of his rights which he
> did not and does not consider fair.[62]

It is questionable that Du Bois acted in good taste when he
published this defensive editorial. If he intended it as an appeal to
the board members, he might have been more direct and made his
plea exclusively in the board room or in private sessions with
individual members. If he meant to arouse public sympathy for
his position, he laid himself open to the charge of going over the
board's head and trying to exert pressure for a decision in his favor.
Villard objected to these tactics as did other officers in the organization. While Du Bois did not identify the "one case" in which he
"yielded to an invasion of his rights," obviously he was implying
one or more board members were guilty of this infringement.[63]
This editorial was another indication that he regarded his editorial
power as so absolute he could accuse his employers publicly and
demonstrate to the ranks that dissension existed among the officers
of the Association. Clearly, the *Crisis* committee did not achieve
complete success in its role as a restraining influence upon the
editor.

The atmosphere of the January, 1916, board meeting was
strained and tense. Villard was agitated and angry. In a letter which
was written three days after the session, the New York *Evening*

Post editor indicated he and Joel Spingarn resigned in protest against Du Bois. According to him, May Nerney even stated that Negroes should direct the Association, and the offices of the executive secretary and the *Crisis* editor should be combined. As Villard recalled the meeting, all three demanded the board recognize that Du Bois "was merely a paid employee, subject to the disciplining of the Chairman, like the poorest paid employee." Spingarn allegedly informed those present about the "ungentlemanly treatment" meted out to him by the colored journalist. As Villard interpreted the situation, the majority of the board decided to rule in favor of the *Crisis* editor.[64] Apparently the conflict was so intense that Villard left the meeting under some misapprehension. When the editor of the New York *Evening Post* offered his resignation, Joel Spingarn, "as a gesture of courtesy," also submitted his resignation. Shortly thereafter, both men agreed to remain, and the session ended in a compromise.[65]

At the board's conference, Spingarn as chairman read the two basic charges against Du Bois. The first was that he had often devoted no small amount of his work-day to his own writings and research and was not always available to help with immediate N.A.A.C.P. projects. After checking Du Bois activities over the previous several years, Spingarn concluded that Villard's old accusation was basically substantiated. While the chairman admitted Du Bois' "personal achievements" were "extraordinary," he asserted that the Association desired more of the leader's time and efforts in N.A.A.C.P. administrative work. Spingarn's rebuke was a gentle one. He reminded the board members that they had never clarified what duties they expected Du Bois to perform. The chairman also took a moderate view in reference to the second charge of dictatorial editorship. He observed that the *Crisis* belonged to the Association, but its editorials must constitute Du Bois own interpretations. He stated it was impossible for all board members to be in accord with the opinions expressed by the editor, but he also emphasized these editorials must not deviate from N.A.A.C.P. administrative policy, nor should they descend in tone or approach to "the level of petty irritations, insulting personalities, or vulgar recriminations."[66]

During these heated debates and exchanges, Du Bois' current *Crisis* criticism of Booker T. Washington was not an issue. The editor was freer to censure the Tuskegean after 1912, because, by then, prominent N.A.A.C.P. board members (like Villard and Joel Spingarn) recognized the hopelessness of gaining the educator's support and were themselves acquiring anti-Washington reputations. In 1913, Du Bois printed a recent Tuskegean complaint against discrimination in schools, but the *Crisis* added a postscript: "In Mr. Washington's case the severeness of his accusations has had its edge taken off by his careful flattery of the South." The N.A.A.C.P. magazine also carried a reprint of a *New York Times* article which praised the Tuskegean for continuing to de-emphasize Negro participation in politics, and Du Bois proclaimed, "No man who advises the black man to sacrifice his well-earned franchise can have the interests—the best interests—of the colored race at heart." During 1914–15, the *Crisis* reprinted several "submissionist" statements of Booker T. Washington—accompanied by critical annotations of Negro newspapers which had originally published the material. For example, the Tuskegean told National Negro Business League delegates that Negroes should stop emphasizing residential sections where they were not wanted, and start improving those neighborhoods which they could occupy. The *Crisis* noted that the editor of the Louisville *Columbian Herald* was stunned by this "obsequious doctrine" promulgated by a man "so servile and spineless in his teachings." The Louisville *News* warned that the Alabama educator was asking Negroes "to passively submit to the humiliation of being pushed aside as though we are a race of lepers because we would seek cleaner and healthier neighborhoods in which to live." Another *Crisis* article charged the Tuskegeean with telling anecdotes, "the butt of which was Negro character."[67]

At least on the subject of Booker T. Washington, Du Bois and Villard had much in common. As early as 1912, the *Crisis* carried an article in which the editor of the New York *Evening Post* admitted that the beliefs of the Alabama educator were not in accord with the policy of the N.A.A.C.P.[68] Villard's complete disenchantment may also be seen in a 1913–14 exchange of letters with the Washingtonians.[69] The journalist invited representatives of several Negro industrial schools to meet at N.A.A.C.P. offices for a discussion of ways to improve and standardize educational practices in the South. For example, Villard hoped these schools could be persuaded to institute a unified system of purchasing and a better method of accounting. Since Booker T. Washington was still convinced that N.A.A.C.P. leaders were masking their "real purpose," he was "in rather an awkward position" when the invitation was delivered. He declined to attend but offered to send a delegate if Villard held the conference anywhere but in the N.A.A.C.P. headquarters ("Du Bois' office"). He did not wish to give "the South" an impression that Negro education had even the remotest connection with the Association.

Villard replied that the field of education was never outside the interest of the Association, especially since Tuskegee and Hampton Institutes did not bother to co-ordinate the rural industrial schools. He rejected the excuse that Tuskegee Institute would be damaged by Washington's attendance at the meeting (which was not sponsored by the N.A.A.C.P.). The New York journalist told the Negro leader that influential whites were present at Association meetings held in the South. Robert R. Moton also turned down Villard's invitation but consented to send someone from Hampton

Institute to represent him. The editor, in pleading with Moton to address the conclave, reported the Tuskegeean refused to co-operate because of a "cowardly reason." Villard even offered to rent a room in neutral territory (which should have been done at first). Moton, doubting "the thing is big enough" for Booker T. Washington to appear in person, also persuaded himself that he was too important to attend. The meeting finally convened at the N.A.A.C.P. offices; no one represented Tuskegee Institute, while Moton sent a delegate from Hampton Institute. Villard's Association of Negro Rural and Industrial Schools aimed to secure financial aid from philanthropic foundations, and Washington's lack of co-operation was related to this goal. The Negro leader, who had long been the intermediary through which funds were channeled for many institutions, probably felt threatened. He doubted the new organization could be controlled and so he withheld his support, thereby weakening it.

In 1915 Booker T. Washington died without making a rap-prochement with the N.A.A.C.P. Du Bois wrote an eloquent obituary for the *Crisis*, representing his appraisal of the Negro leader.[70] In one large respect the piece was well balanced. The Tuskegeean was praised for pushing the race toward economic growth, developing industrial education, and seeking the improve-ment of interracial relations. Du Bois accurately observed that the Alabama educator failed to understand the relationship between politics and economics, minimized the importance of higher education, and in exchange for white aid accommodated himself to a social system based upon caste. However, the *Crisis* editor was too stern in assigning to the Tuskegeean "a heavy responsi-bility" for Negro disfranchisement, the poverty of Negro colleges, and the entrenchment of the caste system in the country. Du Bois' evaluation was based upon his judgment that Washington played a completely determining role in history. But is there actually a way of knowing how much "responsibility" the Tuskegeean must bear for the climate of racism which existed at the time of his death in 1915?

Perhaps if he had placed his weight behind the equalitarians, a larger number of Southern Negroes would have voted and attended better equipped Negro colleges. More probably, his consistent advocacy of these reforms would have lost for him what weight he possessed. The fact is—his power was highly limited. For example, despite the white help he received, he was not even able to establish an adequate vocational educational program in the South because it would have cost too much money and antagonized the whites. Consequently, the majority of Negro institutions "abandoned their dreams" and taught a watered liberal arts curriculum, covered by a veneer of industrial courses.[71] If he had been a consistent exponent of Negro suffrage, a large section of public opinion in the South (and elsewhere) would have opposed him. There were even whites who disapproved of Washington's personal right to cast a ballot. For example, politician J. K. Vardaman said: "I am just as opposed to Booker Washington as a voter, with all his Anglo-Saxon reenforcements, as I am to the coconut-headed, chocolate-colored, typical little coon, Andy Dotson, who blacks my shoes every morning. Neither is fit to perform the supreme function of citizenship."[72]

Gunnar Myrdal in the *American Dilemma* has observed:

> It is a political axiom that Negroes can never, in any period, hope to attain more in the short-term power bargain than the most benevolent white groups are prepared to give them. This much Washington attained.[73]

In other words, Washington sought accommodation for a price, based upon his knowledge of how much whites were willing to pay. Therefore, Du Bois was severe in his judgment, just as later anti-Washingtonians were when they called the Alabama educator a "collaborator" who sold his race down the river. Myrdal has suggested that Washington should not be designated as an "all out accommodating leader" because the Tuskegeean did not believe in permanent inequality. While it is true that the Tuskegeean, at the end of his career, was more favorably disposed toward higher education for Negroes and did repudiate segregation, his conciliatory statements were used by those who accepted the thesis of racial inferiority.[74]

Above all else, it would appear that Washington's limitation was his tight control over Negro leadership. He used his prestige and power to harass and defeat the Du Bois group, which demanded his ultimate equality goals immediately. The Tuskegeean did not permit the establishment of a division of labor—marking off for each group a particular type of program and emphasis. Understandably, he could not speak consistently on behalf of suffrage, higher education, and social equality; but was it necessary for him to work against those who did?

Over the years, prominent people have misunderstood Booker T. Washington's relations with Du Bois and the N.A.A.C.P. Roy Wilkins, present executive secretary of the Association, suggested that the Crisis and the N.A.A.C.P. were created from the contributions of the Tuskegeean.[75] John Haynes Holmes, a long-time member of the N.A.A.C.P. board, called Du Bois and Washington "twin spirits . . . really seeing eye to eye."[76] Such comments are, of course, sentimental and inaccurate—the Tuskegeean always regarded Du Bois and the organization as his enemies. Ideologically, however, in the last few years of his life, Washington "moved considerably toward his opponents." According to Gunnar Myrdal, "Under the influence both of the criticism from the Du Bois group and of much changed conditions, he came increasingly to move toward an ideology which incorporated and expressed the Negro protest in cautious but no uncertain terms."[77]

After 1915, W. E. B. Du Bois was forced no longer to carry the heavy burden of competing with the tremendous prestige of the Alabama educator. The World War I period brought a deluge of democratic propaganda, and, as more and more Negroes fervently embraced the equal rights doctrine, the *Crisis* editor reached the peak of his influence. Paradoxically, during these years, this apostle of protest adopted some accommodationist tactics and was denounced among his race. Apparently, the protest message was well learned by Negroes.

8. Du Bois as Accommodationist: Co-operation with Erstwhile Enemies

With Washington's death, there seemed a possibility that a reconciliation might finally be attained, and leaders of the race might really "close ranks." The N.A.A.C.P. scheduled its annual conference for February 11, 1916, but, after the Tuskegeean's friends announced that on the same day they intended to hold a memorial service for their departed chieftain, Du Bois advised Association officers to postpone their meeting in order to avoid the charge of sponsoring "a counter attraction." The *Crisis* editor, although still suspicious of "certain elements," suggested a "get together meeting" with the leaders of all large Negro organizations, including Tuskegee Institute. N.A.A.C.P. officers agreed immediately. The Association, however, was not seeking alliances because of weakness. The membership had grown rapidly to about 9,000 in 1916, and the monthly circulation of the *Crisis* during the years was between thirty-five and forty thousand.[1] Already, the organization had some success in the field of legal redress. The N.A.A.C.P. claimed "partial victories" in New Jersey where its lawyers attacked the practice of detaining Negro suspects without adequate evidence, and in Maryland where the courts ruled against the residential segregation ordinance. The Association proclaimed its "greatest triumph" in the 1915 United States Supreme Court decision declaring the "grandfather clause" unconstitutional.

When Robert R. Moton succeeded Booker T. Washington as head of Tuskegee Institute, the *Crisis* hoped for "a new era of union and understanding" based upon the race's right to first-class citizenship, and to all the perquisites (political, civil, educational, and social) which accompanied it. In an open letter to Moton—parts of which were condescending—Du Bois acknowledged that the Southern educator "substantially" subscribed to these principles; however, the *Crisis* editor expressed his "deepest solicitude" that Moton would not participate in a conciliation-at-any-cost program.[2] Du Bois was troubled by the undenied reports that the new Tuskegee principal had instructed Mrs. Moton to shun Pullman cars in the South—so whites would not be offended. The *Crisis* editor seemed incredulous when he quoted an account from the New York *Sun* praising the educator for having "respected the feeling of the objectors to Mrs. Moton's presence."[3]

Privately, Du Bois admitted to Joel Spingarn that the "direct frontal attack" did not pay off too well. He agreed "true equality" would not be achieved "for several generations"—in the meantime the race was compelled to endure segregation while making clear the nature of its ultimate goals. In his opinion, it was unnecessary for all Negro leaders "to work in the same lines or for the same things," if they were confident of each other and determined to create a "solid structure." Spingarn also judged the time was propitious to press for a united front and invited influential Negroes of various persuasions to meet at his home in Amenia, New York. Over fifty men and women gathered for the Amenia Conference, which was held from August 24 to August 26, 1916. Among those who attended were Tuskegeeans Emmett J. Scott, Robert R. Moton, and Fred Moore; middle-of-the-roaders Mary Church Terrell, Kelly Miller, James Weldon Johnson, and R. R. Wright, Jr.; and Radicals William M. Trotter, William Sinclair, and W. E. B. Du Bois.[4]

Although the conferees "arrived at a virtual unanimity of opinion," they decided it was not in the race's best interest to reveal what transpired. Almost immediately the decision was reconsidered and the Amenia resolutions were published. The participants recognized no conflict between industrial and college education. The race required "complete political freedom," which could be obtained through "a practical working understanding among the leaders of the colored race." The delegates concluded that Northern leaders should make a better attempt at comprehending the special problems of those Negroes who helped to guide the race in the South. The conferees departed from Amenia resolving to sponsor annual meetings.[5]

The New York *Age* believed an "epoch" had been reached. Fred Moore, the paper's editor (and one of the conferees), wrote: "It marks the birth of a new spirit of united purpose and effort that will have far-reaching results."[6] Recalling the Amenia Conference, Du Bois wrote in 1925: "It not only marked the end of the old things and the old thoughts and the old ways of attacking the race problem, but in addition to this it was the beginning of the new things. Probably on account of our meeting the Negro race was more united and more ready to meet the problems of the world than it could possibly have been".[7]

John Hope Franklin, the distinguished historian of the Negro race in America, concluded in the same vein: "It was a happy prelude to America's entry into the war. With a calm but firm unanimity of opinion among the Negro leaders of the United States, the black citizens of the Western republic could pursue more intelligently and relentlessly the democracy which the allies were seeking to extend to all the world."[8]

Actually, the Amenia Conference has been overrated. Perhaps the conclave sowed a few seeds of understanding—which required years to germinate. Certainly, it was useful for the leaders to confer in the hope that the backbiting and backyard criticism would cease, but such disruptions did not fade away. No real division of labor was worked out and, although the group was supposed to

meet once a year, its members never did. (When the second Amenia
Conference was held in 1933, few of the old conferees were invited
to participate.) Leaders of both wings remained bitter for some
time to come. For example, Emmett J. Scott, in a 1917 biography
of Booker T. Washington, referred to Du Bois' Talented Tenth
in this manner:

> This numerically small and individually unimportant element of
> the Negroes in America would hardly warrant even passing men-
> tion except that the always carping and sometimes bitter criticisms
> of these persons are apt to confuse the well-wishers of the race who
> do not understand the situation. . . . A number of these persons [the
> Talented Tenth] make all or a part of their living by publicly
> bewailing the wrongs and injustices of their race and demanding
> their redress by immediate means. . . .[9]

Scott then attacked Du Bois, although not naming him, as the
"chief exponent" of the Talented Tenth who broke faith with
Booker T. Washington.

Probably Du Bois more than any other racial adviser violated
the Amenia principle of peaceful co-existence. He minimized the
social pressure which was placed upon Southern Negro leaders and
still blamed them for failing to propagandize on behalf of reforms
he favored. Therefore, he continued to deprecate their projects and
programs. For example, in the winter of 1917 Tuskegee Institute
sponsored a conference on Negro migration. Southern newspapers
commended the participants for discouraging Negroes from going
North. Du Bois examined the content of these Tuskegee resolutions
inch by inch and found one-third of the space was devoted to
advising colored people to stay South, while one-sixth dealt with
imploring the region to be kinder to its Negroes. An additional
one-fourth discussed the theme of interracial co-operation, while
only one-thirtieth was concerned with the need for improved
police protection and law enforcement. The *Crisis* editor fumed:

"We do solemnly believe that any system of Negro leadership that today devotes ten times as much space to the advantages of living in the South as it gives to lynching and lawlessness is inexcusably blind."[10]

Du Bois' own views on migration were rather interesting.[11] He recommended immediate migration to resourceful Negroes who cared anything about living in "civilization." For years, he encouraged mass departure as a practical protest against Southern racism, but he demonstrated an inadequate comprehension of the sociological problems arising from such an exodus. He simply asked Northern Negroes to open their hearts to the migrants, whose presence he admitted would create further hardship for the long-time residents of the communities.

Contrary to the Amenia resolutions, he maintained his open war on industrial education. During the months following Amenia, the *Crisis* editor proclaimed Negro high schools and colleges were "ten times" more effective than Tuskegee or Hampton Institutes. He asserted that the Phelps-Stokes Fund was about to issue a report which, in effect, favored the death sentence for higher education. The report was also "dangerous" because it asked leaders of Southern Negro schools to co-operate with the whites.[12] Actually, the Phelps-Stokes survey, while praising the Tuskegee type of education, placed a high value upon secondary and college education. However, the observers noted that since most Negro colleges were small and inadequate, the race would be best served by properly equipping several regional institutions instead of scattering resources. Also recommended was a curriculum change which placed more emphasis upon physical sciences, economics, sociology, and history; and less stress upon the traditional Latin and Greek.[13]

Du Bois blasted away at Hampton Institute and allied himself with "educated Negroes" who charged that this "educational blind alley" was doing incalculable harm. He contended that Hampton was not preparing its students for higher education or the professional schools; he accused the institution of an "illiberal and seemingly selfish attitude toward other colored schools." According to the *Crisis* editor, Hampton Institute was still the pawn of the Northern and Southern racist exploiters.[14] Du Bois' simple remedy: the school should place itself under the tutelage of the Talented Tenth. (If Hampton was a helot of the white supremacists, it is difficult to appreciate how the institution could have accepted his cure. It must also be asked how Negro education in the South could have been operated without co-operating with the whites of the region.)

In view of these attacks *after* the Amenia Conference, one may speculate about the basis for the belief that the conclave was the sunny shedding place of old suspicions and the bedding place of happy unity. Du Bois and the other conferees went to Amenia with strong hopes, and in their great need to *want* a reconciliation they thought they got one. They were only bewitched by the magic of resolutions. Since 1904 there had been fervent talk about a rapprochement, but no one could agree specifically and practically on whose terms it was to take place. Nevertheless, intraracial harmony was a goal around which to rally—nobody was against it in principle. But Booker T. Washington's death did not suddenly remove the suspicion which was nourished over the years. The conferees did not hammer out "a practical working understanding" in Myrdal's sense of a functional interacting division of labor. For example, such an "understanding" would have permitted Southern leaders to stress industrial education while Northerners like Du Bois could have emphasized secondary-college education. Neither group would have tried to demolish the other but simply would have attempted to push its own program. Thus, the race would have achieved as much as possible. But old animosities did not die and old dogmas prevailed. Du Bois and the Radicals were emotionally blinded to a fact of life: Southern Negro education required the co-operation of whites in order to survive. Nor did the *Crisis* editor comprehend that a relatively small proportion of educational funds was warranted for high schools and colleges since most of the Negro youngsters attended grammar schools and industrial schools. Furthermore, because the majority of Negroes did not go beyond grammar school, vocational subjects occupied a justifiable place in its curriculum.

While it is true that the Amenia resolutions gave conservative Negro leaders a rationalization for doing little to propagandize on behalf of suffrage and civil rights, nevertheless these men had attended the reconciliation meeting at Amenia and their fears of the N.A.A.C.P. were lessened considerably. Du Bois should have courted them instead of antagonizing them with hostile editorials.

The Amenia conferees themselves injected the myth of "unanimity," and as such it was preserved by race historians like John Hope Franklin. Actually, the leaders co-operated more closely a few years after Amenia, and the change was due to more earthy reasons than a conference, i.e., World War I, the increase in urbanization and education within the race, *et al.* Undoubtedly, historians used Amenia to signify the place and time at which the schism was healed because it was difficult to know exactly when the rapprochement occurred. It must not be forgotten that a few of the conferees wrote their own historical accounts, and they wished to think their actions were directly responsible for achieving so desirable a goal as intraracial harmony.

Oswald Garrison Villard, who believed in the workability of the Amenia resolutions, was annoyed by the antagonistic *Crisis* editorials following the conclave. He had never given up his profound interest in industrial education and was certain that such training would be even more beneficial to the race if the N.A.A.C.P. and the *Crisis* encouraged the co-operation of "enlightened Southerners."[15] (It seemed to him that Booker T. Washington had been a major obstacle to such an arrangement, and when the leader died the white journalist saw beckoning opportunity.) Of course, such views created another clash with Du Bois. The same Phelps-Stokes report which the *Crisis* editor had described as "dangerous," Villard contended was "remarkable ... the most useful and important thing of the kind that has been made." However, for the time being, Du Bois retained his near-absolute control of the magazine and Villard could only fume. Clearly, the tumultous January, 1916, meeting of the N.A.A.C.P. board had solved nothing—the white journalist still regarded Du Bois as an "employee," and at a board session in 1917 the Negro editor stamped out of the room just as Villard was preparing to criticize him. In view of the differences between the two men, the editor of the New York *Evening Post* talked once more of resigning from his position as N.A.A.C.P. treasurer unless Du Bois departed from the organization.[16]

But the Negro editor was too well entrenched to be discharged. His valuable support still came from Joel Spingarn and Mary White Ovington. During the early days of 1917, after Du Bois underwent a critical operation, Spingarn wrote:

> I walked out of the hospital, thinking of all that it would mean for 12 million people if this champion of theirs were not permitted to live. Others would take up the gauge where he threw it down; others might wield brilliant pens; others would speak with something of his quiet eloquence. But never again could these millions find another leader exactly like him.[17]

Miss Ovington also publicly observed Du Bois and the *Crisis* were indispensable to the N.A.A.C.P. Undoubtedly with the help of his two friends, Du Bois convinced the board that the *Crisis* was a journal "of general circulation" and should not be required to publish N.A.A.C.P. matters which were too parochial. In December, 1916, the Association decided to place material about the organization and the local branches, *not* primarily in the *Crisis*, but in a special *Branch Bulletin*.

The Spingarn-Ovington wing of the N.A.A.C.P. also believed in the value of the Amenia resolutions, but could not bring themselves to stop Du Bois' bitter pen. (However in 1917 Miss Ovington reported to the directors that Du Bois must not possess too much freedom or he would destroy his effectiveness by becoming "rabid.")[18] The interference of these two officers with the work of the *Crisis* editor was infrequent, not only because they had a great deal of affection and admiration for him, but also because they agreed that some of the Southern Negroes did deserve an editorial thrashing now and then.

Since the board recognized, however, that other leaders within the Negro race must be conciliated to some degree, and since it was apparent that Du Bois could not or would not do the job, plans were made to give the task to someone else. Even before the Amenia Conference, the board searched for a middle-of-the-road Negro to serve as its executive secretary. In January of 1916, Du Bois proposed John Hope, his old associate in the Niagara Movement. Hope, who was president of the Atlanta Baptist College, declined the offer.[19] Spingarn considered James Weldon Johnson, and the board chairman was delighted by the thought of capturing one of the few Negro intellectuals associated with the Tuskegeeans. Johnson was the author of *Autobiography of An Ex-Colored Man* and had been a United States consul in Venezuela and Nicaragua. Joel Spingarn viewed the appointment as an absolute "coup d'etat" for the Association—if only it could be brought off. Roy Nash, a white associate in the N.A.A.C.P., also favored Johnson: "He is not academic, is a good mixer with a social bent that Du Bois and Hope lack, he is free from the stigma of religion, is a good talker, and would offend no group nor any audience."[20]

Since Johnson had been friendly to the Booker Washington group, Spingarn especially requested the reactions of Du Bois and Miss Ovington. The latter called the candidate "hopelessly reactionary on labor and other problems," while Du Bois found him "entirely desirable." Amusingly, the leftist *Messenger* magazine was also interested in evaluating Johnson and termed him the choice of "radical opinion."[21]

The *Crisis* editor attempted to persuade Johnson to think seriously about Spingarn's offer and reminded him of an earlier conversation in which they discussed the possibility of forming a "secret organization": "There is no telling what your wide acquaintance as an organizer, etc., might not lead to. We might be able to tie a durable knot to insure the permanency of the main organization."[22]

It is not clear what Du Bois meant, and, in reply to a recent inquiry, he stated that he was unable to recall the plans for his "secret" structure. However, it is probable that he wanted to establish a Negro auxiliary to indirectly influence the white-dominated N.A.A.C.P. The organization could have been kept in readiness to take over the Association machinery should the whites have withdrawn as a result of personality-power clashes, or because of some serious disagreement over policy. Apparently, no such group was created. In November, 1916, Johnson accepted the N.A.A.C.P. offer and Spingarn suggested in a "confidential" memorandum that the new executive secretary seek out Du Bois for immediate discussions.

Just as Du Bois sought to improve the race's bargaining position by co-operating for a short period with the Negro conservatives, when World War I came he pursued the same goal and gave his support to the Allied cause. In both instances he joined with erstwhile enemies; discomfort and dilemmas awaited him.

Until the United States entered the war, Du Bois seemed

completely confused. At the start, he claimed that race prejudice, manifesting itself in the coveting and capturing of the black colonies by imperialistic nations, was the major cause of World War I. As he viewed it, white workers, once having achieved political power, rebelled against the system of exploitation which was unleashed by the industrial revolution. European capitalists were then forced to look beyond their home countries for huge profits, and turned to the African colonies. Rapacity brought about the slaughter of natives and inevitably one European nation challenged another in a struggle over spoils. Thus World War I began. Du Bois, untroubled by consistency, sided with the Allies against the "barbarous" Germans. For him, the Germans were now super-racists who gloried in their suppression of the African natives, while the English and French were conscience-stricken atoners—after they recognized to what degradation their race prejudice and greed had led them. Besides being naive, Du Bois was inconsistent. His commitment to the Allies seemed contradictory, after he had declared the whole "European civilization has failed," and that the war was not the temporary perversion of the cultures of Europe—it was "the real soul of white culture." The next step was an indictment of American society, "the daughter of a dying Europe."[23]

Du Bois stripped the world's whites of all moral resources and was also prepared to divest them of technological contributions, since he wished to arraign them as completely effete and rotten. In accomplishing this task, he returned to an old racist theme—civilization was the product of "the colored races." White civilization had borrowed just about everything without acknowledgment:

> The iron and trade of black Africa; the religion and empire building of yellow Asia; the art and science of the "dago" Mediterranean shore east, south and west as well as north. And where she has

builded securely upon this great past and learned from it she has gone forward to greater and more splendid human triumph; but where she has ignored the past and forgotten and sneered at it she has shown the cloven hoof of poor crucified humanity; she has played, like other empires gone, the world fool.[24]

And the other side of the coin of racism was the glorification and superiority of Negroes. The Negro race was noble and "can stand before Heaven with clean hands." Having been deluded, demoralized, and destroyed, Negroes were called upon to return to "old ideals ... old standards of beauty ... not the blue-eyed, white-skinned types which are set before us in school and literature but rich, brown and black men and women with glowing dark eyes and crinkling hair ... that harks back to the heritage of Africa and the tropics."[25]

For a long time Du Bois had denounced white critics for racism, but it was clear he learned a few lessons from them.

Simultaneously he presented another recurrent and related theme in 1917—Negroes could not survive in the United States unless they united economically. He was aware the ideology smacked of self-segregation, and attempted to make a distinction between "Teamwork" and "Jim Crowism." As he embraced his teamwork vision of Negro men aspiring to be "consecrated" workers instead of millionaires, he predicted capitalists and politicians would oppose it. He realized many "consumers" could buy very little because of insufficient funds, but he did not consider any of these roadblocks impenetrable. Instead, he emphasized that wartime migration had created a Negro concentration in the prosperous North, thus making race identification stronger. He also believed that a cooperative Negro economy was more easily attainable because socio-economic class disparity was smaller than in the white group.[26]

During the same year he introduced a motion at the N.A.A.C.P.

board sessions, asking the Association to embark upon a program of teaching Negroes the value of forming buyers clubs which operated on principles of economic co-operation. Although he wanted the project to be initiated "as soon as possible," the board did not indicate any appreciable interest. In 1918 he met with a group of people and formed the Negro Cooperative Guild. The organization wished to convince various clubs to study economic co-operation and hoped to encourage converts to open co-operative stores under its direction. The *Crisis* editor informed the N.A.A.C.P. board about the recent deliberations of the Guild and the board minutes fail to note any overt antagonism either to Du Bois' profusion of editorials on the racial economy or to his presentation at the September, 1918, meeting.[27]

And so, before the United States entered the war, Du Bois deliciously anticipated the promise of vigorous "race predilections" and had an unabashed desire to "revel in them." He proclaimed the majority of the world's population was "colored" and these people would very likely determine the future of mankind. There was no doubt in his mind that the planet would be in good hands, since the Negro race is "the strongest and gentlest of the races of Men: 'Semper novi quid ex Africa!' "[28] Contradictorily, he also foresaw the inevitable dissolution of the caste line and the arrival of "true Socialism."[29] He predicted the expansion of the American democratic ideals; yet only a few months before, he rather imagined the United States might become a substantial "race exploiter" on an international scale.

Du Bois' contradictions and floundering were the marks of a man's frustration at being in a no-man's land and groping desperately for an exit. His paths in the maze seemed endless and repetitious, frequently tinged with unreality. There was almost nobody inside or outside his race he trusted completely and no political leaders or party to whom he could give his unreserved allegiance. At the 1916 Republican convention, the N.A.A.C.P. requested approval of planks advocating: (1) use of the size of voting population as a basis for Congressional representation, (2) a national anti-lynching law, (3) no discrimination in interstate commerce, (4) "repeal of all statutory recognition of race for residents of this country." Receiving no satisfaction, Du Bois and other N.A.A.C.P. officers tried and failed to secure any promises from Charles Evans Hughes. Within weeks of the election the *Crisis* editor reluctantly considered the establishment of a Negro party and recognized that some would condemn him for advocating segregation. Nevertheless, he advised readers to support only friendly Congressional candidates, and if none could be found, to nominate Negro party candidates. In order to avoid being duped by politicians of both races, Du Bois recommended that N.A.A.C.P. branches assume responsibility for a program of "political education."[30] The *Crisis* editor had been burned badly in 1912 and he did not intend to publicly endorse presidential candidates for a long time to come. William F. Nowlin, examining the political activities of Negroes, observed that, although nothing was done to promote Du Bois' Negro party proposal, "the suggestions appear to have motivated Negroes in working up their own political organizations in centers of colored population."[31]

After the United States joined the Allies in April of 1917, it began to seem that Du Bois had at last found an exit from the maze. Once more "the white world" was no longer the monster. The *Crisis* editor asked American Negroes to participate in the war effort whole-heartedly, and he was especially mindful that the conflict would present tremendous industrial opportunities. While he affirmed his loyalty, he still demanded equal rights.[32] Du Bois' co-operation with the American government may seem sudden when it is recalled that, as late as April of 1917, he termed it "impotent" and described Woodrow Wilson's 1916 victory as a "fraud." But even at that time—despite the harsh words—he added that the United States was "our country and the land of our dreams."[33] His accommodation to the American war effort is also understandable when his long-time interest in a segregated system is considered. Rapid strides—even on a separate basis were desirable. Beyond that, his new line was a reflection of the deluge of democratic propaganda which was unleashed after the American entry into the war. And his affection for Joel Spingarn was also an important factor in accounting for the change.

Spingarn believed it imperative that Negroes show whites they were capable of leadership and he recommended the establishment of a segregated officer candidate school. He disavowed segregation in all areas of American life but knew the army would not permit Negroes to enter white officer schools. He pushed the project as an individual—not in the capacity of N.A.A.C.P. board chairman. The Association prudently decided to take no official stand, in view of the controversy which the segregated camp aroused within the race.[34] Newspapers such as the Boston *Guardian* and the Chicago *Defender* exerted pressure on the N.A.A.C.P. to repudiate the camp idea.[35] Spingarn, who denied he deviated from Association principles, offered to resign as chairman in order not to embarrass his organization.[36]

Since Du Bois administered the *Crisis* independently, he used the magazine to propagandize in favor of Spingarn's camp. As he interpreted it, the chairman and he were caught in the "Perpetual Dilemma." Segregation was an evil, but Negroes had always accepted it in schools, residential areas, and everywhere else. The alternative was to receive no facilities from the whites. Du Bois was charged with selling out to the whites, although he noted that the army privately opposed the camp. He was hurt and disgusted as the contention mounted:

Where in heaven's name do we Negroes stand? If we organize

separately for anything—"Jim Crow!" scream all the Disconsolate; if we organize with white people—"Traitors! Pressure! They're betraying us!" yell all the Suspicious. If, unable to get the whole loaf we seize half to ward off starvation—"Compromise!" yell all the Scared. If we let the half loaf go and starve—"Why don't you *do* something?" yell those same critics, dancing about on their toes.[37]

The *Crisis* also declared many whites wished to bar the Negro from all military service because they knew that he would fight heroically at the front. Du Bois was absolutely enraged that he should have to beg the whites to permit his people to risk their lives for the country, and he sneered:

"We should worry."
If they do not want us to fight, we will work. We will walk into the industrial shoes of a few million whites who go to the front. We will get higher wages and we cannot be stopped from migrating by all the deviltry of the slave South; particularly with the white lynchers and mob leaders away at war. Will we be ousted when the white soldiers come back? THEY WON'T COME BACK!

So there you are, gentlemen, and take your choice—We'll fight or work. We'll fight and work. If we fight we'll learn the fighting game and cease to be so "aisily lynched." If we don't fight we'll learn the more lucrative trades and cease to be so easily robbed and exploited. Take your choice, gentlemen. "We should worry."[38]

The segregated officers training camp was established at Des Moines and the N.A.A.C.P. officially "took active part" in the movement after May, 1917, when the installation actually opened. However, there was some doubt among race leaders whether any of the men would be commissioned. This skepticism was heightened when the Negroes' highest ranking officer, Lt. Colonel Charles Young, was involuntarily retired from active service. (Lt. Colonel Young told Du Bois and the N.A.A.C.P. that his physical condition was excellent.) In July of 1917, Du Bois sought without success an interview with Secretary of War Newton Baker.[39] By late summer, some of the officer candidates were restive and announced they intended to leave Des Moines and go home. N.A.A.C.P. leaders tried to persuade them to remain until the commissions came. Du Bois informed Joel Spingarn, who was then a major in the United States Army, that the Association was still trying to pressure the War Department. The editor's appointment with Secretary Baker was confirmed for early fall. In the interview, the cabinet officer "coldly" announced that the United States government was not at war in order to solve the race problem; the *Crisis* editor replied that racism delayed the successful prosecution of the war. A short time later, hundreds of Negroes received commissions and Joel Spingarn publicly praised Du Bois for vigorous efforts on behalf of the camp. Since this issue was resolved to his satisfaction, the Negro editor was more certain than ever that his race would occupy a new and unprejudiced status in the United States. To prove his point he quoted from favorable comments on Negro soldiers which were written by Southern white editors.[40]

In his purveyor-of-hopefulness role, he produced a revealing editorial when the United States government assumed control of the railroads during the war. He interpreted the move as the probable beginning of the end of the capitalist system and the death blow to the segregated railroad car. According to his reasoning, if the government retained direction in the postwar period, railroad jobs would be placed under civil service and Negroes would receive new opportunities for employment.[41] Apparently he thought that after transportation, other basic industries would come under federal management.

Du Bois' line of accommodation was condemned by Chandler Owen, Negro co-editor (with A. Philip Randolph) of the leftist *Messenger*, which started publication in 1917. Du Bois was charged with supporting causes thwarting his avowed aim of integration. Owen blasted the *Crisis* editor's "superlative sureness" that the Negroes' military and industrial contributions in World War I would efface race prejudice. The *Messenger* editor represented a new breed of the Talented Tenth—consistently oriented toward Marxism and in rebellion against what he judged to be Du Bois' old-fashioned conservatism. Owen placed the *Crisis* editor in the same category with Robert R. Moton and Fred Moore. The *Messenger* was determined to prove Du Bois might even be an all-out reactionary and accused him of possessing an anti-union record. In the old days, critics had always deferred to him as a man of great learning, but Owen was not interested in following any long-established precedents. Eagerly he denounced Du Bois for showing no real understanding of economics, history, or political science; Owen concluded that the race's new leaders must have "scientific education."[42]

Perhaps Du Bois was disturbed by the *Messenger's* pounding and the criticism of other newspapers; in early 1918 he returned to the protest motif. After thirteen Negro soldiers were executed for their crimes in the Houston race riot, he condemned the way of life in the United States which these men, and all other Negroes, had been forced to endure, and he reproached all whites (including President Wilson) who seemed to condone race oppression. Wilson was particularly censured for discussing democracy in Poland and Ireland while ignoring the American color problem. The *Crisis* also indicted the United States Civil Service Commission for racism. Du Bois returned to the case of Charles Young and accused the Adjutant General of discrimination. In May of 1918, the *Crisis* editor attacked the War Department for not enlisting large numbers of technically trained men in the segregated 92nd Division, and he wondered if there were some government leaders working behind the scenes to prevent this Negro outfit from being a success.[43] He ran an advertisement in the magazine, calling upon skilled communications men and truck drivers to join the Ninety-second.

About this time, the United States Department of Justice cautioned that his disparaging statements were harming the war effort, and under proposed legislation such expressions would be illegal. The Negro propagandist recognized prudence was imperative, and the N.A.A.C.P. board was so concerned about this warning that the head of the legal committee was assigned to the *Crisis* editorial board. The editor was instructed in the clearest terms that everything which appeared in the magazine must be submitted to the legal consultant prior to publication. At its June, 1918, meeting, the board ordered Du Bois to present only "facts and constructive criticism."[44] Beginning with the June issue, *Crisis* editorials presented a picture of unblemished optimism. With the Department of Justice and the N.A.A.C.P. board breathing down his neck, he was unusually careful about following instructions. For example, Du Bois, who received a poem in which the United States government was execrated for the deaths of the thirteen Negro soldiers, told the author he "would not dare" publish it in the *Crisis*. When the *Messenger*, which continued in hot pursuit, printed the poem some months later, the editors asked if the N.A.A.C.P. was "for the *advancement of colored people* or for the *advancement of certain people?*"[45]

In the summer of 1918, Du Bois published "Close Ranks"—which became his most controversial editorial because of the following paragraph:

> Let us, while this war lasts, forget our special grievances and close ranks shoulder to shoulder with our own fellow citizens and the allied nations that are fighting for democracy. We make no ordinary sacrifice, but we make it gladly and willingly with our eyes lifted to the hills.[46]

According to the Washington *Eagle*, this piece "raised a storm—a sort of hurricane—among the radicals." Even the Norfolk *Journal and Guide* considered his advice "unfortunate" because "grievances" should be remembered and protests made to correct them. The District of Columbia branch of the N.A.A.C.P. called a special meeting to rebuke Du Bois for abandoning what they adjudged to be the traditional Association position, and the group warned such deviation would not be tolerated if he wished to remain the *Crisis* editor.[47]

The N.A.A.C.P. propagandist denied he had altered his course or that of the Association, whose leaders approved "Close Ranks" before publication. He argued that he never disavowed "full manhood rights," but had simply emphasized victory in the war took precedence over all other considerations. Nor was there any intention to imply "grievances are *not* grievances, or that the temporary setting aside of wrongs makes them right."[48] Du Bois claimed his counsel was no different from the conclusions of a recent Negro leadership conference which was held in Washington. The *Crisis* editor was inaccurate on this last point, although he had authored the Washington resolutions. The conclave, sponsored by the War Department and the Committee on Public Information, pledged "active, enthusiastic and self-sacrificing participation in the war." But the conferees pleaded for the settlement of "minimum" grievances, in order to increase Negro identification with the Allied cause. They asked for improved facilities in public travel and the end of lynching, among other things.[49] The general tone was almost as accommodating as "Close Ranks" but these leaders did not tell anyone to "forget" all grievances during the remainder of the war. Obviously, "Close Ranks" was a colossal blunder and Du Bois tried to squirm out of it.

On the heels of this controversial editorial, Du Bois was offered a commission in the United States Army Intelligence. If "Close

Ranks" caused a "storm and hurricane," the announcement about the captaincy brought on "a cyclone of wrath and denunciation." According to the charges, the War Department bribed the N.A.A.C.P. propagandist, captured the *Crisis*, and demanded support for all government policies, no matter how much these suppressed Negroes.[50] A great deal of the discord resulted from Du Bois' request to retain "general oversight" of the *Crisis* while he was serving in the army. He also asked the N.A.A.C.P. for one thousand dollars a year to supplement his military pay because of the added living expenses in Washington. In the Negro leader's version of the affair, the "Close Ranks" editorial was written many days before the commission was discussed with him. He envisaged his army role as part of "a plan of far-reaching constructive effort to satisfy the pressing grievances of colored Americans."[51] Privately, he was "a little hazy" about the duties he was required to perform. It would appear that the United States Army Intelligence (persuaded by Major Joel Spingarn) thought Du Bois might become its interpreter of accommodation to the Negro people.

At the July, 1918, N.A.A.C.P. board meeting, the *Crisis* editor told of his willingness to serve in Washington and stipulated the two conditions mentioned previously. The Association denied his requests—members feared a growing schism in the organization, and the District of Columbia branch was already in rebellion against the "turncoat" journalist.[52] The following week, the Washington branch held its "stormiest" session; Du Bois was accused of "selfishness," of trying to draw two pay checks, and of other "endearing" terms—as the Chicago *Defender* put it. Joel Spingarn was present but was unable to pacify the local group. (One of the anti-Du Bois observers recorded that Spingarn's appearance "seemed to give us inspiration.") The branch delivered an ultimatum—if the journalist joined the army, he had better withdraw from the *Crisis*! The Washington *Eagle* sardonically congratulated "Captain Du Bois on his choice of Army life" and mockingly anticipated "that he may come out of the conflict as a Brigadier-General, at least."[53]

The *Crisis* editor reconsidered and came up with a compromise, offering to give his services to the government if the N.A.A.C.P. board guaranteed him "control" of the magazine after the Central Powers were beaten. Privately, he claimed he had wanted to retain power over the magazine while in the military service so that Oswald Garrison Villard would not have an opportunity to wreck the Association monthly. Since Joel Spingarn was instrumental in persuading Du Bois to seek the commission and was partially responsible for the Negro's tactical shift toward accommodation, he was saddened by the Association rebuff. In August, at the height "of this personal abuse," he thought of resigning from his position of leadership. Ironically, the army decided it was no longer interested in Du Bois; probably because of the thunderous complaints, the *Crisis* editor was written off as a liability.[54] Although he lost the fight, he played the martyr role with "unruffled serenity. . . . No one who essays to teach the multitude can long escape crucifixion."

Du Bois was hardly circumspect in proposing to control the *Crisis* while working for Army Intelligence. Certainly, it is conceivable that a clash of interest might have arisen. His army-*Crisis* relationship was, from the start, subject to misinterpretation. To his critics, Du Bois did not seem like a man who had decided sincerely to co-operate completely with the government, and had accepted the offer of a commission as the highest expression of this desire. His request for a N.A.A.C.P. subsidy was also questionable, since it was interpreted as proof of a close or binding association between what had long been a protest organization and the United States government, in which white supremacists possessed great power, if not absolute command.

Du Bois failed to gauge the strength of the clamor for equal rights among Negro intellectuals who had mistakenly identified him exclusively as a protest leader. But, after all, this was the first time in nearly thirteen years that he was not *primarily* concerned with producing protest propaganda demanding the immediate elimination of the color line. His wartime accommodation strategy made him seem like an Uncle Tom and disillusioned some Negroes who were unfamiliar with his lifelong paradox by which he found value in some aspects of segregation.

Until the Allies won he did not swerve from his "new Patriotism" and ringingly declared, "If this is OUR country, then this is OUR war."[55] His only slight concession to critics was the admission that there were "present grievances" about which it was proper to "grumble." For instance, he observed it was unfair to draft Negro physicians as privates, and calmly stated that Negroes would be happy if the government "will soon notice" this unjust practice. But he reminded readers that jobs were now plentiful and wages were high. Negroes were accepted as army officers, Red Cross nurses, and officials in the War and Labor Departments. Furthermore, the courts threw out residential segregation ordinances and President Wilson condemned lynching.[56] During the closing days of the war, Du Bois avidly seized a Wilson statement condemning the domination of the weaker peoples by the stronger. The *Crisis* editor realized the comment was "vague" but believed the President meant to reproach racists everywhere, including the South. On this basis, Wilson's remarks were described as "one of the half dozen significant utterances of human history."[57] Du Bois cited other developments to show that the United States government cocked an ear for "just Negro public opinion." The War Service Commission and the Public Information Bureau sent Negro representatives to Europe, Liberia was to receive an American loan (he thought), and Haiti and Liberia "were prominently featured among the Allies during Liberty Loan weeks." Negro troops had finally gone overseas and were serving honorably. Du Bois published a letter from a French mayor, who described "a real brotherhood" between his community and the soldiers of the 349th Field Artillery Regiment. Most of the *Crisis* readers were probably just as satisfied with Negro progress, and it is doubtful if they paid much attention to the editor's critics.

Yet the great Du Boisian paradox appeared through the pages of the magazine. Without any evidence, he anticipated an integrated, Socialist postwar period, while simultaneously he proposed a segregated, socialized economy in the United States. He dreamed of carving out a large socialized African state and forming an international co-operative organization of Negroes. In the decade after World War I, he devoted attention to the Pan-African Movement.

9. The Pan-African Movement: Negroes of the World Unite!

Shortly after the Armistice was signed, Du Bois sailed for France to represent the N.A.A.C.P. as an observer at the Peace Conference. He decided to call a Pan-African congress so that some attention would be focused upon the problems of Negroes in Africa and elsewhere. While he did not originate the Pan-African idea, he had long been interested in such a movement. The Negro leader's work in 1919 will be better understood if consideration is given to previous congresses and to his early concern for African reorganization.

In July of 1900, H. Sylvester Williams, a West Indian lawyer practicing in London, founded the first Pan-African conclave. Only "distinguished" Negroes were invited to the gathering and Du Bois was designated chairman of the "Committee on the address to the nations of the world." The declaration was like his other writings of the period—conciliatory in tone. Repudiating segregation and discrimination, he asked England to yield "as soon as practicable" the responsibility of self-government to African and West Indian natives. Other European powers such as Germany and France were petitioned to grant "justice" to Negroes in the colonies. Du Bois suggested the establishment of "a great central Negro State of the world" in the Congo Free State. He observed that the ideals of the whites would be irreparably tarnished if efforts were not made to improve the lot of Negroes.

The Pan-African Conference, while not geared to social action, brightened immeasurably the social season of the London Negro colony and served as a brilliant intellectual and social diversion for "colored American tourists" abroad that summer. The delegates were notified that Queen Victoria was quite interested in their activities and the Lord Bishop of London entertained them "at his stately palace." Alexander Walters described the scene: "After a magnificent repast had been served we were conducted through the extensive grounds which surround the palace. Prof. Du Bois [and several others] moved about the palace and grounds with an ease and elegance that was surprising; one would have thought they were 'to the manor born.' "[1]

There was also a tea for the delegates at the St. Ermin Hotel ("one of the most elegant in the city ... splendid repast was served"). The Americans of the "professional classes" went home vowing they would recruit "the better classes of our people" in their project. Obviously, "this meeting had no deep roots in Africa itself"; although the group wrote a constitution and elected officers (Du Bois was vice-president), the organization speedily passed from the scene.[2]

T. Thomas Fortune and Booker T. Washington talked about another Pan-African conference in 1906. Fortune claimed his ideas were stolen by Williams in 1900 and ridiculed the earlier conclave. Washington envisioned an organization composed primarily of white scientists, explorers, missionaries, and educators acting as "a sort of guardian of the native peoples." He advised a program of industrial education for Africa, where the Negro race, "whatever [its] faults, is one of the most useful races the world has ever known."[3] Tuskegee Institute actually sponsored a Pan-African conference just before World War I.

Several years earlier, Du Bois suggested that a conclave should be held during the fiftieth anniversary of the Emancipation Proclamation, and he told Negro readers, "The cause of Liberia, the cause of Haiti, the cause of South Africa is our cause, and the sooner we realize this the better."[4] As already mentioned, his personal interest in Africa dates back to the 1890's, when he embraced "Pan-Negroism" and lauded the African continent as the race's "greater fatherland." Around the turn of the century, he believed that some customs of American Negroes were survivals from Africa, e.g., the power of Negro ministers and the strength of the church. He dreamed of gathering a small band to lead Negroes of the world and reorganize Africa. Even before 1900 he asked the Belgian Consul-General in the United States about the possibilities of a Belgian Congo "development program" directed by Negroes of the Congo, West Indies, and the United States. In 1907 he regretted he did not have the opportunity to "work directly in Africa" and told the German Consul-General in the United States that there were other American Negroes who wished to be "economic leaders" in German West Africa.[5] The Niagara Movement maintained its own Pan-African Department and corresponded with African intellectuals.

In 1915 Du Bois concluded that the Pan-African Movement should not exclude whites but should seek to incorporate the working classes of the world. Nevertheless, in the same paragraph in which he spoke about "a new unity of men," he showed reluctance to surrender his desire for a "unity of the colored races" which he claimed was gathering momentum.[6] Two years later, he recommended the formation of a "great free central African state" (the amalgamation of German East Africa and the Belgian Congo) as the practical preventive of a race war.[7] By 1918, he thought the state should be enlarged to include Uganda, French Equatorial Africa, German Southwest Africa, and the Portuguese territories of Angola and Mozambique.[8] Du Bois gave no practical hints about how the black empire was to become a reality. Although the continent was to be "the centralization of race effort," he planned no back-to-Africa movement. Negroes in the United States were primarily Americans and supposedly desired integration. However, in Du Bois' opinion, a belief in the formation and growth of the African state would raise the status of Negro nationals of all countries.

The N.A.A.C.P. did not give the *Crisis* editor much support for the First Pan-African Congress in 1919. (Du Bois designated this conclave as the "first" and his enumeration will be followed for the sake of clarity.) He persuaded the Association to make an official statement, which he wrote, backing his views on Africa, and the paper was published in the *Crisis* about the time he arrived in Europe. After the usual recitation of Africa as a land of exploitation and a cause of war, the N.A.A.C.P. statement warned that the old German colonies should not be given to any of the Allied nations. According to the document, the following groups should be granted "the decisive voice" in the disposition of the territories, since these people constituted "the thinking classes of the future Negro world": African chiefs and educated Negroes in the U.S. and the West Indies, as well as those in French West Africa, Equatorial Africa, British Uganda, Nigeria, Basutoland, and many other parts of Africa. The governments of Abyssinia, Liberia, and Haiti were also to have a "voice." The Pan-African Congress was to be called into session in order to discover the opinions of the above groups. But in the very next line of the N.A.A.C.P. statement, it seemed that the attitudes of world Negrodom were already known. According to this interpretation, the former German colonies in Africa ought to be internationalized, and Portuguese Africa and the Belgian Congo added "by negotiation." For the time being, an "International Commission" of scientists, business-men, and religious leaders was to control the territory, which would become a socialized "industrial democracy" administered by Negro intellectuals.[9]

The N.A.A.C.P. inaugurated the Pan-African Movement in the

United States at the annual meeting in January, 1919, and the theme of the session was distinctly Africa for the African natives. James Weldon Johnson, the Association's secretary, asserted that the N.A.A.C.P. was taking the initiative because no nation seemed desirous of helping the Africans. For the time being, it *appeared* that Du Bois thoroughly convinced the Association to promote the Pan-African Movement.

Du Bois found it immensely difficult to get the First Pan-African Congress off the ground in Paris. For one thing, the American State Department, acting on the premise that the French viewed the gathering as dangerous and ill-timed, refused to issue passports to Negroes who wished to attend.[10] The radical *Messenger* magazine reported that "good niggers" like Du Bois could always receive a passport, since they had "the stamp of approval of President Wilson and his bourbon Southern Democrats."[11] Actually, the *Crisis* editor tried without success to interest President Wilson and his staff in the Pan-African Congress. However, through the help of Blaise Diagne, a Senegalese representative in the Chamber of Deputies, Du Bois was granted permission by Premier Georges Clemenceau to organize the conclave. American State Department officials were absolutely "puzzled" when they received the news—Acting Secretary of State Polk declared he was "officially advised" by the French that the meeting would not be allowed in the country.[12]

Fifty-seven "representatives of the Negro race" assembled in Paris from February 19 to February 21, 1919. Blaise Diagne was elected president and Du Bois was executive secretary. Of the delegates, sixteen were Americans, twenty-one were from the West Indies, and only twelve lived in Africa. The rest came from Europe. The sessions were generally characterized by restraint and accommodation to imperialism. Diagne delivered the first address and lauded French colonialism. One speaker acquainted the conferees with recent reforms in the Belgian Congo, and another spoke about "the opportunities and liberties given the natives in the Portuguese colonies." After they paid tribute to their mother countries, they unanimously passed resolutions which hardly supported colonialism. These statements were sent to the Paris Peace Conference.

The Pan-African delegates recommended that the League of Nations formulate a legal code for the "international protection" of the African Negroes and organize a permanent agency to guarantee political, economic, and social gains. They asked the Paris conferees to admit representatives of the natives to its organization and make certain that Africans were not ignored in "international labor legislation." According to the Pan-African Congress, "the Negroes of the world demand" that the natives be allowed to own all the land in Africa which they could "profitably" cultivate; the exploitation of these people and their land should be stopped through the implementation of controls on the capitalists. The conferees maintained that the Africans also had a right to elementary, vocational, and higher education. In short, "Wherever persons of African descent are civilized and able to meet the tests of surrounding culture, they should be accorded the same rights as their fellow-citizens; they shall not be denied on account of race or color a voice in their own Government, justice before the courts, and economic and social equality according to ability and desert."[13]

Newspaper articles began to appear about the Pan-African Congress in the American white press. Du Bois exaggerated things when he observed that "the entire press of the world has approved" the resolutions. While the New York *Herald* (Paris edition) said, "There is nothing unreasonable in the programme," the Chicago *Tribune* termed the proposals a "dream" of "an Ethiopian Utopia."[14] The *Tenth Annual Report* of the N.A.A.C.P., which was probably written by Du Bois, announced the Pan-African Congress had acquired many powerful supporters and was on the verge of accomplishing a great deal when its limited appropriations were exhausted:

> Colonel House, of the American Peace Commission, received Dr. Du Bois and assured him that he wished these resolutions presented to the Peace Conference. Lloyd George wrote Dr. Du Bois that he would give the demands of the Congress "his careful consideration." The French Premier offered to arrange an audience for the President and Secretary of the Congress. Portugal and Belgium, great colonial powers, offered complete co-operation. The League for the Rights of Man, which freed Dreyfus, appointed a special commission to hear not only of the African, but the facts as to the American race problem.[15]

The African question was a formidable problem to the Peace Conference, and Du Bois contended the conferees were eager for all ideas on the subject. He even asserted that if the Negroes could have supported an office and qualified lobbyists in Paris during the entire Peace Conference, the African problem could have been resolved (along the lines he suggested) for something under ten thousand dollars.[16] Enthusiastically, the *Crisis* editor believed in the power of the League of Nations. He was optimistic about its success and was impressed because Haiti and Liberia were admitted, thereby giving them international prestige. He considered the League a forceful alternative to a race war and especially thought of it as an agency to limit American racism. The Negro leader predicted that the United States would have to join the League "on the terms which the world lays down." But in the next breath, there were some reservations as he pointed out that the organization was dominated by imperialists.[17]

In his desire to unite Negroes around the world, Du Bois hoped to start an international quarterly to be entitled *Black Review*, with

English, French, and possibly Spanish and Portuguese editions. He also suggested American Negroes should study and speak French and Spanish in order to create the *rapprochement pan-africain*. He was certain his program would encourage Negro art and literature in all nations. Du Bois' grand schemes were undoubtedly a reflection of his reception during his stay in France. This visit was characterized—as were previous trips abroad—by a sense of personal liberation, complete social acceptance, and intellectual stimulation.[18]

William Z. Foster appraised the 1919 Pan-African Congress and concluded, "The importance ... was that it emphasized the solidarity of American Negroes with the oppressed colonial peoples, and especially that it expressed the national sentiments of the American Negro people."[19]John Hope Franklin more accurately viewed the effect of the congress as "small," although according to him it served to remind world public opinion that Negroes were interested in the outcome of the Paris Peace Conference and were demanding fairer treatment than they had received previously.[20] Naturally, Du Bois claimed the Pan-African Congress was the beginning of a world-wide race movement and believed his organization was responsible for the establishment of the Mandates Commission of the League of Nations, which was given jurisdiction over the former German colonies in Africa.[21]

Actually, the League appeared to have been unconcerned about the Pan-African resolutions, and it is doubtful that it or any other informed group (including the American press) ever really considered Du Bois or his followers "representatives of the Negro race." Educated Negroes in the United States were not much interested in the Pan-African Congress and the masses did not respond differently. A handful of Negro intellectuals were thinking out loud and resolving even louder. There was no real grass-roots organizational support; none of the N.A.A.C.P. branches seemed to have taken Pan-Africa very seriously, and headquarters gave it only lip service. Operating in such a vacuum, the Pan-African Congress of 1919 could only have accomplished as little as it did.

In the 1920's, Du Bois and his movement clashed with the popular Jamaican Negro leader, Marcus Garvey. Their conflict was inevitable because Du Bois' program competed with Garvey's flashier brand of Negro nationalism. Unlike Du Bois, Marcus Garvey was able to gain mass support and had tremendous emotional appeal. He established the Universal Negro Improvement Association, with New York headquarters and branches in many American cities and several foreign countries. The aim of the organization was the liberation of Africa. He also set up the Black Star Shipping Line and the Negro Factories Corporation. In August, 1920, he called a month-long convention of the U.N.I.A. in New York City. Garvey did not bother to display the restraint which characterized Pan-African Congress leaders and his remarks were frequently inflammatory—for example, he warned that his race would shed its blood to remove the whites from Africa. Garvey's genius was in his showmanship and love of spectacles. His convention delegates and members were paraded through Harlem—hundreds of thousands of Negroes were excited by the massed units of the African Legion in blue and red uniforms and the white-attired contingents of the Black Cross Nurses. The Jamaican's followers sang the new U.N.I.A. anthem, "Ethiopia, Thou Land of Our Fathers," and they proudly waved the Association's flag (black for Negro skin, green for Negro hopes, and red for Negro blood). Never again was the race to have a leader who could produce such wonderful shows.

Du Bois was ambivalent about Garvey and ignored him until late 1920. The *Crisis* editor was profoundly impressed by "this extraordinary leader of men" and acknowledged that Garvey was "essentially an honest and sincere man with a tremendous vision, great dynamic force, stubborn determination and unselfish desire to serve." However, the N.A.A.C.P. journalist also considered him to be "dictatorial, domineering, inordinately vain and very suspicious. . . . The great difficulty with him is that he has absolutely no business sense, no *flair* for real organization and his general objects are so shot through with bombast and exaggeration that it is difficult to pin them down for careful examination."[22]

The following month, after having requested (and failed to receive) a financial statement from the Jamaican on the Universal Negro Improvement Association or the Black Star Line, the *Crisis* editor wrote: "When it comes to Mr. Garvey's industrial and commercial enterprises there is more ground for doubt and misgiving than in the matter of his character.[23]

At first he hoped for Garvey's co-operation. Du Bois thought this mass movement could stir people to effect the realization of his own dreams of a black economy, intricately related to the black colonies of the world, with Africa reclaimed finally for the race. The *Crisis* editor was also interested in the success of the Garvey movement because it had generated so much "spiritual" potential that its demise might destroy racial self-confidence for generations. He was impressed by the "bold effort and some success" of Garvey, who sent ships ("owned by black men") to sea. However, the *Crisis* editor accused the flamboyant Jamaican (who loved public relations as much as buying ships) of using money for current expenses which had been contributed for long-term stock investment. Nevertheless, according to Du Bois, Garvey's future seemed bright if certain old tactics were shunned:

1. Garvey introduced the Jamaican black-mulatto schism to the United States, where Du Bois claimed it had no relevance and caused disunity. One of Du Bois' own errors was the minimizing of this conflict which had a long history in the U.S.

2. Garvey alienated the British by his tactlessness, and the help

of Great Britain was required in his international trade plans.

3. He did not seem to want a friendly relationship with the N.A.A.C.P. and went out of his way to antagonize its officials.

4. His relations with the Liberian government were less than satisfactory, even though he hoped to establish headquarters there.

5. With inadequate material resources, he still made bellicose statements about conquering Africa.

Du Bois' comments showed remarkable temperateness in view of the fact that the Garvey movement had been attacking him for more than a year. Just before the 1919 Pan-African Congress, Garvey alleged that Du Bois talked so mildly and equivocally to French reporters about American race relations that the Jamaican's "High Commissioner" abroad found his own work sabotaged.[24] The *Negro World*, Garvey's newspaper, instructed its readers that the *Crisis* was basically reactionary and was published from an "aristocratic Fifth Avenue" office. After Du Bois' comments about Woodrow Wilson's faithlessness and the postwar imperialist resurgence, the *Negro World* observed that Garvey had foreseen these developments as early as 1918, when the N.A.A.C.P. propagandist was counseling co-operation with the United States government. Du Bois was pictured as a fallen old warrior whose contributions to the race were at an end. With relish the *Negro World* also took up the cry of the *Messenger* that Du Bois was "controlled" by the white capitalists on the N.A.A.C.P. board. And of course Garvey ridiculed the Pan-African Congress.[25]

At the 1920 U.N.I.A. convention, the Jamaican called the *Crisis* editor "the associate of an alien race," and the remark received "the most enthusiastic applause." Du Bois' criticisms were interpreted as evidences of petty jealousy; he was accused of being "more of a white man than a Negro and [he] seems to be only a professional Negro at that." Garvey mounted the platform to chide Du Bois for ignoring the masses and worshipping a "bastard aristocracy." In contrast, the Jamaican recalled how he "always walked among [his own] ordinary humble people ... (cheers)." The U.N.I.A. chieftain demonstrated his demagogic talents:

> Where did he [Du Bois] get this aristocracy from? He picked it up on the streets of Great Barrington, Mass. He just got it into his head that he should be an aristocrat and ever since that time has been keeping his very beard as an aristocrat; he has been trying to be everything else but a Negro. Sometimes we hear he is a Frenchman and another time he is Dutch and when it is convenient he is a Negro (Derisive cheers and laughter). Now I have no Dutch. I have no French, I have no Anglo-Saxon to imitate; I have but the ancient glories of Ethiopia to imitate. (Great applause.) The men who built the Pyramids looked like me, and I think the best thing I can do is to keep looking like them. Anyone you hear always talking about the kind of blood he has in him other than the blood you can see, he is dissatisfied with something, and I feel sure that many of the Negroes of the United States of America know that if there is a man who is most dissatisfied with himself, it is Dr. Du Bois.[26]

The *Negro World*, attempting to demonstrate that Du Bois was unpopular in various quarters of the race, reprinted many comments and editorials from other Negro papers. The Richmond *Planet* and the Oakland *Sunshine* censured the *Crisis* editor for having the audacity to criticize Garvey, "a man of action." Just as in the old Booker T. Washington days, Du Bois was identified as only a talker while his opponents were doers. The *Negro World* resented the *Crisis'* tone of superiority and public omniscience, and Du Bois was castigated for thinking that Negroes who wanted to start race enterprises were obliged to appear before his inquisition.[27] Such remarks brought forth Du Boisian retaliation and the Garveyites were blasted as "scoundrels and bubble-blowers" who caused havoc within the race. He denounced them for exploiting the Negro masses and damning all whites. Du Bois claimed white supremacists were retreating and the N.A.A.C.P. would liberate Negroes within a quarter of a century.[28] In fighting Garvey, the *Crisis* editor—who had also condemned whites in wholesale fashion—tried to appear more optimistic about interracial relations than he actually was.

During the early months of 1921, Du Bois was preparing for the Second Pan-African Congress which was announced for the fall. He promised to invite not only the Negro governments, but "all Negro organizations interested in the peoples of African descent." He also mentioned that colonial powers would be encouraged to send representatives to the conclave which was to be held in Europe again.[29] Realizing his organization would be confused with and compared with the Garveyites, he stressed that the Second Pan-African Congress was not convening to develop a "scheme of migration."[30] Shortly before the Congress, the *Negro World* twitted Du Bois about the small number of African delegates at the first conclave, and the U.N.I.A. newspaper called the term "Pan-African" a misnomer. The Garvey men were striking back at Du Bois who had recently printed an anti-Garvey letter from the President of Liberia. The Liberian chief of state warned that his country would not allow itself to serve as a base of operations from which the U.N.I.A. could harass other governments in Africa.[31]

Du Bois, who found it necessary to make a public statement after it became known that Garvey would not be invited to the coming conclave, informed the New York *Age* that the Jamaican was ignored because the U.N.I.A. movement was "dangerous" and "impracticable." The *Negro World* decided that such studied neglect could only be expected of Du Bois, who ran the Pan-African Congress like "an exclusive college function." The newspaper asked, "Is Dr. Du Bois Misled or Is He Misleading?" After inflicting the usual verbal thrashing, the writer advised Du Bois to join forces against the "white beasts." In the same issue, Garvey personally asked Moton and Du Bois to attend the second convention of the U.N.I.A. The Jamaican also predicted a race war and asserted that old-line leaders were not adequately planning for it.[32]

Garvey plotted to beat Du Bois to the punch and hold his own international convention in New York a few weeks before the Second Pan-African Congress. One of the first pieces of business was the unanimous passage of a resolution (cabled to European newspapers) repudiating the *Crisis* editor's movement. The Jamaican ridiculed the idea of asking white representatives of the colonial powers to be present: "Just imagine that! It reminds me of the conference of rats endeavoring to legislate against the cats and the secretary of the rats convention invites the cat to preside over the convention."[33]

Garvey asserted Du Bois' goal was racial amalgamation, and the U.N.I.A. chieftain, contending that the whites would always hold firmly to their racism, asked the average Negro to develop "a distinct racial type of civilization of his own and . . . work out his salvation in his motherland, all to be accomplished under the stimulus and influence of the slogan, 'Africa for the Africans, at home and abroad!' "[34]

The Second Pan-African Congress met in London on August 28–29, in Brussels on August 31–September 2, and in Paris on September 5–6, 1921. There were 113 official delegates, 25 of whom were from the United States and 41 from Africa.[35] (The African delegation increased proportionally since 1919.) Preceding the actual London meetings were conferences with the Aborigines Protection Society. Du Bois, disappointed with the conclave at the Society, claimed it was under the domination of older, conservative white men. The whites were told pointedly that their "help" in the past had not been accompanied by a concern for the opinions of Negroes. Du Bois declared that in the future, policies ought to be decided by "Negro effort aided by white cooperation." The Aborigines Protection Society proposed an African land resolution which he considered insufficient; nor did he agree when the organization repudiated French conscription of African natives. The *Crisis* editor maintained no rights were violated so long as Negroes were drafted on the same terms as the whites.

Du Bois' group affirmed the mutuality of Negro and white labor at a special session with British Labor party intellectuals. His reaction was a typically mixed one—the white conferees were "deeply sympathetic" even if "they were not perhaps entirely convinced."[36] Sidney Webb said the Labor party opposed "the color bar in labor and elsewhere" all over the world and asked Pan-African delegates for whatever data they compiled on Negro labor. The material was to be brought to the attention of Parliament.

Despite reservations in connection with these two organizations, Du Bois was hopeful when the Pan-African Congress opened in London. Although the delegates sometimes seemed "apologetic," they produced a manifesto and a series of resolutions which were passed unanimously. As in 1919, they asserted a belief in the physical, social, and political equality of all races. African natives were to be given "local self government," and all types of educational opportunities were demanded for them. The Negroes in Africa were to be guaranteed "the ancient common ownership of the land and its natural fruits and defence against the unrestrained greed of invested capital." The League of Nations was asked again to establish an agency for the purpose of studying "Negro problems" and another agency to insure that native labor was not exploited.[37] During the London sessions, the delegates were more explicit in condemning imperialist domination than they had been two years before. England and Belgium were especially criticized for the administration of their African colonies. Although France had an "imperfect" colonial educational system, the nation was credited with a "splendid beginning" in having recognized the equal rights doctrine for educated Negroes.

When the Congress met in Belgium a few days later, whites outnumbered Negroes in the audience. It was quickly apparent to the delegates that "a new spirit was in the air ... Fear." The Belgians were keenly interested in the proceedings because the Congo was their gold mine and they wanted no "interference." During the first and second days, calmness and cliches reigned. No one registered any disapproval of colonialism (two representatives of the Belgian Colonial Office had thoughtfully been invited),[38] and one oration after another was dedicated to demonstrating how far the natives had come under Belgian rule. Du Bois broke the spell of serenity at the last session when he read the London resolutions. His action produced "a serious clash" between the American-British delegation, who favored a critical approach to colonialism, and the French-Belgian delegates, who desired an accommodation to the *status quo*.[39]

Chairman Blaise Diagne, who probably promised the Belgians there would be no trouble, was absolutely furious and charged that the "black American radicals" were courting disaster.[40] He refused to permit the London resolutions to be voted upon, and substituted "an innocuous statement" presented by a white Belgian. The new suggestion agreed that the natives could profit from education and that the colonial powers should establish organizations to study the living conditions of the blacks. Also favored was a "federation" of racial advancement agencies; world headquarters was to be located in Belgium. The proposal was passed and, according to Du Bois, even white spectators were permitted to cast votes. The London *African World* commented that this measure was shoved through the Congress, despite the fact that the American and British delegates, who constituted a big bloc of those with credentials, did not vote in favor of it.[41] The American-British bloc considered Diagne had acted in "bad faith," and they did not think the Belgian climate was the place for a "federation." However, they decided it was strategic to yield temporarily, and the London resolutions were tabled. The Du Bois men also took this position because they recognized that, unless the schism were healed to some degree, the entire organization would end in a complete fiasco. Antagonism seemed everywhere and the delegates were denounced as demagogues. Their movement was confused with Garvey's, while one Belgian newspaper charged that the N.A.A.C.P., and by implication the Congress, was a Communist agency paid to stir up trouble in the Congo.

The Pan-African Congress moved on to Paris; Du Bois described the atmosphere there as filled with "strain," "anger," and "revolt." Diagne confessed he had been dictatorial in Brussels but argued that he was only trying to save the race from destruction. However, his behavior as presiding officer in Paris did not change very much. He was still "unusually autocratic" and refused to recognize many delegates who disagreed with him. Both he and Gratien Candace, the Guadalupian member of the French Chamber of Deputies, told delegates and guests about the good fortune of being "black Frenchmen." One British observer noted that the English-speaking delegation referred to themselves as "we Negroes," while the French representatives always described themselves as "we Frenchmen."[42]

Members of the white press continued to confuse the Pan-African Movement with the U.N.I.A. (much to Garvey's delight)[43] and wanted to know if Du Bois' organization planned to expel the whites from Africa. Time and again, the conferees explained they abhorred "any policy of war, conquest, or race hatred." Du Bois, Diagne, and Candace went on record in opposition to the premise that the Negro race should be removed to Africa, or that the

Africans should be isolated from the whites who lived there.[44] They proposed no large-scale migrations and counseled Negroes to concentrate on improving living conditions in the countries where they lived. But Du Bois often remarked that, in the milieu of race prejudice, "common descent" was very significant because it symbolized "common dangers."[45] Therefore, it was imperative for the race to occupy itself with the plight of the African brethren. Although the delegates displayed anti-Garvey sentiments, they decided it was unwise to reject the Jamaican categorically and agreed he should be invited to explain his views to a future Pan-African Congress.[46]

The London resolutions were finally adopted "with some minor corrections," underscoring once more that there was a decided split between the American and French delegations. The French refused to accept those resolutions critical of capitalism. Diagne disapproved of returning African land to the natives and termed the suggestion "rank communism." It seemed to Du Bois that Diagne reflected the French policy of believing educated Negroes had an equal right "to exploit" black and white workers.[47] In Paris, Gratien Candace was elected president of the Pan-African organization, and Du Bois was retired as secretary, in accordance with his own request. However, he agreed to serve as a member of the committee charged with the task of creating a "permanent organization." For the time being, he favored a "loose" structure until the ideological differences among the members could be resolved.[48] Plans were made for the Congress to convene every two years.

Du Bois left for Geneva, in order to present the Pan-African resolutions to the League of Nations and ask the International Labor Bureau to set up a division to investigate native labor conditions.[49] At the hearing before the League's Mandates Commission, he argued that a Negro should receive an appointment to the Commission since many blacks lived in mandated areas. Although he realized that the League possessed little power to intervene directly in national affairs, Du Bois begged it to employ its "vast moral power of world public opinion" on behalf of race equality. The head of the International Labor Bureau, Albert Thomas, was quite cordial and told Du Bois that the agency was already championing the cause of native labor. Thomas supported the Pan-African Congress suggestion that a special section on native labor should be organized within the International Labor Bureau. However, because of an inadequate budget, he was able to employ only one man to handle the job.[50]

One member of the American delegation to the 1921 Pan-African Congress wrote that whites were "feverishly anxious to know of our thoughts, our hopes, our dreams";[51] actually, interest was only slight. But the Paris *Humanité* was charmed by the conclave: "The black and mulatto intelligentsia which the Congress revealed or permitted us to know better, showed by its very existence that the black race is not naturally or essentially an inferior race, and that it is not destined to remain so forever."

The London *Daily Graphic* found the conferee "so intensely in earnest . . . so absolutely convinced of the justice of their cause." Undoubtedly, some of the journalistic attention was due to curiosity about this strange sight of an international meeting of Negro intellectuals. Perhaps one indication of the feebleness of the Pan-Africa propaganda was the fact that the Congress was so frequently confused with the Garvey movement. If this error were almost inevitable (undoubtedly, in some cases it was part of the colonial powers' smoke screen), Du Bois' group might have anticipated it and carefully documented the differences between both organizations for the benefit of white reporters. The misapprehension was compounded by the flood of anti-Garvey statements originating from Diagne and Candace, while Du Bois was saying publicly that he agreed with the Jamaican's main principles but rejected U.N.I.A. promotional and financial methods.

It was even more difficult for the Pan-African Congress to convince "world public opinion" that Africa should not be exploited, since the conferees could not agree among themselves on this particular point. Du Bois contended he was the spokesman for "civilized" Africans, but they, like Diagne, seemed basically interested in securing a higher social status and a greater share of the profits gained from native labor. Furthermore, although Du Bois repudiated white capitalists in Africa, he presented no practical plan to lessen their influence.

He was generally modest and made no great claims for the accomplishments of the 1921 conclave. He admitted, for example, that only "a few" of the many millions of African Negroes could even identify the Pan-African Congress and he observed that the essential result of the meetings was the exchange of ideas among potential race leaders. Representatives of several African organizations attended, such as the Union Congolaise and the South African Native Congress, but the Pan-African Congress was not a "native movement" and still did not have grass-roots support. In the United States there were only handfuls of people interested enough to contribute time or money to Du Bois' program. The N.A.A.C.P. board decided to confine its activities to the United States and refused to help. White liberals in the Association considered that policing the American milieu was a full-time task and were reluctant to dissipate their limited resources elsewhere. And according to the *Crisis* editor, some of the Negro N.A.A.C.P. board members "had inherited the fierce repugnance toward anything African ... they felt themselves Americans."[52] Since Du Bois was basically not an organizational leader, he did almost nothing (except write editorials) to convince the board to provide support for the Pan-African Movement.

After the Second Pan-African Congress, Marcus Garvey seemed even more determined to undermine the organization and ridiculed those delegates who pleaded that they owed primary allegiance to their mother countries. When Candace said he would "lose everything" if he resided permanently in Africa, Garvey quipped "everything" meant the white women of Paris. The Jamaican predicted the whites would inevitably expel Negroes from all countries, and he viewed African independence as the race's only salvation. He believed race prejudice existed because Negroes were weak and contributed so little to civilization; all was to be changed by the establishment of African cities, empires, armies and navies under the direction of the U.N.I.A. Although Garvey excoriated N.A.A.C.P. leaders like Du Bois, he denied that he hoped for the demise of the Association, which was dubbed "the National Association for the Advancement of (Certain) Colored People." He announced his group would not "originate an attack" upon the N.A.A.C.P., but he was prepared to defend the Negro race against "our bitterest enemies [who] are not so much those from without as within; men who will continue to find faults when there are no faults." He asked the Association to send representatives to the third convention of the U.N.I.A., where "the real leadership" of the race held court.[53]

During all of this time, Du Bois continued to request a financial statement of U.N.I.A. activities, but none was forthcoming. Since he viewed the Black Star Line as the foundation of the leader's fame and influence, he recounted the history of Garvey's mismanagement and stupidity in operating the enterprise. The *Crisis* editor described the sad story of the *Yarmouth* and *Antonio Maceo*, both old and unseaworthy ships which cost fortunes for constant repairs. The first was sold in order to pay off creditors, and the second was beached in Cuba as a total loss. In early 1921, Garvey announced the purchase of the *Phyllis Wheatley*, which was supposed to handle the African trade, and he used the mails to sell passage. Later the Jamaican, who was indicted for fraud, claimed that his associates absconded with funds which had been set aside as a deposit for the ship. By 1922, the Black Star Line was dead and Du Bois wrote feelingly, "Here then is the collapse of the only thing in the Garvey movement which was original or promising."[54]

The *Crisis* editor also attempted to learn how many members actually were in the U.N.I.A. Garvey claimed four million for 1920 and six million for the following year.[55] After the Jamaican was indicted, Du Bois estimated the membership for the period of September, 1920, to July, 1921, and calculated that there were fewer than ten thousand "paid up members," between ten and twenty thousand "active members," and very much less than a hundred thousand "nominal members."[56] His estimates were on the low side, while Garvey's were certainly on the high side. At the Jamaican's trial in 1923, his lieutenants discussed the size of U.N.I.A. locals: New York City, 30,000; Chicago, 9,000; Philadelphia, 6,000; Cincinnati, 5,000–6,000; Detroit, 4,000; Washington, 700. These figures were, of course, incomplete.

Du Bois viewed Garvey as a disoriented victim of the color line: "All his life whites have laughed and sneered at him, and torn his soul. All his life he has hated the half-whites, who rejecting their darker blood, have gloried in their pale shame."[57]

He referred to the U.N.I.A. leader as a "little, fat, black man; ugly, but with intelligent eyes and a big head"; Garvey replied that his physiognomy was "typical of the African" and he placed Du Bois in the category of "pale shame": "Anything that is black, to him is ugly, is hideous, is monstrous, and this is why in 1917 he had but the lightest of colored people in his office, when one could hardly tell whether it was a white show or a colored vaudeville he was running at Fifth Avenue [the offices of the *Crisis* and the N.A.A.C.P.]."[58]

The *Crisis* editor was labeled an apostle of "social equality," which in Garvey's thinking represented the kind of person who demanded to squire a white woman to a dance at the Waldorf-Astoria Hotel. The U.N.I.A., according to its chieftain, was the only organization able to protect the darker-skinned Negro masses against the Du Bois-led "caste aristocracy" of light mulattoes, many of whom were "intellectuals." Garvey refused to accept defeat and in his cell at Atlanta Federal Penitentiary he angrily denounced Du Bois.[59]

Of course, the U.N.I.A. leader's whole program had been unrealistic and escapist. In stressing a back-to-Africa movement, he contributed nothing to the improvement of Negro living conditions either in the United States or in Africa. However, unlike Du Bois, Garvey was a mass leader who gave average Negroes a strong sense of race pride. More clearly than Du Bois, the Jamaican recognized the black-mulatto schism in the United States and capitalized upon it. For blacks in the American society of the 1920's (crushed by ambitious mulattoes and powerful, prejudiced whites), racial chauvinism was a strong antidote to complete hopelessness. Since the *Crisis* editor shunned the uneducated majority within the Negro race, Garvey's wild and absurd accusations against him were widely believed.

During the same years in which the U.N.I.A. attracted hundreds of thousands, the Pan-African Congress barely managed to stay alive, and Du Bois charged Marcus Garvey with sabotage. The *Crisis* editor scheduled another conclave for the fall of 1923, but the new secretary of the movement, I. Beton, sought a postponement and claimed there was simply no interest among the membership. As if to prove his point, he mentioned having spent fifteen thousand francs to obtain one thousand francs in dues. However, Du Bois convinced the executive committee to overrule Beton, and the split between the French and American members was widened.[60] The *Crisis* editor, all too aware the movement was dying, feared that there would be no chance for the organization's survival if the 1923 conference were delayed. He was able to persuade the National Association of Colored Women to sponsor the Third Pan-African Congress, and the delegates met in London near the end of 1923. Few people bothered to attend, although the guest list included Harold Laski and H. G. Wells. The resignations of Candace and Beton were offered and accepted.[61] In view of the hard feelings, Du Bois by-passed Paris and his group moved on to Lisbon for a series of meetings sponsored by the *Liga Africana*, a federated lobby of native organizations from several provinces in Portuguese Africa. The usual resolutions were adopted, e.g., those calling for a democratic and socialized Africa.

When the conferences ended, Du Bois journeyed to Africa for the "greatest" experience of his life. All of the countries he had previously visited were "painfully white," and during this trip to "the Eternal World of Black Folk" he made a characteristic observation—the world brightens as it darkens. His racial romanticism was given free rein:

> The spell of Africa is upon me. The ancient witchery of her medicine is burning my drowsy, dreamy blood. This is not a country, it is a world—a universe of itself and for itself, a thing Different, Immense, Menacing, Alluring.... Africa is the Spiritual Frontier of human kind—oh the wild and beautiful adventures of its taming! But oh! the cost thereof—the endless, endless cost! Then will come a day— an old and ever, ever young day when there will spring in Africa a civilization without coal, without noise, where machinery will sing and never rush and roar, and where men will sleep and think and dance and lie prone before the rising sun, and women will be happy....[62]

After his return to the United States he began to develop plans for the Fourth Pan-African Congress and suggested that the delegates meet in the West Indies. He was reacting to critics who noticed that previous conclaves were held far away from areas in which large numbers of Negroes lived, and he wanted to enlist the co-operation of local groups in the islands who favored home rule. Du Bois proposed to charter a ship and dock at ports in Jamaica, Haiti, Cuba, and the French islands. On learning the ship would cost fifty thousand dollars, he concluded that the steamship companies were ordered by colonial powers to make the price prohibitive. But in a mood of realism he also admitted the project had simply not attracted the support of many Negroes. In 1926, he faced facts and announced that if educated Negroes did not rally around the cause of Pan-Africa, he was ready to give up. The Circle of Peace and Foreign Relations of the National Association of Colored Women agreed to sponsor the Congress for a second time and the sessions were scheduled for August, 1927, in New York City. The demise was postponed a little longer and the elated Du Bois talked of colossal results: "We hope that the coming Congress will be the greatest and most important gathering of representatives of all branches of the black race which the world has yet seen; and that it will settle for all time the question as to whether they must always and everywhere follow the guidance of white folk."[63]

Du Bois was extremely conciliatory in pre-Congress press releases. Other Pan-African leaders shrewdly informed *The New York Times* that their organization had nothing to do with the back-to-Africa movement, and they stated there would be no attempt to drive the whites from their recognized "portion" of Africa. The emphasis was upon "harmony" in race relations and the *Times* lauded the "absence of inflammatory racialism." Among the speakers were Melville Herskovits, the American anthropologist, and Dantes Bellegarde, who had represented Haiti at the

League of Nations. Just as critics predicted, there were few Africans at the conference and Du Bois' large hopes to arouse the Negro race were unrealized again. The old resolutions were reworded and adapted to current situations. For example, the conferees complained about the concession which Liberia granted to the Firestone Rubber Company, and they were "alarmed at the increasing power and influence" of the corporation in the affairs of the people.[64]

Du Bois' own writings on Liberia represent a case study of what had become his personal brand of racism. He romanticized Liberia as the lonely symbol of the Negro race daring to be free, and therefore he glossed over obvious evils which existed in the country. For instance, while he condemned slavery in Liberia, he refused to censure the Negro government for permitting it. Instead, he wrote that the black republic "is no more guilty" than other countries. He even noted that "domestic slavery is discouraged by the government," while he acknowledged simultaneously that Liberia used "forced labor" and the indenture system. He admitted "Liberian labor" was sold to France and Spain, but, speciously, he argued the Europeans were more to blame because they pressured the little nation into selling the natives.[65] George Schuyler, a Negro journalist, penned a devastating reply to Du Bois. He condemned the Liberian government for permitting involuntary servitude and exploiting and terrorizing its people. He also observed that the Liberians were economically inefficient and were losing needed revenue because they neglected to build necessary roads, grade their coffee properly, or clean their palm oil. Schuyler repudiated the idea of a European "trade conspiracy" against the country and lectured the *Crisis* editor for condoning abuses when the culprits were Negroes. Du Bois did not deign to answer and concentrated on damning the Firestone Company.[66]

Although Du Bois accomplished so little in trying to unite

Negroes of various nations, in 1930 he spoke about the possibility of American Negroes joining China, India, Egypt, and Ethiopia in a "world movement of freedom for colored races." This thread was actually an old one in his writings. As early as 1905 he inducted the Asiatics as his allies, and at that time predicted an "awakening" of the black, brown, and yellow peoples. Encouraged by the Russo-Japanese War, which demonstrated the potential of non-Caucasians, he anticipated that unless the whites changed their approach there would be a general race war.[67] A decade later he hoped that an armed struggle would be unnecessary, since "war is Hell"; but at that time he also added that "there are things worse than Hell, as every Negro knows."[68] Again, in 1917 he predicted a militant crusade of the blacks, aided by their "natural" allies, the brown and yellow groups. The "dark world" (Japan, China, India, Egypt, and the Negroes of the United States, the West Indies, South and West Africa) would wage war upon the "white world."[69]

It has been repeatedly shown that there was no evidence of international Negro unity; and even if there had been, the race possessed no power to obtain any objectives by means of war. And it was preposterous that Japan, China, and India would form an alliance with the Negroes to knock out the "white world." The frustrated Du Bois propounded the threat of race war as an ego-defense mechanism and he was trying to bluff the whites. On reconsideration he toned down the talk of violence but did not surrender the dream of India, Africa, China, and Japan developing a "common consciousness" and leading "the labor parties of the world" into a socialized system.[70] Of course these nations were not in sympathy with his economic plans and even he recognized that "there is a vast gulf" between Africa and Asia. Professor Edward M. East, in proposing a reply to Du Bois, portrayed the "gulf" in this graphic fashion: "The Japanese and the Chinese despise each other, and both feel superior to the brown and the black, and the Hindu has more caste tabus than either."[71]

This chapter has examined the Pan-African Congress, one of Du Bois' biggest failures. In his plan for African self-government along socialistic lines he faced the opposition of colonial powers as well as the apathy of Negroes, who ignored the proposal of an international racial co-operative organization. Probably the Pan-African Movement would not have achieved success, no matter what it did, but, under Du Bois' type of leadership, it became a completely hollow effort. He was always fond of writing editorials and conference resolutions and was not disposed to give much attention to creating strong, well-developed social action groups. The movement was composed of small, ineffective organizations which never became more than an exclusive cult—even among African and American Negro intellectuals. The latter, having long been influenced by democratic integrationist propaganda, were not interested in identification with a continent of African natives. Since the Talented Tenth never supported Du Bois' domestic socialized segregated economy, they found his international racial plans even more dubious.

However, the *Crisis* editor was so completely bound to his cosmic concepts that he did not realize he was going against the current of American integrationist propaganda which he had helped to generate and maintain. Consequently, he was not spared enormous pain during the 1930's, when American Negroes rebelled against the segregated economy proposals. Nevertheless, Du Bois did secure some backing for limited race pride projects—such as the attempt to gain greater control of Negro colleges, and the patronize-the-Negroes campaign. The next chapter contains a discussion of his interest in domestic racial chauvinism during the post-World War I period, as well as his further contributions to the integrationist current.

10. The New Negro and the Old Du Bois

After World War I, large numbers of Negroes demanded a "spiritual emancipation" and the "New Negro" movement unfolded. Maurice R. Davie noted:

> The movement has found expression in numerous ways, such as an increasing awareness of the achievements of individual Negroes, support of Negro business enterprises, development of race leadership in the fight for Negro rights, the focusing of economic and political power, the development of morale, the attempt to reconstruct the Negro past, and the glorification of the folk cultural contributions of the Negro.[1]

Various scholars such as E. Franklin Frazier, Horace M. Bond, and Gunnar Myrdal have recognized Du Bois' extensive influence upon the new leadership, although Myrdal contended that the artistic-literary aspects of the New Negro movement were "primarily . . . white-sponsored."[2] Du Bois' expressions in the 1920's did not differ from those of earlier days; however, more Negroes were prepared during the later period to emphasize an aggressive desire for integration and a forceful race pride. Ironically, with the growth of Negro newspapers, even a smaller proportion of educated members of the race were reading Du Bois in the *Crisis*. It is, of course, difficult to estimate precisely how much the editor's writings influenced the New Negro. Certainly, many of the prominent Negro authors and editors regularly examined the *Crisis*; they regarded Du Bois as the father of "militant journalism" and the prophet who had walked in the wilderness almost alone.

Although the *Crisis* editor helped to provide the intellectual framework, the New Negro movement rested on a congeries of social causes. When hostilities in Europe ended, Negro soldiers returned with a new conception of themselves; they fought bravely in battle and had been accepted on equal terms by many of the French people. During the war years other Negroes found good jobs for the first time in their lives. Many migrated to the North, but all were exposed to the wartime democratic propaganda and were reluctant to surrender this promise, and partial fulfillment, of a greater day. Between the years 1910 and 1920, the race experienced an increase in literacy, and, in addition, more Negroes than ever before were attending colleges. Consequently, leaders and followers were ready to assert their rights, and the Negro press influenced and reflected this determination. The growth of the N.A.A.C.P. itself exemplified the new fervor of the race. For instance, by 1919, the organization claimed 91,203 members, which was more than twice the number it had the year before.[3]

Many whites reacted hysterically to these social changes and construed the New Negro as a serious threat to the established social order. The anxieties of both races erupted in bloodshed. In 1919, seventy-seven Negroes were lynched and there were race riots in more than a score of American cities. Du Bois recalled one July day when "a black mob" controlled Washington and battled the whites with hand grenades. He reported that such violence was caused by the "open and secret propaganda" of white migrants from the South.[4] Certainly, the insecure Negroes produced their share of incendiary propaganda. The point which is especially important here, however, is that in such a period of rapid social change people were prepared to believe almost anything—even Du Bois' threat that a race war was imminent.

Almost as soon as World War I ended, Du Bois returned to the old strategy of unmitigated protest and asserted that Negro rights could not possibly be realized "unless we take a desperate, unflinching stand" and make demands.[5] He announced that because of wartime contributions colored people were in a position to exact concessions from the whites. Du Bois held the opinion that Negro soldiers "saved civilization" and were morally upright in France.[6] Consequently, he was very disturbed by the reports that American officers discriminated against these men. While in Europe, he discovered several American-inspired documents, which were issued at the height of the world conflict, advising French officers about the decorum of caste in their encounters with American Negro officers and troops.[7] In the spring of 1919, after he returned to the United States, he became absolutely enraged. The May issue of the *Crisis* (which sold about 100,000 copies and was held up twenty-four hours while the Post Office debated whether to let it go through the mails) contained the documents and another famous flaming editorial, "Returning Soldiers," part of which is quoted:

> By the God of Heaven, we are cowards and jackasses if now that the war is over, we do not marshal every ounce of our brain and brawn to fight a sterner, longer, more unbending battle against the forces of hell in our own land.
>
> We *return*.
> We *return from fighting*.
> We *return fighting*.
> Make way for Democracy! We saved it in France, and by the Great Jehovah, we will save it in the United States of America, or know the reason why.[8]

In August, Representative James Byrnes of South Carolina delivered an address from the floor of the House of Representatives, condemning Du Bois' recent editorials (as well as those of Trotter and the *Messenger* editors, A. Philip Randolph and Chandler Owen) and holding Negro newsmen fully responsible for the numerous postwar race riots. Byrnes declared Du Bois was no longer "conservative" and that the Negro editor's "capacity for evil" had grown substantially. He singled out "Returning Soldiers" as the sort of writing which inspired Negro acts of violence. The South Carolina Congressman interpreted the Federal Espionage Law as prohibiting the publication of material which "encourage[d] resistance" to the government, and he reported to his colleagues that Du Bois had accused the government of lynching and disfranchisement. Byrnes asked the United States Attorney-General for a legal opinion on whether Du Bois committed a violation of the law, and, believing the Negro clearly had, he suggested that the *Crisis* editor be indicted:

> No greater service can be rendered to the Negro to-day than to have him know that this Government will not tolerate on the part of a leader of his race action which constitutes a violation of the law and which tends to array the negro race against the Government under which they live and under which the race has made greater strides than it has under any Government on earth. (Applause.)[9]

Du Bois' explosive editorials continued. While not counseling violence against the whites as an *offensive* policy, he warned Negroes to arm themselves against "the mob." In replying to the Byrnes charges, he reminded readers that the Congressman was chosen by a small electorate because large numbers of citizens were discouraged or prevented from voting. Du Bois complained that men like Byrnes were the ones who helped to cause the race riots, lynchings, and disfranchisement. The Negro editor told his audience he had informed the President, the Attorney-General, and Congress about Mr. Byrnes's behavior and asked that the South Carolina politician be charged with violating the Fourteenth Amendment.[10]

The *Messenger* seemed to have been offended because Byrnes placed it in the same category with Du Bois and the *Crisis*.[11] The

United States Department of Justice investigated the *Crisis* and other Negro periodicals, and published its account, "Radicalism and Sedition Among the Negroes as Reflected in Their Publications." The Department of Justice was provoked because after several race riots the "more radical Negro publications" issued heated statements "which in some cases have reached the limit of open defiance and a counsel of retaliation." Investigators also suspected some Negro newsmen because of the "increasingly emphasized feeling of a race consciousness . . . always antagonistic to the white race and openly, defiantly assertive of its own equality and even superiority."[12] The *Messenger* was viewed as "the most dangerous," and the Justice Department staff noted that the *Crisis* had published nothing "radical" in some months, although the investigators quoted from the "Returning Soldiers" editorials of May, 1919.

President Wilson supported a policy of "watchful waiting" and believed that, if Negro journalists were punished, they might gain public sympathy or perhaps even be driven to take more "radical" measures. However, Congress in January, 1920, considered a vaguely drafted bill outlawing the mailing of any printed material construed as causing race rioting. Du Bois recognized such proposed legislation was a threat to the *Crisis* and freedom of the press, and he urged readers to ask for a congressional amendment permitting "any and all agitation or propaganda to enforce law by Constitutional methods."[13] Negro publications were the source of anxiety, not only for some congressmen, but also for white editors, especially in the South. For example, a Macon newspaper issued a warning: "Du Boise [sic] hates white men because they are white and he is black. . . . There can be no harmony where [the *Crisis* and the Chicago *Defender*] are read either by the whites or the blacks. They must be changed or they must be stopped altogether."[14]

In the early months of 1920, a Mississippi judge fined and imprisoned a Negro minister who sold the *Crisis*, and a lawyer was told by a group of whites that he would be lynched if he took the Negro's case. The acting Governor of the state invited Du Bois to Mississippi and promised the *Crisis* editor would become an "example . . . that would be a lasting benefit to the colored people of the South." About this time an injunction was filed in Arkansas to prevent Negroes from reading certain race publications, and an N.A.A.C.P. official was severely beaten in Texas.[15]

Of course, the fears and tensions were not confined to the South. The Joint Legislative Committee Investigating Seditious Activities in the State of New York issued its own report on "Revolutionary Radicalism." Although it concentrated its fire on the Garvey movement and the Negro Socialists, the N.A.A.C.P. was also named as an organization dominated by Socialist board members. Among the N.A.A.C.P. officials mentioned were Mary White Ovington, John Haynes Holmes, and Archibald H. Grimke.[16] Du Bois was not named, undoubtedly because of his countless disagreements with the *Messenger* editors. Although only a few months before, he wrote that with the ascension of the left-wing Negroes, accommodating leaders of the race had just about lost their influence.

Nevertheless, the *Messenger* men still adjudged Du Bois to be a sterling illustration of the "hand-picked, me-too-boss, hat-in-hand, sycophant, lick spittling" Negroes, who were described as the anointed ones in the race. The *Messenger* editors were angered by his lack of enthusiasm for the Industrial Workers of the World (I.W.W.). Nor could they forgive Du Bois' wartime accommodation. The magazine said the "infamous" editorial, "Close Ranks," would "rank in shame and reeking disgrace with the 'Atlanta Compromise' speech of Booker Washington." According to A. Philip Randolph and Chandler Owen, the race's solemn duty was to overturn American institutions, and they mocked the *Crisis* editor for not viewing revolution as "the only hope of the Negro as well as of mankind."[17]

Du Bois stirred up a real storm when he published *Darkwater* in 1920. In this collection of fairly recent essays, the piece which attracted tremendous attention was one already mentioned, in which the author asserted that the dark world was preparing to meet the white world in battle.[18] After reading the book, the editors of *Current Opinion* published a worried article, "Are We Menaced by a New Race War?" The *Christian Register* of Boston regretted Du Bois' "inflammatory statements" and called upon colored people to return to the sentiments of the Tuskegeean. There was also a warning that the Negro author (a "mixed-blood") could lead his race only to annihilation.[19] *Nineteenth Century and After* published an essay, "Militancy of Colour and Its Leader": "Hatred of the whites has become moral as well as physical, and the American Negro leads the way in a world propaganda for revolt. The leader of the revenge movement of the Negroes is Dr. W. E. Burghardt Du Bois".[20]

The author of this article, Stephen Graham, also espoused the "half-breed" theory and argued that the momentum in Du Bois' movement was to be found in the trauma of the mulatto, whose "white soul [was] imprisoned in the dark mesh." Graham contrasted *Darkwater* with a recent conciliatory book by Robert R. Moton, "the full-blooded Negro." As Graham viewed it, the solution seemed fairly simple—the South should not apply the color line to "near-whites of the complexion of Dr. Du Bois." A white leader of the Southern University Race Commission stated that the organization could not trust Du Bois, who was playing a "vicious and dangerous" game; critics charged that no one was undoing the Commission's accomplishments more than the *Crisis* editor.[21]

Just as the Pan-African Movement represented an effort to integrate Negroes into world civilization by means of an intense race loyalty, Du Bois' postwar aggressive protests for an equal share in the cultural system of the United States also contained what has been described earlier as his segregation paradox. Segregation was "impolitic" because it could never be achieved completely and was a divisive process; however, he also advised Negroes to develop their own racial talents and ideals into one "great ethos," so that colored people might make a larger contribution to civilization than whites had ever made.

Repeatedly, he recognized "the curious paradox" and the "contradictory facts." In 1919 and 1920 Du Bois argued that segregation was evil because it almost invariably meant inferior facilities, but most of the time he emphasized it was wrong because it created more stereotyping and hostilities. Consequently, in 1919 he asked Negroes not to demand or accept separate schools even in the face of mistreatment. Du Bois attempted to prove that alert Northern Negroes could remedy discrimination in educational institutions. For example, in 1920 several Brooklyn Negro high school students were told that their presence was not wanted at the senior prom, but they attended the dance after the *Crisis* editor protested to the superintendent of schools.[22] However, in 1923 Du Bois clearly distrusted integrated schools, even if they were established in the South, "most of the border states, and in some parts of the North." He feared that colored children in non-segregated educational systems would be "abused, browbeaten, murdered, and kept in something worse than ignorance." On the other hand, he described Negro schoolteachers as the very best in the world. But in the same article, he repudiated "compulsory racial segregation" when it was rumored that Pennsylvania planned to institute a Jim Crow normal school as a preparatory measure to establishing a general policy of school segregation. Yet he seemed to condone the separate institutions which already existed in the state but insisted that they operate according to high standards. The *Crisis* editor maintained that whites should be encouraged to attend and that Negro teachers should have opportunities to work in white schools.[23]

Naturally, Du Bois was misunderstood. Negroes were confounded and complained that he seemed to condemn and approve of segregation. For the *Messenger*, segregation was absolute "poison" and anyone who accommodated himself to it was helping to sound "the death knell of the New Negro Manhood Strivings."[24] Du Bois' own ambivalence was always evident, i.e., separation created "race pride" and "race hate." In his opinion, since so many white teachers were hateful and white people were enemies, Negroes were forced to cling to each other for protection. In earlier years, they fought against segregation on grounds that it isolated them from good manners and intellectual stimulation, but recently they found their own people satisfying and even exciting. Nevertheless, he admitted that the wall of separation preserved racial animosities.[25]

In the 1920's Du Bois, exemplifying another aspect of the self-assertiveness of the New Negro, led a movement designed to give the race a voice in setting the policies of Negro colleges. He criticized Lincoln University and Hampton Institute for not having more Negroes on the faculty and in administrative positions. In 1924 he accused Fisk University's white president of being too friendly with white Southerners and ignoring the counsel of the alumni and other Negro leaders. It seemed to the *Crisis* editor that "most" of the Fisk staff were being influenced by Southern whites to discourage Negro students; the student body took the hint and went on strike. Du Bois viewed his efforts at Fisk University as only the beginning of reforms among the colored colleges.[26]

In 1926, when the white president of Howard University

resigned, the editor suggested that a Negro be designated as the next administrator, since no "first class" white man wished to be associated with a Negro school. Actually, Du Bois hoped Howard University would be a showplace and demonstrate to the world that Negroes could successfully operate a great institution. While he admitted "unrest and protest" were not absent in colleges headed by Negroes, he blamed such difficulties primarily upon white philanthropists, white churches, or white state officials.[27] The *Crisis* editor condoned another student strike at Hampton Institute in 1927, which was allegedly caused by the young people's refusal to present a musical program for a visiting white Englishman. However, in an article for the *Nation*, the editor gave a different reason for the disturbance. In this version, the students struck because they were displeased by an inferior faculty and curriculum. Du Bois announced that these segregated institutions ought to reflect Negro "ideals and desires" to become "independent, self-directing, modern men." He asked Negroes to give these colleges greater financial support so that the race would be in a better position to criticize policies and programs.[28]

The financial depression of the 1930's caused the editor to entertain doubts about some of the "ideals and desires" of the Talented Tenth. Du Bois, disturbed by evidences of conspicuous consumption among the delegates at a convention of Negro college fraternities and sororities, condemned the "snobbishness and class distinctions" of those who separated themselves from the masses and became a "closed clan." He scoffed at the elite who replied that their lines were drawn not on the basis of birth or wealth but upon educational achievement.[29] Sadly, the *Crisis* editor addressed the 1932 graduating class of Howard University—the men and women who were to have been the fruits of nearly four decades of toil:

Our college man today, is, on the average, a man untouched by real culture. He deliberately surrenders to selfish and even silly ideals, swarming into semi-professional athletics and Greek letter societies, and affecting to despise scholarship and the hard grind of study and research. The greatest meetings of the Negro college year like those of the white college year have become vulgar exhibitions of liquor, extravagance, and fur coats. We have in our colleges a growing mass of stupidity and indifference.[30]

Re-examining his leadership theory, he indicted the Negro colleges for permitting graduates to acquire a desire for material things which they could not afford. Above all, he charged that institutions of higher education ignored their responsibility of teaching about the economic system. Du Bois was only belatedly recognizing what long-time critics of the Talented Tenth program asserted—that the colleges produced substantial numbers of professionals who had no inclination "to study or solve the economic problem." He was ready to admit that the graduates had become "a white collar proletariat, depending for their support on an economic foundation which does not yet exist."[31] His solution involved a revamping of the curriculum to include "vocational training" and "industrial planning."

Du Bois' increasing emphasis upon a Negro "closed economic circle" in the 1920's and 1930's explained a great deal of his anxiety about the values of Negro higher education and the loyalty of the Talented Tenth, from which the "technical engineers" were to be drawn. Until the envisaged racial manufacturing-distributive system could be worked out, the *Crisis* editor had hoped that organized college graduates, in the sororities and fraternities, would direct economic projects beneficial to the race. For example, he suggested the Talented Tenth could alleviate the slum problem by financing large-scale building developments. Repeatedly he also advised them to establish "consumer co-operation" stores, and some Negroes followed his counsel.[32] However, none of these enterprises practiced two principles he considered important: (1) members should receive profits in accordance with how much they purchased, not in relation to how many shares they owned; (2) members should be allowed one vote each, regardless of the number of shares they owned. Since some sort of "co-operation" existed, he seemed reluctant to be very critical of these stores, and he rejoiced that the Negro race had become "its own *middle man*." But in 1920 he warned of disaster, because the establishments were only "partially cooperative." As he viewed it, the proprietors were attempting to make a fortune by trading on "race loyalty" and were not interested in returning profits to "a mass of people." Later in the year, the ambivalent editor took another look and decided the times made it imperative for Negroes to patronize race enterprises, even though the co-operative principles were ignored. Du Bois, intoxicated by the "New Spirit," asked readers to rely upon Negro businessmen and professionals, even if it meant paying a little more money for products and services.[33]

The *Crisis* editor believed white people prevented the Negro bourgeoisie from earning large incomes, and he concluded illogically that the colored middle class therefore devoted itself primarily to "social service" in order "to help the race." While white banks were subservient to Wall Street, Negro banks represented only "the attempt of Negro Americans to organize their own credit facilities."[34] Du Bois drew upon his Pan-African experiences and proposed a racial co-operative system which would encompass not only Negroes in the United States, but also those in the West Indies, Africa, and elsewhere. Since he announced the world would become socialistic, he thought his program would fit into the new order rather efficiently and provide a basis for inevitable integration of the races. Du Bois received very little support from the Negro bourgeoisie, not only because of the impracticality of a segregated "social service" economy, but because of the crucial factor which he underestimated, i.e., their desire for substantial personal profit. They accepted his message of race pride and were grateful to him for exhorting readers to buy from Negroes. However, they were primarily motivated by the same values as their white counterparts, and some members of the colored upper crust were not only surviving on race prejudice, but thriving upon it. And so the *Crisis* editor was left amid his contradiction of promulgating a socialized system while simultaneously glorifying advocates of private profit.

He tried to secure help from the Negro churches and proposed that the members co-operatively purchase coal, bread, meat, and even apartment houses and farms. His long years of tactlessness had never endeared him to Negro ministers and, when they did not ignore him, they were likely to condemn him. For example, in 1922 the *Crisis* editor was scheduled to deliver an address to the annual convention of the African Methodist Episcopal Church, and a group of clergymen "formed a conspiracy for the purpose of hooting down" the guest speaker. Under pressure, convention leaders withdrew the invitation.[35] Of course, many ministers were conservative and not very interested in seeking any economic solutions, but Du Bois' offensiveness denied him opportunities to receive much consideration for the co-operative program. Belatedly, he made efforts to conciliate the clergymen and in 1925 described the Negro church as "doing the greatest work in social uplift of any present agency." Stretching things, he claimed that, if it had not been for the work of various denominations, the N.A.A.C.P. and the *Crisis* could not have existed or survived.[36] In the era of the New Negro, pride demanded praise for all race institutions.

The artistic renaissance was probably the crowning glory of the Negro society which Du Bois sought to develop. White American culture was portrayed as effete and materialistic, but isolation motivated Negroes to encourage new artistic and creative "stirrings" within themselves. Such sentiments were not new, but during the postwar period he especially exhorted the race along these lines. While admitting Negro art "often lacks careful finish," he admired its honesty and hoped it would be supported within the race.[37] He regarded the *Crisis* as the Negroes' chief talent scout; he helped to sponsor contests and secure prizes for literary works. On *Crisis* covers, he proudly introduced Negro painters Richard Brown and Wilbur Scott; and he "helped to discover" Jesse Fauset the novelist and Langston Hughes the poet.[38] In 1922 Du Bois proposed an annual "Institute of Negro Literature and Art" for purposes of association, recognition, and mutual criticism.[39] The editor, angered that Roland Hayes received no offers to record serious music, announced the formation of a phonograph company dedicated to supporting Negro musical artists.[40] There is no evidence that either of these two projects came to fruition. He also defended "Negro drama" and declared that, in spite of the financial debacle of the Ethiopian Art Players in their Broadway venture during the early 1920's, the company was almost without equal.[41] Du Bois was one of the founders of the *Brownies' Book*, a magazine supposedly for all children, but "written from a Negro standpoint . . . to help foster a proper racial self-respect."[42] He hoped his young readers would eventually advance the Negro renaissance, but the *Brownies' Book* folded in 1922.

The renaissance was essentially directed by mulattoes, and the *Crisis* editor found it difficult to convince them to appreciate *blackness* as a standard of beauty. He was still deluged with protests when he commissioned paintings of darker Negroes for *Crisis* covers. After World War I, Du Bois seems to have placed even greater emphasis on racial endogamy, in order "to build a great black race tradition of which the Negro and the world will be as proud in the future as it has been in the ancient world." The *Messenger* accused Du Bois of rampant racism and on one occasion quoted him as saying, "God speed the breed." To this comment, Randolph and Owen added contemptuously, "God weed the breed." In 1926, while Du Bois demanded the right of racial intermarriage, he reaffirmed that Negro "self respect" should discourage such unions.[43]

It is, of course, very difficult to gauge Du Bois' influence in the artistic movement. He noted, "Practically every Negro author writing today found his first audience through the pages of the *Crisis*."[44] Horace Mann Bond has said, "There can be no denying the fact that most Negro literature of today owes its existence to [the *Crisis* editor's] pioneer work." Bond half-believed the literary movement, which was centered in New York, could be linked to Du Bois' residence there. Such reasoning was specious, but the observer was on stronger ground when he noted a "similarity in style and theme" between the editor's work and that of Negro novelists Jesse Fauset and Jean Toomer.[45] No Negro writer could help but have been stimulated by the *Crisis* editor's lyrical and plaintive pieces. Certainly, Du Bois overestimated his influence as a talent scout and motivator, but, if his magazine did not introduce many of the new writers, it did publish a sampling of their works and by its very existence encouraged them. There is no doubt that the journalist occupied the role of "Negro cultural statesman."[46] However, it is easy to fall into the trap of placing too much importance upon him as *the* great patron-inspirer of Negro arts.

The artistic strands of the New Negro movement, as well as its other aspects, owed much to the sociological influences which were mentioned earlier. Especially crucial was the practical aid of whites, some of whom regarded Negro art as a passing fancy, while others, like Amy Spingarn, were sincere and devoted admirers. In 1933 after the enthusiasm for Negro creative work collapsed, Du Bois recalled how essential white support had been, although his comments were extreme and inaccurate. While he was correct in saying that the artists and writers sought the favor of whites, he was unfair in declaring the movement "did not grow out of the inmost heart and frank experience of Negroes."[47] Such a position contradicted his earlier praise and only reflected his bitterness in perceiving that Negroes were turning their backs on his system of self-segregation. The renaissance foundered because white support waned and there were never enough interested educated Negroes to keep it going. Du Bois neglected to consider that his race was essentially in the lower educated, lower occupational group; such people (white or black) do not patronize serious music, literature, art, and drama.

Tirelessly, ceaselessly, the *Crisis* editor also presented the New Negro with reams of integrationist propaganda and counsel. These encompassed his efforts to achieve an interracial socialized society, interracial industrial unions, and his traditional activities in the political area.

Although Du Bois thought of himself as a Socialist, he continued to criticize the American Socialist party for racist tendencies. (However, there were some Socialists whom he admired, and among them was Eugene Debs.) The *Crisis* editor was still searching for "the right program of socialism," and, as already mentioned, he anticipated a socialized system in the United States and other countries, where the "public" would control business, industry, and income. Behind the hesitations in his theorizing lay the old ambivalent attitude toward white workers. He denied the "dogma" of the class struggle applied to his race, since white workers refused to regard Negroes as fellow members of the proletariat.[48] Chandler Owen was annoyed by this argument: "This is about as asinine as saying we are not human beings or men because in the South we are largely not so recognized. Is manhood dependent upon recognition? Is the proletariat a product of recognition or is it a state of economic position of human beings?"[49]

Du Bois always held the white workers partially responsible for restricting Negroes (nationally and internationally), but in the 1920's he assumed the "Masters of Industry" were more guilty. However, this partisan of "industrial democracy" recognized that his race had profited a great deal under the capitalist system during the war years, and he contended that union exclusion policies had forced Negro workers to be economically and ideologically dependent upon white capitalists.[50]

Heretically, he not only refused to overlook the conflict between white and Negro workers, but, as already shown, he also noted "widespread inter-class sympathy" within the Negro race, and only faint lines between capitalist and worker classes. He maintained that many black capitalists were essentially laborers and many Negro professionals rose from working class homes.[51] One *Crisis* reader was unable to perceive the intraracial "sympathy." She viewed the magazine as the intellectual support of the exploiting class and believed that it was "entirely too 'high brow' " for the working class. The critic complained that the stories and pictures of Negro bankers and businessmen served to strengthen the hold of the capitalist system by giving average Negroes "a certain vicarious satisfaction."[52] Although Du Bois talked of an orientation to the Negro "working classes," he was still seeking the "seldom sort" of *Crisis* reader at the start of the financial depression. Catering to the "aristocracy" of "brains and character," he announced that in coming issues he would feature such articles as "How I Came to Write 'The Green Pastures' " by Marc Connelly and "A Special Message to the American Negro" by the Indian poet, Rabindranath Tagore.

Du Bois was too much in agreement with the ideals of the labor movement to remain anything but a friendly critic. He understood that in spite of its racist leadership, it had improved working conditions of Negro and white laborers. In 1924 he suggested that the N.A.A.C.P., the A.F. of L., and the Railway Brotherhoods organize an interracial labor commission, which was to be essentially a propaganda agency aiming to create strong, integrated unions. Supposedly writing on behalf of the N.A.A.C.P., the *Crisis* editor dispatched an open letter to the annual convention of the American Federation of Labor, reminding the union that Negroes were forced to become strike breakers and were hurting themselves and the entire labor movement. But "the effect of this letter was nil" and the union traditions of exclusion remained rigid. Despite what Du Bois said, the N.A.A.C.P. executive committeemen were uncomfortable in their role of labor organizers and recommended that the promotion of unionism among Negroes "does not come exactly within the scope of the Association's activities."[53] Long before, the *Messenger* and the *Negro World* complained that the N.A.A.C.P. was administered by a "Capitalist Board," and, more recently, George Schuyler remarked that the "bourgeois . . . dilettante" N.A.A.C.P. was not really concerned about organizing the "deah workers."[54] There was more than a little truth in these comments, and, even though one of the Association's avowed aims for 1925 was "industrial democracy,"[55] it is doubtful that more than a few board members really supported a labor union orientation.

However, Du Bois would not give up the idea of the N.A.A.C.P. playing honest broker between the union movement and the Negroes. According to *The New York Times* of January, 1926, both the *Crisis* editor and James Weldon Johnson agreed that the Association "favors organization along conservative trade union lines." Du Bois exploited the fears of white workers, and undoubtedly many members of the N.A.A.C.P. board, and announced that unless there were integrated unions Negroes would be influenced by Communist organizations.[56] Aware he was getting nowhere, the *Crisis* editor condemned racist unions throughout the year. He blasted the barbers' union of Atlanta because members attempted to force Negroes out of the trade, and he added bitterly that William Green "loves the black man like his brother." Yet Du Bois kept trying and in 1928 suggested once more that newspapers and magazines should strive to teach Negro and white workers they had much in common as laborers. He declared both groups would profit if they understood the background of the labor movement. After the depression came he blasted the American Federation of Labor again.[57]

Du Bois wrongly attributed his own economic ideology to the N.A.A.C.P. and declared in 1930 that the Association stood for "increased democratic control of industry" and "cooperation and socialization of wealth." Possibly he was subtly attempting to force the board to redefine its economic position. In the fall of the year, the N.A.A.C.P. did condemn the exclusion policies of labor unions, but it said and did nothing to promote the "socialization of wealth."[58] A little later, Du Bois defended his organization again, but inconsistently argued that its aims were "limited," and "far beyond its program lies ... the economic emancipation of the working classes." After stating that the Association believed in a radical economic program and did not believe in one, he proceeded to lecture it on the necessity of adopting socialized measures. However, by 1931 and 1932, the N.A.A.C.P. was *speaking* in radical tones; its resolutions urged followers to vote as "workers" and "break up the power of corporate wealth." The organization talked of "the future conduct of industry for public weal and not for private profit."[59]

These resolutions were undoubtedly written by Du Bois and were possibly included to pacify him and his supporters. Although the depression was entering the third year, the N.A.A.C.P.'s economic policy was not very developed. The branches were instructed to gather employment statistics on the number of Negroes holding municipal and county jobs, and to bring pressure upon political leaders to assure the race a "fair share" of these positions and an equitable division of the unemployment relief funds. The branches were also asked to do something about increasing the number of jobs available to Negroes in stores located among the black ghettoes.[60]

From the foregoing, it was inevitable that Du Bois should have been sympathetic to the Soviet Union. In 1925, he termed it "the astounding effort which may yet show the world the Upward Path." (However, he still reaped the displeasure of the *Messenger* men, who were angered because he rejected methods of "revolution" and "violence.") The *Crisis* editor maintained that a socialized state should not come into existence through "murder," but should evolve slowly; during its planning and development, people should be carefully educated to accept it. Yet, only a few months earlier, he had called the Russian revolution "a marvelous set of phenomena," although he was cautious about the outcome of the new order.[61] In 1926 some Communists made it possible for him to visit Russia. He concluded the benefactors were secret Soviet agents. Before accepting money to make a fact-finding trip, Du Bois recalled that at his request they signed a statement acknowledging he was under no obligations to them. When he returned from the trip he was absolutely ecstatic: "I stand in astonishment and wonder at the revelation of Russia that has come to me. I may be particularly deceived and half informed. But if what I have seen with my eyes and heard with my ears in Russia is Bolshevism, I am a Bolshevik."[62]

Although he found the houses run-down and shabby, he assured *Crisis* readers that the workers received the best available accommodations. He observed laborers occupying key political positions, also great numbers of them attending the theaters and visiting the museums. In the United States the millionaire was idolized, while Du Bois declared that in Russia the worker was worshipped. He asserted the Communists also believed in cultural pluralism, with each ethnic group permitted to develop its own culture and achieve equal status. Apparently he found no race prejudice there: "In France I was looked at; in England I was regarded with some curiosity, while in Moscow if I happened to sit beside a white woman, no one seemed to notice me. Singular country this."[63]

Du Bois charged that powerful capitalists in other countries were bent on fomenting internal disorders in the Soviet Union, and he accused them of eschewing Russia as a trading partner. The *Crisis* editor also blamed American journalists for not telling the truth about the Communist regime.[64]

At the start of the depression in the 1930's, Du Bois re-examined his position on communism[65] and reaffirmed his support of Karl Marx's program of universal education, redistribution of income, and state industry, among other things. However, as the editor viewed it, Marx had adequately described mid-nineteenth century European society, but the system required substantial modifications for the United States of the twentieth century, especially in relation to Negroes. It seemed to Du Bois that American Communists were slaves to doctrinaire Marxism, and they possessed only a superficial comprehension of race prejudice. He admitted capitalism created economic problems, but he charged American Communists with a failure to recognize that race prejudice, besides being a product of economic exploitation, was also a comprehensive problem in itself.

Revising his earlier view, the *Crisis* editor held white workers responsible for most of the suppressive political and economic measures taken against Negroes. In the depression of the 1930's, he maintained that a sizeable proportion of the white workers constituted a "petty bourgeoisie," while the rest of the laborers upheld the capitalist system because of a belief in social mobility. He could see no proletariat revolution on the "American far horizon." Using many of the same arguments against the Communists as he had employed against the Socialists during the previous decade, Du Bois denied there was a class-mass conflict within the Negro race. However, on this point, he seemed more ambivalent in the later period. While considering the caste system prevented the development of true economic classes, he also acknowledged Negroes were beginning to form their own "petty bourgeois" class. He asserted the race leadership was not dominated by "purely capitalistic ideas," but inconsistently he admitted that Negro business-professional groups possessed capitalistic attitudes. Du Bois agreed that when the opportunity presented itself, these groups were capable of exploitation.

The *Crisis* editor also distrusted the motives of American Communists and doubted they would promulgate integration as their goal if they ever achieved popularity with white workers. Du Bois thought Communists wanted to use Negroes only as "shock troops." In the Scottsboro case (1931), he and the N.A.A.C.P. accused the Communists of plotting to bring about the execution of the defendants for the purpose of furthering the Red cause. The *Crisis* editor tried "to blunt the wedge which the Communist Party is driving into our [Negro] group," and advised his people that, "in the case of the Communists, there is acute danger . . . the Negro vote will be deliberately sacrificed to ulterior purposes." The Eighth American Communist Party Convention struck back and Du Bois was denounced as one of the "chief social supports of imperialist reaction."[66]

At the same time he was attempting to open radical and labor union doors for Negroes, Du Bois continued to try the political portal to integration. Just after World War I, he remarked that voting represented "the greatest Negro problem. . . . Everything else is secondary." He assumed that "industrial democracy" could still be obtained through organized political action. Before the national conventions of 1920 he sent questionnaires to all who were mentioned as possible candidates and asked them to state their position on solving the Negro problem. The irresistible dream of a balance of power ran through his brain again and he predicted a Negro electorate of one million which was open to the highest bidder. The *Crisis* editor still saw little value in voting for the Democrats, since the South "neutralized" the policies of the more liberal Northern wing. However, he served notice that Negroes might place themselves in the Democratic column, because in his opinion Republicans embodied "reaction and privilege" and conspired with the South.

Du Bois anticipated a "large Negro radical vote" because of the sympathetic statements from Socialist and Farmer-Labor party headquarters, but by September he asked readers to ignore these groups since neither had a chance to win. It was the old, old story: recognizing that the race was "in a difficult position," he reluctantly suggested that either Cox or Harding should receive Negro votes in order not to create antagonism and additional disabilities. He was essentially concerned about rewarding sympathetic congressional candidates.[67] The *Messenger* editors were seething because Du Bois turned his back on the Socialists again, and, like the critics of earlier years, Chandler Owen and A. Philip Randolph considered it ridiculous to vote for the "enemy" because the candidate would win anyway. They did not think that Negro support would make the major parties friendlier.[68]

After the election, Du Bois called the entire affair an "unreal campaign"; talk of political independence became an admitted pipe dream, since Negroes had to defeat the Democrats in view of Cox's alleged racism and Wilson's deceit. But the *Crisis* editor, of course, could not believe the Republicans were much different. However, the following month, the resilient Du Bois saw a "political rebirth" since thirteen Negroes had been elected to state legislatures in the North, and many more held posts as councilmen in various cities. He predicted members of his race would win congressional seats in Illinois, Missouri, Pennsylvania, and New York within a few years.[69]

Throughout 1921, aside from Harding's denunciation of lynching, Du Bois found little to praise. When the President was considering William Howard Taft for the Supreme Court, the *Crisis* editor observed, "Mr. Taft is not an enemy of the race, he is worse than that; he is a luke-warm friend whom enemies of the race have used and will use to its hurt." The journalist cautioned that the anti-lynching bill was not being pushed very hard; the White House made few Negro appointments while several lily whites were given jobs. Harding, in a Birmingham speech, declared that the Negro should be encouraged, educated, and given the ballot; but Du Bois was disturbed when the President spoke of preserving "natural segregations." In January, 1922, the *Crisis* charged Harding was attempting to organize his own lily-white movement and was inviting Negroes to leave the Republican party.[70]

In preparation for the coming congressional elections, Du Bois asked readers to watch closely how members of the House of Representatives stood on the Dyer Anti-Lynching Bill, which was soon to come up for a vote. He warned if the bill (part of the Republican platform) were not enacted by the Republican-controlled Congress, Negroes who voted for the party placed themselves in the "gullible fool" category. Utterly desperate, he dusted off the old advice favoring a third party. In January of 1923, after the Dyer Bill was defeated, the *Crisis* editor called for the convening of a "National Political Congress" of Negroes. However Du Bois, writing for the *New Republic*, contended that no third party had a political future in the United States unless it was racist and curried favor with Northern and Southern oligarchic interests. His remark reflected not only hopelessness about a Negro party but also lack of faith in the Farmer-Labor and Socialist organizations.[71] Socialists charged that Du Bois was "contemptible" and they professed sympathy for Negroes. Since the *Crisis* was supposed to be "A Record of the Darker Races," one critic asked why the editor neglected stories about Negro Socialists such as George Frazier Miller, whom the party nominated in 1918 as one of its congressional candidates, or, A. Philip Randolph, who was nominated in 1920 for the office of New York State Controller.[72]

During the early stages of the 1924 presidential campaign, Du Bois gave his standard advice: ignore presidential candidates and concentrate on those men who were running for Congress and the state legislatures. The N.A.A.C.P. took the same position after composing a recital of charges against the Republicans (the Dyer Bill debacle, the failure to end segregation in federal government offices, the refusal to terminate the practice of segregating Negroes on interstate railroad lines, and the denial of the loan to Liberia). The Association longed for a "vigorous third party."[73] Late summer found the *Crisis* editor charging La Follette's Progressive party with "deliberately dodging" a forthright position on the Negro problem and the Ku Klux Klan. By October he publicly endorsed the Progressives and even wrote campaign literature for them. At that time he said he was satisfied that La Follette had condemned the Klan and opposed racial discrimination. However, in the November issue of the *Crisis* he still possessed reservations about the Progressive candidate, but there was no other road to take: "While I wish that the anti-Negro Railway Brotherhood who are supporting La Follette would let him say a plainer, cleaner word on the Negro, I remember that he has said as much as

Coolidge and could scarcely do less if elected president."[74]

After the election, Du Bois estimated an electorate of two million Negroes—one-half voting Republican, one-quarter Progressive, and one-quarter Democratic. The fact that the N.A.A.C.P. officers divided their votes among the various parties also emphasized the frustration and confusion in determining a political choice.

Speaking before the National Inter-racial Conference in 1928, Du Bois reaffirmed his faith in the efficacy of the ballot as a permanent but slow means to end the caste system. The *Crisis* editor thought he was on the right track and recalled that, even though the Dyer Bill failed in the Senate, the House of Representatives approved it. Once more he stressed the desirability of inter-racial unity in the working class; *but only political power could insure economic gains.*[75] As chairman of the N.A.A.C.P. committee to write the 1928 "Address," he maintained the civil libertarian emphasis, while saying little about the economic role the race was forced to play. The important point here is that although he seemed to certify the traditional N.A.A.C.P. approach, *Crisis* editorials about politics disclosed mounting disappointment and cynicism. In 1928 he could not accept Herbert Hoover as a candidate because the editor associated him with the Haitian occupation, lily whites, "big business and the Solid South." He rejected Al Smith on almost the same basis. He defined a political campaign as "an organized effort to stop discussion by the use of money or promise of profit. Money is used for bribes and propaganda." He suggested Negroes cast their ballots for Norman Thomas as a "moral protest." (The Socialist platform mentioned that oligarchic control was perpetuated by denying suffrage to Negroes.) But Du Bois predicted only failure for a third party in the United States.[76]

While neither of the two major candidates made serious public overtures to woo Negroes, the journalist noted secret attempts by politicians to buy colored votes. He was even less enthusiastic than previously in focusing attention on the congressional campaign, and recorded that, while it required something like eighty-five or ninety thousand votes to elect a congressman from California or Ohio, an average of less than ten thousand was needed to elect one in the South.[77] After the election he reported "democracy" definitely lost ground. In the South the Negro was disfranchised and the oligarchy ruled supreme over Negro and white poverty. He considered that problems such as income distribution, corporate control, and the future of unionism had been ignored in the campaign, and he confessed serious error in his early postwar predictions of an increasingly democratic United States. The 1928 campaign was described as "the most humiliating" one the Negro ever experienced. In the last phase, after weeks of racist propaganda, a group of Negro leaders—headed by Robert R. Moton; C. C. Spaulding, president of the North Carolina Mutual Insurance Company; and Du Bois—jointly issued "An Appeal to America" charging that the high command of both parties acted as if it were a "crime" to be a Negro.[78]

Although only a few months before, the *Crisis* editor underscored the fruitlessness of the third party path, he frustratedly returned to the idea when the election was over. He was now ready to believe a third party could be a national success because all the "politically homeless" groups (women, organized labor, pacifists, liberals, farmers, and Negroes) could unite. He also felt heartened by the demonstration of a "union of opinion" among the prominent Negroes who signed the "Appeal."[79] Obviously, the disturbed and harassed journalist was not thinking clearly. There was no evidence, for instance, that American women conceived of themselves as politically homeless, and there was no indication that they or the other groups seriously considered leaving the two major parties and allying with the Negroes, assuming even the colored people would pursue a third party course. And the Negro leaders' protest to the Republicans and Democrats should have given Du Bois no reason to conclude that these men were sympathetic to the political adventure he suggested.

In 1929, Du Bois, the-off-again-on-again Socialist, turned his back on the party once more and counseled Negroes to "become opportunist in politics." Although he called Norman Thomas the best man in the New York City mayoralty campaign, he withheld support because of the desire to pick a winner. The *Crisis* editor became a member of the Colored Citizens Non-Partisan Committee which favored James Walker, who had bestowed political jobs upon the race.[80] (The Committee's mathematician even totaled the Negro payroll in 1929 and came up with the figure of $3,852,375. This statistic was a symbol of Du Bois' disillusionment, for he had always repudiated Negro politicians who were concerned only with patronage.) However, the *Crisis* editor rationalized his behavior by claiming that since the race received so little from political participation, it had better pick up a few jobs.[81] He was also forced to back Illinois Congressman Oscar DePriest, even though Du Bois thought that this Negro politician did not stand for "clean politics." As early as the *Philadelphia Negro* in 1899, he described this dilemma: the reformers outside of the South ignored Negroes while political machines did not; colored people, possessing no other alternative, were cogs in the political machines.

In the 1932 national election, the *Crisis* editor repudiated Herbert Hoover again but did not ask readers to support the Democrats; however, after President Roosevelt was in office for several months, the journalist praised him for condemning lynching and demonstrating a desire "to talk to Haitians as men."[82]

Actually, by the end of the 1920's Du Bois had become completely disenchanted with politics; he was more convinced than ever that republican government was impotent because most

Americans were in "economic slavery." Retrospectively, he credited the trip to Russia with awakening him to a realization that his political emphasis "was justified only in part," and that an economically insecure group was illiterate, sick, criminal, and politically deadened.[83] As frequently indicated in this volume, he had always been interested in economic and political cures and struggled with both simultaneously. After World War I he expended a great deal more energy on economic solutions than previously, but the financial depression of 1929 was responsible for his preoccupation with the subject.

It is necessary to evaluate Du Bois' influence as a political theorist during the fifteen years after the close of the first World War. In 1925 Horace Mann Bond asserted that Negroes were following the *Crisis* editor's blueprint; they were no longer slaves of the Republican party and demanded that political leaders of both parties compete for the race's votes: "Not as an active leader, but as a consistent agitator for political activity of the bloc character, there can be no doubt but that his views have profoundly influenced the course of events, and that his writings first gave impetus to the movement which has gained so much headway in recent years."[84]

Bond did not recognize that the attempt to make the Negroes politically fluid was no great success. Gunnar Myrdal noted, "Before 1933, Negroes voted the Republican ticket in over-whelming proportion."[85] When they finally left the fold in 1932 and, especially in 1936, they did so not because of what Du Bois had said, but because of the New Deal program and the charismatic personalities of Mr. and Mrs. Franklin D. Roosevelt.

Certainly Du Bois' writings constituted a factor in persuading some members of his race to desert the Republicans, but he cannot take much credit for those who voted the national Democratic ticket, since he eschewed that political organization. (In local campaigns however he did praise "Northern Liberal Democrats.")

Furthermore, it is questionable that his confusing and conflicting advice led many into the embrace of the Progressives and Socialists. It should also be remembered that in addition to Du Bois, the N.A.A.C.P. also tried to transform educated Negroes into political independents. And there were other influences involved, including migration and the friendliness of some Northern Democratic candidates. Of course, the *Crisis* editor had often spoken about his dream of the Negro race holding the balance of power in American politics, but such sentiments had also been expressed long before by other Negro leaders, such as Frederick Douglass and Norris Wright Cuney. Maurice R. Davie has said the dream came true "in at least a dozen great Northern states,"[86] but the realization occurred during the Roosevelt administration, many years after Du Bois became a memory in the field of Negro leadership. While no one should wish to underestimate the Negro editor's influence in political affairs, there is danger in yielding to the temptation of overestimating it. Sociological forces were primarily responsible when some of the political changes for which he had long hoped finally came about.

Du Bois' ideological contributions during the postwar years constitute only part of his story; perhaps a more fascinating aspect concerns his relations with the N.A.A.C.P. Throughout this period, in the minds of many Negroes and whites, his name was synonymous with that of the Association. After all, he was one of its founders and was editor of the official magazine. On innumerable occasions he defended the work of the organization and identified himself with it, and at annual conferences he took a bow as an old, brilliant, and level-headed Association spokesman. He was the oracle of the race and not one of its "irrational extremists or ... fire-brands." As an N.A.A.C.P. protector he declared in 1921, "It is foolish for us to give up this practical program."[87] He defended the board against charges of being "undemocratic" and announced that all N.A.A.C.P. members received "a full and effective voice in the conduct of the organization."[88] The *Crisis* editor maintained that all possessed the right to nominate and elect the board at annual meetings, and "this is the method pursued by practically every organization which is permanently effective." In the last years of the decade, he sometimes thought white Americans—especially those in the South—were redefining their attitudes toward Negroes, and he gave the N.A.A.C.P. a large share of the credit for this change.[89] It has already been mentioned that at the start of the depression, he took the side of the Association in the verbal battle with the Communists.

Only infrequently did he publicize his differences with the organization leadership. In 1920, distrusting the white board members, he told readers that Negroes must control the Association, presumably because they knew what was best for the race. To buttress his point about Negro domination he played havoc with the facts and argued that Negroes had always initiated and controlled N.A.A.C.P. policy.[90] Of course, Du Bois did not get along with Negro board members any better than he did with most of the whites. His troubles with the N.A.A.C.P. board were essentially financial and ideological. During the 1920's the circulation of the *Crisis* toppled. In 1919 the magazine sold about 95,000 copies a month, in 1920 less than 65,000, and in 1930, something under 30,000.[91] Around 1921 he blamed his difficulties on a "general financial depression" in the country, a postwar "spiritual reaction," and an upsurge of radicalism. Later, he suggested that the increase in subscription rates, necessitated by higher production costs, had hurt the magazine's circulation.[92] During 1925 and 1926, *Crisis* losses were averaging about two thousand dollars a year.[93]

The editor attempted to rationalize his position and pointed out "the aim of the *Crisis* is not to make a profit." There were those who thought the magazine was expendable, and Du Bois retorted that the organ was necessary to the expansion of the N.A.A.C.P. Claiming to be a pioneer in the systematic gathering of news, pictures, and features about Negroes, he tried to convince the Association that a magazine of uncompromising honesty was a precious commodity in the 1920's. It almost seems that, as the circulation plummeted, his claims soared: "When the *Crisis* has thundered the truth it is no idle boast to say that thieves have gone to jail, imposters have disappeared, colleges have reorganized, governments have stood at attention and Klans have hurried to cover."[94]

The enterprise lost $4,422.96 in 1928.[95]

The *Crisis* was in a sense putting itself out of business because over the years its protest ideology had become accepted by Negroes, who turned to the flamboyant race press for local accounts of themselves and their struggles. These newspapers carried stories of sports, crime, and sex, in addition to news of the N.A.A.C.P., which employed a professional newsman to run its own press service. In the early years the *Crisis* had been a news magazine, but, modifying its format when Negro newspapers became more prominent, it gave greater attention to semi-serious articles. Such a policy may have been necessary and even desirable, but not enough educated Negroes wanted to support it. The *Crisis* might not have lost money if Du Bois had been content with making it more decidedly the house organ of the N.A.A.C.P., and if he had devoted more space to Association news and the activities of the branches. But the editor was not interested; he preferred "to blaze a trail" and perform "a work of education and ideal beyond the practical steps of the N.A.A.C.P."[96] The minutes of the board reveal a steady concern about the plight of the *Crisis*. In 1926, one member demanded that the magazine cater to a mass audience; two years later, the leadership of the

District of Columbia branch blamed Du Bois for the drop in reader interest.[97] In April, 1929, the board held a special meeting to discuss the financial problems of the publication, and the editor announced he might be able to operate without further debts if he received $5,000. However, in the next breath, he noted the *Crisis* might require an equal sum annually for an unstated period.

His request gained little sympathy from N.A.A.C.P. acting secretary, Walter White, who maintained that the organization could not afford to subsidize the publication. The board adjourned and agreed to study the matter carefully; by November, Du Bois, after several sessions with the *Crisis* finance committee, instructed the board that $10,000 was required in order to adjust to "postwar conditions." Association leaders suggested he seek the money from philanthropic foundations and other sources which were not regular N.A.A.C.P. contributors.[98] The *Crisis* income in 1929 was down $2,300 from the preceding year; during 1929 and 1930, the Association gave the ailing magazine nearly $5,000 from the general fund. Du Bois asserted repeatedly that the *Crisis* was not a business but an institution which should not be expected to pay its own way. Aware there was an increase in the number of board members who thought the magazine outlived its usefulness, Du Bois proclaimed again and again that the *Crisis* had played the major role in creating acceptance among Negroes of the race equality doctrine.[99]

His disagreements with Walter White increased as the magazine's losses increased. White was conscious that N.A.A.C.P. income had also dropped during the depression and he maintained that the Association's limited resources should be spent on anti-lynching campaigns, court cases, and legislative lobbying. He viewed the *Crisis* as the organization's tail, while Du Bois regarded it as "the only work" in the N.A.A.C.P. which attracted him. Apparently, the clash between Du Bois and White became so acute that in 1929 Joel Spingarn introduced a motion reminding everyone that the acting secretary was the executive officer, and all employees "shall be subject to his authority." If Spingarn thought the action would somehow create tranquillity, he was much mistaken; the *Crisis* editor demanded that the resolution be rescinded, and it was —over a year later.[100] In April, 1930, Joel Spingarn received a letter from Du Bois, who wished to know what plans the board members were making for the *Crisis*. The Negro journalist considered himself "in an impossible position" after James Weldon Johnson resigned and Walter White received greater powers. Du Bois rebelled at White's membership on the *Crisis* editorial board and threatened to resign if a change were not made. The editor's victory was meager, since the replacement was Roy Wilkins, whom he regarded as White's alter ego.

Between 1930 and 1931, the magazine lost another four thousand dollars and the N.A.A.C.P. was paying Du Bois' salary. He requested the continuation of this arrangement for at least another year,[101] but some people, such as Oswald G. Villard, seriously questioned whether the publication would be alive by then.[102] At the end of 1932, the Crisis Publishing Company was organized as a legal maneuver "to limit the liability of the N.A.A.C.P. for the future debts" of the organ. With this move the Association agreed to assume the outstanding financial obligations of the *Crisis*, and Walter White was made one of the directors of the new company. In an effort to save face, Du Bois reminded the organization that 9,244,979 copies of the magazine had been distributed from 1910 to 1932. While he acknowledged receiving nearly $20,000 from the N.A.A.C.P., he argued that an equal sum was returned in the form of commissions on subscriptions handled by the branches. However, no words could change the fact that, in the preceding twelve months, the *Crisis* suffered an "operated loss" of $2,628.74, even though the editor's entire salary was paid by the Association, which contributed nearly $5,000 "toward operating expenses."[103]

Du Bois was considered by many of the board members as an ideological burden as well as a financial one. It has already been mentioned that the board did not back the Pan-African project and disapproved of all the time he devoted to it.[104] For example, the members were displeased by his five months' absence in 1923–24. His aggressive Socialist-labor orientation annoyed many Association leaders, and he was indirectly reprimanded by the executive committee in 1924. During the summer of that year, the editor was again reminded that the *Crisis* was owned by the N.A.A.C.P., and he would have to make sure his policies did not seriously deviate from those of the Association. The board wanted Du Bois to meet monthly with the executive committee, clear all controversial editorials and articles with the *Crisis* committee at least several days before press time, and participate in "detailed" meetings with the committee four times a year.[105] Four years later, the leadership of the District of Columbia branch accused him of possessing too much control over the *Crisis*.[106] This charge, of course, was hurled at him almost from the beginning of his career as editor of the magazine. The board minutes do not indicate that prior to 1934, Du Bois was censured for editorials on behalf of the segregated economy, although some members certainly disapproved of the subject.

At a 1931 board meeting, the *Crisis* editor attempted to limit the power of the N.A.A.C.P. board and asked for a "larger element of democratic control" in the Association. He thought the general membership should have a greater voice in making new appointments to the board. The request was a contradiction of his long-standing statement that the organization's procedures were democratic. Conditions had changed, however, and now he hoped to pack the board with younger members who would be in agreement with his ideas.[107] Since he was ignored, he took his case to the public in 1932 and recommended that the power of the N.A.A.C.P. be diffused, with less emphasis placed upon the New York headquarters. The New York office was to function as a "clearing house" for the proposals of the branches, especially the suggestions presented by members of the "working class."[108] By 1933 Du Bois decided his financial, organizational, and ideological battles with the N.A.A.C.P. were unendurable, and he recommended that the *Crisis* suspend its operations.

11. Exit From N.A.A.C.P.

The *Crisis* did not die, but Du Bois took a leave of absence and accepted a professorship at Atlanta University. Joel Spingarn was also disappointed with the N.A.A.C.P.'s lack of vigor during the early years of the depression. In his search for a new path he asked for the assistance of younger Negro intellectuals and sponsored the second Amenia Conference.[1] Du Bois, who became chairman of the Amenia organizing committee, asked prominent Negroes to suggest names of possible conferees. It is not known how much co-operation Walter White gave, but, according to rumor, he "was not particularly keen" on the conference. He denied it.[2] From August 18 to August 21, 1933, over thirty Negro lawyers, social workers, and college professors met at the summer estate of Spingarn in New York. Some of the conferees later made names for themselves. Among them were Dr. Ira De A. Reid, chairman of the Sociology Department, Haverford College, and Dr. Ralph Bunche, undersecretary, United Nations.

Both Du Bois and Spingarn gave assurances that N.A.A.C.P. officers would not interfere with the discussions or even suggest any agenda. Above all, no conferee was required to subscribe to the N.A.A.C.P. program. Du Bois, White, Johnson, Spingarn, Miss Ovington, and other Association leaders were invited to attend as observers. Now and then, the participants called upon some of the "older generation" for information, and one of the young men wrote of Du Bois' contribution to the conclave: "The amazing number of facts he knows, and the skill and facility with which he shared them with the conference made Dr. Du Bois the undisputed leader, even though he held himself carefully in the background and came to the fore only when invited and when he was the only man who could 'do the job.' "[3]

Spingarn was hopeful that the conferees would favor a close tie with the labor movement and he believed that the Negroes' salvation lay in "influencing" the policies of the Roosevelt administration. (Henry Morgenthau, Jr. was asked to address the group.) Among the participants themselves, there was a wide difference of opinion; Some were overt revolutionaries while other men were conservatives or union supporters. Many vigorously condemned the approaches of Johnson, White, and Du Bois; for example, Dr. Ralph Bunche recalled the spirited opposition when Du Bois attempted to gain support for the segregated economy theory.[4] Most of the young intellectuals concluded that Negro organizations, especially the N.A.A.C.P., were "short-sighted and inadequate."

At sixty-five, the old *Crisis* editor felt the sting of being shoved aside by the young men who ignored or condemned his separatist concept. Showing his age, he wrote a piece for the magazine criticizing the deportment of the incorrigible conferees:

> There was on the part of a few a certain, not unexpected, but nevertheless startling lack of self-discipline. It has always been interesting to me to see how young people in many countries organized their government and discipline and enforced it with a certain ruthlessness. But here out of twenty-six, five did as they pleased with regard to noise, sleep and enjoyment with utter disregard of the perfectly evident desires of the rest, and to cap the climax, the rest uttered no protest. I have seen evidence of this sort of thing among young colored people elsewhere. It is for us and the race a new and pressing problem.[5]

The delegates were primarily concerned about economic problems and argued that the Negro was essentially a laborer who should identify himself with the white worker; they suggested the formation of a new interracial labor organization composed of skilled and unskilled workers. The "educated" Negroes were given the "primary responsibility" for creating the rapprochement with the whites. The Talented Tenth was advised to surrender any thought of "artificial class differences" and unite with the Negro masses in order to make these interracial overtures more effective. Although Miss Ovington observed a "leaning toward communism," the Amenia resolutions repudiated both communism and fascism.[6]

Just after the conclave ended, Du Bois bravely wrote to Joel Spingarn and noted that, although the results were not "tremendous," the affair might in time be considered as "epoch-making" as the first Amenia Conference. The old leader was accurate in his estimate when one recalls the insignificance of the 1916 assemblage. The young intellectuals of 1933 had passed many resolutions, but they made no attempts to implement them, nor to establish a grass-roots organization. The N.A.A.C.P. subscribed to these resolutions only for propaganda purposes, and the conferees, although they regarded themselves as race spokesmen, were largely isolated from the Negro masses. The conclave demonstrated that Du Bois was standing alone, and some of the participants believed he "was apparently ready to lay his burden down much to the satisfaction of White and Spingarn."[7] But the *Crisis* editor planned to make a fight of it and decided to challenge N.A.A.C.P. board members. Unfortunately for him, the period in which he chose to declare his absolute independence was also the one in which he was most heavily dependent financially.

In late 1933, Du Bois demanded that George Streator and Roy Wilkins (who were directing *Crisis* affairs during the editor's absence) consider themselves under his "general supervision." In December he was absolutely infuriated when N.A.A.C.P. leaders appointed Wilkins to the board of the Crisis Publishing Company;

the old editor found the situation intolerable, not only because White was already a member of that board, but also because Wilkins would now have double-edged powers. By this time there were rumors that the Association was going to discharge Du Bois, and a committee of admirers was formed to demand his retention. The group publicly charged "certain persons acting under the direction of [N.A.A.C.P.] officers" initiated "a most cowardly program of character assault" against the journalist. The N.A.A.C.P. stated it had not any intention of firing its long-time employee and that he was still the official head of the *Crisis*. However, Du Bois repudiated the assertion and informed his supporters that the N.A.A.C.P. board, "without consultation with me," gave Wilkins and Streator "sole and exclusive control" of the magazine. As Du Bois viewed it, Walter White was now virtually the king of the *Crisis*, and the maneuver to place Wilkins on the *Crisis* board along with the executive secretary

> was an action characteristic of a steadily increasing tendency in the N.A.A.C.P. to make the Negro race and its friends in America responsible for the decisions of small committees, and even individual officials of the N.A.A.C.P. who cannot be made answerable to any representative body of opinion. This action, therefore, confirms me in a feeling long growing in my mind that the N.A.A.C.P. needs fundamental and complete reorganization from top to bottom.[8]

Although earlier he had denied that white people made the organization's policy, in 1934 he recommended that Negroes should replace whites as determiners of their own destiny. His counterattack thus became the overture for his own bid to gain control of the N.A.A.C.P. In a February letter to his committee of supporters Du Bois wrote: "I am ready to unite with any persons who think as I do in a determined effort to rescue this great organization and to prepare it for a new and worthy future."

Certainly he possessed a right to an opinion, but his admirers dispatched the letter to the Negro press; it is not known whether he authorized its publication, but in all probability he did. Obviously, the publicizing of this document created an impossible situation.

In a confidential note to James Weldon Johnson, Walter White defended himself: "It is somewhat disheartening when we have cut our force and salaries, gone practically without literature, which has hurt the Association, to pay over to the *Crisis* during the last four years more than thirty thousand dollars from the funds of the Association and then on top of this to be accused of trying to 'oust' him."[9]

The Baltimore *Afro-American* criticized Du Bois for demanding a reorganization of the N.A.A.C.P. board and recalled that the Negro leader worked with the "same type" of associates without complaint for nearly a quarter of a century. The old editor's opponents concluded he was being testy simply because he lost some of his power over the *Crisis*. So far as the newspaper was concerned, the financially-bankrupt magazine belonged in younger hands and Du Bois was invited to "retire."[10]

Frustrated by the economic and organizational problems of the depression, Du Bois made his exit from the N.A.A.C.P. certain by heralding the old segregated economy plan as the only method to ultimately free the race. In the *Crisis* he attacked the integrationists and used the same logic against them which critics had always employed against him: "Never in the world should our fight be against association within ourselves because by that very token we give up the whole argument that we are worth associating with." He tried to show *Crisis* readers that his philosophy did not contradict N.A.A.C.P. teachings. As he argued the case, the Association had never considered the question of segregation abstractly but at times opposed it in various court hearings. Du Bois contended that the organization acquiesced to segregation when its leaders believed there were no other satisfactory alternatives, e.g., the World War I officers training camp, separate schools in the South. But even he was compelled to agree that the N.A.A.C.P. regarded such actions as "a necessary evil." Nevertheless, he asserted, "That race pride and race loyalty, Negro ideals and Negro unity have a place and function today, the N.A.A.C.P. never has denied and never can deny!" The *Crisis* editor announced he would spend the year of 1934 discussing the pros and cons of self-segregation and invited readers to contribute their opinions.[11]

The following issue carried a reply from Joel Spingarn, who claimed that although the N.A.A.C.P. had not repudiated segregation abstractly, it had "always been squarely opposed to" it. The Association maintained that segregation—even voluntary segregation—implied a form of discrimination. The chairman asked the organization's members to reconsider the concept of racial separation and determine whether they wished the N.A.A.C.P. to redefine its own attitudes on the subject. In other words, should segregation be viewed as an evil never to be compromised with, as a necessary evil, or as a social process which would really elevate the race? Spingarn left no doubt where he stood.[12]

The chairman's remarks would have been more impressive if there had been some indication that Du Bois was censured by the Association in previous years for the many editorials on behalf of voluntary segregation. But even if the organization never condemned the *Crisis* editor for these opinions, there was ample evidence demonstrating that over the years the N.A.A.C.P. opposed separation based on race. In 1918 it stated that the lessons of history proved segregation always meant inequality. One of the Association's announced objectives was the "ending of segregation of all sorts based on race and color." Certainly, many Negroes, such as Robert R. Moton, interpreted the N.A.A.C.P. as repudiating "separation of any kind, legal or voluntary."[13]

By April of 1934, it was completely evident that Du Bois was ready to burn the rest of his bridges at the N.A.A.C.P. and he produced the following editorial retort:

> If as Spingarn asserts, the N.A.A.C.P. has conducted a quarter century campaign against segregation, the net result has been a little less than nothing. We have by legal action steadied the foundation so that in the future, segregation must be by wish and will and not by law. But beyond that we have not made the slightest impress on the determination of the overwhelming mass of white Americans not to treat Negroes as men.

He attacked Walter White, who opposed the segregated economy doctrine, and called him more of a white man than a Negro:

> He has more white companions and friends than colored. He goes where he will in New York City and naturally meets no Color Line, for the simple and sufficient reason that he isn't "colored"; he feels his new freedom in bitter contrast to what he was born to in Georgia. This is perfectly natural and he does what anyone else of his complexion would do. But it is fantastic to assume that this has anything to do with the color problem in the United States. It naturally makes Mr. White an extreme opponent of any segregation based on a myth of race.[14]

Although Walter White stated that the *Crisis* should not be censored (he seemed to have forgotten about the *Crisis* editorial board), he concluded that Du Bois' self-segregation articles had been harmful because they were interpreted by some people as official N.A.A.C.P. doctrine. According to him, federal officials, using the editor's comments, were refusing to admit Negroes to a relief project. (White contended integration was especially imperative in government-sponsored programs.) On the other hand, Du

Bois maintained that Negroes would not be accepted in American "subsistence homestead colonies" on equal terms—therefore, colored people should request separate "colonies" and become their own leaders. He warned his colleagues not to acquiesce in a spurious equality, i.e., "submitting to discrimination simply because it does not involve actual or open segregation."[15]

During these months a large section of the Negro press condemned the *Crisis* editor. George Schuyler, of the Pittsburgh *Courier*, criticized Du Bois for implying Walter White was a white man, and the newspaper columnist commented that the remark was redolent of Marcus Garvey: "Imagine the Top Sergeant of the Talented Tenth fouling like a punch drunk pugilist despairing of victory by fair means!"[16]

He reminded readers that previously Du Bois always adopted the whites' racial definition, i.e., one who possesses any Negro "blood" is a Negro. Therefore in the past, the *Crisis* editor opened Negro gates to many prominent light-skinned people such as Alexander Dumas and even Alexander Hamilton. Ironically, Schuyler noted that if Walter White were truly Caucasian, the N.A.A.C.P. executive secretary would be joined by A. Clayton Powell, Mordecai Johnson, John Hope, and thousands of others. The *Courier* writer stated there was nothing wrong with Negroes who were friendly with whites, since whites represented the "salvation" of colored people. Schuyler was one of the few newsmen who understood that Du Bois' segregation position was an old one.

Joseph V. Baker, a columnist for the Philadelphia *Tribune*, wondered if the *Crisis* editor, who "holds no brief for white people," decided to join the "conservatives." The *Tribune* asked, "Is Du Bois slipping?" The newspaper pointed out that the N.A.A.C.P. historically fought for integration, and, even though Du Bois declared his opinions were not the official ones of the

Association, the general public was unable to make the distinction: "The Editor of an official organ must agree with the policies of his organization if there is to be effective work. Because of his former efforts in a glorious cause he should be permitted to resign. But if he refuses he should be fired because all of the honor and glory which are his turn to bitter gall."[17]

Du Bois sought to buttress his position in a Chicago speech, but hardly anyone was listening, and the Chicago *Defender* mourned the passing of a "Race Champion." One reporter intoned: "From his Sunday's speech, Hope no longer sees a star; he admitted defeat and admonished his hearers that he would no longer contend for race equality; that his fight had been a failure, and from now on, as to all things racial, he would travel the path of least resistance. It was a sad Sunday."[18]

Someone in the audience reminded Du Bois about the years spent in the fight against Booker T. Washington's program of separation, and the *Crisis* editor replied: "My opposition to Dr. Washington was not on his program of separation for Colored people, but based upon the fact that he taught Colored children to use certain tools which were almost always obsolete by the time they had finished their courses."

Of course, Du Bois was misrepresenting the whole purpose of the Niagara Movement—which was integrationist. While many critics professed to see no difference between the Washingtonian and Du Boisian positions, the Chicago *Defender* went one step further and argued that, if the Tuskegeean were living in 1934, he would have advocated "a more militant" policy than that of Du Bois.[19]

A Chicago N.A.A.C.P. leader also demanded the *Crisis* editor's resignation. He maintained that Du Bois was no longer accepted by "his white folks" as "the Negro superman" and was therefore being spiteful. Another critic diagnosed the old editor as "a neurotic personality." However, Du Bois still retained some supporters. One produced an article for the Philadelphia *Tribune*, in which the "defeatists" were admonished to "Stop Whining" and accept segregation as a fact of life. He suggested there could be profit from segregation and contended that the Jews gained a great deal from their separateness. A Negro college student wrote to the *Defender*:

> For the intelligent Negro student Dr. Du Bois is still a champion. He is a far greater champion now than he ever was. Like a wise general, he has seen that the point of attack can be made from a more advantageous point. Rather than lead his army blindly on, he has chosen to turn and seek other courses that offer surer and quicker means of [success]. Dr. Du Bois has realized that by being bound together the Negro presents a more consolidated front; a more concentrated movement.[20]

The N.A.A.C.P. was deluged by Negro newspapers that wanted to know once and for all what was the official position of the Association. Walter White, who asked for the "guidance" of the administrative committee, was reluctant to make a public statement because he wished to avert a battle with Du Bois. At least one newsman reported that "the debate is one of W. E. B. Du Bois vs. Walter White." The newspapers accused the executive secretary of nonco-operation, but James Weldon Johnson advised him to say nothing to the press.[21] Yet it was obvious that the board would have to do something to clarify its position to the public. After several months of campaigning to stir up Negro public opinion on behalf of his ideology, Du Bois went before the board to ask for its formal adoption. At its meeting the N.A.A.C.P. leaders passed their own resolution repudiating "enforced segregation." As the *Crisis* editor pointed out, the resolution was almost meaningless. He had always opposed "enforced segregation"—his vision was organized, systematic, voluntary separation. Publicly he inquired if the N.A.A.C.P. did or did not support Negro churches, schools, newspapers, etc.—*"And if it does believe in these things is the Board of Directors of the N.A.A.C.P. afraid to say so?"*[22]

The board placed itself on record as repudiating all forms of segregation and also resolved that, henceforth, no paid N.A.A.C.P. official could criticize the Association in the *Crisis* without prior approval.[23] Du Bois chose to ignore the ruling and proclaimed that the magazine was meant for greater things than "simply reflecting" the official N.A.A.C.P. platform. Of course it was true that he always exercised a large amount of freedom in editing the monthly and he *had* often introduced subjects which the Association's leadership did not actively support; however, it was unrealistic of him to expect that he could espouse causes which clearly contradicted the board's ideological approach.

Basically, Du Bois and his opponents differed on the level of policy not principle. For tactical purposes he changed his emphasis from protest to Negro nationalism. In his conception the climate of racism was just too strong for Negroes to do anything but systematically develop their own resources. After this had been accomplished, they would be in a stronger position to demand integration. However, he possessed no adequate answer to critics who observed that even if the segregated economy were feasible, both races would come to accept organized separation as an unalterable fact of life, thus lessening the possibilities of establishing an integrated society. Of course he was correct when he pointed out that the N.A.A.C.P. supported segregated institutions such as Negro schools, but, unlike Du Bois, the Association did not seem to glory in them. Nor was the organization prepared to surrender its tactics of protest.

Negro newspapers were increasingly disturbed by this "obvious division" in the Association, and one journalist warned that the

N.A.A.C.P. needed to keep the confidence of the press. In June, the Philadelphia *Tribune* threatened to withdraw its help unless the board removed either Walter White or Du Bois. The paper complained that "the stench of the argument" proved the weakness and inadequacy of the N.A.A.C.P. board. [24] A few days later, Du Bois submitted his resignation, but the board, still hoping for a compromise, refused to accept it. On June 26, 1934, he formally terminated his relationship with the organization and announced the decision to the Negro press.[25] In his version, censorship and not segregation was the essence of the dispute. He argued that this suppression was symptomatic of the spiritual poverty of the N.A.A.C.P. leadership and he hoped the dramatic exit might cause Negroes to rally to his side, creating a new organization or over-throwing the old one. He believed that some day in the immediate future a wiser leadership would turn to voluntary segregation. His departure brought a collective sigh of relief from the board— "Now we are rid of our octopus."

After Du Bois' exit, Negro intellectuals carefully analyzed the segregated economy conception and completely discarded it. E. Franklin Frazier noted: "With thousands of Negroes being displaced from the farms of the South while many more thousands are depending upon relief in the cities, a cooperative program could only adopt 'Share Your Poverty' as a slogan."[26]

Others observed that whites owned and directed the American financial and industrial system, and Negroes—a marginal economic group—were without the ability to manufacture and distribute their own products on a large, centralized scale. But even if colored people embarked upon the racial program—with or without the help of white capital—the majority group could apply "counter-boycotts" at any time. Ralph Bunche asserted "the legal and police forces of the state would inevitably be aligned against them [the Negroes]." James Weldon Johnson considered that Negro success would only make whites envious and therefore even more suppressive in their treatment of the blacks.[27]

Even though the segregated economy was impractical, Du Bois' resignation made it imperative for the N.A.A.C.P. to re-examine its program. The Association appointed Abram L. Harris as chairman of the Committee on Future Plan and Program, and this study group searched for ways in which the N.A.A.C.P. could help the race meet the economic crisis more effectively. Like the Amenia conferees of two years before, the Harris committee recommended that the organization encourage Negroes "to view their special grievances as a natural part of the large issues of American labor as a whole." The branches were advised to create and control industrial and agricultural councils to educate workers for economic and political action.

The Harris committee also favored a reorganization of the N.A.A.C.P. power structure. Under the new proposals, the New York headquarters was to possess less authority, while the branches were to receive more influence. At the time Harris made his survey, "the Association membership and branches had no voice in the selection of the Board members." "The highly centralized organization had developed into a personal clique which runs the Association from New York."[28] Thus, although Du Bois' solution to the race's economic problem was repudiated, his demand for structural reorganization of the Association was vindicated.

In 1935 the N.A.A.C.P. board voted to adopt the Harris report, but its provisions were not followed.[29] Negro business and professional men refused to adopt the trade union orientation as a way to advance the economic interests of the Negro masses. Within the Negro race there was also a convergence of color and class, and some mulatto leaders announced their love for the blacks, but really despised them and shunned them.[30] The colored masses were more immediately plagued by economic problems than were the

Negro business-professional classes, who wanted the N.A.A.C.P. to retain its traditional emphasis on political-civil equality, because racial discrimination in these areas especially affected them. In addition to their own interests, they were also influenced by white board members who "wanted the Association to keep its skirts free of the grime and bitterness of economic strife."[31] The N.A.A.C.P. desired to be "radical" only in the respect that it demanded Negro rights as granted by the Constitution. While it may have been true that the Association would have forfeited some white and Negro support if a labor union orientation were established, it seemed even more true that an economic de-emphasis during the Great Depression represented a blind alley. In any case, Du Bois had seriously miscalculated. Some of his prized theories were used by the Talented Tenth as a rationalization for its own advancement.

12. The Recent Years: An Epilogue

Even before leaving the N.A.A.C.P., Du Bois resumed his duties at Atlanta University's Department of Sociology. In 1939 he founded the magazine *Phylon*, Atlanta University's "Review of Race and Culture." While his ultimate goal was to discover "a general view of human beings," basically he sought to revive his old program of research on the American Negro. With the help of the Carnegie Foundation, Du Bois sponsored the First Phylon Institute, and at a meeting in the early 1940's he asked representatives of Negro colleges to cooperate in a systematic study of the race's status.[1] In 1941 he became "official coordinator" of a sociological research program which Negro land-grant colleges planned to underwrite. In 1945 the Phelps-Stokes Fund published the "Preparatory Volume" of a projected Encyclopedia of the Negro, for which Du Bois had been appointed editor-in-chief. It almost seemed that the old Atlanta studies were coming alive again, but in the end nothing happened.[2]

During the early years of his return to Atlanta University, Du Bois produced his last two major books. *Black Reconstruction* attempted to relate Marxist theory to the post-Civil War period. He asserted that by escaping from the cotton fields and joining the Union Army, Southern Negroes engaged in a "general strike" and helped to defeat the Confederacy. After the war, Negroes and poor whites supposedly united in a dictatorship of the proletariat, forcing upon the region such programs as the extension of suffrage and the establishment of public schools. Although this book impressed Communist historians,[3] others scathingly criticized it.[4] One reviewer noted, "I have never come across a more completely fantastic attempt at applying Marxian dogma to history." Abram L. Harris commented that the Negro migrations from the farms were unorganized and never resembled a "general strike." Furthermore, Negro political power in the Reconstruction governments depended upon the presence of Northern armies sent to the South by Northern capitalist interests. Henry Lee Moon declared that Negroes and poor whites in the Southern governments were devoted to capitalist goals and did not seek to socialize industry, banking, or the railroads. *Black Reconstruction*'s merit was in its portrayal of Negro contributions during an era previously depicted as completely disorganized and chaotic. The volume was an antidote to the usual characterization of postwar Southern Negroes as ignorant and dishonest men who created a nightmare for supporters of good government. It remains to this day the best summary of Negro participation in the governments of the Southern states during Reconstruction.

In 1940 appeared *Dusk of Dawn*, subtitled, "An Essay Toward an Autobiography of a Race Concept." In this book Du Bois sought to explain his role in both the African and Afro-American struggles for freedom. He viewed his own career as an ideological case study illuminating the varied and complex facets of the Negro-white conflict. Reviewing the volume, Oswald Garrison Villard, Du Bois' colleague in the founding of the N.A.A.C.P., called attention to "the very real egotism which shines through these pages in which few others are praised—chiefly those who contributed to his success."[5]

During the decade after his resignation from the N.A.A.C.P., Du Bois' writings revealed the old blend of organized self-segregation and Marxism. For *Current History* he wrote "A Negro Nation Within the Nation," in which he called Negroes "idiotic" if they ignored his economic plans and turned instead to "await the salvation of a white god."[6] Yet shortly after the article appeared, Du Bois addressed the National Negro Baptist Convention and found much race salvation in Franklin D. Roosevelt's seeming desire to give

Negro labor "its due share of recognition." He eloquently lauded the New Deal's concern for "the masses of workers," and commented that "the Negro was envisaged in practically all of the plans adopted."[7] Ironically, Du Bois' praises came in the period when N.A.A.C.P. leaders like Walter White, despite an evident sympathy for Roosevelt, were charging that racist governmental officials had excluded Negroes from the benefits of many New Deal programs.

As in years past, Du Bois never relented in attacks upon imperialism, especially in Africa. In 1944 he reaffirmed his recommendation for an international mandates commission "with native representation."[8] His book *Color and Democracy: Colonies and Peace*, published in 1945, dealt extensively with racism and imperialism and denounced the Dumbarton Oaks Conference for refusing "to emphasize the rights of colonial peoples."[9] He maintained that the proposed United Nations Security Council would be controlled almost entirely by imperialist nations. About this time he joined the staff of the N.A.A.C.P. for the second time, and was asked to prepare Association memoranda for the opening sessions of the United Nations. In 1945 he served as an associate consultant to the American delegation at the founding conference of the U.N. in San Francisco.

Du Bois returned from San Francisco in disappointment, charging that the U.N. Charter effectively blocked the world organization from intervening in the administration of colonies, thereby leaving hundreds of millions disinherited and disfranchised.[10] He announced that the Fifth Pan-African Congress would convene to allow representatives of Black Africa to determine what "joint pressure" they could use on the World Powers.

The Fifth Pan-African Congress met in England in the fall of 1945, under the leadership of George Padmore, Kwame Nkrumah, and other West Indian and African intellectuals. The Congress elected Du Bois International President, but cast him largely in a ceremonial role as "Father of Pan-Africanism." To a new generation of African leaders he was now basically a symbol, an "Elder Statesman."[11] His pronouncements still rated a mention in *The New York Times*, where he was quoted as saying, "The tempo of the colored peoples has changed. Either the British Government will extend self-government in West Africa and the West Indies or face open revolt."[12] He was contemptuous of British Labor Party leaders whose colonial policy was "sometimes worse than the Tories and at no time better." A year later, Du Bois presided at a New York conference which urged the U.N. Assembly to permit "participation of designated representatives of the African colonial peoples in such business of the United Nations as concerns them." He asserted that various African organizations had asked American Negroes like himself "to lay before the United Nations abuses against the African people which do not occur against Negroes in the most backward areas of the United States."[13] In 1947 he was back at the U.N. again, this time to plead for American Negroes. As editor of the N.A.A.C.P. "Appeal to the World," he petitioned the United Nations to marshal world public opinion for pressure on the United States "to be just to its own people" of dark skin.[14]

Surveying the postwar world, Du Bois viewed the Soviet Union as the only World Power which practiced racial egalitarianism and opposed colonialism (whose tide he thought was rising).[15] His line of thinking became increasingly similar to the foreign policy of that nation. In an appearance before the 1947 N.A.A.C.P. convention, where as he rose to speak he received a standing ovation, Du Bois announced that only the Marxists were seeking to abolish world poverty.[16] N.A.A.C.P. leaders ignored his pro-Soviet slant, but the far-left wing, which in the Depression decade had harshly condemned him, now described him as a "New Moses." Facing rejection again by the mainstream of the civil rights movement, this old but very proud man became the Communists' ornament.[17] He entered his last phase as a protest propagandist, committed beyond "a single social group" to a "world conception" of proletarian liberation.

In 1948 he made appearances for the Progressive Party, seeking unsuccessfully to win Negro votes for Henry Wallace. Shortly before the election, he created a bitter controversy that resulted in his final separation from the N.A.A.C.P. In September, after Walter White was appointed a consultant to the American delegation of the United Nations, Du Bois charged that acceptance of the post would bind the N.A.A.C.P. to "the reactionary, war-mongering colonial imperialism of the present [Truman] administration." Within hours his accusations, contained in a memorandum to White and the N.A.A.C.P. board, were leaked to the press.[18]

After his employment with the Association ended, he became vice-chairman of the Council on African Affairs, an organization listed as subversive by the United States Attorney General.[19] Although *The New York Times Magazine* had printed a Du Bois article in late 1948, by the following year he was publishing exclusively in far-left publications such as *Masses and Mainstream*, *New Africa*, and the *National Guardian*. In 1949 he wrote, "Drunk with power, we [the United States] are leading the world to hell in a new colonialism with the same old human slavery which once ruined us and to a third world war which will ruin the world."[20] He denounced as imperialistic the Marshall Plan and European rearmament. ("We want to rule Russia and cannot rule Alabama."[21]) During the year he attended the All-Union Conference of Peace Proponents in Moscow; in August of 1950, he went to Prague as one of the honored guests of the "Partisans of Peace."[22] The following month, the left-wing American Labor Party nominated Du Bois as its candidate for the U.S. Senate from New York. During the campaign he discussed segregation in military and civilian life, but the issue which he stressed was war and peace. He charged that his opponents stood by while "Big Business drove the United States into the Korean War." Republicans and Democrats alike pursued a "bipartisan policy of war," and only he and the American Labor Party offered the New York electorate an alternative. On election day Du Bois and his entire ticket were resoundingly defeated.[23]

In the meantime he had accepted the chairmanship of the Peace Information Center, a position which almost landed him in a federal prison. According to the United States Attorney General, this Center handled the publicity for the executive committee of the World Congress of the Defenders of Peace and circulated the "Stockholm Peace Appeal." Secretary of State Dean Acheson denounced the Appeal, which demanded the outlawing of atomic weapons, as pure Soviet propaganda. The United States Department of Justice ordered Du Bois and other Peace Information Center officers to register as agents of a "foreign principal." When the eighty-three-year-old Du Bois refused, he was indicted under the Foreign Agents Registration Act. Federal Judge Matthew F. McGuire decided that sufficient evidence was lacking and consequently directed the acquittal of the Negro leader. In effect, it was one thing to conclude that Du Bois' propaganda was similar to that of the Soviet Union, and quite another to prove he was a foreign agent.[24]

After the trial, Du Bois became more alienated both from American society and from the thinking of American Negroes. Only the far left continued to claim this man whom one observer described as a "Prophet in Limbo."[25] Invited to deliver the keynote address at the Progressive Party convention of 1952, he told those assembled that "working class" whites and Negroes wanted no part of the Cold War and were contemptuous of "the two old parties."[26] Yet even Du Bois[27] saw that the Progressive Party had far less appeal in 1952 than four years earlier when Henry Wallace had won only about two percent of the national vote. At times Du Bois showed an awareness that most American Negroes were ignoring his message. On a speaking tour in 1953 he commented that Negroes were enthralled by American materialism: "our idea of heaven is to be rich Americans." Negroes should drop these "distorted ideals" and remember that they belong to the working class of the world.[28] A few years later, when sociologist E. Franklin Frazier satirized the Negro middle class in his famous *Bourgeoisie Noire*, Du Bois found himself largely in agreement.[29]

The unanimous Supreme Court school-desegregation decision of 1954 caught Du Bois by surprise and he exclaimed, "I have seen the impossible happen."[30] After all, as late as 1948, writing of his timetable for "complete equality," he had anticipated "slow" progress along Freedom Road: "The Negro does not expect to reach these goals in a minute or in ten years. He is long-suffering and patient. But whether it takes thirty years or a thousand, equality is his goal and he will never stop until he reaches it."[31] Yet, despite the elation over the Brown Decision, he cautioned that "we are not yet free" until the color line is effaced not only in schools but in every other institution of American society.

By the 1956 election campaign Southern school boards clearly were using massive subterfuge to maintain segregation. Du Bois blamed Eisenhower and the Republican party for doing "exactly nothing" to encourage integration in schools or anywhere else. But he also denounced Eisenhower's opponent, Adlai Stevenson, as the leader of "the party of Talmadge, Eastland, and Ellender."[32] Du Bois charged that in large parts of the country, Negroes still received "less consideration than a dog."[33] He did not bother to register and vote in this "phony election" and counseled others to boycott the ballot box in 1956. He mused that if twenty-five million fellow Americans followed his example, neither the Democrats nor the Republicans would ever be the same.

From the sidelines during his last years, he avidly followed the work of the direct actionists in their bus boycotts and lunch-counter sit-ins. While these demonstrations did not comprise a basic assault on the economic system, he was proud that the participants in the Montgomery boycott had been "the black workers."[34] Shortly after the lunch-counter sit-ins began in 1960, Du Bois wrote how "uplifted" he was by the revolt of the Negro students, who acted, he said, without even the assistance and encouragement of adult Negroes: "Black students—not agitators, not even radicals . . . just honest, clear-headed youth."[35]

His interest in the rising Negro activism notwithstanding, Du Bois' estrangement from America was just about complete. A few years earlier, at the age of eighty-eight, he had declared: "American culture is rotting away; our honesty, our human sympathy. . . . Our manners are gone and the one thing we want to be is rich—to show off. . . . Democracy is dead in the United States."[36] Hardly anyone was listening on this side of the Iron Curtain. On the other side, however, Du Bois was regarded as a towering figure to be courted with great attentiveness. In 1953 the Communist-sponsored World Peace Council at its Budapest meetings awarded him a $7,000 peace prize, and later in the decade the Soviet Lenin Prize.[37]

In 1958–59, on journeys to Russia and China, he was feted by the highest governmental officials: Nikita Khrushchev, Mao Tse-tung, and Chou En-lai. And he reciprocated by lavishly complimenting his hosts while scornfully portraying life in America. After a few weeks in China he reported that the nature of the people there had changed—"envy and class hate" had just about disappeared since Chiang Kai-shek was ousted. On the other hand, the nature of America was inflexible. Celebrating his ninety-first birthday in Peking, he told a large audience that "in my own country for nearly a century I have been nothing but a 'nigger.' "[38]

In October 1961, only a few months before his ninety-fourth birthday, Du Bois officially joined the Communist Party. Making application for membership to Gus Hall, general secretary of the party in the United States, Du Bois wrote that he had been "long and slow in coming to this conclusion, but at last my mind is settled."[39] By the time the press published an announcement of the event, Du Bois was residing in Ghana, an expatriate from the United States. Earlier he had received Prime Minister Nkrumah's personal invitation to visit Ghana when the new African nation became a member of the British Commonwealth in 1957. However, at that time the American government had denied Du Bois a passport to leave the country because of his refusal to sign a non-Communist affidavit. The following year when Nkrumah convened the All-African People's Conference at Accra, Du Bois was again invited, but ill health prevented his attending. Nkrumah used the occasion to praise Du Bois and Marcus Garvey as "Sons of Africa" who "fought for African national and racial equality . . . long before many of us were conscious of our own degradation. . . ."[40] Finally, in 1960, Du Bois set foot on African soil for the second time in his life when he attended the celebration of Ghana's new status as an independent republic. Obviously moved by the world recognition of black African leaders, Du Bois remarked that he had never dreamed he would live to see "this miracle." Later he declared that American Negroes might have to learn from Africans the way to obtain freedom.[41] President Nkrumah urged Du Bois to return to Ghana permanently and direct the government-sponsored Encyclopedia Africana. Both because of Du Bois' alienation from America, and because of the opportunity to fulfill a scholarly dream cherished for half a century, the offer was a welcome one and he accepted it late in 1961.[42] Over a year later, in the final months of his life, Du Bois became a Ghanian citizen.[43]

On August 27, 1963, at the age of ninety-five, Du Bois died in Accra. Arrangements were made for a state funeral; the official mourners were headed by President Nkrumah, members of his cabinet and the parliament. The honor was heightened, and Du Bois' role as a pioneering Pan-Africanist memorialized, with the selection of a burial site located just outside the historic Christianborg Castle, the Ghanian Government House.[44]

Across the world in Washington, D.C., the American civil rights movement was reaching a climax, as a quarter of a million people gathered at the March on Washington. Moments before the mammoth March departed from the Washington Monument, the actor Ossie Davis announced Du Bois' death. The vast assemblage stood bowed in silent tribute. Later, at the Lincoln Memorial, Roy Wilkins, executive secretary of the N.A.A.C.P., referred to Du Bois' passing and his earlier work in the long struggle for Negro freedom. To the younger generation of Negro activists, Du Bois was a symbol of dedicated, uncompromising militance. From the viewpoint of the old-timers at the March, Du Bois, having trod the course of the far left, had cut himself off from the main stream of Negro protest. Yet they, too, understood that his last, Communist period could not diminish the enormous contribution he had made to the civil rights movement in America.

13. Conclusions

Growing up in the second half of the nineteenth century, Du Bois heard Negroes asking themselves if a prophet or a messiah would appear among their number and help them. Many others were sure that Frederick Douglass was the race leader who had been sent to bring unity and self-respect. But the task was left undone, and Negroes continued to pray for someone to release them from despair. Du Bois, as a young man of imagination and intelligence, began to think he might be the man to redeem his people. He was determined to prepare himself for the role. Since Harvard was the oldest and greatest college in the United States, that was where he felt compelled to go. Because of financial obstacles, he took an undergraduate degree at Fisk University, but he also managed to attend Harvard and qualify for another bachelor of arts degree. He needed more specialized intellectual tools and studied abroad, but he returned to take a Ph.D. degree at Harvard.

When he came back from Europe his ideological system was already propounded. He believed that the Negro race would be saved through its own self-development and through the good will of the whites. He considered it essential to convince Negroes that they should be interested in education (more schooling, literary societies, community centers) and organization (social services, industrial enterprises). He also set out to persuade whites that Negroes were worthy of help. Du Bois maintained that both tasks would be facilitated by Negro intellectuals who cajoled and harangued their own race, while simultaneously seeking stimulation from whites. The Talented Tenth was to be the *avant-garde*, the first wave of Negroes who were to lower the color barriers.

Du Bois offered whites his propositions and shrewdly, if not accurately, painted a picture of Negro impatience and revolutionary undercurrents.

But he did not ask for complete assimilation or amalgamation. He was opposed to homogeneity and wanted to see racial-cultural differences preserved. However, he objected to the pariah role which American Negroes were assigned. He refused to be "a stranger in mine own house." He chose the "Veil" as the symbol of racial barriers and depicted the Negro as one who was

> gifted with second-sight in this American world—a world which yields him no true self-consciousness, but only lets him see himself through the revelation of the other world. It is a peculiar sensation, this double-consciousness, this sense of always looking at one's self through the eyes of others, of measuring one's soul by the tape of a world that looks on in amused contempt and pity. One ever feels his two-ness—an American, a Negro; two souls, two thoughts, two unreconciled strivings; two warring ideals in one dark body, whose dogged strength alone keeps it from being torn asunder.[1]

Du Bois wanted to give his race a sense of its own self-consciousness, and he sought to end the "unreconciled strivings" by synthesizing them and creating an organized group of American Negroes who could be proud of themselves as Negroes and as Americans. In effect, he was enunciating the theory of cultural pluralism, whereby peoples of diverse backgrounds "live together on a basis of equality, tolerance, justice, and harmony." However, cultural pluralism was rejected by many whites, who ethnocentrically and racistly affirmed the inherent superiority of their own group, and who maintained that accommodation between the races could be established only on the basis of dominance and submission. They demanded separateness, but not equality.

Du Bois, on the other hand, desired not only organized self-segregation, but also insisted that his people should be allowed to participate *fully* in the common political, spiritual, and social life of the nation. But these goals were contradictory, since they ignored the realities of the American milieu. A highly disciplined, almost bureaucratic, Negro social and economic system would have preserved in the minds of both races a sense of detached destinies and fostered among the colored people a glorification of separateness, thereby making it impossible for them to achieve full participation in the larger society.

When he sought to fuse these "unreconciled strivings," critics ignored his dedication to a Negro ethos and condemned his request for social and political equality. He was constantly accused of being ashamed of his race and wanting to be a white man. Especially in the early decades of his career, Du Bois readily admitted the cultural inferiority of his race, but he proclaimed his intentions to direct the road to advancement. By personality he was reticent and did not associate freely with Negroes (or whites). Since he did not join many Negro clubs or organizations, he was often called a "stranger" in his race. Certainly, this exclusiveness was a distinct limitation in a man who proposed to lead his people, but it represents no evidence that he wanted to be white. Even social scientists misinterpreted him on this last point. Edward B. Reuter, for example, used Du Bois as an illustration of the humiliated mulatto who nourished a longing to be included in the "superior [white] race" which "deracialized" him by its rejection.[2]

At the beginning of the twentieth century, Du Bois wanted to discover more about Negro living conditions and embarked upon a series of empirical studies sponsored by Atlanta University. These investigations were to possess the certified sanctity of science, and he appeared before the public as a skilled specialist—the man with research training, the objective observer who had amassed reams of information. Because of methodology and insufficient funds, many of his investigations left much to be desired, but these published monographs provided him with another platform to espouse his program to solve the Negro problem. A forum—not a scientific laboratory—was what he came to require more than anything else. The Atlanta studies were filled with his propaganda messages to Negroes and whites. He restated the theories of the Talented Tenth and the segregated economy. He contributed to race pride by asserting that Negroes were rising, and he emphasized race prejudice to account for the fact that they were not rising as fast and as far as he wished. He attempted to reform the world's conception of Africa. He depicted the natives as people who used iron and had developed complex tools. The Negroes were presented as victims of slave traders, geographical isolation, and oppressive climatic conditions. In short, he was providing his race with a respectable pedigree.

Until shortly after the turn of the century, Du Bois was a conciliationist who pleaded for the good will of the whites. He had condemned Negroes for whining and refusing to identify themselves with whites. He had criticized those who relied primarily on legislation to raise the race's status. However, when he saw Negro higher education starving and colored people being denied suffrage, he changed tactics and became a protest propagandist. He held whites responsible for the Negro problem. His tone changed and his calm, quiet requests became loud, insistent demands. He called for immediate action and asked Congress to coerce the South into complying with the Constitution. He came into conflict with Booker T. Washington and accused the Tuskegeean of accepting Negro inferiority and blaming Negroes excessively for their difficulties. Du Bois, the propagandist with a powerful pen, was pushed to the helm of the Niagara Movement and was forced to become an executive-administrator in order to compete with Washington, who was a formidable opponent.

The Tuskegeean was the conciliationist par excellence. He believed that Negroes should acquiesce to the demands of the "better class" of Southern whites because these people were the true friends of the subordinate race. Since he held that progress could be attained only by enlisting the good will of the dominant power group, Washington avoided antagonism and concentrated on emphasizing harmony within the framework of the caste system. When he did complain, it was in terms of the effect which the inequity had, not upon the Negroes, but upon the whites. He viewed everything from the whites' point of view. Since they opposed Negro voting, he opposed it for the present. Since Southerners saw no usefulness in encouraging Negro higher education, the sage of Tuskegee saw none. He concluded that Negroes must prepare themselves for the privileges of the law and he proposed a Spartan philosophy of humility and hard work. His shibboleth was industrial education.

Whites rushed to give prestige and financial resources to the man who expressed such an ideology. To them he was the only *bona fide* representative of the Negro race. Booker T. Washington was well aware of the opportunity which was given him, and he became the most powerful executive leader the race had had. He ruled with a firm and knowing hand. His moralizing impressed white sponsors, who placed him upon a pedestal and rarely questioned the manner in which he administered his domain. He made Tuskegee Institute his headquarters and the institution possessed a substantial private endowment plus a subsidy from the state of Alabama. With such money he was able to attract devoted lieutenants and a large following. He could influence Negro education because of his important voice on the General Education Board and the Southern Education Board. He occupied a key position in Negro politics because of his close connection with the White House and Republican party leaders. He exerted pressure on the Negro press through effective public relations, judicious placement of advertisements, purchase of large quantities of particular issues, bestowal of occasional or regular gifts, and, in some cases, through investment of large sums of money. The man possessed a genius for organization. In various communities, friendly Negro political clubs were established and maintained under the supervision of trusted associates. In an effort to control Negroes who were interested in civil rights, he became the power behind the Afro-American Council. Negro businessmen were shepherded into the National Negro Business League and hundreds of farmers convened regularly at the annual Tuskegee Farmers Conference.

Washington was a brilliant tactician. He enticed members of the opposition to confer with him and he tried to divide them and isolate them from their leadership. He was able to win some converts to his cause by pretending to embrace the doctrine of immediate political rights and higher education. His success was based upon his power to reward and punish. It was essential for him to know the opinions of prominent Negroes and his followers transmitted information to headquarters for evaluation. The Radicals' speeches were monitored and he even employed spies who were in the secret councils of the New England Suffrage League and the Niagara Movement. Many men who co-operated were given political jobs and positions in Negro schools. He took steps to remove opposition members from political positions and he helped to prevent others from securing employment. Having access to the White House as well as the State House in New York, he could convince political leaders that his enemies were their enemies. Institutions which offered his opponents sympathy or sanctuary were intimidated. When Storer College permitted the Niagara Movement to use its campus for the Harpers Ferry conference in 1906, the school experienced a loss of income during the following year. Atlanta University would probably have received more financial aid had it not harbored Du Bois. All the time Washington was exerting tremendous power, he cannily appeared before his public as a simple former slave who was as humble as the average Negro. His platform manner was captivating, and he punctuated his speeches with farm stories which uneducated Negroes loved.

Du Bois, as general secretary of the Niagara Movement, simply could not match the skill and resources of Booker Washington. He "hated the role" of being a social action leader. His personality was aloof and many Negroes considered him conceited. He never attempted to appeal directly to large numbers of colored people, although he said that he represented the race. He was satisfied to assemble a small group of educated men and he assumed these people would carry his message to the masses. However, most of the Niagara men were psychologically isolated from average Negroes. Many regarded the masses as inferiors and considered their own college diplomas as symbols of social prestige instead of tools to raise the race.

Du Bois and his lieutenants were able to devote only part of their time to the Niagara Movement, and financial resources were almost nonexistent. Local Niagara chapters were autonomous and there was little central direction. Emphasis was placed on annual conferences. A schism occurred which hurt the movement and Du Bois seemed unable to convince William Monroe Trotter and other disputants to resolve their differences. Du Bois' reputation as an administrator was hardly enhanced by the failure of various Radical organizations to merge. Considering his lack of success in this type of leadership, it is a wonder that the Niagara Movement lasted as long as it did and accomplished anything.

The answer in no small part lies in Du Bois' skill as a protest propagandist. The Niagara addresses were masterpieces. His demands for equality were simply, sharply, and often lyrically written. He repeatedly reminded Negroes and whites of their heritage of freedom and Christianity—and of the contradictions inherent in the caste system. His editorials antagonized but they attracted attention. His words gave followers a reason to fight as well as the verbal ammunition to battle. Despite the weaknesses of the Niagara Movement, it was the first national organization of Negroes which aggressively and unconditionally demanded civil rights. At a time when Negroes were asked to eschew higher education and the ballot, the Niagara men categorically embraced these goals. They attempted to create a political lobby composed of informed, independent, and articulate citizens.

An essential failure of the Niagara Movement was its inability to attract the support of more than a handful of whites. However, by 1909, liberal whites were willing to aid the equal rights movement, and Du Bois' propaganda was one of the factors which brought about that support. The whites who formed the N.A.A.C.P. decided not only to work for the Negro race, but also to work with it. They attempted to appeal to the Washingtonians as well as to the Du Boisians. However, the Washingtonians disapproved of the N.A.A.C.P. campaign of agitation for civil rights and tried to weaken the organization.

When Booker T. Washington died in 1915, Du Bois admitted that the Alabama educator helped to promote industrial training, pushed the race toward economic growth, and sought the improvement of interracial relations. But the Tuskegeean failed to understand the relationship between politics and economics, minimized the importance of higher education, and, in exchange for white aid, accommodated himself to a social system based upon caste. However, the *Crisis* editor was too stern in assigning to Washington "a heavy responsibility" for Negro disfranchisement, the poverty of Negro colleges, and the entrenchment of the caste system in the country. Washington's power was limited by the whites, and, rather than determining their behavior, he was their spokesman. His great error lay in his tight control over Negro leadership. He used prestige and power to harass and defeat the Du Bois group, which demanded the immediate realization of the equality goals Washington espoused. The Tuskegeean did not allow the establishment of a division of labor—marking off for each group a particular type of program and emphasis. Understandably, he could not speak consistently on behalf of suffrage, higher education, and social equality; but was it necessary for him to work against those who did? Washington's implacability made Du Bois uncompromising and short-sighted on some issues. For example, the sociologist condemned those seeking the co-operation of whites who controlled Southern Negro education. Du Bois wanted Negroes to have an important voice in the operation of segregated schools, but it should have been obvious to him that the aid of white Southerners was required if colored schools were to continue in any form.

Since the platform of the N.A.A.C.P. was one of racial equality, Du Bois' presence was deemed essential. His advocacy of the cause had been successful enough for him to become the very personification of it. By choice, his leadership in the Association was basically that of protest propagandist instead of executive leader. Rather than hammer out policies at board sessions, he preferred to make his influence felt as editor of the *Crisis*, the official magazine of the organization. However, as *Crisis* editor, Du Bois was repelled by the thought that the journal should become a house organ. He preferred "to blaze a trail" and go beyond the "practical steps" of the Association. He was under the impression that the *Crisis*, rather than serving the N.A.A.C.P. as its interpreter to the public, was actually the pre-eminent division which would "make the N.A.A.C.P. possible." His influence was considerably weakened by such a view.

Frequently, an advocate leader is authoritarian to the extent that he is certain that his propaganda is the panacea. This type tends to have an omniscient conception of his role and frequently believes in the omnipotence of his ideas. As *Crisis* editor, Du Bois felt free to lecture the race on a wide array of subjects from consumer co-operation to migration to the Northwest. He told Negroes what to read and even how to behave at the theater. He continued to criticize Negro ministers and made intemperate attacks on the Negro editors. Both of these groups were influential with average Negroes, whom Du Bois claimed he wanted to reach. In the case of the editors, the N.A.A.C.P. realized Du Bois' error and passed a resolution of confidence in the press. The Association recognized that it required the colored newspapers as an outlet for its propaganda, even if the *Crisis* editor did not.

The height of his influence occurred during the period immediately preceding and following World War I. In these years there was a deluge of democratic propaganda and his own integrationist line fitted the "American creed," which was pushed forward as a rallying cry of the war effort. No longer did Du Bois have to compete with Booker T. Washington. The Washingtonians, without their leader, lost a great deal of their esprit de corps, and for the time being the old point of view seemed outdated. Even before the Tuskegeean died, he "moved considerably toward his opponents" because of societal changes and Du Bois' propaganda. More Negroes were acquiring an education and were migrating to the North. They were finding better jobs and were concerned about keeping them. Racial equalitarianism became a more practical philosophy. Furthermore, during the war period, Du Bois had no other important competitors. The Negroes of the far left, led by Chandler Owen and A. Philip Randolph, were only starting to be heard and Marcus Garvey was a complete unknown.

Du Bois' propaganda had always moved in two directions— integrationist and Negro nationalist; he could move in either direction and still seem to be a prophet or oracle. Since the United

States was thumping for the American creed—on a verbal level at least—he found little trouble accommodating to it. Temporarily, he changed his tactics, with a little prodding from the Department of Justice and the N.A.A.C.P. board, and dropped the protest line. Changing conditions required a shift in other propaganda presentations. Before the United States entered the war, Du Bois said that the conflagration was caused by a maddened imperialist white world. Later, he was able to convince himself that Germany was the evil nation, while England and France were conscience-stricken sinners who had just been saved. Furthermore, he assumed that America would lead the world to a new day of integrationist socialism.

He could even have his cake and eat it too, since his Negro nationalist needs were satisfied as he viewed Negro progress—within the framework of segregation. (Example: Negro officers leading Negro troops.) But Du Bois was led to propaganda excesses, and the erstwhile protest chieftain went too far for some Negroes when he asked them to forget their "present grievances." They had learned the integrationist lessons (which he had helped to teach) only too well. His interest in an Army commission also nauseated those who feared that the *Crisis* was to be annexed by the racist Wilson administration.

His Negro nationalist aspirations brought him to Europe in 1919 to convene the Pan-African Congress. He was still the talented editorialist and pamphleteer, but his propaganda outlets continued to be confined to the *Crisis* and to short articles in magazines with limited circulations, such as the *New Republic*. If these outlets were to be increased and the Pan-African Movement transformed into a working organization, the services of a skilled administrator were required. Du Bois was not such a person. (In this examination, as in previous ones, we are not dealing with his success or chances of success—only with his efforts as a leader. Obviously, his goal of a world organization of Negroes—in a milieu of imperialism—was a formidable one to achieve in the 1920's, even if he had been a capable executive.) He repeated the errors of the Niagara Movement. He still seemed to equate an organization with a conference and a conference with a short, well-screened guest list of Negro intellectuals. Although he said he spoke for the Negro race, he made no real attempt to discover the desires of these people, or to encourage them to adopt his ideological positions.

Du Bois was the race prophet with gigantic ideas which were never implemented. He was the man in a big center chair at an international conclave—playing a role he seemed to like best of all. The Pan-African organizations in various countries were tenuous groups which met infrequently. There was no evidence that they ever made any genuine efforts to expand and they were perennially without funds to finance their plans. Although Du Bois wrote resolutions condemning imperialism, many of the leaders in the movement were unwilling to support his conceptions. From the start, the movement possessed the organizational seeds of its destruction. In order to convene the Pan-African Congress in 1919, he required the help of conservative French-Negro political leaders (such as Blaise Diagne), but these men were dedicated to the way of life which Du Bois sought to undermine. Diagne and his colleagues were not really interested in racial socialism; they identified themselves with French colonialism. This schism doomed the movement. It also helped to foster and maintain contradictions in Du Bois' own propaganda and tactics—in addition to the major paradox of desiring the creation of an international Negro organization while simultaneously pleading for integration. Du Bois stated that the whites should have their "recognized portion" of Africa, but also that the natives should control the land they could "profitably" cultivate. He did not wish to see the African natives isolated from the white settlers, but he also desired the continent to be organized along racial lines. He was unable to make incendiary demands, not only because he did not possess support from members of his own organization, but also because he recognized the need to adopt moderate tactics in order to differentiate his program from the raucous Universal Negro Improvement Association. He was unsuccessful in this latter aim, due to the determination of some colonialists to equate the two movements and thereby discredit Du Bois' group, and also because of the ineffectiveness of the propaganda and administration of the Pan-African Congress.

There was no indication that the organization had any influence, either among Negroes or whites. Despite this fact, Du Bois asked Negroes of the world to go one step further and join a mutual aid pact with oriental nations. He not only saw an impending Negro-oriental alliance which had no basis in fact, but he also refused to see other facts which did exist. For example, while he condemned slavery in Liberia, he did not censure the Liberian government which permitted it. In his view, Liberia was a Negro nation (therefore pure in heart) which was the prey of white colonial powers (impure in heart). He possessed his own brand of racism and was reluctant to complain about colored culprits.

The N.A.A.C.P. decided to confine its activities to the American race problem, and, after 1921, the Association gave no financial aid to the Pan-African Movement. Perhaps Du Bois was correct when he said that Negro board members were ashamed of their African heritage and therefore convinced white members to eschew Pan-Africa. Certainly, N.A.A.C.P. resources were limited, and there were justifiable fears that the Association might be weakened by subsidizing the Pan-African organization. But the important point here was that Du Bois did little to convince key N.A.A.C.P. board members—either in board sessions or in private conferences —of the value of his project. He simply editorialized and announced. He still viewed himself as the man with all the facts; he did not feel the need to elicit ideas from the board and possibly modify his program. In addition to by-passing the board, he also did nothing to organize the N.A.A.C.P. branches behind his movement.

Du Bois came into direct conflict with Marcus Garvey, the Negro nationalist whose leadership rested upon an ability to dramatize himself. He understood the race's need for the flamboyant and the tangible. While Du Bois' and Washington's public statements were limited by their white associates as well as by their own restraint, Garvey was completely unfettered. His irresponsibility was the first step to his great attraction. Unresponsive to reason, he openly battled all the forces which the downtrodden blacks hated. For these people, crushed by prejudiced whites and ambitious mulattoes, racial chauvinism seemed the only antidote to complete hopelessness.

On their own level, Garvey shrilly presented them with a miracle of a black man—who was unashamedly black—unabashedly proclaiming the past greatness of the black race and the unbounded glories awaiting a marching people who were on the verge of conquering their place in the world. His deeds were his words and his words were absolutely exhilarating. He was no conciliationist like Booker T. Washington. Nor was he a protest leader like Du Bois, who surrounded himself with "the very best class" of Negroes. Garvey's appeal was to the uneducated blacks who had previously felt ignored or, worse, condemned. He claimed to be one of them and they claimed him; his followers desperately wanted a hero whom they could worship, in order that they might worship themselves.

Black was the standard for his propaganda system. Since he realized that average Negroes loved religion, he created the African Orthodox Church—with a black God, Madonna, and bishop. Christmas and Easter were celebrated as the birth and resurrection of the Negro race. He gave his people a flag (black for Negro skin, green for their hopes, and red for their blood), a national anthem, and an "African homeland." He understood the blacks' need for pomp and formed his own marching corps—complete with batons, uniforms, medals, and ranks. He founded units of the "African" army and navy and the Black Cross Nurses. He established local organizations of the Universal Negro Improvement Association and appointed lieutenants to carry his message to the rank and file. He owned a central meeting hall in Harlem and held regular meetings and conventions.

However, his talents as an administrator did not match those as a propagandist. He was a pompous man who attracted fawning and inept associates. Garvey was especially ignorant in financial matters and could not account for much of the money he received. (Some of it was embezzled by friends.) He was incapable of operating the Black Star Line; for example, he paid too much money for old ships which were constantly in need of extensive repairs. His incendiary manner made it impossible for him to deal with colonial powers, even on the most preliminary levels. But the career of this charismatic nationalist proved that a large number of average Negroes could be reached, stirred, and united in a movement dedicated to race pride. Garvey represented the extreme outbursts of the New Negro era.

Although the New Negro movement of the 1920's emphasized race pride and Negro rights—the two large themes which Du Bois had always espoused—the *Crisis* editor's influence was on the downgrade. The reasons for this paradox stemmed from the type of propaganda Du Bois chose to stress in his role as a "race journalist." Secondly, he possessed obvious shortcomings as an executive leader, and, thirdly, Negro society had changed.

The integration philosophy had a powerful hold on many Negroes and they eschewed his propaganda which favored a planned, separate economy. Since he could not develop the kind of personality which inspired complete loyalty, he was unable to develop a large following. While he was respected for his intellect, he was also considered a stranger in the race. His influence was lessened by the fact that he never consciously worked at creating disciples. His withdrawn introvertive manner made it impossible for him to cultivate a "Du Bois school." (Various writers have been inaccurate when they referred to James Weldon Johnson, Walter White, and other prominent N.A.A.C.P. men as members of a Du Bois coterie. These people never recognized Du Bois as their "master." They were never personally indoctrinated by him, never accepted the whole cloth of his doctrines, and the parts of which they approved were never exclusive with the *Crisis* editor.)[3]

Although Du Bois viewed himself as the savior of his race, by the 1920's American Negroes had acquired a greater degree of heterogeneity of interests (due to occupational differentiation, urbanization, increased education, etc.), and they were unwilling to submit to any one Great Race Leader type. Not only was the *Crisis* editor obliged to compete with other aspirants such as Marcus Garvey, Chandler Owen, A. Philip Randolph, and James Weldon Johnson, among others, but, in a large sense, he also competed with scores of community leaders. These local Negro politicians, editors, and labor union leaders were primarily concerned not so much with ideological systems as with local problems.[4] During these difficult years for Du Bois, the *Crisis* circulation was consistently declining as Negroes turned more and more to their community race papers.

In the 1920's, he made integrationist efforts along three old fronts, i.e., the labor unions, Socialists, and the two major political parties. His rebuffs created many contradictions besides the basic one of simultaneously promulgating demands for Negro nationalism and integration. For example, he threatened the two major parties with the balance of power weapon, while he admitted after each election that colored people did not possess the necessary political strength to do any balancing. He sought to identify himself with a third party, but he also said that the solid South made such an adventure fruitless.

After the depression of the 1930's, Du Bois could no longer support integration as present tactics and relegated it to a long-range goal. Unable to trust white politicians, white capitalists, or white workers, he invested everything in the segregated socialized economy. He believed that since Negroes were compelled to live in a separate environment for a long, long time, at least they should have the satisfaction of planning it. The Talented Tenth revolted against him and correctly observed that his ideology was economically impractical and might bring about a permanent caste status. Many of the serious intellectuals in the race were thumping for an interracial labor rapprochement. Negro businessmen refused to devote their lives in Spartan service and had no desire to surrender their anticipation of personal profits. Du Bois was forsaken by those to whom he had devoted his propaganda messages for four decades. The signposts had always been there, but he either ignored or minimized them.

Despite all of the resistance, Du Bois still demanded the right to use the *Crisis* as his separatist platform. However, N.A.A.C.P. board members decided to embrace civil libertarianism more fervently, and they refused to turn to the segregated economy on the one hand or to a labor rapprochement on the other. His quarter of a century relationship with the N.A.A.C.P. disintegrated completely. Standing almost alone in his struggle with the Association, he finally came to realize that he had erred in not attempting to influence the organization more directly. Since he had preferred to be a propagandist leader, the executive powers went to other men by default. He had given little attention to the importance of organizing people to translate ideas into action, and his ideas were neglected. The *Crisis* had been subsidized only grudgingly and Du Bois' requests for larger appropriations received little sympathy from the board and Walter White, whose administrative leadership was in accord with the Association's thinking. White believed in centralized control of the N.A.A.C.P. and justified the old methods of conducting anti-lynching campaigns, fighting court cases, and lobbying in Congress.

In affirming the absolute supremacy of the Association over the *Crisis*, the board members rejected Du Bois' leadership in the roles he most cherished. They made it only too clear that he was to be rejected as the expert and propagandist. They refused to pretend any longer that he was the national race leader who could stand as representative of the Negro people in the United States. Ironically, in the final phase of the struggle, Du Bois made one last attempt to assert himself in the role in which he had proved weakest—that of the executive leader. He asked the N.A.A.C.P. to decentralize and offered to reconstruct the organization in his own image. His resignation followed.

During the 1940's, he redefined his position for what may be the final time. Believing that the Soviet Union is the only haven of equalitarianism and cultural pluralism, he now embraces the far-left wing. He has paid no attention to those who deny that cultural pluralism actually exists in Russia. He is no longer of any influence in the field of contemporary American race relations. He made this shift at the very time that the status of his race was rapidly rising. Many of the things for which he fought so long were being realized. But Du Bois had removed himself from old ties. He became a figure of pathos, if not tragedy—talented, even brilliant, but hurt beyond repair after a long life of battling racism.

Over the decades, Du Bois made some impressive contributions. He was a pioneer in Negro research. He helped to limit the excesses of Booker T. Washington and was founder-prophet of the Niagara Movement. He was an important booster of Negro morale. He encouraged his people to seek a college education and improve themselves generally. For many, he exemplified the heights the race could reach. Moreover, he demonstrated that colored people were making progress and he provided reasons and rationalizations for the failure to achieve. His life represented a struggle to prove that a man need not be ashamed of being a Negro, and he regularly recorded the contributions of Negroes to American society. He even provided his race with a pedigree and encouraged members to be proud of their African past.

During his long career as a propagandist, some of the social changes he favored actually became part of the American scene: a Negro political balance of power, Negro Congressmen, a split between the Northern and Southern wings of the Democratic party, a congressional investigation committee on Negro suffrage, interracial labor unions, among many others. While he certainly did not create these developments, his voice was surely among the strongest in helping to promote an ideological climate which fostered them.

On other matters he was not so prescient; he never realized how close was the 1954 Supreme Court decision and he erred in predicting that the N.A.A.C.P. would turn to organized voluntary segregation. He was also mistaken in foreseeing a socialistic world; yet during the past generation socialism has attained wider influence, and the American government has established a greater degree of economic control over its citizens. Nevertheless, Du Bois did not realize that the United States capitalist system would not only survive the depression, but also gain increasing strength and vigor.

Although he erred in predicting a general race war between the whites on one side and the Negroes and orientals on the other, the

world may some day witness his concept of a "common consciousness" among India, Africa, China, Egypt, and Japan. When he
promulgated the idea over forty years ago, it seemed preposterous
and there was no evidence suggesting its possibility. And yet in
1955, the Asian-African Conference convened in Bandung with
twenty-nine governments represented. The conclave repudiated
race discrimination and colonialism, although it gave little attention
to Communist colonialism. At the end of 1957, the Afro-Asian
Peoples' Solidarity Conference was held in Cairo under the
blessings and guidance of Nasser. While the delegates were not
official representatives of their governments, they gained a great
deal of publicity and demonstrated their affection for world
communism.

Du Bois foresaw the awakening of Africa and although his Pan-
African Congresses were failures, they are linked in a small sense
with prominent African nationalist leaders such as Dr. Kwame
Nkrumah, Prime Minister of Ghana, and Dr. Nnamdi Azikiwe,
Prime Minister of Eastern Nigeria. These men were not only
familiar with his propagandist writings, but both attended the
Fifth Pan-African Congress which met in Manchester, England, in
1945. Nkrumah organized the West African delegates into the
West African National Secretariat, and the group was charged
with implementing the Pan-African principles.[5] He announced an
intention to call a Sixth conclave on the Gold Coast. In 1958, he
sponsored an All Africa Peoples' Conference which "was ostensibly
organized as one more step toward the creation of 'an ultimate
commonwealth of free, independent, United States of Africa.' "
While Nkrumah has been denounced as an upstart by other
African leaders, the continent is stirring, and, as time passes, Du
Bois may well become beatified as a saint in the new Africa.

Du Bois' contributions, while substantial in themselves, seem
pale beside his affirmations that he was primarily responsible for

the acceptance among Negroes of the equal rights doctrine and that he was the key policy-maker of the N.A.A.C.P.[6] Probably, if he had been more of an executive leader as well as a protest propagandist, or if he had been a propagandist who worked closer with the Association, his influence would have been more substantial. It may be suggested that the organization possessed a "natural history"[7] which other social movements have shared, and in its earliest phase—"The Stage of Collective Excitement"—Du Bois' protest advocate leadership was especially important. At that time, he expressed the basic ideological themes and helped to make the public aware of the new group's mission. However, as the Association developed and passed through succeeding stages—"The Stage of Formal Organization" and "The Institutional Stage"—the demand for administrative-executive leadership became apparent. Diverse forces inside and outside the group needed to be conciliated, further membership drives required systematic planning, and greater smoothness of operation became a crucial value.

However, Du Bois refused to become an organization man. He did not comprehend that N.A.A.C.P. policy was made in board sessions and in private conclaves with key board members. While the *Crisis* presented issues and clarified them for the Association, in the last analysis, social power, however limited, resided in the organization, which physically united Negroes (and their white friends) in face-to-face contacts at regular meetings across the country. At such sessions, the position which the Association intended to take was explained and money was collected to finance test cases in the courts, anti-lynching campaigns, and congressional lobbying.

Du Bois, in emphasizing projects which did not have the support of the N.A.A.C.P., such as Pan-Africa and the segregated economy, sacrificed much of the influence he might have possessed. In making frontal assaults on values which society considers inviolate, such as the Christian church and the capitalist system, he probably hurt the Association by creating the impression that the cause of race equalitarianism possessed some inherent connection with these attacks. Although he did not initiate N.A.A.C.P. policies and frequently deviated from some of them, for twenty-five years he was the organization's most prominent equal rights propagandist. There can be no doubt that in the field of race relations, W. E. B. Du Bois, despite his individualism, was the dean of the protest advocate leaders during the first half of the twentieth century.

NOTES

I

1. Robert A. Warner, *New Haven Negroes* (New Haven, 1940), pp. 86–87. Alexander Du Bois listed incorrectly by the author as a great-uncle of W. E. B. Du Bois. See also, Du Bois, *Darkwater* (Washington, 1920), p. 6. Du Bois, *Dusk of Dawn* (New York, 1940), p. 11.

2. Du Bois, *Darkwater*, p. 9.

3. W. E. B. Du Bois, *Pageant in Seven Decades* (Atlanta, 1938), p. 4; *Dusk of Dawn*, p. 10.

4. W. E. B. Du Bois, *Souls of Black Folk* (Chicago, 1903), p. 2.

5. W. E. B. Du Bois, "My Evolving Program for Negro Freedom," a contribution to Rayford Logan's symposium, *What the Negro Wants* (Chapel Hill, 1944), p. 34.

6. New York *Globe*, April 14, 1883. This material comes from the Du Bois Papers. I wish to express my appreciation to Dr. Francis Broderick for sharing his transcriptions of some of the original Du Bois Papers used in this volume. Naturally, I bear responsibility for all interpretation.

7. New York *Globe*, May 17, 1884.

8. Du Bois, *Dusk of Dawn*, pp. 23, 25.

9. *Ibid.*, p. 24.

10. *Catalogue of the Officers of Fisk University*, 1884–85.

11. Du Bois in Logan, *op. cit.*, p. 36.

12. W. E. B. Du Bois, "A Negro Schoolmaster in the New South," *Atlantic Monthly*, LXXXIII (1899), 100.

13. W. E. B. Du Bois, "The Religion of the American Negro," *New World*, IX (1900), 615.

14. W. E. B. Du Bois, "An Open Letter to Southern People," MS, 1888: Du Bois Papers.

15. W. E. B. Du Bois, "Political Serfdom," MS, 1887: Du Bois Papers.

16. W. E. B. Du Bois, "Bismarck," MS, 1888: Du Bois Papers.

17. W. E. B. Du Bois, "Diuturni-Silenti," *Fisk Herald*, XXXIII (1924), 1–12.

18. *Crisis*, XLI (1934), 134.

19. W. E. B. Du Bois, "Account Book and Diary," MS, 1888–90 and "Harvard and Democracy," MS, *circa* 1920: Du Bois Papers; *Dusk of Dawn*, p. 101.

20. Supplied by Mrs. Maude Trotter Stewart in an interview, April, 1954.

21. Du Bois in Logan, *op. cit.*, p. 40.

22. W. E. B. Du Bois, "What The Negro Will Do," MS, 1889: Du Bois Papers.

23. W. E. B. Du Bois, "Harvard and the South," MS, 1891: Du Bois Papers.

24. Du Bois was proposed for membership in the Harvard Graduate Club, but was "said to have been blackballed because of color." Three white students, who were accepted at the time of his rejection, decided to remain outside of the organization in protest. (Thomas E. Will to Du Bois, 1906: Du Bois Papers).

25. W. E. B. Du Bois, "Does Education Pay?" MS, 1891: Du Bois Papers.

26. Du Bois in Logan, *op. cit.*, p. 41.

27. *Crisis*, XV (1917-18), 169.

28. W. E. B. Du Bois, "Burghardt," MS, *circa* 1894-96: Du Bois Papers.

29. Frederick A. McGinnis, *A History and an Interpretation of Wilberforce University* (Wilberforce, 1941), p. 164.

30. Du Bois in Logan, *op. cit.*, p. 44; *Dusk of Dawn*, p. 57.

31. His dissertation was entitled, *The Suppression of the African Slave Trade to the United States of America*, 1638-1870 (New York, 1896). Loggins estimated that Du Bois' work was "by far the greatest intellectual achievement which had by 1900 come from any American Negro." (Vernon Loggins, *The Negro Author* [New York, 1931], p. 282.) See also *Nation*, LXIII (1896), 498-99.

32. Telegram from Dr. Charles C. Harrison to Du Bois, June 8, 1896: Du Bois Papers.

33. Minutes of the University of Pennsylvania Board of Trustees, October 5, 1896, p. 385. University Archives.

34. Letter appears in Du Bois' *Philadelphia Negro* (Philadelphia, 1899), p. viii.

35. On the first page of the monograph, he announced that he intended to capitalize the word, "Negro." He asserted that "eight million Americans are entitled to a capital letter."

36. Du Bois, *Philadelphia Negro*, pp. 368-84.

37. *Ibid.*, p. 177.

38. *Ibid.*, p. 397.

39. *Nation* LXIX (1899), 310.

40. *Yale Review*, IX (1900), 110.

41. *Outlook*, LXIII (1899), 647-48.

42. *American Historical Review*, VI (1900-01), 162-64.

43. W. E. B. Du Bois, "The Negroes of Farmville, Virginia," *Bulletin of the United States Department of Labor* (Washington, 1898), No. 14, pp. 1–38.
44. W. E. B. Du Bois, "The Study of Negro Problems," *Annals of the American Academy of Political and Social Science*, XI (1898), 1–23.
45. Brewton Berry, *Race and Ethnic Relations* (Boston, 1958), p. 337.

II

1. Willard Range, *The Rise and Progress of Negro Colleges in Georgia, 1865–1949* (Athens, Georgia, 1951), pp. 77, 112, 164.
2. *Ibid.*, p. 153. Chicago *Whip*, April 11, 1925. John H. Adams, "Rough Sketches," *Voice of the Negro*, II (1905), 180; Darkwater, p. 20.
3. W. E. B. Du Bois, "A Program for a Sociological Society," MS, 1897: Du Bois Papers.
4. *Mortality Among Negroes in Cities* (Atlanta, 1896), p. 5.
5. *Social and Physical Conditions of Negroes in Cities* (Atlanta, 1897), p. 69.
6. W. E. B. Du Bois, "The Atlanta University Studies of Social Conditions Among Negroes, 1896–1913," MS, 1940: Du Bois Papers and "The Atlanta University Conferences," *Charities*, X (1903), 436.
7. W. E. B. Du Bois (ed.), *Economic Cooperation Among Negro Americans* (Atlanta, 1907), p. 2.
8. *Outlook*, LXXIII (1903), 593.
9. *Publications of the Southern History Association*, VIII (1904), 459.
10. *Political Science Quarterly*, XIX (1904), 702–03.
11. W. E. B. Du Bois, "The Study of Negro Problems," *Annals of the American Academy of Political and Social Science*, XI (1898), 7–11.
12. W. E. B. Du Bois (ed.), *The Negro Church* (Atlanta, 1903), p. 154.
13. W. E. B. Du Bois, "Atlanta Conferences," *Voice of the Negro*, I (1904). 85–90.
14. Horace Bumstead to W. E. B. Du Bois, November 26, 1904: Du Bois Papers.
15. W. E. B. Du Bois (ed.), *A Select Bibliography of the Negro American* (Atlanta, 1905), p. 6.
16. President Ware to W. E. B. Du Bois, April 22, 1908: Du Bois Papers.
17. W. E. B. Du Bois and A. Dill, *Morals and Manners Among Negro Americans* (Atlanta, 1914), p. 44.

18. W. E. B. Du Bois, *The Negro Common School* (Atlanta, 1902), pp. 89–92. Also W. E. B. Du Bois and A. Dill (eds.), *The Common School and the Negro American* (Atlanta, 1911), pp. 120–26.

19. *Outlook*, LXXI (1902), 676–77. *Dial*, XXXII (1902), 353. *Publications of the Southern History Association*, VI (1902), 350.

20. Du Bois and Dill, *Morals and Manners Among Negro Americans*, p. 67.

21. Du Bois, *The Negro Church*, p. 3.

22. W. E. B. Du Bois, *The Negro in Business* (Atlanta, 1899). p. 50.

23. W. E. B. Du Bois to William M. Trotter, May 20, 1905: Du Bois Papers. Booker T. Washington, "The National Negro Business League," *World's Work*, IV (1902), 2672. Also Booker T. Washington, "The Negro in Business," *Gunton's Magazine*, XX (1901), 215.

24. Du Bois, *Darkwater*, pp. 21–22.

25. W. E. B. Du Bois, "Relation of the Negro to the Whites in the South," *Annals of the American Academy of Political and Social Science*, XVIII (1901), 140.

III

1. W. E. B. Du Bois, *Memorial to the Legislature of Georgia on the Hardwick Bill*, pamphlet, November, 1899: Du Bois Papers, and "The Suffrage Fight in Georgia," *Independent*, LI (1899), 3226–28.

2. Du Bois, *et al.*, *A Memorial to the Georgia Legislature on Negro Common Schools*, circa 1900: Du Bois Papers.

3. W. E. B. Du Bois, "The Opening of the Library," *Independent*, LIV (1902), 809–10.

4. W. E. B. Du Bois, "The Spawn of Slavery," *Missionary Review of the World*, XXIV (1901), 737, 745.

5. W. E. B. Du Bois, "The American Negro at Paris," *Review of Reviews*, XXII (1900), 575–77; "The Freedmen and Their Sons," *Independent*, LIII (1901), 2709; and "The Savings of Black Georgia," *Outlook*, LXIX (1901), 128–30.

6. W. E. B. Du Bois, quoted in Herbert Aptheker, *A Documentary History of the Negro People in the United States* (New York, 1951), p. 775.

7. Du Bois, "Relation of the Negro to the Whites in the South," p. 131. See also, Du Bois, "The Negro and Crime," *Independent*, LI (1899), 1355–57.

8. W. E. B. Du Bois, "The Storm and Stress in the Black World," *Dial*, XXX

(1901), 262–64; "The Negro as He Really Is," *World's Work*, II (1901), 848-63 and "The Religion of the American Negro," *New World*, IX (1900), 614–25.

9. The following letters are found in the Du Bois Papers:
Du Bois to Washington, April 17, 1901. Washington to Du Bois, November 28, 1902. W. H. Smith to Du Bois, December 1, 1902. Telegram from Du Bois and others to Robert T. Lincoln, October 29, 1903. Washington to Du Bois, December 14, 1903.
The following letters are found in the Washington Papers:
Washington to J. Napier, November 2, 1903. Washington to Du Bois, November 5, 1903. Du Bois to Washington, January 24, 1904. Washington to J. Napier, January 27, 1904. Washington to Du Bois, February 27, 1904. Washington to Du Bois, June 4, 1904.

10. The following letters are found in the Du Bois Papers:
Du Bois to G. R. Parkin, January 21, 1903. G. R. Parkin to Du Bois, January 28, 1903. Washington to Du Bois, February 3, 1903.

11. Du Bois *et al.*, "Resolutions of the Third Hampton Conference," *Hampton Negro Conference*, III (*circa* 1899), 7–9. W. E. B. Du Bois, "Results of the Ten Tuskegee Conferences," *Harper's Weekly*, XLV (1901), 641.

12. W. E. B. Du Bois, "The Evolution of Negro Leadership," *Dial*, XXXI (1901), 53–55.

13. W. E. B. Du Bois to Booker T. Washington, September 2, 1901: Washington Papers.

14. W. E. B. Du Bois to Booker T. Washington, March 4, 1902: Washington Papers.

15. *Negro Artisan* (Atlanta, 1902), pp. 5–7.

16. Du Bois, *Dusk of Dawn*, pp. 77–79.

17. Booker T. Washington, *Up From Slavery* (Garden City, 1901), p. 226.

18. *Ibid.*, pp. 192–93. Washington, *Future of the American Negro* (Boston, 1899), pp. 153–54 (1907 edition) and "Signs of Progress Among the Negroes," *Century*, LIX (1899), 474. See also, E. Davidson Washington (ed.), *Selected Speeches of Booker T. Washington* (Garden City, 1932), pp. 5, 6, 45.

19. Washington, *Future of the American Negro*, p. 141.

20. Basil Mathews, *Booker T. Washington, Educator and Interracial Interpreter* (Cambridge, 1948), p. 206. Booker T. Washington to F. J. Garrison, February 27, 1900. Garrison to Washington, March 11, 1900. These letters are found at the Schomburg Collection.

21. Lyman B. Stowe and Emmett J. Scott, *Booker T. Washington Builder of a Civilization*, 1917, pp. 50–55.

22. Edith A. Talbot, *Samuel C. Armstrong* (New York, 1904), p. 155. See Washington, *Up From Slavery.*

23. Booker T. Washington, "The Salvation of the Negro," *World's Work*, II, (1901), 961–64 and "Problems in Education," *Cosmopolitan*, XXXIII (1902), 506.

24. Booker T. Washington, "Education Will Solve the Race Problem,"*North American Review*, CLXXI (1900), 228.

25. Booker T. Washington, speech in *Thirty-Ninth Annual Report of the Michigan State Board of Agriculture* (Lansing, 1899–1900), p. 452.

26. Washington, *Future of the American Negro*, p. 79.

27. Washington, *Up From Slavery*, pp. 121–23. Washington in *Thirty-Ninth Annual Report of the Michigan State Board of Agriculture*, p. 451 and "Problems in Education," p. 508.

28. Kelly Miller, "The Negro and Education," *Forum*, XXX (1900–01), 700.

29. Booker T. Washington, "Education of the Negro," N. M. Butler (ed.), *Monographs on Education*, II (1900).

30. See W. E. B. Du Bois, *Conservation of Races*, Occasional Papers of the American Negro Academy, 1897.

31. *Independent*, LIII (1901), 2547.

32. Francis E. Leupp, "Why Booker Washington Has Succeeded," *Outlook*, LXXI (1902), 330. See also, Du Bois, "Training of the Negroes for Social Power," *Outlook*, LXXV (1903), 410.

33. W. D. Howells, "An Exemplary Citizen," *North American Review*, CLXXIII (1901), 285.

34. E. Davidson Washington, *op. cit.*, p. 52.

35. Boston *Guardian*, September 13, 1902. For other Trotter criticisms, see Boston *Guardian*, September 6, 20; November 1; November 15; December 6, 20, 1902, and April 4, 1903. Also see Ruth Worthy, "A Negro in Our History—William Monroe Trotter" (M.A. thesis, Columbia University, 1952).

36. Kelly Miller, *Race Adjustment* (New York, 1908), p. 14. Kelly Miller's unpublished autobiography, MS, n.d., Kelly Miller Papers. I am indebted to Professor August Meier, who saw the material and sent me this note as well as others.

37. Boston *Guardian*, November 1, 1902.

38. Supplied by Mrs. Maude Trotter Stewart in an interview, May, 1954.

39. W. E. B. Du Bois, "Of the Training of Black Men," *Atlantic Monthly*, XC (1902), 292–95.

40. Boston *Guardian*, September 6, 1902.

41. Boston *Guardian*, January 3, 10, 1903.

42. James Weldon Johnson, *Along This Way* (New York, 1933), p. 203.

43. James Weldon Johnson, *Black Manhattan* (New York, 1930), p. 134.

44. Mathews, *op. cit.*, p. 281.

45. William H. Ferris, *African Abroad* (New Haven, 1913), p. 277.

46. W. E. B. Du Bois, *Souls of Black Folk* (Chicago, 1903), pp. 43–59.

47. *Outlook*, LXXIV (1903), 214.

48. Washington *Colored American*, March 21, 1903.

49. J. S. Bassett, "Two Negro Leaders," *South Atlantic Quarterly*, II (1903), 267–72. Boston *Guardian*, July 25, 1903.

50. W. E. B. Du Bois, "Possibilities of the Negro: The Advance Guard of the Race," *Booklover's Magazine*, II (1903), 7.

51. Washington *Colored American*, July 18, 1903.

52. Washington *Bee*, July 11, 1903. See August Meier, "Booker T. Washington and the Rise of the N.A.A.C.P.," MS, 1953, pp. 1, 8. William Ferris, *op. cit.*, pp. 372, 375–76.

53. *Crisis*, XLI (1934), p. 134.

54. The following materials come from the Du Bois Papers: Du Bois to Clement Morgan, October 19, 1903. Horace Bumstead to Du Bois, December 5, 15, 1903.

55. The following materials come from the Du Bois Papers: Du Bois to George F. Peabody, December 28, 1903. Horace Bumstead to Du Bois, January 26, 1904.

56. Booker T. Washington to F. J. Garrison, August 3, 1903: Schomburg Collection.

57. John Daniels, *In Freedom's Birthplace* (New York, 1914), p. 122. Ferris, *op. cit.*, p. 371. Worthy, *op. cit.*, p. 64.

58. Boston *Guardian*, August 1, 1903.

59. Booker T. Washington to F. J. Garrison, August 3, 1903: Schomburg Collection. Emmett J. Scott to Booker T. Washington, August 3, 1903: Washington Papers. Scott to Washington, August 13, 1903: Washington Papers.

60. Booker T. Washington to Whitfield McKinlay, August 3, 1903: Carter Woodson Papers, Library of Congress.

61. Worthy, *op. cit.*, p. 69.

62. Booker T. Washington to Theodore Roosevelt, September 15, 1903: Theodore Roosevelt Papers, Library of Congress.

63. Booker T. Washington, *My Larger Education* (New York, 1911), pp. 112–26.

64. The following materials come from the Du Bois Papers: Du Bois, "Notes for Autobiography," MS, May 14, 1930. Du Bois to R. S. Baker, February 5, 1907.

65. Emmett J. Scott to Booker T. Washington, August 3, 1903: Washington Papers.

66. Worthy, *op. cit.*, pp. 27–29. G. W. Andrews to Du Bois, November 2, 1903 and Du Bois to G. W. Andrews, November 3, 1903: Du Bois Papers. See the following letters in Washington Papers: J. C. May (Wilford Smith) to R. C. Black (Emmett J. Scott), June 3 and August 31, 1903. Also, W. H. Lewis to Booker Washington, September 16, 1903. Washington to Scott, November 23, 1903.

IV

1. Form letter from Booker T. Washington, February 12, 1903, in Herbert Aptheker, "The Washington-Du Bois Meeting of 1904," *Science and Society*, XIII (1949), 346.

2. W. E. B. Du Bois to Kelly Miller, February 25, 1903: Du Bois Papers.

3. Booker T. Washington to F. J. Grimke, November 19, 1903. Carter Woodson (ed.), *Works of F. J. Grimke*, IV (Washington, 1942), 88.

4. The following are found in the Washington Papers: Washington to Du Bois, October 28, 1903. Washington to Du Bois, November 8, 1903. Du Bois to Washington, November 14, 1903. See also, Washington to F. J. Grimke, November 19, 1903 in Woodson, *op. cit.*, p. 88.

5. See Woodson, *op. cit.*, p. 89.

6. Washington *Bee*, January 16, 23, 30, 1904.

7. Kelly Miller, "Conference of Prominent Colored Men—Summary of Proceedings," MS, January, 1904: Washington Papers.

8. The following are found in the Washington Papers: W. H. Baldwin to Booker T. Washington, January 18, 1904. Washington to Baldwin,

January 19, 1904. Moton to Washington, January 14, 1904. Washington to Moton, January 18, 1904. Washington to Moton, January 22, 1904, Moton to Washington, January 28, 1904. Anderson to Washington, January 26, 1904.

9. Washington to Du Bois, February 27, 1904: Washington Papers.

10. Washington to Du Bois, March 5, 1904: Washington Papers. See also the following letters in Washington Papers: Washington to A. B. Humphrey, June 4, 1904. Humphrey to Washington, June 9, 1904. Washington to Anderson, August 15, 1904. Washington to Villard, October 10, 1904.

11. See Washington Papers: Washington to Du Bois, January 27, 1904. Washington to Du Bois, February 23, 1904. Du Bois to Washington, February 25, 1904. Washington *Bee*, March 19, 1904.

12. Washington Papers: Emmett J. Scott to R. W. Thompson, March 11, 1904. Thompson to Scott, March 20, 1904.

13. Anderson to Washington, June 27, 1904: Washington Papers.

14. Washington Papers: Scott to Washington, July 5, 1904. Anderson to Washington, July 12, 1904.

15. Du Bois to Oswald G. Villard, March 24, 1905: Villard Papers.

16. Hugh Browne to Du Bois, July 28, 1904: Du Bois Papers.

17. Aptheker, "The Washington-Du Bois Meeting of 1904," p. 350.

18. Washington to Villard, November 16, 1904: Villard Papers.

19. Du Bois to Villard, November 16, 1904: Villard Papers.

20. Villard to Du Bois, April 18, 1905: Villard Papers.

21. Mary White Ovington, *The Walls Came Tumbling Down* (New York, 1947), p. 76.

22. Du Bois, *Dusk of Dawn*, p. 75.

23. August Meier, "Booker T. Washington and the Rise of the N.A.A.C.P.," *Crisis*, LXI (1954), 70 and "Booker T. Washington and the Negro Press," *Journal of Negro History*, XXXVIII (1953), 67–90.

24. Reprinted in Cleveland *Gazette*, January 5, 1905.

25. New York *Age*, January 19, February 16, and March 2, 1905.

26. Du Bois to Villard, March 24, 1905: Villard Papers. Du Bois to W. H. Ward, March 10, 1905: Du Bois Papers.

27. O. G. Villard to Du Bois, April 18, 1905: Villard Papers.

28. F. J. Garrison to Booker T. Washington, May 8, 1905: Washington Papers.

29. Washington to Garrison, May 17, 1905: Schomburg Collection.

30. See the following letters in the Washington Papers: Charles Alexander to Booker Washington, February 19, 1905. Washington to Alexander, March 25, 1905. Alexander to Washington, April 2, 1905. Alexander to Washington, April 15, June 9, 1905.

31. Meier, "Booker T. Washington and the Negro Press," p. 71. A few years later, Washington invested another $3,000 in the New York *Age*. See Fred Moore to Booker Washington, March 23, 1910: Washington Papers.

32. See following in Washington Papers: R. W. Thompson to Emmett Scott, February 18, 1905. Thompson to Scott, July 3, 1905. Scott to Gilmer, July 6, 1905.

33. Washington to B. J. Davis, April 21, 1904. Davis to Washington, April 22, 1904: Washington Papers.

34. See following in Washington Papers: R. W. Thompson to Scott, February 23, 1905. Scott to Thompson, February 25, 1905. Scott to Thompson, March 2, 1905. Thompson to Scott, May 9, 1905.

35. Cleveland *Gazette*, March 11, 1905. See also W. M. Trotter to Du Bois, February 27, 1905: Du Bois Papers. The following materials are found in the Washington Papers: Washington to Charles Alexander, March 25, 1905. R. W. Thompson to Scott, February 18, 1905. Scott to Thompson, March 25, 1905. Washington to Roscoe Simmons, May 13, 1905.

36. Washington *Bee*, February 11, 1905. Boston *Guardian*, February 16, 1905. See also Cleveland *Gazette*, April 1, 1905.

37. Washington to Scott, March 11, 1905. Thompson to Scott, March 21, 1905: Washington Papers.

38. Villard to F. J. Garrison, May 23, 1905: Villard Papers.

V

1. Ralph J. Bunche, "The Programs, Ideologies, Tactics and Achievements of Negro Betterment and Interracial Organizations," unpublished memorandum for the Myrdal study (1940), I, 16. Located in the Schomburg Collection, New York City.

2. J. Max Barber, "The Niagara Movement," *Voice of the Negro*, II (1905), 617. Cleveland *Gazette*, 'March 19, 1904. Jesse Fauset to W. E. B. Du Bois, 1905, in Herbert Aptheker, *A Documentary History of the Negro People in the United States* (New York, 1951), p. 900.

3. J. Max Barber, "What is the Niagara Movement," *Voice of the Negro*, II (1905), 647.
4. The following letters come from the Du Bois Papers and were examined by Dr. Francis Broderick: Albert Bushnell Hart to W. E. B. Du Bois, April 24, 1905. John S. Brown to W. E. B. Du Bois, May 15, 1905. W. E. B. Du Bois to John S. Brown, May 18, 1905. W. E. B. Du Bois to Albert Bushnell Hart, October 9, 1905.
5. Mathews, *op. cit.*, p. 285.
6. Ferris, *African Abroad*, pp. 276–77.
7. Johnson, *Along This Way*, p. 313.
8. *What's the Niagara Movement?* pamphlet, 1905, Howard University Library.
9. *Niagara Movement Declaration of Principles*, pamphlet, 1905, Howard University Library. See also, Barber, "The Niagara Movement," p. 522.
10. *Outlook*, LXXX (1905), 796.
11. Chicago *Law Register*, reprinted in the Washington *Bee*, August 12, 1905. Cleveland *Gazette*, July 22, 1905.
12. Washington *Bee*, September 9, 1905.
13. W. E. B. Du Bois, "Growth of the Niagara Movement," *Voice of the Negro*, III (1906), 43.
14. Booker T. Washington to Charles W. Anderson, July 11, 1905, and Charles W. Anderson to Booker T. Washington, July 14, 1905: Washington Papers.
15. Emmett J. Scott to R. W. Thompson, July 18, 1905, and see also Emmett J. Scott to Booker T. Washington, July 18, 1905: Washington Papers.
16. Emmett J. Scott to Booker T. Washington, July 24, 1905, and see also R. W. Thompson to Emmett J. Scott, July 28, 1905: Washington Papers.
17. Roscoe Simmons to Booker T. Washington, July 25, 1905, and Emmett Scott to R. W. Thompson, July 31, 1905: Washington Papers.
18. Booker T. Washington to Emmett J. Scott, July 27; August 7, 1905: Washington Papers.
19. R. W. Thompson to Emmett J. Scott, July 28, 1905: Washington Papers.
20. Emmett J. Scott to R. W. Thompson, July 31, 1905: Washington Papers.
21. W. E. B. Du Bois, "What Is the Niagara Movement," reprint from Boston *Guardian*, 1905. W. E. B. Du Bois to L. C. Jordan, April 16, 1905: Du Bois Papers.

22. Booker T. Washington to Charles W. Anderson, December 30, 1905: Washington Papers. The Tuskegeean was familiar with this approach; for more than a year, he had been using an informer against Trotter in the New England Suffrage League. See the following communications in the Washington Papers: Booker T. Washington to Clifford Plummer, September 29, 1904. Washington to Plummer, September 30, 1904. Plummer to Washington, September 30, 1904. Washington to Plummer, October 1, 1904. Plummer to Washington, October 24, 1904. Washington to Plummer, October 27, 1904. Plummer to Emmett J. Scott, September 25, 1905. Scott to Plummer, September 29, 1905.

23. Charles W. Anderson to Booker T. Washington, January 8, 1905: Washington Papers.

24. Oswald Garrison Villard to F. J. Garrison, November 8, 1905: Villard Papers.

25. Booker T. Washington to Emmett J. Scott, August 7, 1905, and Scott to Washington, August 10, 1905: Washington Papers.

26. See the following letters in the Washington Papers: Charles W. Anderson to Booker T. Washington, September 18, 1905. Anderson to Scott, November 1, 1905. Anderson to Washington, December 27, 1905. Anderson to Washington, January 12, 1906. Anderson to Washington, January 8, 1906.

27. Booker T. Washington to John E. Milholland, September 18, 1905: Washington Papers.

28. Meier, "Booker T. Washington and the Rise of the N.A.A.C.P.," p. 74. See the following letters in the Washington Papers: John Milholland to Booker Washington, February 3, 1903. Milholland to Washington, February 7, 1903. Washington to Milholland, February 9, 1903. Washington to Milholland, February 20, 1903. Washington to Milholland, November 25, 1903.

29. Charles W. Anderson to Booker T. Washington, October 16, 1905: Washington Papers.

30. See the following letters in the Washington Papers: Charles W. Anderson to Booker T. Washington, September 27, 1905. Fred Moore to Washington, September 28, 1905. Roscoe Simmons to Washington, October 2, 1905. Anderson to Washington, October 3, 1905. Washington to Moore, October 5, 1905. Anderson to Washington, October 12, 1905.

31. John E. Milholland, *The Nation's Duty* (New York, 1906), pamphlet, p. 5.

32. John E. Milholland, *The Negro and the Nation* (New York, 1906). See also, A. B. Humphrey, "Statement of Principles of the Constitution League," January 23, 1906: Du Bois Papers. New York *Age*, February 8, 1906. Barber, "The Niagara Movement," p. 476.

33. *Voice of the Negro*, III (1906), 239.

34. Gilchrist Stewart to Booker Washington, February 13, 1906: Washington Papers.

35. Supplied by Mr. Mercer Daniel in an interview in February, 1954.

36. See the following letters in the Washington Papers: Richard Greener to "My dear Friend," July 31, 1906. Booker T. Washington to Richard Greener, August 11, 1906. Telegram from Greener to Washington August 11, 1906. Washington to Greener, October 20, 1906.

37. See J. Max Barber, "The Niagara Movement at Harpers Ferry," *Voice of the Negro*, III (1906), 403–11. "Minutes of the Niagara Movement," August 18, 1906: Du Bois Papers.

38. "Report on the Committee on Education—2nd Annual Meeting," 1906: Du Bois Papers.

39. *Outlook*, LXXXIV (1906), pp. 3–4, 54–55.

40. John Hope Franklin, *From Slavery to Freedom* (New York, 1948), p. 437.

41. New York *Age*, August 16, 23, 30; November 22, 1906. Also see New York *Age*, February 8, 1906.

42. Barber, "The Niagara Movement at Harpers Ferry," p. 411.

43. Washington *Bee*, August 25, 1906. Also the following letters in Du Bois Papers: Clement Morgan to W. E. B. Du Bois, May 13, 1906. Du Bois to "Niagara Membership," May 16, 1906.

44. The Jamestown appropriation was also opposed because Virginia disfranchised Negroes and segregated them on railroads. According to the Washington *Bee*, the Negro Annex of the Exposition informed newspapers that Du Bois would send a sociological exhibit. Du Bois angrily replied that the statement was "an impudent lie." Washington *Bee*, March 30, 1907. See also, Barber, "The Niagara Movement at Harpers Ferry," p. 408. Arther Gary, "Story of the Niagara Movement" (unpublished MS from *Negroes of New York*, W. P. A. Project, New York, 1939). Located in Schomburg Collection, New York City.

45. Washington *Bee*, June 30, July 14, 1906.

46. Washington *Bee*, September 23, October 28, 1905; and August 18, 1906.

47. *African Methodist Episcopal Review*, XXIII (1906), 184.

48. New York *Age*, August 30, 1906.

49. New York *Age*, September 13, October 11, 1906.

50. Booker Washington to Charles W. Anderson, October 4, 1906: Washington Papers. New York *Age*, October 18, 1906.

51. Booker Washington to T. Thomas Fortune, April 9, 1906: Washington Papers.

52. Booker T. Washington, "Golden Rule in Atlanta," *Outlook*, LXXXIV (1906), 913.

53. W. E. B. Du Bois, "The Tragedy of Atlanta—from the Point of View of the Negroes," *World Today*, XI (1906), 1175.

54. New York *Age*, November 22, 1906.

55. W. E. B. Du Bois, "Litany of Atlanta," *Independent*, LXI (1906), 856–58.

56. Crawford's report may be found in Aptheker's *Documentary . . .* , p. 911.

57. The following are found in the Du Bois Papers: W. E. B. Du Bois to John E. Milholland, March 27, 1907. A. C. Humphrey to Du Bois, April 25, 1907. Du Bois to Humphrey, May 2, 1907. "Niagara Movement's Civil Rights Department Report," 1906–07.

58. "Abstracts of Minutes, Niagara Movement," August 15–18, 1906: found in Howard University Library. Washington *Bee*, August 25, 1906. L. M. Hershaw, "Pope Case," *Horizon* (May 1907), p. 17. W. E. B. Du Bois to "Dear Colleagues," April 10, 1907: Du Bois Papers.

59. "Secretary and Committee Reports of the Niagara Movement," April 1, 1907: Du Bois Papers.

60. Charles W. Anderson to Booker T. Washington, February 19, 1907; Anderson to Emmett J. Scott, February 25, 1907; and Anderson to Washington, May 27, 1907: Washington Papers.

61. W. E. B. Du Bois to Henry T. McDonald, March 18, 1907: Du Bois Papers.

62. For example, see New York *Age*, September 7, 1907.

63. R. W. Tyler to Booker T. Washington, August 29, 1907: Washington Papers.

64. "Minutes of the Third Niagara Conference," August 29, 1907: Du Bois Papers. 1907 *Boston Meeting of Niagara* (pamphlet), Howard University Library. Washington *Bee*, September 14, 1907.

65. Niagara Movement to the Constitution League, August 29, 1907, and Niagara Movement to Senator Foraker, August 29, 1907: Du Bois Papers. See also Cleveland *Gazette*, December 15, 1906; and June 22, 1907.

66. 1907 *Boston Meeting of Niagara* (pamphlet), 1907: located at Howard University Library.
67. "Minutes of the Third Niagara Conference": Du Bois Papers.
68. *Ibid.*
69. W. E. B. Du Bois to I. M. Rubinow, November 17, 1904: Du Bois Papers. Du Bois, "Socialist of the Path," *Horizon*, February, 1907; "The Negro and Socialists," *Horizon*, February, 1907; and *The Negro in the South* (Philadelphia, 1907), p. 116. Du Bois, "A Field for Socialists," MS, 1907: Du Bois Papers.
70. Indianapolis *Freeman*, September 21, 1907. (This material comes from the scrapbook collection at the library of Hampton Institute. Hereafter, this source will be referred to as "Hampton.")
71. *Address to the World of the Third Niagara Conference*, pamphlet, 1907. Located at Howard University Library. See also, Cleveland *Gazette*, September 7, 1907.
72. New York *Age*, September 19, 1907.
73. *Outlook*, LXXXVII (1907), 48.
74. L. M. Hershaw, "With a Grievance," *Horizon* (October 1907), p. 15.
75. Washington *Bee*, September 14, 1907. "Minutes of the Third Niagara Conference": Du Bois Papers.
76. Mary White Ovington to W. E. B. Du Bois, October 8, 1907: Du Bois Papers, courtesy of Ruth Worthy. See also, Mary White Ovington to Ray Stannard Baker, October 17, 1907: Baker Papers, Library of Congress.
77. Clement Morgan to Charles E. Bentley, November 20, 1907: Du Bois Papers.
78. New York *Age*, November 14, 1907. The following material comes from the Du Bois Papers: J. Max Barber to W. E. B. Du Bois, November 9, 1907. Du Bois to Executive Committee and Sub-Committee, *circa* December, 1907. Du Bois to F. L. McGhee, *circa* late 1907. Du Bois to Executive Committee, *circa* late 1907. "Report of the Executive Committee and Sub-Executive Committee of the Niagara Movement," January 11, 1908.
79. Charles W. Anderson to Emmett J. Scott, February 15, 1908: Washington Papers. Oswald G. Villard to F. J. Garrison, January 15, 1908: Villard Papers.
80. W. E. B. Du Bois, "To Black Voters," *Horizon* (February 1908), p. 17.
81. W. E. B. Du Bois, "Bryan," *Horizon* (March 1908), p. 7. New York *Age*, April, 2 1908. See also, Springfield *Republican*, March 28, 1908: Hampton.

82. Reprinted in New York *Age*, April 2, 1908. See also New York *Age* April 16, 1908.

83. Booker T. Washington to Fred Moore, *circa* June, 1908: Washington Papers.

84. W. E. B. Du Bois, "Talk No. Three," *Horizon* (August 1908), pp. 5-7. W. E. B. Du Bois to Harry S. New, June 1, 1908: Du Bois Papers.

85. W. E. B. Du Bois, "The Negro Vote," *Horizon* (September 1908), pp. 4-6, and "Talk No. Five," *Horizon* (September 1908), pp. 7-8.

86. Washington *Bee*, September 19, 1908. New York *Age*, November 12, 1908.

87. Aptheker, *Documentary* . . . , p. 848.

88. W. E. B. Du Bois to John E. Milholland, March 20, 1908: Du Bois Papers.

89. W. E. B. Du Bois, "The Negro Vote," *Horizon* (October 1908), p. 6, and "Politics," *Horizon* (November–December 1908), p. 11.

90. The following material comes from Du Bois Papers: J. M. Waldron to Du Bois, February 11, 1908. Niagara circular letter (no name), March 14, 1908.

91. The following material comes from Du Bois Papers: Alexander Walters to Du Bois, March–April, 1908. Du Bois to Walters, March 31, 1908. Walters to Du Bois, April 4, 1908. Du Bois to Walters, April 7, 1908. Du Bois to Walters, April 16, 1908. Walters to Du Bois, April 11, 1908. Du Bois to Walters, June 12, 1908.

92. Mary White Ovington to W. E. B. Du Bois, April 24, 1908: Du Bois Papers.

93. "Report of the Niagara Secretary for Pennsylvania," August–September, 1908: Du Bois Papers.

94. *Independent*, LXV (1908), 676. See also Richmond *Planet*, September 19, 1908. *Horizon* (September 1908), p. 1.

95. Savannah *Tribune*, September 19, 26, 1908: Hampton.

96. Booker T. Washington to Fred Moore, September 7, 8, 1908: Washington Papers.

97. W. E. B. Du Bois, "Little Brother of Mine," *Horizon* (February 1908), p. 18.

98. New York *Age*, July 29, 1909. Hampton.

99. W. E. B. Du Bois to George W. Crawford, July 31, 1909: Du Bois Papers.

100. "Report of the Fifth Niagara Movement Convention by F. L. McGhee, Secretary of the Legal Department," August 14, 1909: Du Bois Papers.

101. W. E. B. Du Bois, "Niagara Movement," *Horizon* (November 1909), p. 9. See also, *Fisherman's Net*, September 17, 1909: Hampton.
102. Indianapolis *Freeman*, October 2, 1909; Hampton.
103. W. E. B. Du Bois, "Subscribers," *Horizon* (May 1910), p. 1. *Crisis*, V (1912–13), 27.
104. Arnold M. Rose, *The Negro's Morale* (Minneapolis, 1949), p. 32. See also, Henry Lee Moon, *The Balance of Power: The Negro Vote* (New York, 1948), p. 100.

1. Mary White Ovington, *How the N.A.A.C.P. Began*, pamphlet, New York, 1914.
2. Booker T. Washington to O. G. Villard, September 7, 1908, and Villard to Washington, September 10, 1908: Villard Papers.
3. O. G. Villard to F. J. Garrison, February 24, 1909, and Villard to Garrison, April 15, 1909: Villard Papers.
4. Ovington, *How the N.A.A.C.P. Began*, pp. 2–3. Bunche, "Programs, Ideologies, Tactics . . . ," pp. 26–28.
5. Ovington, *The Walls Came Tumbling Down*, p. 105. O. G. Villard to Washington, May 26, 1909: Washington Papers.
6. The following materials come from the Villard Papers: Washington to Villard, May 28, 1909. Villard to Washington, June 4, 1909. F. J. Garrison to Villard, June 6, 1909.
7. *The New York Times*, June 1, 1909. W. E. B. Du Bois, "National Committee on the Negro," *Survey*, XXII (1909), 407.
8. *Outlook*, XCII (1909), 342.
9. Du Bois, "National Committee on the Negro," p. 408. *Proceedings of the National Negro Conference*, 1909, pp. 21, 39–40.
10. *Ibid.*, pp. 80–87.
11. O. G. Villard to F. J. Garrison, June 4, 1909: Villard Papers. Ovington, *The Walls Came Tumbling Down*, p. 106.
12. Du Bois, "National Committee on the Negro," p. 409.
13. *Proceedings of the National Negro Conference*, 1909, p. 223.
14. New York *Post*, June 2, 1909: Hampton.
15. Anderson to Washington, May 30, 1909, and telegram from Anderson to Washington, May 31, 1909: Washington Papers.
16. Mary White Ovington to Villard, June 2, 1909: Villard Papers.

17. New York *World,* June 1, 1909: Hampton.
18. *The New York Times,* June 1, 1909.
19. Baltimore *Sun,* June 3, 6, 1909, and Raleigh *Observer,* June 4, 1909: Hampton.
20. O. G. Villard to F. J. Garrison, June 7, 1909: Villard Papers. John Graham Brooks, *An American Citizen—The Life of William H. Baldwin* (Boston, 1910), pp. 206, 214.
21. O. G. Villard to F. J. Garrison, November 15, 1909: Villard Papers.
22. Booker T. Washington to R. H. Terrell, April 27, 1910: Washington Papers. *The New York Times,* May 15, 1910.
23. Emmett Scott to H. T. Kealing, May 16, 1910, and Kealing to Scott, May 27, 1910: Washington Papers.
24. Springfield *Republican,* May 10, 1910, and New York *Evening Post,* May 13, 1910: Hampton. See also New York *Age,* May 19, 1910.
25. Villard to Garrison, May 17, 1910: Villard Papers.
26. *The New York Times,* May 13, 15, 1910.
27. Booker T. Washington to Ray Stannard Baker, May 24, 1910: Baker Papers. Booker T. Washington to Charles Anderson, July 11, 1910: Washington Papers.
28. Edwin R. Embree, 13 *Against the Odds* (New York, 1944), p. 164.
29. W. E. B. Du Bois, "Atlanta University Studies of Social Conditions Among Negroes, 1896–1913," MS, 1940: Du Bois Papers.
30. Range, *op. cit.,* p. 160.
31. New York *Age,* December 8, 1910. (Reprint from Atlanta *Independent.*)
32. F. J. Garrison to O. G. Villard, November 19, 1910: Villard Papers. Moorfield Storey to Du Bois, October 13, 20, 1910, and Storey to Trotter, October 25, 1910: Storey Papers. Garrison to Villard, November 19, 1910: Villard Papers. Storey to Du Bois, November 19, 1910: Storey Papers. Garrison to Villard, March 21, 1911, and Villard to Garrison, March 22, 1911: Villard Papers. Storey to Villard, October 17, 1911; Villard to Storey, October 19, 1911; and Storey to Villard, October 19, 1911: Storey Papers.
33. Cleveland *Gazette,* October 1, 1910 (reprinted from London *Standard*).
34. Booker Washington to R. R. Moton, October 24, 1910; Moton to Villard, November 15, 1910; and Moton to Washington, November 17, 1910: Washington Papers. O. G. Villard to Moton, November 23, 1910: Villard Papers.

35. W. E. B. Du Bois, *Race Relations in the United States: An Appeal to England and Europe*, pamphlet, October, 1910: Nathan Mossell Papers. See also, Helen Maria Chesnutt, *Charles W. Chesnutt, Pioneer of the Color Line* (Chapel Hill, 1952), pp. 241–43.

36. Booker Washington to O. G. Villard, December 11, 1910: Washington Papers.

37. The following materials come from Washington Papers: Villard to Moton, November 23, 1910. Villard to Washington, December 13, 1910. Moton to Washington, December 2, 1910.

38. *Crisis*, I (January 1911), 9. *Amsterdam News, circa* January, 1911: Hampton.

39. *Crisis*, I (January 1911), 10. See also, *Crisis*, I (December 1910), 15, 28.

40. Philadelphia *Bulletin*, December 2, 1910: Mossell Papers.

41. Washington's letter of January 10, 1911 to Villard is found in Mathews, *op. cit.*, p. 290. Washington to Anderson, January 19, 1911, and Anderson to Washington, January 16, 1911: Washington Papers.

42. Villard to Washington, January 19, 1911: Washington Papers.

43. Washington to Anderson, January 23, 1911, and see also Anderson to Washington, January 16, 1911: Washington Papers.

44. The following letters are from Washington Papers: Anderson to Washington, February 14, 20, 1911. Joel Spingarn to Anderson, February 25, 1911. Washington to Anderson, February 28, 1911.

45. O. G. Villard to F. J. Garrison, March 24, 1911: Villard Papers.

46. O. G. Villard to F. J. Garrison, March 20, 21, 1911: Villard Papers.

47. M. A. DeWolfe Howe, *Portrait of an Independent—Moorfield, Storey* (Boston, 1932), p. 252.

48. Telegram from O. G. Villard to Booker Washington, March 27, 1911: Washington Papers.

49. The following letters are from Washington Papers: Washington to Anderson, March 28, 1911. Anderson's telegram to Washington, March 29, 1911. Anderson to Washington, March 29, 1911. Moton to Washington, March 29, 1911. Washington's telegram to Villard, March 30, 1911. Anderson to Washington, March 31, 1911.

50. Villard to Washington, March 31, 1911: Washington Papers.

51. Washington to Villard, April 19, 1911: Washington Papers. Villard to Seth Low, April 13, 1911: Villard Papers.

52. *Crisis*, II (May 1911), 12, 25, 28–32.

53. The following letters are from Washington Papers: Villard to Moton, April 5, 1911. Washington to Moton, April 10, 1911. Moton to Washington, April 17, 1911. Washington to Villard, April 19, 1911.

54. Washington to Anderson, May 24, 1911: Washington Papers.

55. *Crisis*, II (1911), 112, 243.

56. *First Annual Report of the N.A.A.C.P.* (New York, 1910), p. 8. These reports are published in the year following the one about which they give information. Therefore, in order to avoid confusion, the date used by the present writer is the *reported* year not the *publication* year.

57. Du Bois, "Universal Races Conference," *Horizon* (May 1910), p. 2.*Crisis*, I (December 1910), 17. *Crisis*, II (1911), 196. Du Bois, "The First Universal Races Congress," *Independent*, LXXI (1911), 401. G. Spiller (ed.), *Papers on Inter-racial Problems: First Universal Races Congress* (London, 1911), pp. v, xiii.

58. The following letters are from the Washington Papers: Moton to Washington, May 13, 1911. Scott to Moton, May 17, 1911. Washington to Moton, May 23, 1911. Moton to Scott, May 20, 1911. Moton to Washington, July 23, 1911. Moton to Fred Moore, July 24, 1911. Washington to Moton, August 5, 1911. Moton to Washington, August 11, 1911. Scott to Moton, December 26, 1911. See Du Bois' address entitled, "The Negro Race in the United States of America," in Spiller, *op. cit.*, pp. 362–64.

59. Du Bois, "The First Universal Races Congress," pp. 401–03. *Crisis*, II (1911), 157.

60. *Independent*, LXXI (1911), 403.

61. *Crisis*, II (1911), 209.

62. Ovington, *The Walls Came Tumbling Down*, p. 132.

63. *Crisis*, II (1911), 207. Boston *Transcript*, *circa* 1911: Hampton. Spiller, *op. cit.*, pp. xiii–xiv.

64. *Crisis*, VIII (1914), 166.

65. *The New York Times*, July 26, 1911.

66. *Afro-American Ledger*, November 26, 1910; Washington *American*, July 29, 1911; and *Amsterdam News*, July 29, 1911: Hampton.

67. *Crisis*, II (1911), 154.

68. *Crisis* II (1911), 208.

69. W. E. B. Du Bois, "Social Evolution of the Black South," *American Negro Monographs*, I (March 1911), 7.

70. W. E. B. Du Bois, "Forty Years of Freedom," *Missionary Review of the World*, XXXIV (1911), 460–61.
71. W. E. B. Du Bois, "The Upbuilding of Black Durham," *World's Work*, XXIII (1911–12), 338.
72. Du Bois, "Forty Years of Freedom," p. 461. See also, W. E. B. Du Bois, *College-Bred Negro Communities*, pamphlet, Atlanta University, 1910, and "The Souls of White Folk," *Independent*, LXIX (1910), 339.

VII

1. *Crisis*, III (1911–12), 157. *Crisis*, V (1912–13), 130.
2. Supplied by Mr. Arthur Spingarn, Mr. Walter White, and Mr. George Crawford in interviews, February and April, 1954.
3. *Twenty-First Annual Report of the N.A.A.C.P.*, 1930, p. 68.
4. Ovington, *The Walls Came Tumbling Down*, p. 108.
5. *Third Annual Report of the N.A.A.C.P.*, 1912, p. 15.
6. J. Saunders Redding, "Portrait: W. E. Burghardt Du Bois," *American Scholar*, XVIII (1949), 93.
7. *Crisis*, I (November 1910), 10.
8. *Crisis*, VI (1913), 184–85.
9. *Ibid.*, p. 236.
10. *Crisis*, III (1911–12), 244–45.
11. *Crisis*, I (January 1911), 20. *Crisis*, II (1911), 197. *Crisis*, III (1911–12), 197. See also *Crisis*, I (February 1911), 20.
12. *Crisis*, I (February 1911), 20.
13. *Crisis*, II (1911), 189.
14. *Crisis*, V (1912–13), 289–90.
15. *Crisis*, VI (1913), 290–91.
16. *Crisis*, VII (1913–14), 83.
17. *Crisis*, III (1911–12), 25.
18. *Crisis*, IV (1912), 24.
19. *Crisis*, III (1911–12), 113.
20. *Crisis*, V (1912–13), 127, 129, 239.
21. *Crisis*, IV (1912), 74. See also *Crisis*, II (1911), 195.
22. *Crisis*, III (1911–12), 197.
23. *Crisis*, V (1912–13), 290–91.

24. W. E. B. Du Bois, "From McKinley to Wallace," *Masses and Mainstream*, I (1948), 7. See Philadelphia *Tribune*, December 23, 1911, and Albany *Press*, February 23, 1913: Hampton. William Z. Foster, *The Negro People in American History* (New York, 1954), pp. 404–05.

25. *Crisis*, IV (1912), 180–81.

26. *Ibid.*, pp. 235–36.

27. *Ibid.*, pp. 180–81.

28. Arthur S. Link, *Wilson, The Road to the White House* (Princeton, 1947). p. 502.

29. The New York *Age* scoffed at the figure. *Age*, August 22, 1912.

30. See the following: *Crisis*, V (1912–13), 29. Arthur S. Link, "The Negro as a Factor in the Campaign of 1912," *Journal of Negro History*, XXXII (1947), 89–93. Woodrow Wilson to O. G. Villard, August 23, 1912, and Villard to Wilson, August 28, 1912: Villard Papers.

31. *Crisis*, V (1912–13), 75–76.

32. New York *Age*, November 28, 1912.

33. *Ibid.*, December 12, 1912.

34. *Crisis*, V (1912–13), 236.

35. Villard to Wilson, July 21, 1913, and Wilson to Villard, July 23, 1913: Villard Papers.

36. New York *Age*, August 14, 1913.

37. *Crisis*, VI (1913), 267. Jane Addams, W. E. B. Du Bois, Moorfield Storey, and O. G. Villard to Woodrow Wilson, August 15, 1913: Villard Papers.

38. *Crisis*, VI (1913), 181, 184.

39. *Fourth Annual Report of the N.A.A.C.P.*, 1913, pp. 12–13. Woodrow Wilson to O. G. Villard, August 21, 1913: Villard Papers. O. G. Villard to Moorfield Storey, September 10, 1913: this letter, among others, is found in the manuscript division of the Princeton University Library.

40. *Crisis*, VI (1913), 232–33.

41. *Crisis*, VII (1913–14), 171. See also *Crisis*, IX (1914–15), 119. Ruth Worthy, *op. cit.*, p. 114. *Crisis*, IX, 82, 129.

42. O. G. Villard to F. J. Garrison, September 23, 1913, and W. E. B. Du Bois to O. G. Villard, March 18, 1913: Villard Papers.

43. See Villard Papers: F. J. Garrison to O. G. Villard, February 5, 1913. O. G. Villard to F. J. Garrison, February 7, 1913. O. G. Villard to F. J. Garrison, February 11, 1913. O. G. Villard to F. J. Garrison, March 14, 1913.

44. *Crisis*, VII (1913–14), 186–87.

45. *Crisis*, VI (1913), 182–83.

46. O. G. Villard to the N.A.A.C.P. Board of Directors, November 19, 1913: Villard Papers.

47. Mary White Ovington to O. G. Villard, November 23, 1913: Villard Papers.

48. *Crisis*, VII (1913–14), 188–89.

49. *Crisis*, VII (1913–14), 239. *Crisis*, VIII (1914), 17, 177–78. See the following from the Hampton Clippings: Richmond *Planet*, *circa* 1914; Washington *Bee*, *circa* 1914; New York *Age*, March 12, 1914; *Advocate* (Jacksonville?), March 14, 1914; Utica *Press*, March 14, 1914.

50. *Crisis*, IX (1914–15), 312. *Crisis*, X (1915), 31, 33.

51. *Crisis*, IX, 312.

52. W. E. B. Du Bois to O. G. Villard and Joel Spingarn, November 10, 1914: Villard Papers. Moorfield Storey to O. G. Villard, November 19, 1914. and Storey to Villard, November 21, 1914: Storey Papers.

53. Minutes of the N.A.A.C.P. Board of Directors, December 1, 1914. These minutes are in the Association's New York office and were seen by Dr. Francis Broderick, who shared his notes with the present writer.

54. William E. Benson, "Kowaliga: A Community With a Purpose," *Charities*, XV (1905), 22–24. New York *Age*, April 2, 1908: Hampton.

55. *Crisis*, XI (1915–16), 79.

56. *Crisis*, X (1915), 116. See also, Mary White Ovington to O. G. Villard, August 10, 1915: Villard Papers.

57. Personal communication from Dr. Du Bois, March 24, 1955.

58. *Crisis*, XI (1915–16), 79.

59. Mary White Ovington to O. G. Villard, August 10, 1915: Villard Papers. See also, Villard to Ovington, August 11, 1915: Villard Papers.

60. *Crisis*, XI (1915–16), 80.

61. Minutes of the N.A.A.C.P. Board of Directors, December 13, 1915.

62. *Crisis*, XI (1915–16), 27. See also p. 25.

63. In response to an inquiry, Du Bois said he was unable to name the individual (or individuals) who exerted this interference. Personal communication from Dr. Du Bois, March 24, 1955.

64. Villard Papers: Roscoe Conkling Bruce to Villard, January 4, 1916. Villard to Bruce, January 6, 1916.

65. Personal communication from Du Bois, July 12, 1955; from Arthur Spingarn, July 14, 1955.
66. Minutes of the N.A.A.C.P. Board of Directors, January 3, 1916.
67. *Crisis*, V (1912–13), 72, 128. *Crisis*, VI (1913), 215–16. *Crisis*, IX (1914–15), pp. 17, 173–74. *Crisis*, X (1915), pp. 144–45.
68. O. G. Villard, "The Objects of the National Association for the Advancement of Colored People," *Crisis*, IV (1912), 81–82.
69. Booker T. Washington to R. R. Moton, March 21, 1913: Washington Papers. Seth Low to O. G. Villard, April 9, 1913; Villard to Washington April 5, 1913; and Villard to Moton, March 31, 1913: Villard Papers. Scott to Moton, April 3, 1913, and Moton to Scott, April 11, 1913: Washington Papers. See also, *Crisis*, VI (1913), 37. *Fourth Annual Report of the N.A.A.C.P.*, 1913, p. 18.

Some of the 1914 letters are found in the Washington Papers: Villard to Washington, May 21, 1914. Moton to Fred Moore, March 5, 1914. Villard to Moton, March 9, 1914. Moton to Moore, March 11, 1914. Scott to Moton, March 11, 1914. Moton to Scott, March 18, 1914.
70. *Crisis*, XI (1915–16), 82.
71. Range, *op. cit.*, p. 78. Myrdal, *op. cit.*, pp. 890, 898. W. Farrison, "Booker T. Washington—A Study in Educational Leadership," *South Atlantic Quarterly*, XLI (1942), 317.
72. Roi Ottley, *Black Odyssey* (New York, 1948), p. 216.
73. Myrdal, *op. cit.*, p. 740.
74. Edward B. Reuter, *The Mulatto in the United States* (Boston, 1918), p.354.
75. Mathews, *op. cit.*, p. 288.
76. John Haynes Holmes, "On Presenting the Spingarn Medal," *Crisis*, XXXII (1926), 232.
77. Myrdal, *op. cit.*, p. 743.

VIII

1. *Crisis*, XI (1915–16), 255. James E. Pierce, "The N.A.A.C.P.—A Study in Social Pressure" (M.A. thesis, 1933, Ohio State University), p. 49.
2. *Crisis*, XII (1916), 136.
3. *Ibid.*, p. 185.
4. *Amenia Conference*, pamphlet, 1916. Located in files at Howard University Library.

5. "Amenia Report," MS, August 26, 1916. Located at Howard University Library. Final draft published in New York *Age*, September 7, 1916.

6. New York *Age*, September 14, 1916.

7. W. E. B. Du Bois, *The Amenia Conference*, pamphlet (Troutbeck, New York, 1925), p. 17. See also *Crisis*, XL (1933), 226.

8. Franklin, *From Slavery To Freedom*, p. 447.

9. Scott and Stowe, *op. cit.*, pp. 24–25.

10. *Crisis*, XIII (1916–17), 219.

11. *Crisis*, XII (1916), 270. *Crisis*, XIII (1916–17), 115. *Crisis* XIV (1917), 8, 63.

12. *Crisis*, XIII (1916–17), 111. *Crisis*, XV (1917–18), 173–77.

13. *Negro Education, A Study of the Private and Higher Schools for Colored People in the United States*, Bulletin, 1916, No. 38–39 [Washington, 1917]).

14. *Crisis*, XV (1917–18), 10–12.

15. O. G. Villard to Mary White Ovington, October 6, 1917: Villard Papers.

16. Villard to F. J. Garrison, May 10, 1916, and Villard to Ovington, October 6, 1917: Villard Papers.

17. *Crisis*, XIII (1916–17), 163–64.

18. Annual Report of the Chairman of the *Crisis* Committee to the N.A.A.C.P. Board, contained in Minutes of the N.A.A.C.P. Board of Directors, January 2, 1917.

19. Ridgely Torrence, *The Story of John Hope* (New York, 1948), p. 199.

20. The following letters are from the Spingarn Papers, Howard University Library: Spingarn to Roy Nash, October 21, 1916. Nash to Spingarn, October 27, 1916.

21. *Messenger*, December, 1920, p. 163.

22. W. E. B. Du Bois to James Weldon Johnson, November 1, 1916: Johnson Papers, Yale University Library.

23. *Crisis*, IX (1914–15), 28. *Crisis*, X (1915), 28. Du Bois, "African Roots of War," *Atlantic Monthly*, CXV (1915), 707–14. *Crisis*, IX (1914–15), 29. *Crisis*, X (1915), 81. *Crisis*, XI (1915–16), 186. *Crisis*, XII (1916), 216–17.

24. W. E. B. Du Bois, "Of the Culture of White Folk," *Journal of Race Development*, VII (1917), 438.

25. *Crisis*, XII (1916), 216–17.

26. *Crisis*, XIV (1917), 165–66, 215, 284. See also *Crisis*, XV (1917–18), 9. W. E. B. Du Bois, "The Passing of 'Jim Crow'," *Independent*, XCI (1917), 53–54.

27. Minutes of the N.A.A.C.P. Board of Directors, October 8, 1917. *Ninth Annual Report of the N.A.A.C.P.*, 1918, p. 56. *Crisis*, XVI (1918), 215, 268. Minutes of the N.A.A.C.P. Board of Directors, September 9, 1918.

28. W. E. B. Du Bois, *The Negro* (New York, 1915), p. 242.

29. *Crisis*, XII (1916), 216–17.

30. *Crisis* XII (1916), 135, 268, 269.

31. William F. Nowlin, *The Negro in American National Politics* (Boston, 1931), p. 141.

32. *Crisis*, XIV (1917), 165, 217.

33. *Crisis*, XIII (1916–17), 268.

34. Joel Spingarn to "The Educated Colored Men of the United States," February 15, 1917: Joel Spingarn Papers, James Weldon Johnson Memorial Collection, Yale University. See also, *Eighth Annual Report of the N.A.A.C.P.*, 1917, p. 9.

35. Du Bois, *Dusk of Dawn*, p. 250. Ruth Worthy, *op. cit.*, p. 118. See also, New York *Age*, March 1, 22, 1917.

36. Joel Spingarn Papers, James Weldon Johnson Memorial Collection, Yale: Spingarn to A. H. Grimke, April 3, 1917, and Spingarn to Mrs. J. E. McClain, April 12, 1917.

37. *Crisis*, XIV (1917), 61. See also *Crisis*, XIII (1916–17), 270–71.

38. *Crisis*, XIV (1917), p. 62.

39. Mary White Ovington to Joel Spingarn, July 5, 1917: Spingarn Papers, James Weldon Johnson Memorial Collection, Yale.

40. *Crisis*, XV (1917–18), 61, 77–78.

41. *Ibid.*, p. 164.

42. *Messenger* (January 1918), p. 23.

43. *Crisis*, XV (1917–18), 114, 165, 216, 218, 268. *Crisis*, XVI (1918), 7.

44. Minutes of the N.A.A.C.P. Board of Directors, May 13, June 10, 1918.

45. *Messenger*, October, 1919, pp. 8, 25.

46. *Crisis*, XVI (1918), 111.

47. Washington *Eagle*, July 27, 1918; Norfolk *Journal and Guide*, July 27, 1918; and Chicago *Defender*, July 20, 1918: Hampton. See also, *Crisis*, XVI (1918), 218.

48. *Crisis*, XVI (1918), 216.

49. W. E. B. Du Bois to Joel Spingarn, June 24, 1918: Spingarn Papers, James Weldon Johnson Memorial Collection, Yale. *Crisis*, XVI (1918), 163, 232.

50. New York *Age*, July 13, 1918; Washington *Eagle*, July 27, 1918; and Richmond *Planet*, September 7, 1918: Hampton.

51. *Crisis*, XVI (1918), 215.

52. Minutes of the N.A.A.C.P. Board of Directors, July 8, 1918.

53. Chicago *Defender*, July 20, 1918; and Washington *Eagle*, July 27, 1918: Hampton. See also, Neval H. Thomas to O. G. Villard, September 13. 1918: Villard Papers.

54. Supplied by Mr. Arthur Spingarn in an interview, April, 1954.

55. *Crisis*, XVI (1918), 164. See also, *Crisis*, XVII (1918–19), 10.

56. *Crisis*, XVI (1918), 217. See also, *Crisis*, XVII (1918–19), 7.

57. *Crisis*, XVII (1918–19), 7.

IX

1. Alexander Walters, *My Life and Work* (London, 1917), pp. 253–62, and "The Pan-African Conference," *A.M.E. Zion Quarterly Review*, XI (1901), 164–65.

2. Du Bois in George Padmore's *History of the Pan-African Congress* (Manchester, 1945), p. 13.

3. New York *Age*, March 12, 1906.

4. *Horizon* (November–December 1908), p. 13.

5. Du Bois Papers: Du Bois to Paul Hageman, *circa* 1896–97. Du Bois to Joseph Booth, February 5, 1907. Du Bois to Moritz Schanz, October 24 1907.

6. Du Bois, *The Negro*, pp. 241–42.

7. W. E. B. Du Bois, "The Negro's Fatherland," *Survey*, XXXIX (November 1917), 141.

8. *Crisis*, XV (1917–18), 114.

9. *Crisis*, XVII (1918–19), 119–20.

10. *Ibid.*, p. 237. See also *The New York Times*, February 2, 1919.

11. *Messenger* (March 1919), p. 4.

12. *The New York Times*, February 16, 1919.

13. *Crisis*, XVII (1918–19), 271–74.

14. *Crisis*, XVIII (1919), 7. Du Bois in Padmore, *op. cit.*, pp. 13, 16.

15. *Tenth Annual Report of the N.A.A.C.P.*, 1919, pp. 65–67.

16. *Crisis*, XVIII (1919), 8–9.

17. *Ibid.*, pp. 10–11. *Crisis*, XIX (1919–20), 173. *Crisis*, XX (1920–21), 199.

18. *Crisis*, XVII (1918–19), 268–70.

19. William Z. Foster, *op. cit.*, p. 435.

20. Franklin, *op. cit.*, p. 462.
21. W. E. B. Du Bois, *The World and Africa* (New York, 1947), p. 11.
22. *Crisis*, XXI (1920–21), 58–60.
23. *Ibid.*, pp. 112–115.
24. *Ibid.*, pp. 58–60, 112–15.
25. *Negro World*, May 24, 1919; March 13, April 3, June 12, 19, 1920.
26. *Ibid.*, January 8, 1921.
27. *Ibid.*, January 29, March 5, May 14, 21, 1921.
28. *Crisis*, XXII (1921), 8.
29. *Crisis*, XXI (1920–21), 101. *Crisis*, XXII (1921), 5.
30. New York *Call*, April 25, 1921: Hampton.
31. *Crisis*, XXII (1921), 53.
32. *Negro World*, July 2, 23, 30, 1921.
33. *Ibid.*, August 6, 1921.
34. *Ibid.*, September 17, 1921.
35. Du Bois in Padmore, *op. cit.*, p. 17.
36. W. E. B. Du Bois, "A Second Journey to Pan Africa," *New Republic*, XXIX (1921–22), 39.
37. *Crisis*, XXIII (1921–22), 5–8.
38. *Twelfth Annual Report of the N.A.A.C.P.*, 1921, pp. 70–73.
39. Jesse Fauset, "Impressions of the Second Pan-African Congress," *Crisis.*, XXIII (1921–22), 15.
40. Du Bois in Padmore, *op. cit.*, p. 18.
41. Jesse Fauset, "What Europe Thought of the Pan-African Congress," *Crisis*, XXIII (1921–22), 65–66.
42. New York *Age*, January 21, 1922.
43. *Negro World*, October 8, 1921.
44. New York *Age*, September 10, 1921. See also, New York *Sun*, September 5, 1921: Hampton.
45. W. E. B. Du Bois, "The Object of the Pan-African Congress," *African World* (1921–22), p. 99.
46. *Negro World*, December 17, 1921.
47. W. E. B. Du Bois, "Second Journey to Pan-Africa," *New Republic*, XXIX (1921–22), 40–42.
48. *Crisis*, XXII (1921), 120.
49. "Second Pan-African Congress," League of Nations Mandates (A. 148, Geneva, August–September, 1921).

50. Albert Thomas, "The International Bureau of Labor of the League of Nations," *Crisis*, XXIII (1921–22), 69–70.

51. Fauset, "Impressions of the Second Pan-African Congress, pp. 12–18.

52. Minutes of the N.A.A.C.P. Board of Directors, July 21, 1921. Du Bois in Logan, *op. cit.*, p. 59. Du Bois, *Dusk of Dawn*, p. 275.

53. *Negro World*, September 17, October 29, 1921; February 4, 1922.

54. *Crisis*, XXIV (1922), 210–14. In a recent study of Garvey, Cronon had access to the transcript of the Jamaican's trial for mail fraud. Cronon was able to see various records of the U.N.I.A. and the Black Star Line. His sources, indicating Garvey's mismanagement, strikingly confirm Du Bois, 1922 appraisal. (Edmund D. Cronon, *Black Moses* [Madison, 1955], pp. 54, 79, 82.)

55. Marcus Garvey, "The Negro's Greatest Enemy," *Current History*, XVIII (1923), 955–56.

56. *Crisis*, XXV (1922–23), 120.

57. W. E. B. Du Bois, "Back to Africa," *Century*, CV (1922–23), 544.

58. *Negro World*, February 10, 17, 1923.

59. *Ibid.*, March 3, 1923; March 1, 1924; March 14, 1925.

60. Du Bois in Padmore, *op. cit.*, p. 22.

61. *Negro World*, November 3, 1923.

62. *Crisis*, XXVII (1923–24), 274.

63. *Crisis*, XXXII (1926), 284.

64. *The New York Times*, August 14, 23, 24, 1927. *Crisis*, XXXIV, 264.

65. *Crisis*, XXVIII (1924), 9–11. *Crisis*, XXXVIII (1931), 102.

66. *Crisis*, XXXIX (1932), 92. *Crisis*, XL (1933), 202–03, 236.

67. W. E. B. Du Bois, "Atlanta University," Kelly Miller *et al.*, *From Servitude to Service* (Cambridge, 1905), pp. 196–97.

68. *Crisis*, XII (1916), 166–67. See also, *Crisis*, XIII (1916–17), 63.

69. Du Bois, "Of the Culture of White Folk," pp. 440–45.

70. W. E. B. Du Bois, "The Negro Mind Reaches Out," Alain Locke (ed.), *The New Negro* (New York, 1925), p. 409.

71. Edward M. East, *Mankind at the Crossroads* (New York, 1928), p. 120.

X

1. Maurice R. Davie, *Negroes in American Society* (New York), 1949, p. 446.

2. E. Franklin Frazier, "The American Negro's New Leaders," *Current History*, XXVIII (1928), 57. Horace M. Bond, "Negro Leadership Since

Washington," *South Atlantic Quarterly*, XXIV (1925), 123–24. Myrdal, *op. cit.*, p. 750.

3. *Crisis*, XIX (1919–20), 241.

4. Du Bois, *Dusk of Dawn*, p. 264. *Crisis*, XIX (1919–20), 106.

5. *Crisis*, XVII (1918–19), 111.

6. *Ibid.*, p. 267. *Crisis*, XVIII (1919), 12.

7. *Crisis*, XVII (1918–19), 218–23. *Crisis* XVIII (1919), 16–21.

8. *Crisis*, XVIII, 13–14.

9. *Congressional Record*, First Session of the Sixty-sixth Congress, LVIII, Part 5, August 25, 1919, p. 4303.

10. *Crisis*, XVIII (1919), 231, 284.

11. *Messenger* (October 1919), p. 11.

12. "Radicalism and Sedition Among the Negroes as Reflected in Their Publications," in *Investigation Activities of the Department of Justice*, Sixty-sixth Congress, First Session, U. S. Senate Documents (1919), XII, 161–62,

13. *Crisis*, XIX (1919–20), 169.

14. Indianapolis *Freeman*, November 1, 1919: Hampton. (Reprint from Macon. *Telegraph*.)

15. Newport News *Star*, April 29, 1920, and New York *Age*, May 8, 1920: Hampton. *Crisis*, XX (1920), 165.

16. "Revolutionary Radicalism," *Report of the Joint Legislative Committee Investigation of Seditious Activities*, filed April 24, 1920, in the Senate of The State of New York, Part 1, Vol. II, pp. 1518–19. See also pp. 1481–82,

17. *Messenger* (November 1919), pp. 7–8. See also *Messenger* (May–June 1919). p. 9 and (July 1919), pp. 10–12.

18. Du Bois, *Darkwater*, p. 49.

19. *Current Opinion*, LXIX (1920), 82–85.

20. Stephen Graham, "Militancy of Colour and Its Leader," *Nineteenth Century and After*, LXXXVIII (1920), 909–13.

21. *Crisis*, XXI (1920–21), 247.

22. *Eleventh Annual N.A.A.C.P. Report*, 1920, p. 53. See also, *Crisis*, XVII (1918–19), 112–13. *Crisis*, XVIII (1919), 130. *Crisis*, XIX (1919–20), 109.

23. *Crisis*, XXVI (1923), 172.

24. *Messenger* (August 1923), p. 781. See also, *Negro World*, July 14, August 4, 1923.

25. W. E. B. Du Bois, "Dilemma of the Negro," *American Mercury*, III (1924), 180–81, and "The Hosts of Black Labor," *Nation*, CXVI (1923), 539–41.

26. *Crisis*, XXIV (1922), pp. 104–05. *Crisis*, XXVIII (1924), pp. 251–52. *Crisis*, XXIX (1924–25), pp. 247–50. *Fifteenth Annual Report of the N.A.A.C.P.*, 1924, p. 65.
27. *Crisis*, XXXII (1926), p. 7. W. E. B. Du Bois, "Negroes in College," *Nation*, CXXII (1926), 229.
28. *Crisis*, XXXIV (1927), 347–48. W. E. B. Du Bois, "The Hampton Strike," *Nation*, CXXV (1927), 471–72.
29. *Crisis*, XXXIX (1932), 59.
30. W. E. B. Du Bois, "Education and Work," *Journal of Negro Education*, I (1932), 64.
31. *Crisis*, XL (1933), 175–77.
32. *Crisis*, XXXV (1928), 240. Du Bois, *Dusk of Dawn*, pp. 280–81.
33. *Crisis*, XIX (1919–20), 50, 171–72. *Crisis*, XXI (1920–21), 5–6.
34. *Crisis*, XXXVI (1929), 374–75. Chicago *Defender*, March 5, 1927: Schomburg Scrapbooks.
35. New York *Age*, July 1, 1922.
36. *Crisis*, XXX (1925), 7–9.
37. *Crisis*, XXXII (1926), 296–97. *Crisis*, XXXVI (1929), 168.
38. *Crisis*, XIX (1919–20), 299. Telegram from Langston Hughes to W. E. B. Du Bois, *circa* 1951: James Weldon Johnson Memorial Collection, Yale.
39. *Crisis*, XXIV (1922), 58–59.
40. *Crisis*, XXI (1920–21), 152.
41. *Crisis*, XXVI (1923), 103.
42. *Crisis*, XXII (1921), 75.
43. See following: *Crisis*, XX (1920), 266. *Crisis*, XXI (1920–21), 18. *Crisis*, XXXI (1925–26), 218. *Messenger* (May 1925), p. 210.
44. *Sixteenth N.A.A.C.P. Annual Report*, 1925, p. 50.
45. Bond, "Negro Leadership Since Washington," pp. 121–22.
46. Van Wyck Brooks, *The Confident Years* (New York, 1952), pp. 547–48.
47. *Crisis*, XL (1933), 176.
48. *Crisis*, XVII (1918–19), 114. *Crisis*, XXII (1921), 103, 151, 199. *Crisis*, XXXIII (1926–27), 65.
49. *Messenger* (September 1921), p. 246.
50. *Crisis*, XIX (1919–20), 235. *Crisis*, XXII (1921), 151–52, 246. *Crisis*, XXXI (1925–26), 60. *Crisis*, XXXV (1928), 98.
51. *Crisis*, XXII (1921), 151–52.
52. *Crisis*, XXXV (1928), 134.

53. *Fifteenth Annual Report of the N.A.A.C.P.*, 1924, pp. 48–49. Sterling D. Spero and Abram L. Harris, *The Black Worker* (New York, 1931), p. 145. Minutes of the N.A.A.C.P. Board of Directors, October 14, 1924.

54. *Messenger* (September 1919), pp. 9–10, and (November 1925), p. 346.

55. *Sixteenth Annual Report of the N.A.A.C.P.*, 1925, p. 39.

56. *The New York Times*, January 17, 1926.

57. *Crisis*, XXXII (1926), 64, 180. *Crisis*, XXXV (1928), 98. *Crisis*, XXXVII (1930), 160. *Crisis*, XXXIX (1932), 234. *Crisis*, XL (1933), 292.

58. *Crisis*, XXXVII (1930), 137, 174, 305–06.

59. *Crisis*, XXXVIII (1931), 314–15. *Crisis*, XXXIX (1932), pp. 218–19, 236. *Twenty-Second N.A.A.C.P. Annual Report*, 1931, p. 25.

60. R. W. Bagnall, "N.A.A.C.P. Branch Activities," *Crisis*, XXXIX (1932), 457.

61. *Crisis*, XIX (1919–20), 46. *Crisis*, XXII (1921), 103, 245. *Crisis*, XXXI (1925–26), 60. *Messenger* (September 1921), p. 246.

62. *Crisis*, XXXIII (1926–27), 8, 189. See also, *Dusk of Dawn*, pp. 286–88.

63. *Amsterdam News*, January 12, 1927: Schomburg Scrapbooks.

64. *Crisis*, XXXIII (1926–27), 189–90. *Crisis*, XXXIV (1927), 240, 348.

65. *Crisis*, XXXVIII (1931), 313–20. *Crisis*, XXXIX (1932), 190. *Crisis*, XL (1933), 104, 140–41. *Twenty-Second N.A.A.C.P. Annual Report*, 1931, p. 12. *National News*, February 25, 1932, and Baltimore *Afro-American*, May 20, 1933: Schomburg Scrapbooks.

66. Wilson Record, *The Negro and the Communist Party* (Chapel Hill, 1951), p. 92.

67. *Crisis*, XIX (1919–20), 44, 298. *Crisis*, XX (1920), 69, 213–14. *Crisis* (1921), 245–46. W. E. B. Du Bois, "The Republicans and the Black Voter," *Nation*, CX (1920), 757–58.

68. *Messenger* (November 1920), p. 141.

69. *Crisis*, XXI (1920–21), 56, 104.

70. *Crisis*, XXII (1921), 7, 101. *Crisis*, XXIII (1921–22), 53–56, 105.

71. *Crisis*, XXIII (1921–22), 248. *Crisis*, XXIV (1922), 11. *Crisis*, XXV (1922–23), 105. W. E. B. Du Bois, "The South and a Third Party," *New Republic*, XXXIII (1922–23), 138–41.

72. *Messenger* (August 1923), pp. 793–94.

73. *Crisis*, XXVIII (1924), 104, 151–54. *Fifteenth Annual Report of the N.A.A.C.P.*, 1924, p. 48.

74. *Crisis*, XXIX (1924–25), 13. See the following: *Crisis*, XXVIII (1924), 154. *Crisis*, XXIX, 55, 103. *The New York Times*, October 21. 1924.

75. W. E. B. Du Bois, "The Negro Citizen," a contribution to Charles S. Johnson, *The Negro in American Civilization* (New York, 1930), pp. 463–70.

76. *Crisis*, XXXV (1928), 257, 346, 368, 381.

77. *The New York Times*, June 28, 1928.

78. *Crisis*, XXXV (1928), 416, 336.

79. *Crisis*, XXXV (1928), 418.

80. Spero and Harris, *op. cit.*, p. 412.

81. *Crisis*, XXXV (1928), 168. *Crisis*, XXXVI (1929), 387.

82. *Crisis*, XXXIX (1932), 362. *Crisis*, XL (1933), 140–41. *Crisis*, XLI (1934), 20.

83. *Crisis*, XXXVI (1929), 349. Du Bois in Logan, *op. cit.*, p. 61.

84. Bond, "Negro Leadership Since Washington," p. 126.

85. Myrdal, *op. cit.*, pp. 493–94.

86. Davie, *op. cit.*, p. 283. Moon, *The Balance of Power: The Negro Vote*, p. 84.

87. *Crisis*, XXII (1921), 104. See also, *Crisis*, XX (1920), 5.

88. *Crisis*, XXXIII (1926–27), 129–30.

89. *Crisis*, XXXIV (1927), 193.

90. *Crisis*, XX (1920), 6–8.

91. Pierce, "The N.A.A.C.P.—A Study in Social Pressure," p. 49.

92. *Twelfth N.A.A.C.P. Annual Report*, 1921, pp. 80–82. *Twentieth N.A.A.C.P. Annual Report*, 1929, pp. 69–71.

93. *Sixteenth N.A.A.C.P. Annual Report*, 1925, p. 39. *Seventeenth N.A.A.C.P. Annual Report*, 1926, p. 45.

94. *Sixteenth N.A.A.C.P. Annual Report*, 1925, pp. 48–50.

95. *Nineteenth Annual N.A.A.C.P. Report*, 1928, p. 47.

96. *Twentieth Annual N.A.A.C.P. Report*, 1929, p. 70.

97. Minutes of the N.A.A.C.P. Board of Directors, December 13, 1926.

98. Minutes of the N.A.A.C.P. Board of Directors, April 18, November 11, 1929.

99. *Twenty-First N.A.A.C.P. Annual Report*, 1930, pp. 66–67.

100. Minutes of the N.A.A.C.P. Board of Directors, May 13, 1929, February 9, 1931.

101. *Twenty-Second N.A.A.C.P. Annual Report*, 1931, pp. 42–45.

102. O. G. Villard to Mary W. Ovington, January 22, 1932: Villard Papers.

103. *Twenty-Third N.A.A.C.P. Annual Report*, 1932, pp. 53, 60, 61.

104. Minutes of the N.A.A.C.P. Board of Directors, April 14, 1924.

105. Minutes of the N.A.A.C.P. Board of Directors, July 14, 1924.
106. Minutes of the N.A.A.C.P. Board of Directors, December 10, 1928.
107. Minutes of the N.A.A.C.P. Board of Directors, April 13, 1931.
108. *Crisis*, XXXIX (1932), 218.

XI

1. Joel Spingarn's "Memorandum No. 2" on Amenia Conference, 1933: Spingarn Papers, James Weldon Johnson Memorial Collection, Yale.
2. Walter White to James Weldon Johnson, April 3, 1933: Johnson Memorial Collection, Yale.
3. W. Bond, "Impressions of the Second Amenia Conference," *circa* 1933 (unpublished memorandum): Howard University Library.
4. Bunche, "Programs, Ideologies, Tactics, ... ," II, 209. Personal communication from Dr. Bunche, May 2, 1955.
5. *Crisis*, XL (1933), 226–27.
6. *Ibid.* Mary W. Ovington to Joel Spingarn, August 22, 1933: Spingarn Papers, Howard University Library.
7. Bunche, "Programs, Ideologies, Tactics, ... ," II, 209. Personal communication from Dr. Abram L. Harris, April 4, 1954. *Twenty-Fourth N.A.A.C.P. Annual Report*, 1933, p. 38. *Opportunity* (October 1933), p. 295.
8. *Amsterdam News*, February 21, 1934. See also Philadelphia *Tribune*, January 18, 1934. Minutes of the N.A.A.C.P. Board of Directors, January 8, 1934.
9. Walter White to James Weldon Johnson, February 28, 1934: James Weldon Johnson Memorial Collection, Yale.
10. Baltimore *Afro-American*, February 24, 1934: Schomburg Scrapbooks.
11. *Crisis*, XLI (1934), 20, 52–53.
12. Joel Spingarn, *Crisis*, XLI (1934), 79–80.
13. *Ninth N.A.A.C.P. Annual Report*, 1918, pp. 77–78. *Sixteenth N.A.A.C.P. Annual Report*, 1925, p. 39. Robert R. Moton, *What the Negro Thinks* (Garden City, 1929), p. 115.
14. *Crisis*, XLI (1934), 115.
15. Walter White, "Segregation—A Symposium," *Crisis*, XLI (1934), 80–81, *Crisis*, XLI, 85.
16. Pittsburgh *Courier*, April 7, 1934: Schomburg Scrapbooks.
17. Philadelphia *Tribune*, March 8, 1934. See also, Philadelphia *Tribune*. January 18, April 12, 1934.
18. Chicago *Defender*, March 24, 1934: Schomburg Scrapbooks.

19. *Ibid.*, August 4, 1934: Schomburg Scrapbooks.
20. *Ibid.*, April 14, 1934. See also Philadelphia *Tribune*, January 25, 1934.
21. Walter White's Memorandum to N.A.A.C.P. Committee on Administration, April 3, 1934, and James Weldon Johnson to Walter White, April 6, 1934: Johnson Collection, Yale.
22. *Crisis*, XLI (1934), 149.
23. Minutes of the N.A.A.C.P. Board of Directors, April 9, 1934. James Weldon Johnson to Walter White, May 15, 1934: Johnson Collection, Yale. Du Bois to N.A.A.C.P. Board, June 1, 1934, in Minutes of the N.A.A.C.P. Board of Directors, June 11, 1934.
24. Joseph V. Baker, "The N.A.A.C.P. and the Negro Press," *Crisis*, XLI. (1934), 131. Philadelphia *Tribune*, June 7, 1934.
25. Du Bois to N.A.A.C.P. Board, June 26, 1934—read to board, Minutes of the N.A.A.C.P. Board, July 9, 1934.
26. E. Franklin Frazier, "Dr. Du Bois Dons a New Suit," *Race* (1935-36), p. 13.
27. From Abram L. Harris' statement which appears in Donald R. Young, *Research Memorandum on Minority Peoples in the Depression*, Social Science Research Council Bulletin, XXXI (New York, 1937), ix. Ralph J. Bunche, "A Critical Analysis of the Tactics and Programs of Minority Groups,'. *Journal of Negro Education*, IV (1935), 313. James Weldon Johnson, *Negro Americans, What Now?* (New York, 1934), p. 16.
28. Bunche, "Programs, Tactics, Ideologies . . . ," I, 156. See also Pierce, *op. cit.*, pp. 39, 168. Personal communication from Dr. Abram L. Harris, April 4, 1954.
29. Bunche, "Programs, Tactics, Ideologies, . . . ," I, 155-67.
30. *Ibid.*, p. 145. See also, F. C. Covington, "Color a Factor in Social Mobility," *Sociology and Social Research*, XV (1930), 152. Myrdal, *op. cit.*, pp. 696-97. Robert H. Brisbane, "The Rise of Protest Movements Among Negroes Since 1900" (Ph.D. thesis Harvard, 1949), p. 66.
31. Bunche, "A Critical Analysis of the Tactics and Programs of Minority Groups," p. 315.

XII

1. Frank G. Davis, "Nature, Scope, and Significance of the First Phylon Institute," *Phylon*, II (1941), 280. Mozell C. Hill, "The Formative Years of Phylon Magazine," *Freedomways*, V (1965), 129–132.

2. W. E. B. Du Bois (ed.), *Report of the First Conference of Negro Land Grant Colleges For Coordinating a Program of Cooperative Social Studies* (Atlanta, 1943), pp. 6–18.

3. Record, *op. cit.*, p. 174.

4. New York *Post*, June 14, 1935. Abram L. Harris, "Reconstruction and the Negro," *New Republic*, LXXXIII (1935), 367–68. Henry Lee Moon, *Race*, IV (1935–36), 60.

5. Oswald G. Villard, "World Problem No. 1," *Saturday Review of Literature*, October 12, 1940, pp. 26, 28.

6. W. E. B. Du Bois, "A Negro Nation Within the Nation," *Current History*, XLII (1935), 265–270.

7. *The New York Times*, September 7, 1935.

8. W. E. B. Du Bois, "Prospect of a World Without Race Conflict," *American Journal of Sociology*, XLIX (1943–44), 450–56. For examples of articles on Africa during the late 1930's and early 1940's see the following by Du Bois: "Inter-racial Implications of the Ethiopian Crisis," *Foreign Affairs*, XIV (1935–36), 82–92; "Black Africa Tomorrow," *Foreign Affairs*, XVII (1938–39), 100–10; "The Realities in Africa," *Foreign Affairs*, XXI (1942–43), 721–32.

9. W. E. B. Du Bois, *Color and Democracy: Colonies and Peace* (New York, 1945), pp. 1–16.

10. *The New York Times*, June 6, 1945.

11. George Padmore (ed.), *History of the Pan-African Congress* (Manchester, 1945), pp. 11–26. Richard B. Moore, "Du Bois and Pan Africa," *Freedomways*, V (1965), 183.

12. *The New York Times*, November 28, 1945.

13. *Ibid.*, October 6, 1946.

14. W. E. B. Du Bois (ed.), *An Appeal to the World* (New York, 1947), pp. 1–14. See also *The New York Times*, October 12, 19, 24, 1947.

15. Du Bois to Joel Spingarn, May 30, 1945: Spingarn Papers, Howard University Library.

16. *The New York Times*, June 27, 1947.

17. Harold R. Isaacs, "Du Bois and Africa," *Race*, November 1960, p. 5. Record, *op. cit.*, p. 305. George W. Streator, "Working on The Crisis," *Crisis*, LVIII (1951), 160.

18. W. E. B. Du Bois' Memorandum to Executive Secretary and N.A.A.C.P. Board, September 7, 1948: Spingarn Papers, Howard University Library. Philadelphia *Tribune*, September 11, 1948.

19. Memorandum from W. A. Hunton, Secretary of Council on African Affairs, November 16, 1953: Howard University Library. The House Committee on Un-American Activities has published material about Du Bois and some movements in which he was interested. All were printed by the U.S. Government Printing Office: *The Communist "Peace Petition" Campaign*, 1950, p. 1; *Review of the Scientific and Cultural Conference for World Peace*, 1949, p. 1; *Statement on The March of Treason*, 1951, p. 2; and *Report on the Communist "Peace" Offensive—A Campaign to Disarm and Defeat the United States*, 1951, pp. 17, 21, 42, 43, 45.

20. *New Africa*, May 1949, p. 3.

21. *New Africa*, April 1949, p. 2. California *Eagle*, August 18, 1949: Howard University Scrapbooks.

22. *New Africa*, October 1949, p. 1; July–September 1950, p. 1.

23. *The New York Times*, September 5, 7, 25, October 6, 10, 23, November 2, 22, 1950.

24. Philadelphia, *Tribune*, February 13, 1951. *The New York Times*, April 19, 21, 23, 1949; June 2, 20, August 27, 1949; July 17, August 25, 1950; November 8, 19, 21, 1951. For Du Bois' version of the case, see his book entitled *In Battle for Peace* (New York, 1952).

25. Truman Nelson, "W. E. B. Du Bois: Prophet in Limbo," *Nation*, CLXXXVI (1958), 76–79.

26. *The New York Times*, July 5, 1952.

27. *National Guardian*, September 11, 1952.

28. W. E. B. Du Bois, "On the Future of the American Negro," *Freedomways*, V (1965), 117–124.

29. *National Guardian*, May 20, 1957.

30. *Ibid.*, May 31, 1954.

31. W. E. B. Du Bois, "The Negro Since 1900: A Progress Report," *The New York Times Magazine*, November 21, 1948, p. 59.

32. W. E. B. Du Bois, "I Won't Vote," *Nation*, CLXXXIII (1956), 325. See also *National Guardian*, November 4, 1957.

33. *National Guardian*, January 16, 1956.

34. *Ibid.*, February 11, 1957.

35. *Ibid.*, May 23, 1960.

36. W. E. B. Du Bois, "I Won't Vote," *Nation*, CLXXXIII (1956), 325.

37. *The New York Times*, June 21, 1953, and September 25, 1959.

38. *National Guardian*, June 8, 1959. W. E. B. Du Bois, "China and Africa," *New World Review*, April 1959, p. 28.

39. *Political Affairs*, October 1963, pp. 31–32. *The Worker*, November 26, 1961.

40. St. Clair Drake, "Pan Africanism, What Is It?" *Africa Today*, January–February 1959, p. 7. Harold R. Isaacs, "Du Bois and Africa," *Race*, November 1960, p. 20.

41. *National Guardian*, September 19, 1960, and February 13, 1961.

42. W. E. B. Du Bois, "Conference of Encyclopedia Africana," *Freedomways*, III (1963), 28–30.

43. *The New York Times*, February 20, 1963.

44. *The New York Times*, August 28, 30, 1963. Pittsburgh *Courier*, September 7, 1963. *Amsterdam News*, September 7, 1963. *National Guardian*, September 26, 1963. *The Worker*, September 2, 1963.

XIII

1. Du Bois, *Souls of Black Folk*, p. 3.

2. Reuter, *The Mulatto in the United States*, pp. 11, 102–04, 315, 317, 319, 339–40, 346.

3. Bond, "Negro Leadership Since Washington," p. 120. T. G. Standing, "Nationalism in Negro Leadership," *American Journal of Sociology*, XL (1934–35), 185.

4. E. Franklin Frazier, *The Negro in the United States* (New York, 1949), pp. 547–63. The search for the Great Leader type did not die, but it had lost much of its fervor. As late as 1937, Guy B. Johnson predicted that unless economic conditions improved, radical Negroes would unite behind The Race Leader. (Guy B. Johnson, "Negro Racial Movements and Leadership in the United States," *American Journal of Sociology*, XLIII, 68–70.) However, other writers besides Frazier have repudiated such a conception. Oliver C. Cox argued that no "great leader" would arise because Negroes really did not want such a figure. Cox believed that if he did appear, he would hurt the cause of the Negroes by uniting the race as

a separate group. Such a situation, Cox concluded, would unleash chauvinism and delay inevitable integration. (O. C. Cox, *Caste, Class, and Race* [Garden City, 1948], p. 572.) Hugh Smythe concurred and held that in the past, such a leader demanded uniformity—the very thing that would destroy race "initiative and strength." (Hugh H. Smythe, "Changing Patterns of Negro Leadership," *Social Forces*, XXIX [1950–51], 191–97.)

5. George Padmore, *Pan Africanism or Communism* (New York, 1956).
6. *Dusk of Dawn*, p. 303. W. E. B. Du Bois, "Editing 'The Crisis,'" *Crisis*, LVIII (1951), 213.
7. The "Natural History" conception was taken from Robert E. L. Faris, *Social Disorganization* (New York, 1955), pp. 438–49.

SOURCES CONSULTED

I. Du Bois Articles and Books.

The Suppression of the African Slave-Trade to the United States of America, 1638–1870. New York: Longmans, Green, 1896.

"Strivings of the Negro People," *Atlantic Monthly*, LXXX (August 1897), 194–98.

The Conservation of Races. Pamphlet. Washington, 1897.

"The Study of the Negro Problems," *Annals of the American Academy of Political and Social Science*, XI (January 1898), 1–23.

The Negroes of Farmville, Virginia: A Social Study. Bulletin of the United States Department of Labor, III (January 1898), 1–38.

"Careers Open to College-Bred Negroes," in *Two Addresses Delivered by Alumni of Fisk University.* Pamphlet, Nashville, 1898.

Some Efforts of Negroes for Their Own Social Betterment. Atlanta: Atlanta University Press, 1898.

"A Negro Schoolmaster in the New South," *Atlantic Monthly*, LXXXIII (January 1899), 99–104.

The Negro in the Black Belt: Some Social Sketches. Bulletin of the United States Department of Labor, IV (May 1899), 401–17.

"The Negro and Crime," *Independent*, LI (May 18, 1899), 1355–57.

"Two Negro Conventions," *Independent*, LI (September 7, 1899), 2425–27.

"The Suffrage Fight in Georgia," *Independent*, LI (November 30, 1899), 3226–28,

"Resolutions of the Third Hampton Negro Conference," in *Hampton Negro Conferences*, III (1899), 7–9.

Memorial to the Legislature of Georgia on the Hardwick Bill. Pamphlet. 1899.

The Negro in Business. Atlanta: Atlanta University Press, 1899.

Philadelphia Negro: A Social Study. Philadelphia: University of Pennsylvania, 1899.

"The Twelfth Census and the Negro Problem," *Southern Workman*, XXIX (May 1900), 305–09.

"The American Negro at Paris," *American Monthly Review of Reviews*, XXII (November 1900), 575–77.

"The Religion of the American Negro," *New World*, IX (December 1900), 614–25.

The College-Bred Negro. Atlanta: Atlanta University Press, 1900.

"The Freedmen's Bureau," *Atlantic Monthly*, LXXXVII (March 1901), 354–65.

"The Storm and Stress in the Black World," *Dial*, XXX (April 16, 1901). 262–64.

"The Negro As He Really Is," *World's Work*, II (June 1901), 848–66.

"Results of Ten Tuskegee Conferences," *Harper's Weekly*, XLV (June 22, 1901), 641.

"The Relation of the Negroes to the Whites in the South," *Annals of the American Academy of Political and Social Science*, XVIII (July 1901), 121–40.

"The Burden of Negro Schooling," *Independent*, LIII (July 18, 1901), 1667–68.

The Negro Landholder of Georgia. Bulletin of the United States Department of Labor, VI (July 1901), 647–777.

"The Savings of Black Georgia," *Outlook*, LXIX (September 14, 1901), 128–30.

"The Spawn of Slavery," *Missionary Review of the World*, XXIV (October 1901), 737–45.

"The Freedmen and Their Sons," *Independent*, LIII (November 14, 1901), 2709.

The Negro Common School. Atlanta: Atlanta University Press, 1901.

"The Opening of the Library," *Independent*, LIV (April 3, 1902), 809–10.

"Of the Training of Black Men," *Atlantic Monthly*, XC (September 1902), 289–97.

"Hopeful Signs for the Negro," *Advance*, XLIV (October 2, 1902), 327–28.

The Negro Artisan. Atlanta: Atlanta University Press, 1902.

"The Atlanta University Conferences," *Charities*, X (May 2, 1903), 435–39.

"The Laboratory in Sociology at Atlanta," *Annals of the American Academy of Political and Social Science*, XXI (May 1903), 160–63.

"Possibilities of the Negro: The Advance Guard of the Race," *Booklovers*, II (July 1903), 2–15.

"The Talented Tenth" in Booker T. Washington *et al.*, *The Negro Problem*. New York: James Pott & Co., 1903, pp. 31–75.

"The Training of Negroes for Social Power," *Outlook*, LXXV (October 17, 1903), 409–14.

Souls of Black Folk. Chicago: A. C. Mc Clurg, 1903.

The Negro Church. Atlanta: Atlanta University Press, 1903.

"The Atlanta Conferences," *Voice of the Negro*, I (March 1904), 85–90.

Heredity and the Public Schools. Pamphlet. Washington, 1904.

"The Negro Problem From the Negro Point of View: The Parting of the Ways,". *World Today*, VI (April 1904), pp. 521–23.

"What Intellectual Training Is Doing For The Negro," *Missionary Review of the World*, XXVII (August 1904), 578–82.

"Credo," *Independent*, LVII (October 6, 1904), 787.

The Negro Farmer, Negroes in the United States. United States Department of Commerce and Labor, Bureau of the Census, Bulletin VIII (1904), Washington, pp. 69–98.

Notes on Negro Crime. Atlanta: Atlanta University Press, 1904.

"Debit and Credit," *Voice of the Negro*, II (January 1905), 677.

"The Beginning of Slavery," *Voice of the Negro*, II (February 1905), 104–06.

"The Southerners' Problem," *Dial*, XXXVIII (May 1, 1905), 315–18.

"The Negro South and North," *Bibliotheca Sacra*, LXII (July 1905), 500–13.

"The Niagara Movement," *Voice of the Negro*, II (September 1905), 619–22.

"The Black Vote of Philadelphia," *Charities*, XV (October 7, 1905), 31–35.

"Garrison and the Negro," *Independent*, LIX (December 7, 1905), 1316–17.

et al., *Niagara Movement—Declaration of Principles*. Pamphlet. 1905.

A Select Bibliography of the American Negro. Atlanta: Atlanta University Press, 1905.

"Atlanta University," in Kelly Miller et al., *From Servitude to Service*. Boston, 1905, pp. 153–97.

"The Growth of the Niagara Movement," *Voice of the Negro*, III (January 1906), 43–45.

"The Economic Future of the Negro," *Publications of the American Economic Association*, 3rd series, VII (February 1906), 219–42.

"Vardaman," *Voice of the Negro*, III (March 1906), 189–94.

"Litany of Atlanta," *Independent*, LXI (October 1906), 856–58.

"Tragedy of Atlanta," *World Today*, XI (November 1906), 1173–75.

Health and Physique of the Negro American. Atlanta: Atlanta University Press, 1906.

"The Value of Agitation," *Voice of the Negro*, IV (March 1907), 109–10.

"Sociology and Industry in Southern Education," *Voice of the Negro*, IV (May 1907), pp. 170–75.

Horizon: A Journal of the Color Line, I–VI (January 1907–July 1910).

et al., *Address to the World of the Third Niagara Conference*. Pamphlet. 1907.

The Negro in the South. Philadelphia, 1907.

Economic Cooperation among Negro Americans. Atlanta: Atlanta University Press. 1907.

"Race Friction Between Black and White," *American Journal of Sociology*, XIII (May 1908), 834–38.

The Negro American Family. Atlanta: Atlanta University Press, 1908.

"Georgia Negroes and Their Fifty Millions of Savings," *World's Work*, XVIII (May 1909), 11550–554.

John Brown. Philadelphia: G. W. Jacobs & Co., 1909.

"Politics and Industry" and "Evolution of the Race Problem" in *Proceedings of the National Negro Conference*. 1909, pp. 79–88, 142–58.

"National Committee on the Negro," *Survey*, XXII (June 12, 1909), 407–09.

"Long in Darke," *Independent*, LXVII (October 21, 1909), 917–18.

Efforts for Social Betterment among Negro Americans. Atlanta: Atlanta University Press, 1909.

'Reconstruction and Its Benefits," *American Historical Review*, XV (July 1910) 781–99.

"Negro Property," *World Today*, XIX (August 1910), 905–06.

'The Souls of White Folk," *Independent*, LXIX (August 18, 1910), 339–42.

"Marrying of Black Folk," *Independent*, LXIX (October 13, 1910), 812–13.

(Ed.). *Crisis: A Record of the Darker Races*, I–XLI (November 1910–July 1934)

College-Bred Negro Communities. Pamphlet. 1910.

Race Relations in the United States: An Appeal to England and Europe. Pamphlet 1910.

The College-Bred Negro American. Atlanta: Atlanta University Press, 1910.

"The Social Evolution of the Black South," *American Negro Monographs*, I, iv (March 1911).

"Forty Years of Freedom," *Missionary Review of the World*, XXXIV (June 1911), 460–61.

"A Hymn to the Peoples," *Independent*, LXXI (August 24, 1911), 400.

"The First Universal Races Congress," *Independent*, LXXI (August 24, 1911), 401–03.

"The Negro Race in the United States of America," in G. Spiller (ed.), *Papers on Inter-Racial Problems*. London, 1911, pp. 348–64.

The Common School and the Negro American. Atlanta: Atlanta University Press, 1911.

"Upbuilding of Black Durham," *World's Work*, XXIII (January 1912), 334–38.

"The Rural South," *Publications of the American Statistical Association*, XIII (March 1912), 80–84.

The Negro-American Artisan. Atlanta: Atlanta University Press, 1912.

"Some Effects of Emancipation," *Survey*, XXIX (February 1, 1913), 570–73.

"Negro in Literature and Art," *Annals of the American Academy of Political and Social Science*, XLIX (September 1913), 233–37.

Morals and Manners Among Negro Americans. Atlanta: Atlanta University Press, 1914.

"African Roots of War," *Atlantic Monthly*, CXV (May 1915), 707–14.

The Negro. New York: Henry Holt, 1915.

"Of the Culture of White Folk," *Journal of Race Development*, VII (April 1917). 434–47.

"The Passing of Jim Crow," *Independent*, XCI (July 14, 1917), 53–54.

"The Negro's Fatherland," *Survey*, XXXIX (November 1917), 141.

(Ed.). *The Brownies' Book*, I–II (January 1920–December 1921).

"On Being Black," *New Republic*, XXI (February 18, 1920), 338–41.

"The Republicans and the Black Voter," *Nation*, CX (June 5, 1920), 757–58.

"Eternal Africa," *Nation*, CXI (September 25, 1920), 350–52.

Darkwater. New York: Harcourt, Brace, & Howe Co., 1920.

"E. D. Morel," *Nation*, CXII (May 25, 1921), 749.

"A Second Journey to Pan-Africa," *New Republic*, XXIX (December 7, 1921), 39–42.

"The Object of the Pan-African Congress," *African World* (1921–22), p. 99.

"The South and a Third Party," *New Republic*, XXXIII (January 3, 1923), 138–41.

"Back to Africa," *Century*, CV (February 1923), 539–48.

"The Hosts of Black Labor," *Nation*, CXVI (May 9, 1923), 539–41.

"The Negro as a National Asset," *Homiletic Review*, LXXXVI (1923), 52–58.

"The Negro Takes Stock," *New Republic*, XXXVII (January 2, 1924), 143–45.

"The Dilemma of the Negro," *American Mercury*, III (October 1924), 179–85.

"The Primitive Black Man," *Nation*, CXIX (December 17, 1924), 675–76.

"Diuturni Silenti," *Fisk Herald*, XXXIII (1924), 1–12.

The Gift of Black Folk. Boston: Stratford Co., 1924.

"Georgia: Invisible Empire State," *Nation*, CXX (January 21, 1925), 63–67.

"Britain's Negro Problem in Sierra Leone," *Current History*, XXI (February 1925), 690–700.

"What is Civilization?" *Forum*, LXXIII (February 1925), 178–88.

"The Black Man Brings His Gifts," *Survey*, LIII (March 1, 1925), 655–57.

"Worlds of Color," *Foreign Affairs*, III (April 1925), 423–44.

"France's Black Citizens in West Africa," *Current History*, XXII (July 1925), 559–64.

"Liberia and Rubber," *New Republic*, XLIV (November 18, 1925), 326–29.

Amenia Conference. Pamphlet. Amenia, New York, 1925.

"Negroes in College," *Nation*, CXXII (March 3, 1926), 228–30.

"The Shape of Fear," *North American Review*, CCXXIII (June 1926), 291–304.

"The Hampton Strike," *Nation*, CXXV (November 2, 1927), 471–72.

"Is Al Smith Afraid of the South?" *Nation*, CXXVII (October 17, 1928), 392–94.

"Race Relations in the United States," *Annals of the American Academy of Political and Social Science*, CXL (November 1928), 6–10.

"Will the Church Remove the Color Line?" *Christian Century*, XLVIII (December 9, 1931), 1554–56.

"Education and Work," *Journal of Negro Education*, I (April 1932), 60–74.

"Liberia, the League, and the United States," *Foreign Affairs*, XI (July 1933), 682–95.

"A Negro Nation Within the Nation," *Current History*, XLII (1935), 265–70.

"Does the Negro Need Separate Schools?" *Journal of Negro Education*, IV (July 1935), 328–35.

"Inter-racial Implications of the Ethiopian Crisis," *Foreign Affairs*, XIV (October 1935), 82–92.

Black Reconstruction. New York: Harcourt Brace, 1935.

What the Negro Has Done for the United States and Texas. Pamphlet. Washington, 1936.

"Social Planning for the Negro, Past and Present," *Journal of Negro Education*, V (January 1936), 110–25.

Race Philosophy and Policies for Negro Life in the North. Mimeographed speech. New York, 1936.

"Black Africa Tomorrow," *Foreign Affairs*, XVII (October 1938), 100–10.

A Pageant in Seven Decades. Atlanta, 1938.

"The Negro Scientist," *American Scholar*, VIII (Summer 1939), pp. 309–20.

"The Position of the Negro in the American Social Order: Where Do We Go From Here?" *Journal of Negro Education*, VIII (1939), 551–70.

Revelation of Saint Orgne The Damned. Nashville: Hemphill Press, 1939.

Black Folk Then and Now. New York: Henry Holt, 1939.

(Ed.). *Phylon: The Atlanta University Review of Race and Culture*. I–V (1940–44).

Dusk of Dawn. New York: Harcourt Brace, 1940.

"The Future of Wilberforce University," *Journal of Negro Education*, IX (October 1940), 553–70.

"Federal Action Programs and Community Action in the South," *Social Forces*, XIX (March 1941), 375–80.

"The Realities in Africa," *Foreign Affairs*, XXI (July 1943), 721–32

(Ed.). *Report of the First Conference of Negro Land-Grant Colleges for Co-ordinating a Program of Cooperative Social Studies.* Atlanta: Atlanta University Publications, 1943.

(Ed.). *Report on the Second Conference of Negro Land-Grant Colleges for Co-ordinating a Program of Cooperative Social Studies.* Atlanta: Atlanta University Publications, 1944.

"Prospect of a World Without Race Conflict," *American Journal of Sociology,* XLIX (March 1944), 450–56.

"My Evolving Program for Negro Freedom," in Rayford Logan (ed.), *What the Negro Wants.* Chapel Hill: University of North Carolina Press, 1944, pp. 31–70.

Color and Democracy: Colonies and Peace. New York: Harcourt Brace, 1945.

(Ed.), with Guy B. Johnson. *Encyclopedia of the Negro: Preparatory Volume.* New York: Phelps Stokes Fund, 1945.

"The Black Man and Albert Schweitzer," in A. A. Roback (ed.), *The Albert Schweitzer Jubilee Book.* Cambridge, 1945, pp. 119–27.

"The Future and Function of the Private Negro College," *Crisis,* LIII (1946), 234–36, 254.

"The Freeing of India," *Crisis,* LIV (1947), 301–04, 316–17.

"Three Centuries of Discrimination," *Crisis,* LIV (1947), 362–64, 379–80.

(Ed.). *Appeal to the World.* New York, 1947.

The World and Africa. New York: Viking Press, 1947.

"A Program of Emancipation for Colonial People," *Howard University Studies in the Social Sciences,* VI, No. 1 (1948), 96–103.

My Relations with the N.A.A.C.P. Mimeographed. 1948.

"From McKinley to Wallace: My Fifty Years as a Political Independent," *Masses and Mainstream,* I (August 1948), 3–13.

"John Hope: Scholar and Gentleman," *Crisis,* LV (September 1948), 270–71.

"The Negro Since 1900: A Progress Report," *The New York Times Magazine,* November 21, 1948, pp. 54–57, 59.

"The Freedom to Learn," *Midwest Journal,* II (Winter 1949), 9–11.

"Government and Freedom," *Harlem Quqrterly,* I (Spring 1950), 29–31.

"The Role of West Africa," *Crescent* (Spring 1950).

"Editing the Crisis," *Crisis,* LVIII (March 1951), 147, 213.

"I Take My Stand For Peace," *Masses and Mainstream* (June 1951).

In Battle For Peace. New York: Masses and Mainstream, 1952.

(During the past few years, Du Bois has published many short pieces in such places as *New Africa,* the *National Guardian,* and *Harlem Quarterly.*)

II. **Other Articles and Books.**

Abrahams, Peter. *Tell Freedom*. New York: Alfred A. Knopf, 1954.

Abromowitz, Jack. "Accommodation and Militancy in Negro Life, 1870–1915." Unpublished doctoral thesis, Columbia University, 1951.

Adams, John Henry. "Rough Sketches," *Voice of the Negro*, II (March 1905), 176–81.

Adams, Julius J. *The Challenge: A Study in Negro Leadership*. New York: W. Malliet, 1949.

Allen, James S. *Negro Liberation*. New York, 1932.

Aptheker, Herbert. "The Washington-Du Bois Conference of 1904," *Science and Society*, XIII (Fall 1949), 344–51.

———. *A Documentary History of the Negro People in the United States*. New York: Citadel Press, 1951.

Aron, Burgit, "The Garvey Movement." Unpublished M.A. thesis, Columbia University, 1952.

Baker, Joseph V. "The N.A.A.C.P. and the Negro Press," *Crisis*, XLI (May 1934).

Baker, Ray S. "An Ostracized Race in Ferment," *American*, LXVI (May 1908), 60–70.

———. *Following the Color Line*. New York: Doubleday, Page, 1908.

Barber, J. Max. "In the Sanctum," *Voice of the Negro*, II (September 1905), 647–48.

———. "Macon Convention," *Voice of the Negro*, III (March 1906), 163–66.

———. "The Niagara Movement at Harpers Ferry," *Voice of the Negro*, III (October 1906), 403–11.

Bassett, John Spencer. "Two Negro Leaders," *South Atlantic Quarterly*, II (July 1903), pp. 267–72.

Benson, William E. "Kowaliga: A Community with a Purpose," *Charities*, XV (October 7, 1905), 22–24.

Berry, Brewton. *Race and Ethnic Relations*. Boston: Houghton Mifflin, 1958.

Blake, Jean. "The N.A.A.C.P. at the Crossroads," *Fourth International*, (May-June 1950).

Bogardus, E. S. *Fundamentals of Social Psychology*. New York: The Century Co., 1924.

———. "Tuskegee and Booker T. Washington," *Sociology and Social Research* XVI (May-June 1932), 466–71.

Bond, Horace M. "Negro Leadership Since Washington," *South Atlantic Quarterly*, XXIV (April 1925), 115–30.

———. *Education of the Negro in the American Social Order*. New York: Prentice-Hall, 1934.

———. "The Influence of Personalities on the Public Education of Negroes in Alabama," *Journal of Negro Education*, VI (April 1937), 172–87.

Braithwaite, William S. "A Tribute to W. E. Burghardt Du Bois," *Phylon*, X (1949), 302–06.

Brawley, Benjamin. *The Negro in Literature and Art in the United States*. New York: Duffield Co., 1929.

———. *Negro Builders and Heroes*. Chapel Hill: University of North Carolina Press, 1937.

Brisbane, Robert H. "The Rise of Protest Movements Among Negroes Since 1900." Unpublished doctoral thesis, Harvard University, 1949.

Broderick, Francis. "W. E. B. Du Bois: The Trail of His Ideas." Unpublished doctoral thesis, Harvard University, 1955.

Brooks, John G. *An American Citizen—The Life of William H. Baldwin, Jr.* Boston: Houghton Mifflin, 1910.

Brooks, Van Wyck. *The Confident Years*. New York: Dutton Co., 1952.

Buckler, Helen. *Doctor Dan*. Boston: Little, Brown, 1954.

Bunche, Ralph J. "A Critical Analysis of the Tactics and Problems of Minority Groups," *Journal of Negro Education*, IV (July 1935), 308–20.

———. "The Programs of Organizations Devoted to the Improvement of the Status of the American Negro," *Journal of Negro Education*, VIII (July 1939), 539–50.

———. "Conceptions and Ideologies of the Negro Problem; The Programs, Ideologies, Tactics, and Achievements of Negro Betterment and Inter-racial Organizations; A Brief and Tentative Analysis of Negro Leadership." Unpublished memoranda for the Myrdal study, 1940.

Calverton, V. F. "The New Negro," *Current History*, XXIII (February 1926), 694–98.

Carnegie, Andrew. *The Negro in America*. Pamphlet. 1907.

Cayton, Horace and Mitchell, George S. *Black Workers and the New Unions*. Chapel Hill: University of North Carolina Press, 1939.

Chesnutt, Helen M. *Charles W. Chesnutt, Pioneer of the Color Line*. Chapel Hill: University of North Carolina Press, 1952.

Collins, Leslie M. "W. E. B. Du Bois's Views on Education." Unpublished M.A. thesis, Fisk University, 1937.

Covington, F. C. "Color a Factor in Social Mobility," *Sociology and Social Research*, XV (December 1930), pp. 145–52.

Cox, Oliver C. *Caste, Class, and Race:* Garden City: Doubleday, 1948.

——. "New Crisis in Leadership Among Negroes," *Journal of Negro Education*, XIX (Fall 1950), 459–65.

——. "Leadership Among Negroes in the United States," in Alvin W. Gouldner (ed.), *Studies in Leadership.* New York: Harpers, 1950, pp. 228–71.

——. "Patterns of Race Relations," *Midwest Journal*, III (Winter 1950–51), 31–38.

——. "The Leadership of Booker T. Washington," *Social Forces*, XXX (1951), 91–97.

Cronon, Edmund D. *Black Moses.* Madison: University of Wisconsin Press, 1955.

Curti, Merle. *The Social Ideas of American Educators.* New York: Scribners, 1935.

Daniels, John. *In Freedom's Birthplace.* New York: Houghton Mifflin, 1914.

Davie, Maurice R. *Negroes in American Society.* New York: McGraw Hill, 1949.

Davis, Frank G. "Nature, Scope and Significance of the First Phylon Institute," *Phylon*, II (1941), 280–88.

Detweiler, Frederick G. *The Negro Press in the United States.* Chicago: University of Chicago Press, 1922.

Dorsey, Emmett E. "The Negro and Social Planning," *Journal of Negro Education* V (January 1936), 105–09.

Doyle, Bertram W. *Etiquette of Race Relations in the South:* Chicago: University of Chicago Press, 1937.

East, Edward M. *Mankind at the Crossroads.* New York: Scribners, 1928.

Edwards, Newton. "A Critique: The Courts and the Negro Separate School," *Journal of Negro Education*, IV (July 1935), 442–55.

Embree, Edwin R. *Brown America.* New York: Viking Press, 1931.

——. 13 *Against the Odds.* New York: Viking Press, 1944.

Faris, Robert E. L. *Social Disorganization.* New York: Ronald Press, 1955.

Farrison, W. Edward. "Booker T. Washington: A Study in Educational Leadership," *South Atlantic Quarterly*, XLI (July 1942), 313–19.

Fauset, Jesse. "Impressions of the Second Pan-African Congress," *Crisis*, XXIII (November 1921), 12–18.

Fauset, Jesse. "What Europe Thought of the Pan-African Congress," *Crisis*, XXIII (December 1921), pp. 60–67.

Ferris, W. H. *African Abroad*. New Haven: Tuttle, Morehouse, & Taylor Press, 1913.

Fisk University Catalogue, 1884–85.

Foster, William Z. *The Negro People in American History*. New York: International Publishers, 1954.

Frank, Glenn. "Clash of Color," *Century*, XCIX (November 1919), 86–98.

Franklin, B. J. "Politico-Economic Theories of Three Negro Leaders." Unpublished M.A. thesis, Howard University, 1936.

Franklin, John Hope. *From Slavery to Freedom*. New York: Alfred A. Knopf, 1948.

Frazier, E. Franklin. "Garvey: A Mass Leader," *Nation*, CXXIII (August 18, 1926), 147–48.

———. "The American Negro's New Leaders," *Current History*, XXVIII (April 1928), 56–59.

———. "The Du Bois Program in the Present Crisis," *Race*, I (1935–36), 11–13.

———. *The Negro in the United States*. New York: Macmillan, 1951.

Garvey, Amy-Jacques (ed.). *Philosophy and Opinions of Marcus Garvey*. 2 vols. New York: Universal Publishing House, 1923–25.

Garvey, Marcus. "The Negro's Greatest Enemy," *Current History*, XVIII (September 1923), 951–57.

Goldman, Morris. "The Garvey Movement." Unpublished M.A. thesis, New School for Social Research, 1940.

Gorman, William. "W. E. B. Du Bois and His Work," *Fourth International* (May–June 1950), pp. 80–85.

Grady, Henry. *The New South*. New York: R. Bonner's Sons, 1890.

Graham, Shirley. "Why Was Du Bois Fired?" *Masses and Mainstream*, I (November 1948), 15–26.

———. "Eighty-Two Years Alive! W. E. B. Du Bois," *Harlem Quarterly*, (Spring 1950), pp. 17–19.

Graham, Stephen. "Militancy of Colour and Its Leaders," *Nineteenth Century and After*, LXXXVIII (November 1920), 909–13.

Grimke, F. J. "Segregation," *Crisis*, XLI (June 1934), 173–74.

———. "The Battle Must Go On," *Crisis*, XLI (August 1934), 240–41.

Harris, A. L. "The Negro Problem as Viewed by Negro Leaders," *Current History*, XVIII (June 1923), 410–18.

Harris, A. L. "Reconstruction and the Negro," *New Republic*, LXXXIII (August 7, 1935), 367–68.

Hill, Mozell C. "Re-View of the Review—Editorial," *Phylon*, X (1949), 297–301.

Holmes, John H. "On Presenting the Spingarn Medal," *Crisis*, XXXII (September 1926), 231–34.

Howe, M. A. DeWolfe. *Portrait of an Independent—Moorfield Storey.* New York: Houghton Mifflin, 1932.

Howells, W. D. "An Exemplary Citizen," *North American Review*, CLXXIII (August 1901), 280–88.

Jack, Robert L. *History of the N.A.A.C.P.* Boston: Meador Publishing Co., 1933.

Johnson, Arthur L. "The Social Theories of W. E. B. Du Bois." Unpublished M.A. thesis, Atlanta University, 1949

Johnson, Charles S. *The Negro in American Civilization.* New York: Henry Holt, 1930.

———. *The Economic Status of Negroes:* Nashville: Fisk University Press, 1933.

Johnson, Guy B. "Negro Racial Movements and Leadership in the United States," *American Journal of Sociology*, XLIII (July 1937), 57–71.

Johnson, James W. *Black Manhattan.* New York: Alfred A. Knopf, 1930.

———. *Along This Way.* New York: Viking Press, 1933.

———. *Negro Americans, What Now?* New York: Viking Press, 1934.

Jones, Dewey R. "The Effect of the Negro Press on Race Relationships in the South." Unpublished M.A. thesis, Columbia University, 1931.

Jones, Harry H. "The Crisis in Negro Leadership," *Crisis*, XIX (March 1920), pp. 256–59.

Jones, Lester M. "The Editorial Policy of Negro Newspapers of 1917–1918 as Compared With That of 1941–1942," *Journal of Negro History*, XXIX (January 1944), 24–31.

Jones, William H. "Some Theories Regarding the Education of the Negro," *Journal of Negro Education*, IX (January 1940), 39–43.

Kerlin, Robert. *The Voice of the Negro.* New York: E. P. Dutton Co., 1919.

Leupp, Francis E. "Why Booker Washington Has Succeeded in His Life Work," *Outlook*, LXXI (May 31, 1902), 326–33.

Link, Arthur S. *Wilson, The Road to the White House.* Princeton: Princeton University Press, 1947.

———. "The Negro As A Factor In The Campaign Of 1912," *Journal of Negro History*, XXXII (January 1947), 81–99.

Locke, Alain. *The New Negro.* New York: Albert & Charles Boni, 1925.

Logan, Rayford. *What the Negro Wants*. Chapel Hill: University of North Carolina Press, 1944.

———. *The Negro in American Life and Thought*, 1877–1901. New York: Dial Press, 1954.

Loggins, Vernon. *The Negro Author*. New York: Columbia University Press, 1931.

Lovett, Robert M. "Du Bois," *Phylon*, II (1941), 214–17.

McGinnis, Frederick A. *A History and an Interpretation of Wilberforce University*. Wilberforce: Wilberforce University Press, 1941.

Mathews, Basil. *Booker T. Washington, Educator and Interracial Interpreter*. Cambridge: Harvard University Press, 1948.

Meier, August. "The Emergence of Negro Nationalism," *Midwest Journal*, IV (Winter 1951–52), 96–104.

———. "The Emergence of Negro Nationalism," *Midwest Journal*, IV (Summer 1952), 95–111.

———. "Booker T. Washington and the Negro Press," *Journal of Negro History*, XXXVIII (January 1953), 67–90.

———. "Booker T. Washington and the Rise of the N.A.A.C.P.," *Crisis*, LXI (February 1954), 69–76, 117–23.

Milholland, John. *The Nation's Duty*. Pamphlet. New York, 1906.

———. *The Negro and the Nation*. Pamphlet. New York, 1906.

Miller, Kelly. "The Negro and Education," *Forum*, XXX (February 1901), 693–705.

———. *Race Adjustment*. New York: Neale Publishing Co., 1908.

———. *Out of the House of Bondage*. New York: Neale Publishing Co., 1914.

———. "After Marcus Garvey—What of the Negro," *Contemporary Review*, CXXXI (April 1927), 492–500.

Moon, Henry Lee. "Du Bois Looks at Reconstruction," *Race* I (1935–36), 60–61.

———. *The Balance of Power: The Negro Vote*. New York: Doubleday & Co., 1948.

Morris, C. S. "Booker Washington," *Independent*, LIV (March 6, 1902), 565–68.

Moton, R. R. *What the Negro Thinks*. Garden City: Doubleday, Doran, 1929.

———. "Negro Higher and Professional Education in 1933," *Journal of Negro Education*, II (July 1933), 397–402.

Myrdal, G. *An American Dilemma*. New York: Harpers, 1944.

N.A.A.C.P. Annual Reports, 1909–34.

Nowlin, William F. *The Negro in American National Politics*. Boston: Stratford Co., 1931.

Ottley, Roi. *New World A-Coming*. Boston: Houghton Mifflin, 1943.

———. *Black Odyssey*. New York: Charles Scribners, 1948.

Ovington, Mary W. *Half a Man*. New York: Longmans, Green, 1911.

———. *How the National Association for the Advancement of Colored People Began*. Pamphlet. New York, 1914.

———. "The National Association for the Advancement of Colored People," *Journal of Negro History*, IX (April 1924), 107–16.

———. *The Walls Came Tumbling Down*. New York: Harcourt, Brace, 1947,

Owens, Dorothy E. "W. E. Burghardt Du Bois: A Case Study of a Marginal Man." Unpublished M.A. thesis, Fisk University, 1944.

Padmore, George (ed.). *History of the Pan-African Congress*. Manchester, 1945.

———. *Pan Africanism or Communism*. New York: Roy Publishers, 1956.

Paschal, Andrew G. "The Paradox of Negro Progress," *Journal of Negro History*, XVI (July 1931), 251–56.

Pickens, William. "Africa for the Africans—The Garvey Movement," *Nation*, CXIII (December 28, 1921), 750–51.

Pierce, James E. "The N.A.A.C.P.—A Study in Social Pressure." Unpublished M.A. thesis, Ohio State University, 1933.

Randolph, A. Philip and Owen, Chandler (eds.). *Messenger* (1917–27).

Range, Willard. *The Rise and Progress of Negro Colleges in Georgia 1865–1949*. Athens: University of Georgia Press, 1951.

Record, Wilson. *The Negro and the Communist Party*. Chapel Hill: University of North Carolina Press, 1951.

Redding, J. Saunders. "Portrait of W. E. Burghardt Du Bois," *American Scholar*, XVIII (Winter 1948–49), 93–96.

———. *They Came in Chains*. Philadelphia: Lippincott, 1950.

Reid, Ira De A. "Negro Movements and Messiahs," *Phylon*, X (1949), 362–69.

Reuter, Edward B. *The Mulatto in the United States*. Boston: R. G. Badger Co., 1918.

Robinson, Carrie C. "A Study of Literary Subject-Matter of the Crisis." Unpublished M.A. thesis, Fisk University, 1934.

Rose, Arnold M. *The Negro's Morale*. Minneapolis: University of Minnesota Press, 1949.

Scott, Emmett J. "Twenty Years After: An Appraisal of Booker T. Washington," *Journal of Negro Education*, V (October 1936), 543–54.

Seligman, H. J. "The Negro Protest Against Ghetto Conditions," *Current History*, XXV (March 1927), 831–33.

———. "N.A.A.C.P. Battlefront," *Crisis*, XXXV (1928), 49–50.

———. "Twenty Years of Negro Progress," *Current History*, XXIX (January 1929), 614–21.

Smythe, H. H. "The N.A.A.C.P. Petition on the Denial of Human Rights and the United Nations," *Journal of Negro Education*, XVII (1948), 88–90.

———. "Negro Masses and Leaders," *Sociology and Social Research*, XXXV (September 1950), 31–37.

———. "Changing Patterns of Negro Leadership," *Social Forces*, XXIX (1950–51), 191–97.

Spencer, Samuel. *Booker T. Washington and the Negro's Place in American Life.* Boston: Little Brown, Co., 1955.

Spero, Sterling D. and Harris, Abram L. *The Black Worker.* New York: Columbia University Press, 1931.

Spiller, G. (ed.). *Papers on Inter-Racial Problems: First Universal Races Congress.* London: King & Son, 1911.

Standing, T. G. "Nationalism in Negro Leadership," *American Journal of Sociology*, XL (1934–35), 180–92.

Stolberg, Benjamin. "Black Chauvinism," *Nation*, CXL (May 15, 1935), 570–71.

Stowe, Lyman B. and Scott, Emmett J. *Booker T. Washington, Builder of a Civilization.* Garden City: Doubleday, Page, 1917.

Streator, George. "In Search of Leadership," *Race*, I (1935–36), 14–20.

———. "A Negro Scholar," *Commonweal*, XXXIV (May 2, 1941), 31–34.

———. "Working on the Crisis," *Crisis*, LVIII (1951), 159–61.

Talbot, Edith A. *Samuel C. Armstrong.* New York: Doubleday, Page, 1904.

Talley, Truman H. "Marcus Garvey—The Negro Moses," *World's Work*, XLI (December 1920), 153–66.

Terrell, Mary Church. *A Colored Woman in a White World.* Washington: Ransdell, Inc., 1940.

Thomas, V. P. "Mr. Booker T. Washington in Louisiana," *Crisis*, X (1915), 144–46.

Thrasher, Max B. "Booker Washington's Personality," *Outlook*, LXIX (November 9, 1901), 629–33.

Torrence, Ridgely. *The Story of John Hope.* New York: Macmillan, 1948.

Van Deuson, John G. *The Black Man in White America.* Washington: Associated Publishers, 1938.

Villard, Oswald G. "Objects of the N.A.A.C.P.," *Crisis*, IV (June 1912), 81–84.

Walling, William E. "Science and Human Brotherhood," *Independent*, LXVI (June 17, 1909), 1318–27.

Walters, Alexander. "The Pan-African Conference," *A.M.E. Zion Quarterly Review*, XI (1901), 164–65.

———. *My Life and Work*. London: Fleming H. Revell Co., 1917.

Warner, Robert A. *New Haven Negroes*. New Haven: Yale University Press, 1940.

Washington, Booker T. Speech printed in the *Thirty-Ninth Annual Report of the Michigan State Board of Agriculture*, Lansing, 1899–1900.

———. "Signs of Progress Among the Negroes," *Century*, LIX (January 1900), 472–78.

———. "The Montgomery Race Conference," *Century*, LX (August 1900), 630–32.

———. "Education Will Solve the Race Problem, A Reply," *North American Review*, CLXXI (August 1900), 221–32.

———. *Up From Slavery*. Garden City: Doubleday, Page, 1900.

———. *Future of the American Negro*. Boston: Small, Maynard Co., 1900.

———. *Sowing and Reaping*. New York: L. C. Page, Co., 1900.

———. "The Negro in Business," *Gunton's Magazine*, XX (March 1901), 209–19.

———. "The Salvation of the Negro," *World's Work*, II (July 1901), 961–71.

———. "Problems in Education," *Cosmopolitan*, XXXIII (September 1902), 506–14.

———. "The National Negro Business League," *World's Work*, IV (October 1902), 2671–75.

———. *Character Building*. New York, Doubleday, Page, Co., 1902.

———. "Industrial Education for the Negro," in *The Negro Problem*. New York, 1903.

———. "The Golden Rule in Atlanta," *Outlook*, LXXXIV (December 15, 1906), 913–16.

———. "A University Education for Negroes," *Independent*, LXVIII (March 24, 1910), 613–18.

———. *My Larger Education*. New York: Doubleday, Page, Co., 1911.

———. "The Negro and the Labor Unions," *Atlantic Monthly*, CXI (June 1913), 756–67.

———. "My Views of Segregation Laws," *New Republic*, V (December 4, 1915), 113–14.

Washington, E. Davidson. *Selected Speeches of Booker T. Washington.* Garden City: Doubleday, Doran, Co., 1932.

Watson, J. B. "Recalling 1906," *Crisis,* XLI (April 1934), 100–01.

White, Walter. *A Man Called White.* New York: Viking Press, 1948.

Wilkins, Roy. "The Negro Wants Full Equality," in Logan, *What the Negro Wants.* Chapel Hill: University of North Carolina Press, pp. 113–32.

———. "The Crisis 1934–1939," *Crisis,* LVIII (March 1951), 154–56.

Winston, Robert W. "Should the Color Line Go?" *Current History,* XVIII (September 1923), 945–51.

Woodson, Carter G. (ed.). *The Works of Francis J. Grimke.* 4 vols. Washington: Associated Publishers, 1942.

Worthy, Ruth. "A Negro in Our History: William M. Trotter." Unpublished M.A. thesis, Columbia University, 1952.

Young, Donald R. *Research Memorandum on Minority Peoples in the Depression.* Social Science Research Council Bulletin, XXXI, New York, 1937.

Zickefoose, Harold E. "The Garvey Movement: A Study in Collective Behavior." Unpublished M.A. thesis, University of Iowa, 1931.

III. Documents, Government and Private.

A. CONGRESSIONAL DOCUMENTS.

Report Number 311, "Semicentennial Anniversary of the Act of Emancipation," pp. 1–7, in *Senate Documents,* Volume I, 62nd Congress, 2nd Session, 1911–12.

Congressional Record, First Session of the 66th Congress, LVIII, Part 5, August 25, 1919, p. 4303.

Review of the Scientific and Cultural Conference for World Peace, House Committee on Un-American Activities, Washington, 1949.

The Communist "Peace Petition" Campaign, House Committee on Un-American Activities, Washington, 1950.

Statement on The March of Treason, House Committee on Un-American Activities, Washington, 1951.

Report on The Communist "Peace" Offensive—A Campaign to Disarm and Defeat the United States, House Committee on Un-American Activities, Washington, 1951.

B. U.S. DEPARTMENT OF JUSTICE DOCUMENT.

"Radicalism and Sedition Among the Negroes as Reflected in Their Publications," pp. 161–87, found in Investigation Activities of Department of Justice, 66th Congress, 1st Session, U.S. *Senate Documents*, XII, 1919.

C. NEW YORK SENATE DOCUMENT.

"Propaganda Among Negroes," pp. 1476–1520, found in "Revolutionary Radicalism"—*Report of the Joint Legislative Committee Investigating Seditious Activities*, filed April 24, 1920, in the Senate of the State of New York. Part I, Vol. II.

D. PRIVATE DOCUMENTS.

Minutes of the Board of Directors of the National Association for the Advancement of Colored People, 1910–34. (These Minutes were seen by Dr. Francis Broderick, who graciously shared his transcriptions. Mr. Walter White, executive secretary of the association, had refused me access to the material.)

Abstracts of Minutes of the Second Niagara Conference, August 15–18, 1906. Located at the Howard University Library, Washington D.C.

Minutes of the Board of Trustees of the University of Pennsylvania, 1896. Located at the University Archives, Philadelphia.

IV. PERSONAL CORRESPONDENCE.

Ray Stannard Baker Papers, Library of Congress.

John Edward Bruce Papers, Schomburg Collection, New York City.

Du Bois' Papers, in his possession.

(Unfortunately, I did not receive very much help from Dr. Du Bois. Since his 1951 federal indictment, he has been unco-operative to researchers. Although he refused me access to his papers, through the courtesy of Dr. Francis Broderick I examined transcriptions of the Du Bois Papers prior to 1910. Dr. Broderick examined some materials before the indictment, but permission was revoked shortly thereafter.)

Du Bois Papers, James Weldon Johnson Memorial Collection, Yale University Library.

James Weldon Johnson Papers, Johnson Collection, Yale Library.

Nathan Mossell Papers, courtesy of Mrs. Gertrude Williams, Philadelphia.
Theodore Roosevelt Papers, Library of Congress.
Joel Spingarn Papers, Johnson Collection, Yale Library.
    (There are also some Spingarn letters at Howard University Library.)
Moorfield Storey Papers, courtesy of Mr. Charles Storey, Boston.
Oswald Garrison Villard Papers, Harvard University Library—Houghton
    Collection.
Booker T. Washington Papers, Library of Congress.
Carter Woodson Collection, Library of Congress.

V. NEWSPAPERS.

Boston *Guardian*, 1902–03.
Cleveland *Gazette*, 1902–10.
Indianapolis *Freeman*, 1907–10.
Negro World, 1919–30.
New York *Age*, 1906–12.
The New York Times, 1901–51.
Portland *New Age*, 1902–07.
Washington *Bee*, 1903–11.
Washington *Colored American*, 1902–04.

INDEX

377